Communications in Computer and Information Science 2468

Series Editors

Rationale
The CCIS series is devoted to the publication of proceedings of computer science conferences. Its aim is to efficiently disseminate original research results in informatics in printed and electronic form. While the focus is on publication of peer-reviewed full papers presenting mature work, inclusion of reviewed short papers reporting on work in progress is welcome, too. Besides globally relevant meetings with internationally representative program committees guaranteeing a strict peer-reviewing and paper selection process, conferences run by societies or of high regional or national relevance are also considered for publication.

Topics
The topical scope of CCIS spans the entire spectrum of informatics ranging from foundational topics in the theory of computing to information and communications science and technology and a broad variety of interdisciplinary application fields.

Information for Volume Editors and Authors
Publication in CCIS is free of charge. No royalties are paid, however, we offer registered conference participants temporary free access to the online version of the conference proceedings on SpringerLink (http://link.springer.com) by means of an http referrer from the conference website and/or a number of complimentary printed copies, as specified in the official acceptance email of the event.

CCIS proceedings can be published in time for distribution at conferences or as post-proceedings, and delivered in the form of printed books and/or electronically as USBs and/or e-content licenses for accessing proceedings at SpringerLink. Furthermore, CCIS proceedings are included in the CCIS electronic book series hosted in the SpringerLink digital library at http://link.springer.com/bookseries/7899. Conferences publishing in CCIS are allowed to use Online Conference Service (OCS) for managing the whole proceedings lifecycle (from submission and reviewing to preparing for publication) free of charge.

Publication process
The language of publication is exclusively English. Authors publishing in CCIS have to sign the Springer CCIS copyright transfer form, however, they are free to use their material published in CCIS for substantially changed, more elaborate subsequent publications elsewhere. For the preparation of the camera-ready papers/files, authors have to strictly adhere to the Springer CCIS Authors' Instructions and are strongly encouraged to use the CCIS LaTeX style files or templates.

Abstracting/Indexing
CCIS is abstracted/indexed in DBLP, Google Scholar, EI-Compendex, Mathematical Reviews, SCImago, Scopus. CCIS volumes are also submitted for the inclusion in ISI Proceedings.

How to start
To start the evaluation of your proposal for inclusion in the CCIS series, please send an e-mail to ccis@springer.com

Pasquale Ardimento · Raffaele Di Fuccio ·
Giovanni Fulantelli · Pierpaolo Limone ·
Riccardo Pecori · Paolo Raviolo ·
Marco Rondonotti · Daniele Schicchi ·
Davide Taibi · Gianluca Zaza
Editors

Higher Education Learning Methodologies and Technologies Online

6th International Conference, HELMeTO 2024
Rome, Italy, September 25–27, 2024
Revised Selected Papers, Part II

Springer

Editors
Pasquale Ardimento
University of Bari Aldo Moro
Bari, Italy

Raffaele Di Fuccio
Università Telematica Pegaso
Rome, Italy

Giovanni Fulantelli
National Research Council of Italy
Palermo, Italy

Pierpaolo Limone
Università Telematica Pegaso
Rome, Italy

Riccardo Pecori
eCampus University
Novedrate, Italy

Paolo Raviolo
eCampus University
Novedrate, Italy

Marco Rondonotti
eCampus University
Novedrate, Italy

Daniele Schicchi
National Research Council of Italy
Palermo, Italy

Davide Taibi
National Research Council of Italy
Palermo, Italy

Gianluca Zaza
University of Bari Aldo Moro
Bari, Italy

ISSN 1865-0929 ISSN 1865-0937 (electronic)
Communications in Computer and Information Science
ISBN 978-3-031-93998-3 ISBN 978-3-031-93999-0 (eBook)
https://doi.org/10.1007/978-3-031-93999-0

This Springer imprint is published by the registered company Springer Nature Switzerland AG
The registered company address is: Gewerbestrasse 11, 6330 Cham, Switzerland

If disposing of this product, please recycle the paper.

Preface

Volumes 2467 and 2468 of Communications in Computer and Information Science (CCIS) contain the post-proceedings of HELMeTO 2024, the sixth International Conference on Higher Education Learning Methodologies and Technologies Online. The conference took place in Rome, Italy, from September 25 to 27, 2024, and was organized through a joint collaboration between E-Campus University and Università Telematica Unipegaso. The conference focused on learning methodologies and technologies in higher education and featured 101 submissions from over 262 authors representing 22 countries (Argentina, Austria, Belgium, Canada, Chile, Cyprus, Denmark, Germany, Greece, Italy, Latvia, Lithuania, Malta, Morocco, Netherlands, Nigeria, Slovakia, Spain, Sweden, Ukraine, UK, and USA). The conference has become a pivotal gathering for researchers and practitioners engaged in higher distance education institutions and exploring online learning methodologies. This year's conference was organized into two main tracks: one focused on online pedagogy and learning methodologies (General Track 1), and the other on learning technologies, data analytics, and educational big data mining (General Track 2). Specifically, authors presenting papers in General Track 1 reported on the strategies, techniques, and practices used to facilitate effective teaching and learning in digital environments; they dealt with the adaption of traditional pedagogical approaches to online platforms while leveraging digital tools. General Track 2 focused on how learning technologies, data analytics, and educational big data mining are transforming education by using digital tools and large-scale data to enhance teaching, learning, and decision-making.

In addition, 7 special tracks focused on various topics related to education and technology.

Special Track 1, "*Inclusion and Immersive Approaches for Higher Education*", looked at the transformative roles of immersive technologies in enhancing inclusion within higher education. Special Track 2, "*Artificial Intelligence and Innovative Technology for Special Education*", focused on how Artificial Intelligence (AI), Augmented Reality (AR), and Virtual Reality (VR) are transforming education, particularly for students with Special Educational Needs (SEN). Special Track 3, "*Learning Technologies and Faculty Development in the Digital Framework*", focused on the transformative impact of digital technologies in higher education. Special Track 4, "*Critical Pedagogy, Art, Affect as Method, and Performativity in Online Higher Education*", analysed how to integrate critical pedagogy, art, and performativity in online higher education. Special Track 5, "*Intelligent Tutoring Systems and Conversational Pedagogical Agents in Higher Education*", investigated the integration of intelligent tutoring systems and adaptive conversational agents within the context of higher education, with a focus on personalized learning and administrative support. Special Track 6, "*Rethink Education: The Opportunities and Challenges of Artificial Intelligence*" focused on exploring the potential and challenges of integrating Artificial Intelligence into education. Finally, Special Track 7,

"*Laboratory Teaching and Experiential Learning in Digital Environments*", discussed the impact of distance learning on education.

An international Program/Scientific Committee, consisting of members from 13 different countries including Austria, China, Cyprus, Croatia, France, Germany, Greece, Italy, Poland, Portugal, Slovakia, Spain, and Turkey, was responsible for reviewing 101 papers submitted for HELMeTO 2024. After a separate double-blind peer-review process conducted by at least three members of the Program/Scientific Committee, a final set of the best 46 papers (45% of the original submissions) were chosen for publication in this book. We would like to express our gratitude to all the authors for their contributions, presentations, and efforts, as well as for their attendance at the event. We also extend our thanks to all the committee members, organizers, and contributors for their help and involvement in preparing and hosting both the conference and this book.

March 2025

Paolo Raviolo
Pierpaolo Limone
Riccardo Pecori
Pasquale Ardimento
Raffaele Di Fuccio
Giovanni Fulantelli
Marco Rondonotti
Daniele Schicchi
Davide Taibi
Gianluca Zaza

Organization

Organizing Committee

General Chairs

Pierpaolo Limone	Pegaso University, Italy
Riccardo Pecori	eCampus University, Italy

Permanent Steering Committee

Daniel Burgos	Universidad Internacional de La Rioja, Spain
Gabriella Casalino	University of Bari Aldo Moro, Italy
Marta Cimitile	Unitelma Sapienza University, Italy
Giosuè Lo Bosco	University of Palermo, Italy
Riccardo Pecori	National Research Council of Italy; eCampus University, Italy
Pietro Picerno	Sassari University, Italy
Paolo Raviolo	eCampus University, Italy
Pier Cesare Rivoltella	University of Bologna, Italy
Christian Stracke	European Institute for Learning, Innovation and Cooperation, Germany
Davide Taibi	CNR – Institute for Educational Technology, Italy

Program Chairs

Paolo Raviolo	eCampus University, Italy
Raffaele Di Fuccio	Pegaso University, Italy
Marco Rondonotti	eCampus University, Italy
Davide Taibi	CNR – Institute for Education Technology, Italy

Publication Chairs

Pasquale Ardimento	University of Bari Aldo Moro, Italy
Giovanni Fulantelli	CNR - Institute for Educational Technology, Italy

Daniele Schicchi	CNR - Institute for Educational Technology, Italy
Gianluca Zaza	University of Bari Aldo Moro, Italy

Publicity and Communication Chairs

Joanna Kic-Drgas	Adam Mickiewicz University, Poland
Alberto Fornasari	University of Bari Aldo Moro, Italy
Lia Daniela Sasanelli	Pegaso University, Italy
Gianluca Zaza	University of Bari Aldo Moro, Italy
Daniele Schicchi	CNR - Institute for Educational Technology, Italy

Local Organization Chairs

Arianna Giuliani	eCampus University, Italy
Emanuele Marsico	Pegaso University, Italy
Amin Muhammad Nadim	Pegaso University, Italy
Fabiana Sasso	Università San Raffaele, Italy
Ilaria La Penna	Pegaso University, Italy

Web Master

Luca De Matteis	Italy

Program Committee

Pasquale Ardimento	University of Bari Aldo Moro, Italy
Federica Baroni	Università degli Studi di Bergamo, Italy
Fabrizio Barpi	Politecnico di Torino, Italy
Giorgia Bassi	IIT CNR, Italy
Mario Luca Bernardi	University of Sannio, Italy
Salvatore Calderaro	University of Palermo, Italy
Nadia Carlomagno	Università Suor Orsola Benincasa, Italy
Maria Concetta Carruba	Università Telematica Pegaso, Italy
Gabriella Casalino	Università degli Studi di Bari Aldo Moro, Italy
Marta Cimitile	Unitelma Sapienza University, Italy
Giuseppa Compagno	University of Palermo, Italy
Mario Covarrubias Rodriguez	Politecnico di Milano, Italy
Davide Dalmazzo	Politecnico di Torino, Italy

Antonella De Blasio	Università eCampus, Italy
Grazia De Angelis	Università Telematica Pegaso, Italy
Emiliano Del Gobbo	University of Foggia, Italy
Raffaele Di Fuccio	University of Foggia, Italy
Marco di Furia	University of Foggia, Italy
Valeria Di Martino	University of Palermo, Italy
Daniele Di Mitri	Leibniz Institute for Research and Information in Education, Germany
Benedetto Di Paola	Università degli Studi di Palermo, Italy
Yannis Dimitriadis	University of Valladolid, Spain
Gregor Donabauer	University of Regensburg, Germany
Martin Drlik	Constantine the Philosopher University in Nitra, Slovakia
Xu Du	Central China Normal University, China
Stefano Faralli	Sapienza University of Rome, Italy
Simona Ferrari	Università Cattolica, Italy
Francesca Finestrone	University of Foggia, Italy
Michele Fiorentino	University of Bari Aldo Moro, Italy
Dominik Froehlich	University of Vienna, Austria
Marc Fuertes-Alpiste	Universitat de Barcelona, Spain
Giovanni Fulantelli	National Research Council of Italy, ITD, Italy
Sandra Gama	University of Lisbon, IST, Portugal
Isabel Gonzalez Enrıquez	Universidad Complutense de Madrid, Spain
Annalisa Guarini	University of Bologna, Italy
Elif Gulbay	University of Palermo, Italy
Sara Havzi	University of Novi Sad, Serbia
Ümit İzgi Onbaşılı	Mersin University, Turkey
Sebastien Jacques	University of Tours, France
Udo Kruschwitz	University of Regensburg, Germany
Sandra Kucina Softic	University of Zagreb, Croatia
Ilaria La Penna	Università Telematica Pegaso, Italy
Carla Limongelli	Università Roma Tre, Italy
Giosuè Lo Bosco	Università di Palermo, Italy
Rene Lobo	Universitat Pompeu Fabra, Spain
Renato Lombardo	Università degli Studi di Palermo, Italy
Leonarda Longo	University of Palermo, Italy
Riccardo Magni	GLIC Centri Ausili, Italy
Jacek Marciniak	Adam Mickiewicz University, Poland
Ronald Marquez	North Carolina State University, USA
Stefania Massaro	University of Bari Aldo Moro, Italy
Ilaria Matteucci	National Research Council of Italy, IIT, Italy
Maria Meletiou-Mavrotheris	European University Cyprus, Cyprus

Domenico Monacis	Università Telematica Pegaso, Italy
Eric Monfroy	University of Nantes, France
Debora Montano	Università del Sannio, Italy
Antonella Montone	University of Bari, Italy
Guendalina Peconio	University of Foggia, Italy
Riccardo Pecori	eCampus University, Italy
Pietro Picerno	University of Sassari, Italy
Paolo Raviolo	eCampus University, Italy
Angelo Rega	Università Telematica Pegaso, Italy
Manuela Repetto	Università degli Studi di Torino, Italy
Grazia Romanazzi	Università Telematica Pegaso, Italy
Marco Rondonotti	eCampus University, Italy
Martina Rossi	University of Foggia, Italy
Domenico Santoro	University of Foggia, Italy
Lia Daniela Sasanelli	Università Telematica Pegaso, Italy
Daniele Schicchi	National Research Council of Italy, ITD, Italy
Lidia Scifo	National Research Council of Italy; Lumsa University, Italy
Burcu Sezginsoy Şeker	Balıkesir University, Turkey
Maria Grazia Simone	eCampus University, Italy
Davide Taibi	National Research Council of Italy, ITD, Italy
Melania Talarico	Università degli Studi di Torino, Italy
Gaetano Tieri	Unitelma Sapienza, Italy
Ottavia Trevisan	Università degli Studi di Padova, Italy
Stefano Triberti	Università Telematica Pegaso, Italy
Christos Troussas	University of West Attica, Greece
Fiorella Vinci	eCampus University, Italy
Viviana Vinci	University of Foggia, Italy
Gianluca Zaza	University of Bari Aldo Moro, Italy

Learning Methodologies and Technologies Online. HELMeTO 2024 Editorial: Introduction to the Scientific Contributions (Editorial)

Pasquale Ardimento[1], Giovanni Fulantelli[2], Daniele Schicchi[2], Gianluca Zaza[1], Raffaele Di Fuccio[3], Riccardo Pecori[4], Paolo Raviolo[5], Marco Rondonotti[5], Davide Taibi[2], and Pierpaolo Limone[3]

[1] University of Bari Aldo Moro, Bari, Italy
[2] National Research Council of Italy, Palermo, Italy
[3] Università Telematica Pegaso, Napoli, Italy
[4] National Research Council of Italy; eCampus University, Novedrate, Italy
[5] eCampus University, Novedrate, Italy

Abstract. The HELMeTO 2024 Conference Proceedings highlight the transformative role of Artificial Intelligence (AI) and emerging technologies in reshaping higher education. The 46 accepted research papers explore a wide spectrum of themes including AI in education, digital transformation, inclusion and student well-being, educational policy, ethics, and teacher development. The contributions examine how AI tools foster student engagement, personalize learning, support accessibility, and streamline educational processes, while also addressing critical concerns such as ethical governance, algorithmic bias, and data privacy. Emerging technologies like augmented and virtual reality, game-based learning, and robotics are shown to enhance interactivity and motivation in diverse learning environments. The proceedings also emphasize the importance of inclusive education and mental well-being, calling for holistic approaches that integrate emotional and cognitive development. In parallel, the role of educators is redefined through AI-driven practices, necessitating targeted professional development and ethical training. Policy frameworks such as UNESCO's guidance on generative AI and the European Union's AI Act are examined for their potential to guide responsible implementation.

Keywords. Higher Education · Artificial Intelligence · Online Learning · Educational technologies · Educational methodologies.

1 Introduction

The Higher Education Learning Methodologies and Technologies Online (HELMeTO) 2024 conference serves as a platform for researchers, educators, and practitioners to discuss advancements in artificial intelligence (AI), emerging technologies, and inclusive educational strategies within higher education. As digital transformation reshapes academia, HELMeTO 2024 fosters collaboration to ensure technology-driven education remains effective, accessible, and ethically responsible. This year's conference features 46 accepted research papers exploring AI in education, digital transformation, inclusion and well-being, as well as policy, ethics, and teacher pedagogy. The presented research examines AI's role in pedagogy, student engagement, assessment, and computational thinking, alongside emerging technologies such as augmented reality, virtual reality, game-based learning, and robotics. The ethical implications of AI, governance frameworks, and professional development for educators are also central topics of discussion. AI's impact extends beyond personalized learning, influencing student engagement, automating administrative processes, and supporting faculty in course design. However, ethical concerns such as bias, data privacy, and algorithmic decision-making require careful scrutiny. Governance frameworks, including the European Union's AI Act, underscore the need for robust ethical guidelines to regulate AI's educational applications. Emerging technologies continue to reshape learning paradigms by fostering immersive and interactive experiences. Virtual and augmented reality enhance spatial learning and practical training, while game-based learning platforms promote student motivation and collaboration. Beyond technology, HELMeTO 2024 highlights the importance of student well-being and inclusive education, showcasing AI's potential in providing personalized support and stress management interventions. Teacher development and educational policy remain crucial to the successful integration of AI and digital technologies. As these tools become embedded in pedagogy, educators must develop digital literacy and adapt to evolving instructional methods. Professional development programs emphasizing AI literacy, ethics, and adaptive teaching strategies are essential to ensure that technology enhances, rather than replaces, human-centered learning. Discussions on policy frameworks, including UNESCO's guidelines on AI in education, offer insights into regulatory strategies to ensure ethical and equitable AI implementation. The presented papers can be grouped in four main thematic areas that reflect the evolving priorities of technology-enhanced education. The theme of AI in Education focuses on AI-driven pedagogical strategies, engagement methodologies, and assessment techniques, demonstrating how AI can personalize and enhance learning experiences. Emerging Technologies and Digital Transformation highlights innovations such as AR, VR, robotics, and game-based learning, emphasizing their role in creating immersive and interactive learning environments. Inclusion and Well-being addresses the significance of equitable access to digital education, the role of AI in supporting students with diverse needs, and the integration of well-being initiatives in academic settings. Finally, the theme of Policy, Ethics, and Teacher Pedagogy explores governance frameworks, AI literacy among educators, and the ethical considerations necessary to ensure responsible implementation of technology in education.

2 The Role of Artificial Intelligence in Education

The growing usage of artificial intelligence (AI) into educational settings is transforming learning environments, promoting active engagement, personalized learning experiences, and streamlined course organization. Research on AI-driven strategies for active learning demonstrates that tools such as ChatGPT and other interactive AI systems significantly enhance student engagement [27]. In the realm of computer science education, AI-related activities are being integrated into the curriculum to foster students' computational thinking and problem-solving skills, thereby bridging the gap between traditional pedagogical methods and contemporary AI applications [17]. Concurrently, investigations into teacher training and AI literacy highlight the necessity of equipping future educators with the competencies required to effectively utilize AI [34]. AI is making significant contributions to personalized learning and assistive education, particularly for students with disabilities [15]. Adaptive learning models and intelligent tutoring systems are designed to provide tailored educational experiences that ensure accessibility for a diverse range of learners [3]. Additionally, the interplay between AI and human agents within educational feedback mechanisms is vital for enhancing student autonomy and motivation [10]. However, these advancements also necessitate critical discussions surrounding AI ethics and governance. Ongoing research on the AI Act [9] and the establishment of ethical frameworks are essential to ensure the responsible and equitable implementation of AI in educational contexts. As artificial intelligence continues to transform the landscape of academia, there has been a growing emphasis on student well-being [21]. Research indicates that interventions incorporating physical activity, Internet of Things (IoT) technologies, and biometric monitoring can significantly assist students in coping with stress and anxiety, particularly in de manding situations such as public speaking and higher education environments [2, 5]. Furthermore, AI's capacity to automate course organization and develop tailored learning tasks is alleviating administrative demands on educators [14]. This shift enables a more personalized and efficient approach to teaching. For instance, large language models facilitate the dynamic creation of educational resources [1]. Higher education institutions increasingly integrate artificial intelligence in their processes, research focused on the perspectives of faculty and students regarding this integration is playing a pivotal role in shaping the future of academia [37]. While AI presents significant opportunities for innovation, it also raises important challenges, including ethical considerations, faculty skepticism, and regulatory uncertainties, all of which warrant thorough examination [6].

Engaging in an ongoing dialogue surrounding generative AI is crucial for addressing its effects on academic integrity, assessment methodologies, and institutional policies. This discourse is vital in defining the role of AI within contemporary educational frameworks. By exploring AI's potential across diverse domains—such as engagement, accessibility, stress management, course organization, and ethical governance—these studies not only underscore AI's transformative capabilities but also highlight the necessity for thoughtful, inclusive, and ethical implementation in educational settings.

3 Emerging Technologies and Digital Transformation in Education

The rapid advancement of technology is changing the way education is delivered, introducing new approaches to teaching and learning. Emerging tools such as Augmented Reality (AR), Virtual Reality (VR), game-based learning, robotics, and online learning platforms are improving student engagement, motivation, and knowledge retention.

These innovations create interactive, personalized, and immersive learning experiences that support different learning styles and needs. AR and VR technologies are improving education by providing engaging environments that help students understand complex topics more easily. AR applications add digital elements to real-world interactions, while VR simulations allow learners to explore abstract or potentially hazardous concepts in a safe and controlled setting. Research has shown that AR and VR significantly improve students' spatial awareness and participation, particularly in STEM subjects [30]. Building on immersive experiences, game-based learning has proven to be an effective method to increase student motivation and participation. Platforms like Fortnite Creative provide interactive spaces where students can collaborate, build, and solve problems in a dynamic way. In addition, eye tracking technology is used to analyze usability and engagement levels in digital learning, ensuring that educational games keep students mentally stimulated and focused [20]. As interactive learning continues to grow, robotics is also becoming an important tool in early education. Robots like NAO are being introduced in classrooms to teach computational thinking, social skills, and problem-solving. These technologies give children, including those with special educational needs, unique opportunities to engage with learning materials and develop essential skills for the future [7]. The rise of interactive and engaging learning methods is further supported by the increasing availability of digital education. The growth of e-learning platforms, Massive Open Online Courses (MOOCs), and blended learning strategies is making education more accessible to people around the world. These digital approaches provide flexible, self-paced learning, allowing students to access quality resources beyond traditional classroom settings. Blended learning, in particular, combines online lessons with in-person instruction, offering a well-balanced mix that enhances both independent learning and classroom discussions [36]. The HELMeTO 2024 conference aims to explore these evolving trends and opportunities in educational technology. Educators can create inclusive and engaging learning environments by adapting teaching methods, providing accessible content, training faculty, and effectively integrating technology. Reflecting on these developments is crucial to fostering informed discussions on the latest trends and innovations in the field. By embracing these emerging technologies, educators can make learning more interactive, inclusive, and effective. The integration of AR/VR, game-based learning, robotics, and digital education represents a significant change in the way knowledge is acquired and applied, shaping the future of education in the digital age.

4 Inclusion, Well-Being, and Student Support

In recent years, artificial intelligence (AI) has emerged as a transformative force in education, enabling greater accessibility and fostering personalized learning experiences. These advancements hold particular promise for students with special needs, allowing them to engage with educational content tailored to their abilities. AI can provide individualized learning plans for students with disabilities and create interactive materials that adapt to diverse learning styles. By prioritizing inclusivity, e-learning platforms offer new opportunities for self-directed learning and empowerment, ensuring no student is left behind. Recent research highlights the role of AI and inclusive education models in promoting student empowerment and equitable access to learning. For instance, [19] explores technologies such as intelligent tutors and adaptive systems, addressing their benefits and ethical challenges, including privacy, algorithmic fairness, and the digital divide. It also suggests strategies for responsible AI integration in education, fostering collaboration among researchers, educators, and policymakers to enhance learning experiences. Similarly, [18] emphasizes the importance of a positive school climate in supporting student achievement and well-being, reinforcing inclusivity as a key factor in educational success. Beyond accessibility, contemporary studies underscore the necessity of a holistic approach that incorporates students' emotional and physical well-being alongside cognitive development. As academic pressures increase, embedding well-being initiatives into educational frameworks becomes essential. For example, [28] analyzes PhD students' psychological well-being, stressing the need for comprehensive academic mental health support systems. Furthermore, discussions in this field consistently highlight technology's fundamental role in facilitating inclusion and well-being. Thoughtfully leveraging AI and digital tools enables educators and policymakers to design learning environments that accommodate diverse student needs, nurture emotional resilience, and foster a genuinely inclusive academic experience. Additionally, the connection between environmental factors and mental health further illustrates the significance of a supportive educational climate. For instance, [39] examines how teacher self-efficacy and school climate influence student learning and emotional well-being, underscoring the need for adaptable educational environments. Similarly, [32] investigates the impact of pass/fail grading systems in medical schools, advocating for assessment methods that reduce stress while maintaining academic rigour. AI-driven educational solutions not only have the potential to revolutionize learning environments but also to pave the way for a more inclusive, equitable, and adaptive educational paradigm. By integrating AI in an evidence-based and ethically responsible manner, educators and policymakers can foster an education system that not only enhances academic achievement but also holistically supports students' cognitive, emotional, and social development. Future research and collaborative efforts should continue exploring innovative applications of AI to maximize its positive impact while mitigating ethical and accessibility concerns.

5 Educational Policy, Ethics, and Teacher Development

As artificial intelligence (AI) and digital tools increasingly permeate educational practices, the ethical implications and policy considerations surrounding their use demand rigorous examination. Research presented at this conference underscores the importance of embedding ethical principles such as transparency, accountability, and human oversight into AI and emerging technologies adoption strategies in education, finding strong support both in the scientific literature [11] and in the numerous guidelines that have recently been published by independent international organizations. Amongst the others, the UNESCO's Guidance for Generative AI in Education and Research [12] outlines recommendations for the responsible use of generative AI technologies in academic settings. UNESCO emphasizes the need for clear governance frameworks, advocating for regulations that protect students and teachers from algorithmic discrimination, misinformation, and unethical data practices. The report also underscores the importance of aligning AI-driven educational tools with human rights principles, ensuring that such systems enhance learning rather than replace human educators. Notably, UNESCO warns against overreliance on AI-driven grading and assessment tools, as these may reinforce systemic biases if not properly calibrated and monitored. Moreover, the guidance stresses that AI should be developed in open, transparent, and accountable ways, allowing educational institutions to assess the quality and reliability of AI-generated content. Beyond AI, technologies that are emerging or that in recent years are becoming increasingly prevalent in educational settings, such as Augmented Reality (AR), Virtual Reality (VR), metaverse, and robotics introduce additional ethical considerations in education. AR/VR, for example, can provide immersive experiences for students, allowing them to explore historical sites, conduct virtual science experiments, or engage in medical simulations. However, ethical challenges such as data privacy, accessibility, and potential cognitive overload must be carefully managed [8, 16, 33]. Similarly, robotics and the use of metaverse in education offers opportunities for hands-on education but may also introduce concerns about excessive screen time, gamification addiction, and digital equity [13, 29]. To ensure ethical implementation, educational policies must address issues of content moderation, informed consent, and the psychological effects of immersive and gamified environments. Equally significant is the transformation of education itself, which necessitates a concurrent shift in teacher training and professional development. Studies have demonstrated that while AI-assisted tools such as adaptive learning platforms and intelligent tutoring systems offer novel opportunities to enhance classroom engagement, their successful implementation depends heavily on educators' digital competence and confidence [38, 4]. For example, AI can support teachers by automating administrative tasks, enabling them to focus on pedagogy, or by providing actionable insights through learning analytics to tailor instruction to student needs [23]. However, educators often experience anxiety about integrating AI technologies into their teaching due to perceived threats to their professional autonomy and concerns about being replaced by machines [35]. These challenges underscore the pressing need for comprehensive, ongoing professional development programs that not only enhance digital literacy but also equip teachers with critical skills to navigate the ethical and pedagogical implications of AI use in education. UNESCO's Guidance for Generative AI also highlights the urgent need for teacher training in AI literacy, advocating for targeted professional development programs that help educators understand both the potential and risks of AI tools in the classroom [12]. The document calls for governments and educational institutions to establish clear policies on AI integration, ensuring that educators are empowered rather than overwhelmed by technological change. One of the key recommendations is that AI education should not be confined to technical disciplines but should be embedded across curricula, enabling students and teachers alike to critically engage with AI as a socio-technological phenomenon. The UNESCO report also suggests that AI ethics should be a core component of teacher training, helping educators develop strategies to mitigate AI-driven biases and uphold the values of equity, inclusion, and fairness in digital learning environments. Teacher professional development must also evolve to incorporate training in emerging technologies beyond AI. AR/VR tools and robotics require specialized pedagogical strategies, yet many teachers lack access to structured training in these areas. Furthermore, ethical dilemmas arise when teachers are expected to integrate tools that they have not been properly trained to evaluate for risks such as biased algorithms, data privacy violations, or mental health implications of immersive learning environments. Moreover, the integration of AI requires rethinking traditional pedagogical models to align with the capabilities and limitations of these technologies. Research suggests that AI can enable interactive and immersive learning experiences, fostering creativity and critical thinking in students [22, 25, 26]. However, the effective design of such learning environments requires collaboration between AI developers and educators to ensure that technological tools support—not dictate—educational goals. Studies further highlight the importance of establishing institutional support systems, such as peer mentoring, access to technical resources, and clear guidelines for AI use in classrooms, to help teachers transition into AI-enabled practices [31]. By addressing these needs, educational institutions can create a culture of innovation where technology enhances teaching and learning rather than becoming a source of stress or inequity. Central to this discourse around the policy considerations surrounding the adoption of AI-based technologies in education is the European Union's proposed AI Act [24], which classifies AI systems based on risk and outlines stringent requirements for their deployment, including in education. The AI Act, that officially entered into force on 1 August 2024 and will become fully applicable in August 2026 (with the exception of few specific indications), raises critical concerns about how to regulate AI technologies in ways that uphold data privacy, protect student rights, and foster equitable access to resources in diverse learning environments. For instance, AI-based assessment tools, while capable of delivering personalized feedback, often rely on vast amounts of sensitive student data, raising questions about data security and consent. Addressing these challenges requires an ethically grounded approach to AI integration, ensuring that educational policies promote not only technological innovation but also inclusivity and fairness. Finally, both the AI Act and UNESCO's guidelines emphasize the need for multi-stakeholder collaboration, ensuring that AI policies are not designed in isolation but reflect the voices of educators, students, policymakers, and technology developers. UNESCO's report highlights the global digital divide as a major ethical concern, warning that without proactive intervention, AI in education could exacerbate existing inequalities, leaving students in low-income regions at a disadvantage due to lack of access to AI-powered resources. Addressing this challenge requires investment in digital infrastructure, open access AI tools, and teacher capacity-building initiatives, ensuring that all learners, regardless of geography or socioeconomic background, benefit from AI-enhanced education.

6 Conclusion

The research presented in this year's proceedings provides valuable insights into the evolving landscape of education. While AI and emerging technologies offer unprecedented opportunities for personalized learning, engagement, and accessibility, they also present challenges that must be addressed through ethical considerations, policy development, and teacher support. As we look to the future, it is clear that the role of educators, researchers, and policymakers will be pivotal in ensuring that technology serves as an enabler of meaningful, inclusive, and high-quality education. This conference serves as a platform to foster dialogue, share innovations, and pave the way for a more equitable and technologically empowered learning environment.

References

1. Abd-alrazaq, A.A., et al.: Large language models in medical education: Opportunities, challenges, and future directions. JMIR Med. Educ. **9** (2023). https://doi.org/10.2196/48291
2. AG, A.G., Su, H.K., Kuo, W.K.: Monitoring panic situations in students and alerting using artificial intelligence. Sens. Mater. **34** (2022)
3. Alrakhawi, H.A., Jamiat, N., Abu-Naser, S.S.: Intelligent tutoring systems in education: a systematic review of usage, tools, effects and evaluation. J. Theor. Appl. Inf. Technol. **101**(4), 1205–1226 (2023)
4. Celik, I., Dindar, M., Muukkonen, H., Järvelä, S.: The promises and challenges of artificial intelligence for teachers: a systematic review of research. TechTrends **66**(4), 616–630 (2022)
5. Fernandes, J., Querido, J., Duarte, P.: Exploring the potential of AI tools in promoting and monitoring public speaking skills in higher education students. In: ICERI2024 Proceedings, pp. 6797–6803. IATED (2024)
6. Ferrara, E.: Should ChatGPT be biased? Challenges and risks of bias in large language models. First Monday 28 (2023). https://doi.org/10.5210/fm.v28i11.13346
7. Garcia, P., Singh, R.: Using robotics to enhance early childhood education. Int. J. Early Learn. **29**(4), 89–104 (2021)
8. Giaretta, A.: Security and privacy in virtual reality: a literature survey. Virtual Reality **29**(1), 10 (2024)
9. Helberger, N., Diakopoulos, N., et al.: ChatGPT and the AI act. Internet Policy Rev. **12** (2023)
10. Hmoud, M., Swaity, H., Hamad, N., Karram, O., Daher, W.: Higher education students' task motivation in the generative artificial intelligence context: the case of ChatGPT. Information **15**(1), 33 (2024)
11. Holmes, W., Bialik, M., Fadel, C.: Artificial intelligence in education promises and implications for teaching and learning. Cent. Curriculum Redesign (2019)
12. Holmes, W., Miao, F., et al.: Guidance for generative AI in education and research. UNESCO Publishing (2023)
13. Kaddoura, S., Al Husseiny, F.: The rising trend of Metaverse in education: Challenges, opportunities, and ethical considerations. PeerJ Comput. Sci. **9**, e1252 (2023)
14. Kasneci, E., et al.: ChatGPT for good? On opportunities and challenges of large language models for education. Learn. Individ. Differ. **103**, 102274 (2023)
15. Kato, M., Koshino, M., Ogoshi, S., Ogoshi, Y.: Educational support system for children with developmental disabilities through offline large language models and retrieval-augmented generation. Int. J. Inf. Educ. Technol. **14**(7) (2024)

16. Kenwright, B.: Virtual reality: ethical challenges and dangers [opinion]. IEEE Technol. Soc. Mag. **37**(4), 20–25 (2018)
17. Kuhail, M.A., Mathew, S.S., Khalil, A., Berengueres, J., Shah, S.J.H.: "Will I be replaced?" assessing ChatGPT's effect on software development and programmer perceptions of AI tools. Sci. Comput. Program. **235**, 103111 (2024)
18. Kutsyuruba, B., Klinger, D.A., Hussain, A.: Relationships among school climate, school safety, and student achievement and well-being: a review of the literature. Rev. Educ. **3**(2), 103–135 (2015)
19. Lata, P.: Towards equitable learning: exploring artificial intelligence in inclusive education (2024)
20. Lee, M., Chang, A.: Game-based learning and its impact on student engagement. In: Proceedings of the International Conference on Digital Education, pp. 112–125 (2022)
21. Lee, M.J., Zhang, R.: Human-centric artificial intelligence of things–based indoor environment quality modeling framework for supporting student well-being in educational facilities. J. Comput. Civil Eng. **38**(2), 04024002 (2024)
22. Lo, C.K.: What is the impact of ChatGPT on education? A rapid review of the literature. Educ. Sci. **13**(4), 410 (2023)
23. Luckin, R., Holmes, W.: Intelligence unleashed: an argument for AI in education (2016)
24. Madiega, T.: Artificial intelligence act (2021)
25. Malik, A.R., et al.: Exploring artificial intelligence in academic essay: higher education student's perspective. Int. J. Educ. Res. Open **5**, 100296 (2023)
26. Muthmainnah, Ibna Seraj, P.M., Oteir, I.: Playing with AI to investigate human-computer interaction technology and improving critical thinking skills to pursue 21st century age. Educ. Res. Int. **2022**(1), 6468995 (2022)
27. Pahi, K., Hawlader, S., Hicks, E., Zaman, A., Phan, V.: Enhancing active learning through collaboration between human teachers and generative AI. Comput. Educ. Open **6**, 100183 (2024)
28. Scott, H., Takarangi, M.K.: Measuring Phd students' well-being: Are we seeing the whole picture? Student Success **10**(3), 14–24 (2019)
29. Smakman, M., Vogt, P., Konijn, E.A.: Moral considerations on social robots in education: a multi-stakeholder perspective. Comput. Educ. **174**, 104317 (2021)
30. Smith, J., Doe, J.: The role of augmented and virtual reality in modern education. J. Educ. Technol. **35**(2), 45–60 (2023)
31. Southworth, J., et al.: Developing a model for AI across the curriculum: transforming the higher education landscape via innovation in AI literacy. Comput. Educ.: Artif. Intell. **4**, 100127 (2023)
32. Spring, L., Robillard, D., Gehlbach, L., Moore Simas, T.A.: Impact of pass/fail grading on medical students' well-being and academic outcomes. Med. Educ. **45**(9), 867–877 (2011)
33. Steele, P., Burleigh, C., Kroposki, M., Magabo, M., Bailey, L.: Ethical considerations in designing virtual and augmented reality products—virtual and augmented reality design with students in mind: designers' perceptions. J. Educ. Technol. Syst. **49**(2), 219–238 (2020)

34. Valeri, F., Nilsson, P., Cederqvist, A.M.: Exploring students' experience of ChatGPT in stem education. Comput. Educ.: Artif. Intell. **8**, 100360 (2025)
35. Wang, Y., Liu, C., Tu, Y.F.: Factors affecting the adoption of AI-based applications in higher education. Educ. Technol. Soc. **24**(3), 116–129 (2021)
36. Wilson, E., Brown, T.: MOOCs and Blended Learning Strategies: The Future of Digital Education. Springer (2020)
37. Yan, L., et al.: Practical and ethical challenges of large language models in education: a systematic scoping review. Br. J. Educ. Technol. **55**, 90–112 (2023). https://doi.org/10.1111/bjet.13370
38. Zawacki-Richter, O., Marín, V.I., Bond, M., Gouverneur, F.: Systematic review of research on artificial intelligence applications in higher education–where are the educators? Int. J. Educ. Technol. High. Educ. **16**(1), 1–27 (2019)
39. Zee, M., Koomen, H.M.: Teacher self-efficacy and its effects on classroom processes, student academic adjustment, and teacher well-being: a synthesis of 40 years of research. Rev. Educ. Res. **86**(4), 981–1015 (2016)

Contents – Part II

Contents – Part I

Inclusion, Well-Being, and Student Support

Artificial Intelligence in Special Education: Enhancing IEP Design with CONALI & ChatGPT

Dario Lombardi[1](✉), Luigi Traetta[1], Fan Mo[2,3], and Antonio Maffei[4]

[1] University of Foggia, Foggia, Italy
{dario.lombardi,luigi.traetta}@unifg.it
[2] Faculty of Engineering, University of Nottingham, Nottingham, UK
Fan.Mo@nottingham.ac.uk
[3] Department of Computer Science, University of Oxford, Oxford, UK
[4] KTH Royal Institute of Technology, Stockholm, Sweden
maffei@kth.se

Abstract. Artificial intelligence (AI) has demonstrated significant utility in education, particularly in providing feedback, personalised learning paths, and reducing costs [1]. Despite its potential [2, 3], there is a notable gap in the literature on AI's role in inclusive educational planning and IEP (Individualised Education Plan) compilation [4]. This study presents the results of interventions aimed at assessing the perceived usefulness of AI and the CONALI Ontology by trainee special education teachers during IEP compilation. Conducted with teachers across all educational levels, the study investigates whether AI and CONALI are beneficial for IEPs for students of all ages. The research verifies the effectiveness of AI combined with the CONALI Ontological framework by Maffei [5–7], guiding teachers to identify Specific, Measurable, Achievable, Realistic, and Time-bound (SMART) educational goals. Exercises and validated questionnaires were administered to 391 teachers from early childhood, primary, lower secondary, and upper secondary education. Initially, teachers were introduced to the IEP's Section 5, emphasising SMART objectives. They then completed this section for a hypothetical student with disabilities. Next, the CONALI Ontology was introduced, showing its utility in aligning educational objectives with teaching activities and assessment methods. Teachers then completed a second IEP with CONALI support and evaluated their design experience via a questionnaire. Finally, they used the AI tool ChatGPT, in conjunction with CONALI, to compile a final IEP. Results showed that teachers perceived ChatGPT and CONALI as useful and effective. The Ontology was confirmed as a valuable tool for identifying SMART objectives aligned with intervention strategies and assessment methods. AI, supported by CONALI, effectively accelerated the IEP compilation process, enhancing engagement, motivation, and learning quality.

Keywords: AIEd · ChatGPT · IEP · CONALI

P. Ardimento et al. (Eds.): HELMeTO 2024, CCIS 2468, pp. 3–27, 2025.
https://doi.org/10.1007/978-3-031-93999-0_1

1 Introduction

Artificial Intelligence (AI) systems are software and hardware designed by humans that, given a complex objective, act in the physical or digital dimension by perceiving their environment through data acquisition, interpreting the collected structured or unstructured data, reasoning on the knowledge or processing the information derived from such data, and deciding the best action(s) to take to achieve the set goal [8].

AI is transforming the landscape of education and teaching, offering innovative solutions to enhance students' learning experiences and providing educators with tools to simplify administrative tasks, improve strategies, and reshape teaching methodologies [9].

Literature studies have demonstrated that AI can offer significant benefits to teachers, enhancing their work efficiency, teaching skills, and professional development support [10–12] (Meng & Sumettikoon, 2022; Chen et al., 2020; Lin, 2022), as well as fostering a positive attitude towards the use of technologies in teaching contexts [13].

AI-based personalized learning systems with timely feedback have shown significant potential for improving students' learning outcomes [14]. Despite the proven effectiveness of AI in teaching practices, improving student interaction and learning [15], there is a lack of evidence on how it can contribute to the inclusion of marginalized and minority students [11], as well as to inclusive educational design and, specifically, the development of Individualized Education Programs (IEPs).

The integration of AI into inclusive teaching is a delicate challenge requiring a multifaceted and complex approach. It is essential to understand how AI technologies can be used to identify students' individual needs, adapt teaching materials in real-time, and monitor progress accurately. Therefore, further research is needed to explore the implementation of AI in inclusive educational contexts, with particular attention to the benefits and limitations these technologies may present [16].

Teachers must receive adequate training not only on AI implementation but also on effectively integrating it with traditional and taxonomic pedagogical methodologies. This training should aim to equip teachers with the skills to identify educational pathways within IEPs that include targeted teaching activities, specific learning objectives, and evaluation methods that ensure the inclusion of all students, regardless of their abilities [12].

Integrating AI into the IEP development process, supported by appropriate taxonomic tools, can significantly enhance the personalization of educational pathways for students with disabilities. This not only allows for the creation of more inclusive learning environments but also ensures that students actively participate in the learning process, thereby promoting their right to self-determination and improving their academic and personal outcomes [17].

The integration of AI into the educational planning process offers a significant opportunity to make education more inclusive and accessible for students with disabilities [18].

Moreover, AI can greatly simplify the workload for teachers when creating project documentation, serving as a valuable support tool for planning personalized and inclusive educational paths.

In this context, the main objective of this study is:

RO1 – To analyze the perceptions of pre-service teachers in nursery school, primary school, and lower and upper secondary school regarding the use of ChatGPT and the CONALI Ontology to complete Section 5 of the Individualized Education Plan (IEP).

Therefore, the research question guiding this study is:

RQ1 – What are teachers' perceptions regarding the applications of AI in IEP design, particularly with the support of a taxonomic tool such as the CONALI Ontology? Specifically, how do these perceptions differ among teachers from various educational levels (nursery school, primary school, lower secondary school, and upper secondary school) regarding the implementation of AI and taxonomy in the design of Section 5 of the IEP?

2 Methods

The personalization of the educational path for students with disabilities is determined by identifying educational objectives, methodological strategies, and cognitive evaluation criteria that enable students to actively engage in learning and achieve significant results [19].

Given that these elements are reported in Section 5 of the Individualized Education Plan (IEP), we decided to have teachers complete this section. The objectives included in the document must be SMART, i.e., Specific, Measurable, Attainable, Realistic, and Time-bound [20, 21].

Furthermore, they must be aligned with teaching and learning activities and the methods used to verify the achievement of these objectives by students. Such alignment is guaranteed by the CONALI Ontology, which focuses on identifying educational objectives for planning constructively aligned activities [5, 6]. Therefore, we chose to use it to support teachers during the design and completion of Section 5 of the IEP.

The experimental sample involved 391 teachers enrolled in the specialization course on educational support (Active Formative Apprenticeship - TFA) at the University of Foggia, including: 88 attending courses pertaining to the preschool and primary grades; 199 those in secondary school; and 104 those in secondary school.

To familiarize teachers with inclusive planning and the identification of SMART objectives through Bloom's taxonomy (1956), a frontal lecture was conducted. Teachers were then given the task of completing Section 5 of the IEP for an imaginary student with autism spectrum disorder. They were provided with a detailed clinical picture of the student to ensure clarity about the conditions for which they needed to plan.

Following this 45-minute exercise, a discussion was conducted to address any issues experienced by the teachers during the planning phase.

Since the teachers were not familiar with the Ontology, the first part of the intervention involved explaining and presenting the methods to apply the CONALI Ontology and Constructive Alignment (CA).

Teachers then used the Ontology to complete Section 5 of the IEP for the same student as in the initial task. This exercise was completed individually within 45 minutes, followed by a 30-minute discussion to assess whether teachers had mastered the use of the Ontology and to clarify any doubts.

At the end of the discussion, a questionnaire was distributed to assess teachers' perceptions of the application of the Ontology. Teachers had 15 minutes to complete the questionnaire.

After assessing teachers' perceptions of using the CONALI Ontology for IEP design through the questionnaire, the sample was divided into an experimental group and a control group based on their preferences. For the completion of the third exercise, teachers who chose to use ChatGPT accessed the platform to complete the task in combination with the CONALI Ontology, while those who preferred not to use ChatGPT completed the exercise with the support of only the CONALI Ontology.

Both groups had 1 hour to complete the exercise. At the end of it, a questionnaire was handed out to the groups to verify their perceptions during the planning phase. The questionnaire assessed the extent to which ChatGPT supported teachers in identifying objectives, teaching and learning activities (TLA), and verification methods to understand whether the educational objectives had been achieved. Teachers were also asked if they would integrate ChatGPT into their educational planning and to note any advantages or disadvantages observed during the planning phase.

2.1 Intervention Summary Syllabus

To ensure the reproducibility of the study, the intervention summary syllabus is provided below:

- **Introduction and Context (1 hour)**: Trainees were explained the importance of personalizing the educational path for students with disabilities, focusing specifically on Section 5 of the IEP. The purpose was to help teachers define SMART educational objectives and align them with teaching and learning activities, as well as verification methods.
- **Exercise 1 (45 minutes)**: Teachers filled in Section 5 of the IEP for an imaginary student with autism spectrum disorder to become familiar with inclusive planning and SMART objectives.
- **Introduction to the CONALI Ontology (30 minutes):** The CONALI Ontology was presented to teachers to help ensure educational objectives are aligned with teaching and learning activities.
- **Application of the CONALI Ontology** (45 minutes for the exercise; 30 minutes for the discussion): Teachers used the CONALI Ontology to fill in Section 5 of the IEP for the same imaginary student. This was followed by a classroom discussion.
- **Assessment Questionnaire (20 minutes)**: Teachers completed a questionnaire to assess their perceptions of using the CONALI Ontology for IEP design.
- **Introduction to ChatGPT (30 minutes)**: Following the initial assessment, teachers were introduced to ChatGPT technology.
- **Final Exercise (60 minutes)**: Teachers from both experimental and control groups filled in Section 5 of the IEP for a new imaginary student with Trisomy 21. The experimental group used ChatGPT and the Ontology, while the control group used only the Ontology.
- **Intervention Assessment (20 minutes)**: Teachers completed a final questionnaire to assess their perceptions of the exercise. The experimental group's questionnaire

explored the extent to which ChatGPT supported them in identifying objectives, TLAs, and verification methods, while the control group's questionnaire gathered feedback on their overall experience.

The questions and answers from the questionnaire are reported in the Sect. 3.

3 Results

In this section, we present the results of the questionnaires distributed to teachers during the intervention. The discussion follows the order of questionnaire distribution.

It should be noted that the number of teachers who responded to the questionnaires may vary from one exercise to another due to technical and personal issues encountered during the intervention, such as temporary unavailability of the network and technological devices, or the need to leave the classroom for personal reasons.

We will begin by examining the questionnaire administered after the exercise that involved the application of the CONALI Ontology. The presentation of the results will compare the different responses and their respective percentages across the different levels of education of the study participants.

Responses were received from: 88 teachers from nursery and primary schools (Inf. + Prim.), who participated in the same session for logistical reasons; 199 teachers from lower secondary schools (Sec I); and 104 teachers from upper secondary schools (Sec II).

3.1 Results on the Application of CONALI for IEP Design

After the explanation and prior exercise on the application of the CONALI Ontology, a questionnaire was distributed to the teachers to evaluate the effectiveness of the Ontology for inclusive design.

Across all levels of education, the results clearly show that Constructive Alignment (CA) and the CONALI Ontology were appreciated and considered effective by teachers for aligning objectives, teaching strategies, and assessment methods.

The collected data indicate that, before using CA, many teachers felt only moderately capable of designing an Individualized Education Plan (IEP) with aligned learning objectives, methods, and assessment modalities. However, nursery and primary school teachers felt more confident than secondary school teachers (Fig. 1).

Over 90% of teachers across all levels reported that they effectively understood the principles of CA during the course and found the instructional materials clear and easy to understand.

After the course, many teachers felt more capable of aligning the learning objectives of the IEP with teaching and assessment methods, though there was a higher level of neutrality in responses from lower secondary school teachers (Fig. 2).

Additionally, teachers highlighted that the course provided practical examples applicable to IEP design. The graphs indeed show peaks of strong agreement among nursery, primary, and upper secondary school teachers, and agreement among lower secondary school teachers (Fig. 3).

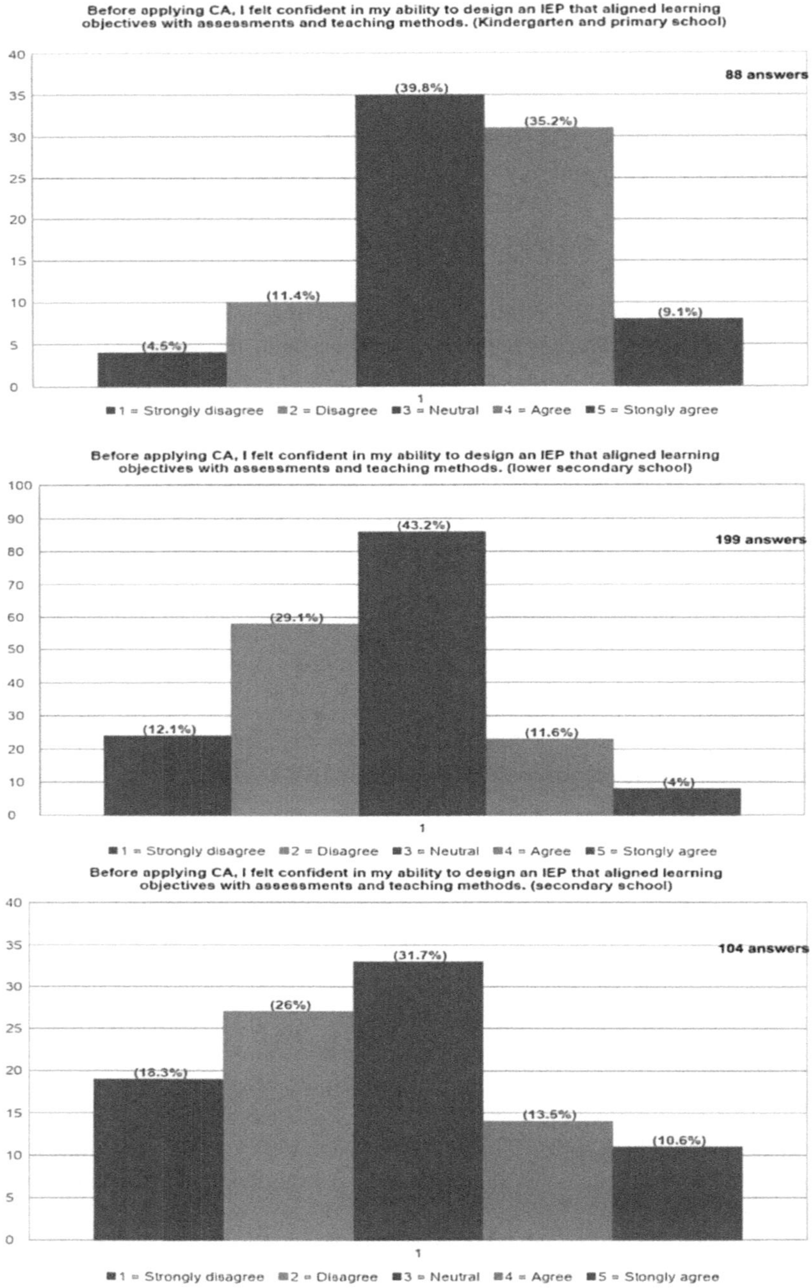

Fig. 1. Teachers' confidence levels in designing an IEP before and after using Constructive Alignment (CA) and the CONALI Ontology.

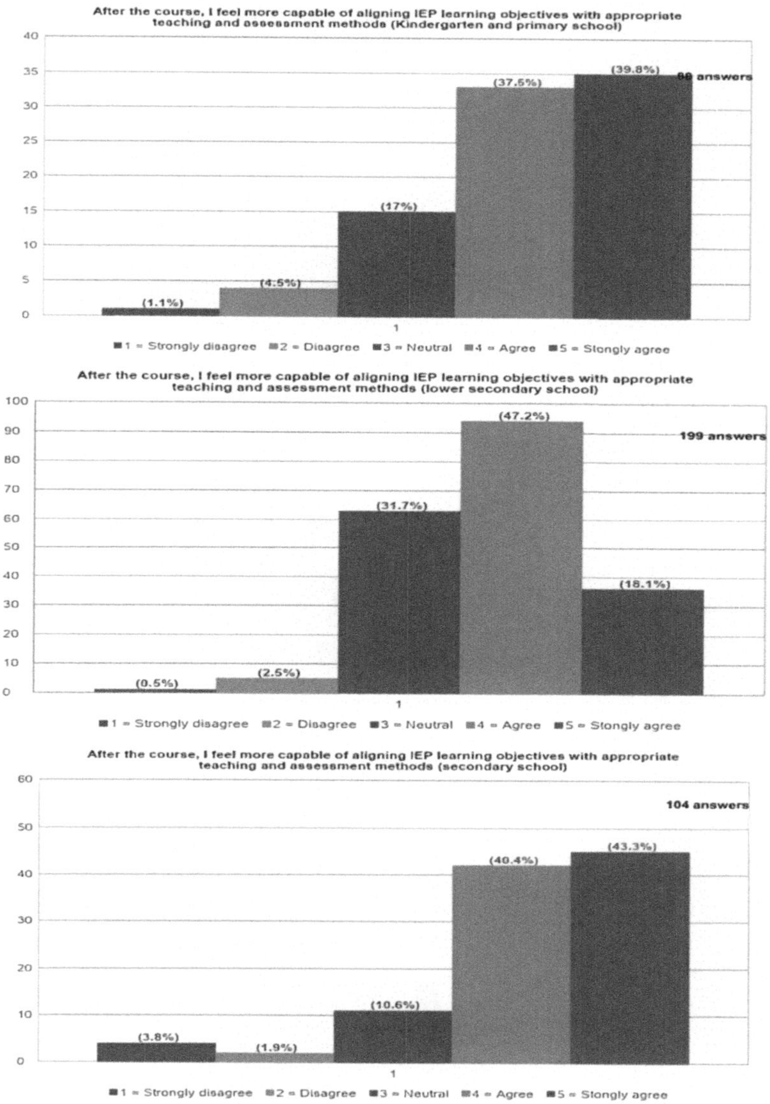

Fig. 2. Teachers' self-assessment on their ability to align learning objectives with teaching strategies and assessment methods after training on CA and the CONALI Ontology.

Several teachers also believe that using CA will improve student learning outcomes (8% Inf + Prim; 26.1% Sec I; 9.6% were neutral; 40.9% Inf + Prim, 50.8% Sec I, 36.5% agreed; and 46.6% Inf + Prim, 22.1% Sec I, and 52.9% Sec II strongly agreed) and intend to apply CA principles in their future course design (Fig. 4).

During the course, teachers received adequate support and resources to understand and apply the concepts (39.8% Inf + Prim, 38.7% Sec I, 27.9% Sec II agreed and 51.1% Inf + Prim, 39.7% Sec I, 67.3% Sec II strongly agreed); the course encouraged

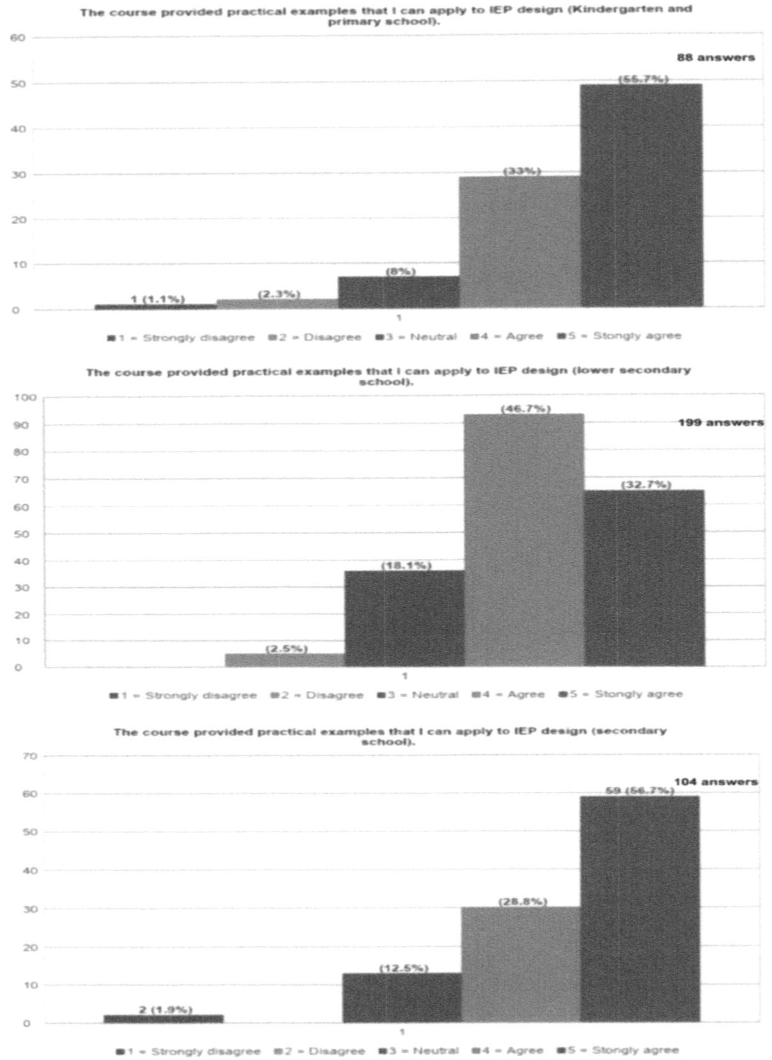

Fig. 3. Teachers' perceptions of the practical applicability of Constructive Alignment (CA) in IEP design across different educational levels.

collaboration and idea exchange among participants (42% Inf + Prim, 36.2% Sec I, 25% Sec II expressed a positive opinion; and 44.3% Inf + Prim, 44.2% Sec I, and 54.8% Sec II expressed a very positive opinion).

Overall, almost all teachers were satisfied with the CA lesson and its content (39.8% Inf + Prim, 41.2% Sec I, 23.1% Sec II agreed; 54.5%, 42.2% Sec I, and 74% Sec II strongly agreed) and believe that the lesson met their learning expectations regarding CA and that CA will have a positive impact on their teaching practices (38.6% Inf +

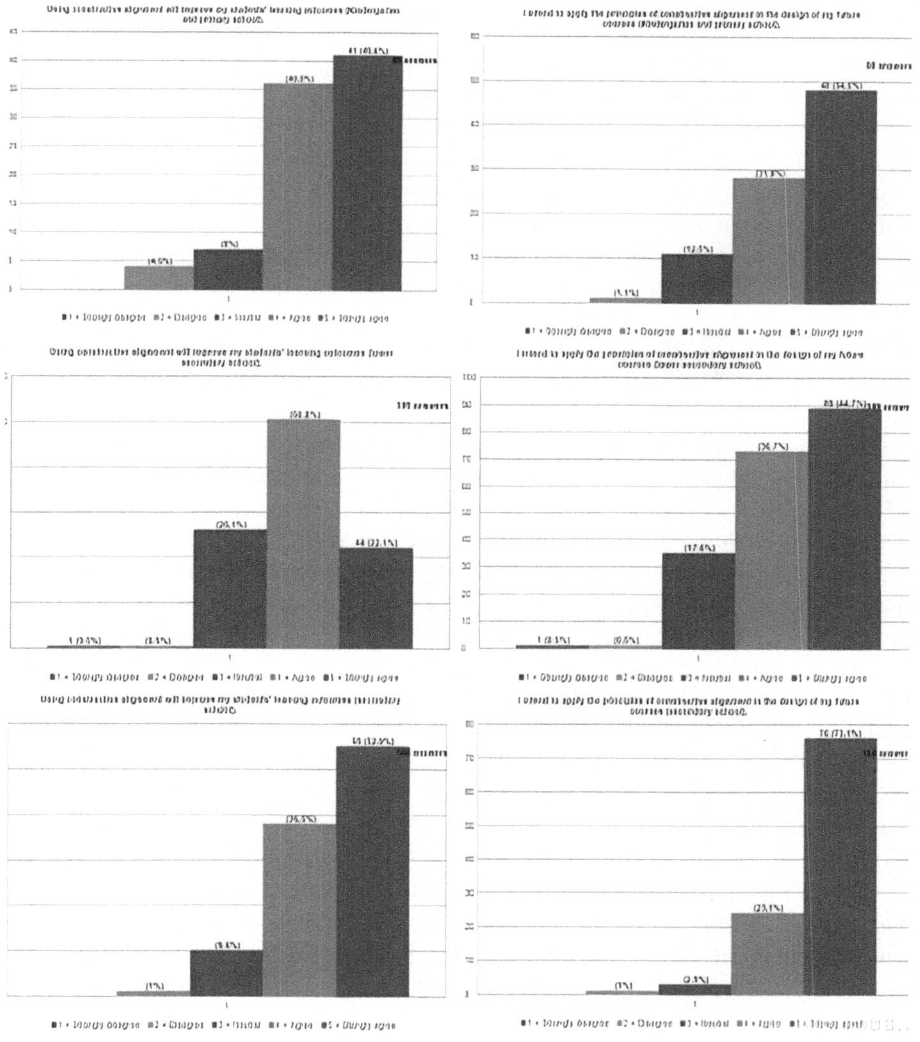

Fig. 4. Teachers' agreement on the impact of Constructive Alignment (CA) on student learning outcomes and their intention to apply CA principles in future course design.

Prim, 48.7% Sec I, 30.8% Sec II agreed and 37.5% Inf + Prim, 25.1% Sec I, 63.5% Sec II strongly agreed).

In light of the above, CA appears to be an effective tool for inclusive educational design and a support that is perceived as extremely valuable by pre-service teachers in teaching support activities.

3.2 Results on the Application of ChatGPT for IEP Design

The group of teachers who utilised ChatGPT for planning Section 5 of the IEP consisted of: 8 teachers from Nursery and Primary schools (Inf + Prim); 57 from Lower Secondary schools (Sec I); and 81 from Upper Secondary schools (Sec II).

In the kindergarten, primary, and lower secondary levels, many teachers did not use the artificial intelligence system, a phenomenon that will be discussed later. Additionally, in the kindergarten and primary school levels, nearly half of the participants left the session before the end of the intervention.

Consequently, the number of respondents to the questionnaire was significantly reduced.

Turning to the results, all teachers reported understanding the task, and many were satisfied with how they completed it (37.5% Inf + Prim, 42.1% Sec I, 40.7% Sec II were satisfied, 62.5% Inf + Prim, 10.5% Sec I, 39.5% Sec II were very satisfied).

More than half of the participants completed the task in less than an hour (50% Inf + Prim, 54.4% Sec I, 54.3% Sec II), a substantial portion completed it in an hour (25% Inf + Prim, 17.5% Sec I, 34.6% Sec II), and the remaining took more time. All participants used the free version of ChatGPT, except for 1.8% of Sec I.

Many participants (37.5% Inf + Prim, 21.1% Sec I, 48.1% Sec II) had never used ChatGPT before. However, by the end of the exercise, despite a significant percentage expressing neutrality (62.5% Inf + Prim, 50.9% Sec I, 28.4% Sec II), many stated that the system helped them generate objectives, strategies, and systems consistent with the IEP (12.5% Inf + Prim, 31.6% Sec I, 38.3% Sec II agreed, and 25% Inf + Prim, 8.8% Sec I, 29.6% Sec II strongly agreed).

Despite many neutral responses, ChatGPT enabled teachers to organise their ideas during IEP planning and find more congruent objectives, strategies, and assessment systems than they would have on their own (25% Inf + Prim, 35.1% Sec I, 33.3% Sec II agreed; and 25% Inf + Prim, 5.3% Sec I, 21% Sec II strongly agreed) (Fig. 5).

ChatGPT assisted teachers with the less interesting parts of planning, allowing them to focus on the quality of objectives and the search for strategies and assessment systems to include in the IEP (37.5% Inf + Prim, 52.6% Sec I, 33.3% Sec II were neutral; 37.5% Inf + Prim, 33.3% Sec I, 37% Sec II agreed; 12.5% Inf + Prim, 3.5% Sec I, 18.5% Sec II strongly agreed) (Fig. 6).

Thanks to ChatGPT, teachers spent less time completing the planning (12.5% Inf + Prim, 38.6% Sec I, 30.9% Sec II agreed; 75% Inf + Prim, 24.6% Sec I, 46.9% Sec II strongly agreed) (Fig. 5); moreover, the planning of the IEP was more enjoyable and interesting (75% Inf + Prim and 37% Sec II strongly agreed, while Sec I had 38.6% neutral and 33.3% agreed) and was praised by almost all participants.

Many teachers positively evaluated the accuracy of ChatGPT's feedback (37.5% Inf + Prim, 21.1% Sec I, 44.4% Sec II agreed; 12.5% Inf + Prim, 3.5% Sec I, 16% Sec II strongly agreed), but many gave a neutral response to this question (50% Inf + Prim, 52.6% Sec I, 37% Sec II).

Furthermore, many participants stated that ChatGPT is capable of understanding and providing relevant responses. However, many participants believe that when completing tasks with the support of ChatGPT, it is inevitable and important to apply their own

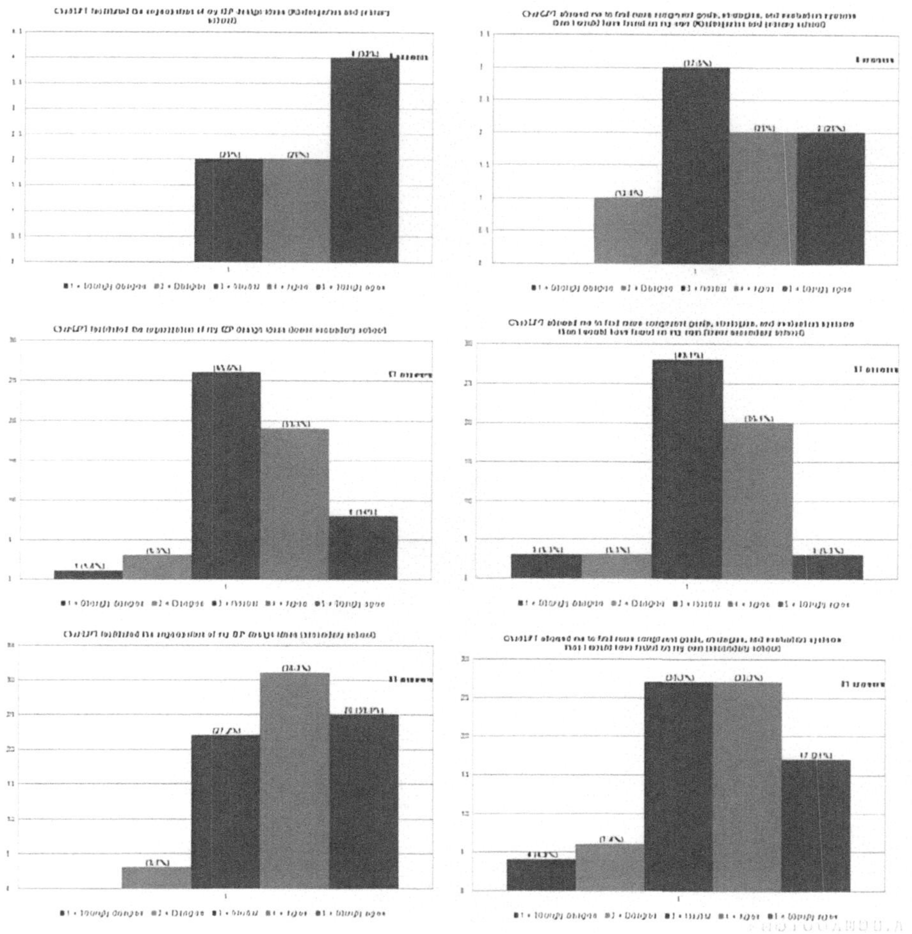

Fig. 5. Teachers' perceptions of ChatGPT's support in organizing ideas and generating IEP-aligned objectives, strategies, and assessment methods.

critical thinking (37.5% Inf + Prim, 15.8% Sec I, 13.6% Sec II agreed; 12.5% Inf + Prim, 24.6% Sec I, 79% Sec II strongly agreed) (Fig. 7).

Finally, many of the teachers (48.1% Inf + Prim, 45.6% Sec I, 48.1% Sec II) stated that they would not have found the same objectives, methodological strategies, and assessment systems without the use of ChatGPT, and the majority (62.5% Inf + Prim, 78.9% Sec I, 92.6% Sec II) consider the system a useful tool for IEP design (Fig. 8).

3.3 Teachers Who Didn't Use Chat GPT

The group of teachers who did not use ChatGPT to complete the IEP consisted of 31 participants in the kindergarten and primary levels, 115 in the lower secondary level, and 9 in the upper secondary level.

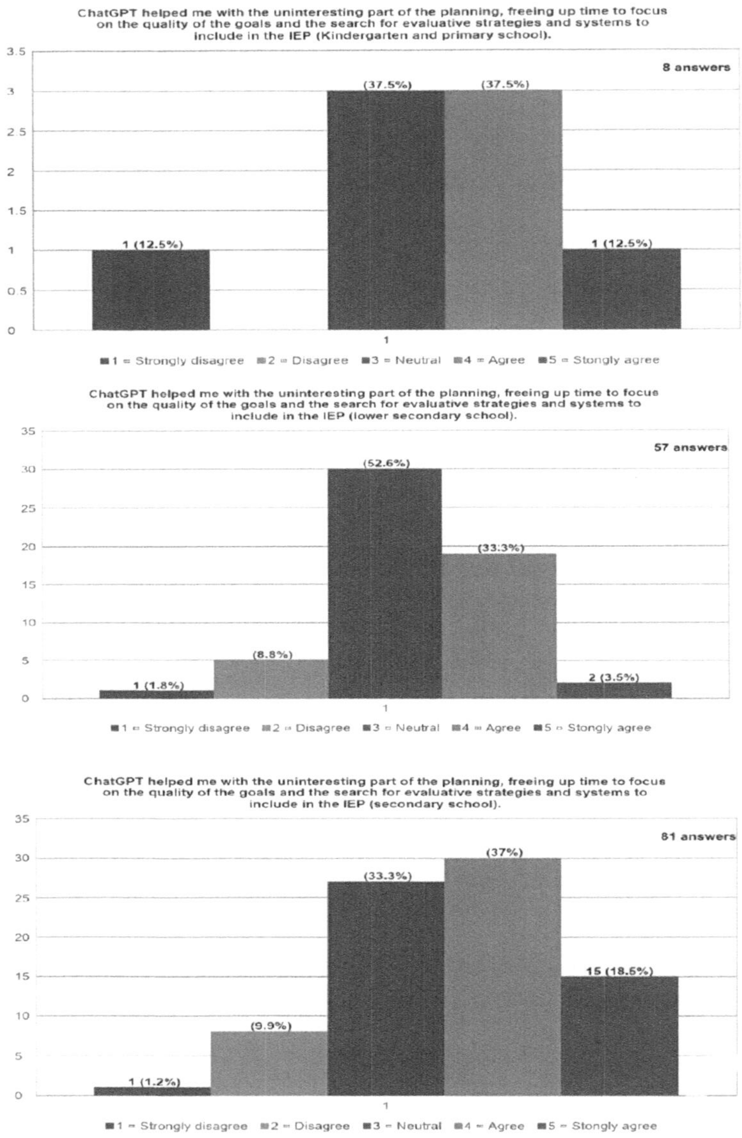

Fig. 6. Teachers' feedback on ChatGPT's role in reducing workload and allowing more focus on refining IEP objectives and strategies.

Most of them were satisfied with how they completed the task (35.5% in kindergarten and primary, 41.7% in lower secondary, and 33.3% in upper secondary were in agreement, and 25.8% in kindergarten and primary, 14.8% in lower secondary, and 33.3% in upper secondary were in complete agreement).

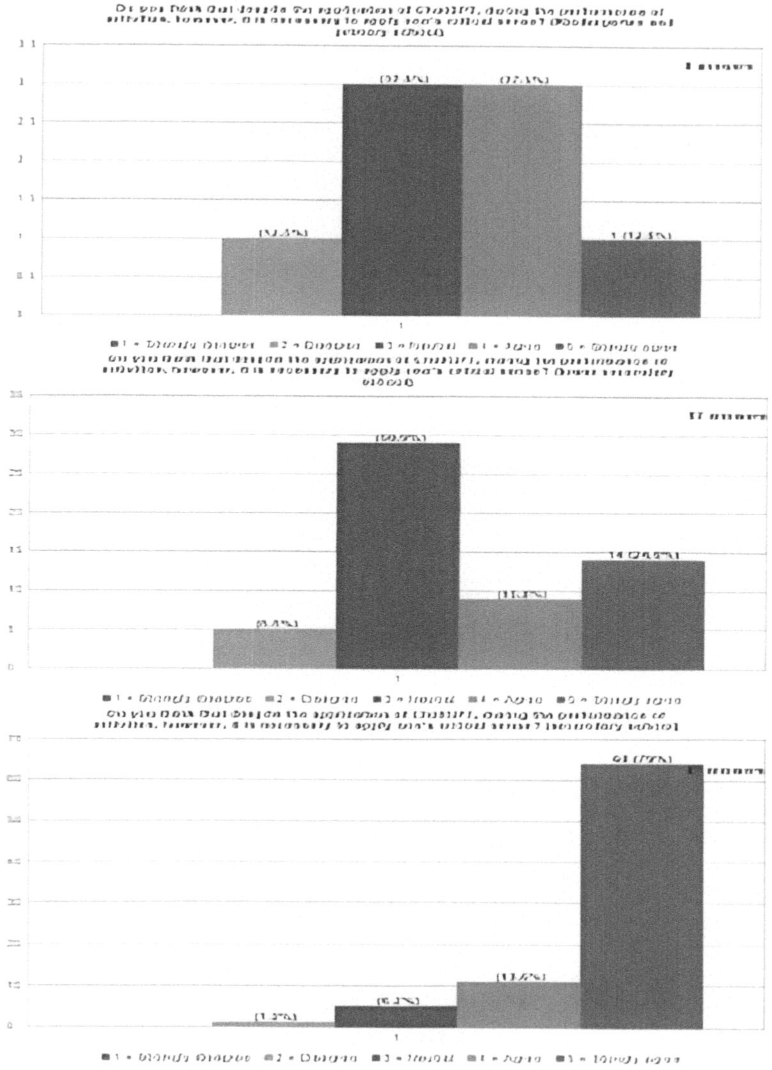

Fig. 7. Teachers' views on the necessity of applying critical thinking despite ChatGPT's assistance in IEP design.

In the kindergarten and primary levels, many teachers regretted not using ChatGPT (87.1%); in the other levels, only 23.5% in lower secondary and 22.2% in upper secondary expressed regret.

Interestingly, many of them ended up using the OpenAI system anyway (54.8% in kindergarten and primary; 39.1% in lower secondary; 33.3% in upper secondary) (Fig. 9), and many believe that the system could be useful for IEP design (77.4% in kindergarten and primary; 31.3% in lower secondary; 66.7% in upper secondary).

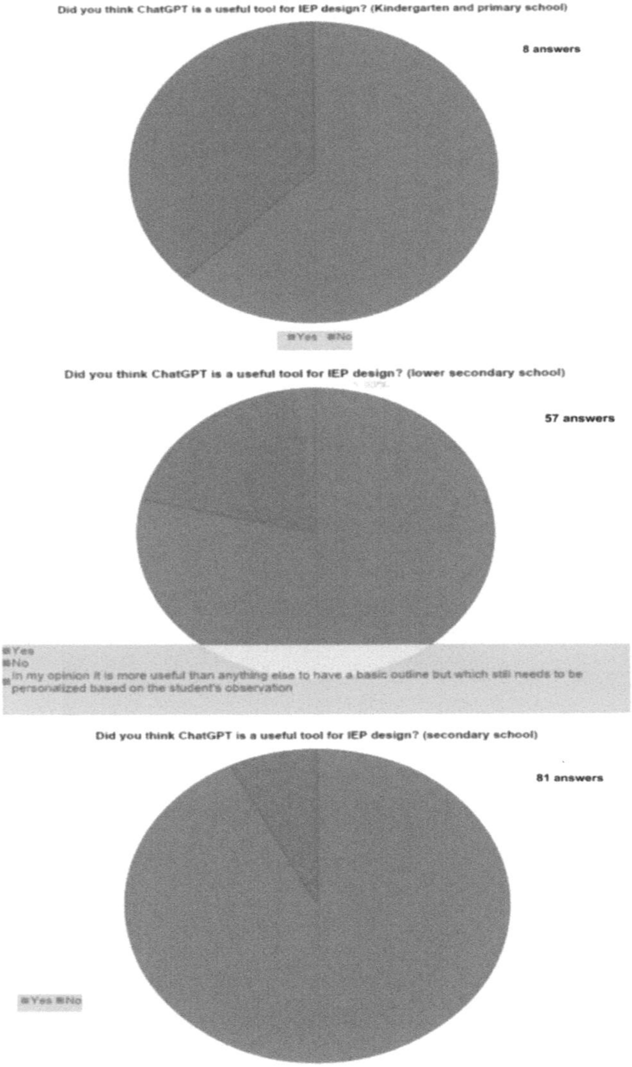

Fig. 8. Percentage of teachers who consider ChatGPT a useful tool for IEP design.

Indeed, many stated that they would adopt it for IEP design in the future (83.9% in kindergarten and primary; 37.4% in lower secondary; 55.6% in upper secondary).

Finally, almost all participants considered the activity useful for IEP design (90.3% in kindergarten and primary; 81.7% in lower secondary; 88.9% in upper secondary).

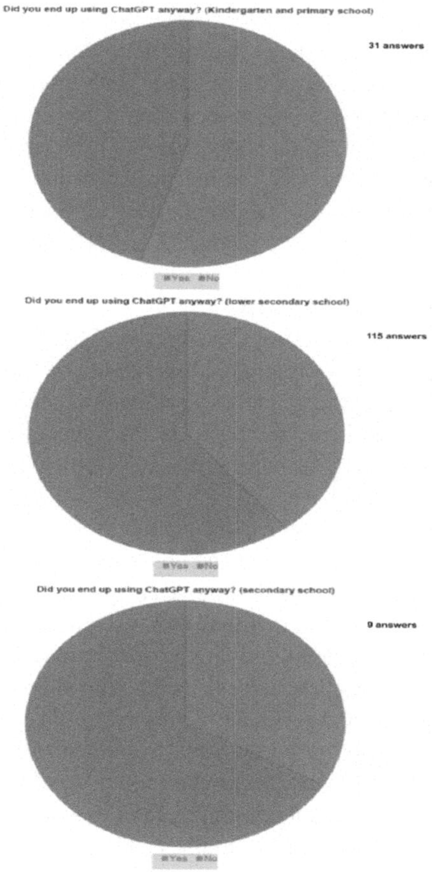

Fig. 9. Percentage of teachers who initially did not use ChatGPT but later adopted it for IEP design and their perceptions of its utility.

4 Discussion

The results of the study reveal significant appreciation for the application of ChatGPT and the CONALI Ontology across various educational levels. Teachers from different grades expressed distinct perceptions and experiences regarding these tools, highlighting both their benefits and discrepancies. Additionally, the findings underscore key challenges in AI integration, particularly in terms of technical accessibility, teacher training, and the necessity of a critical approach to educational AI tools.

4.1 Appreciation of ChatGPT and CONALI by Teachers

Overall, ChatGPT and the CONALI Ontology were well-received by teachers across all educational levels. Constructive Alignment (CA) and the CONALI Ontology were particularly valued for their effectiveness in aligning objectives, teaching strategies, and assessment methods. More than 90% of teachers reported understanding CA principles effectively and found the instructional materials clear. Many teachers felt more capable of aligning IEP learning objectives with teaching and assessment methods after the course, indicating a substantial increase in their confidence.

Teachers from nursery, primary, and upper secondary schools showed strong agreement on the practical applicability of CA in IEP design, while lower secondary teachers displayed a higher level of neutrality. This suggests a variance in confidence levels and perceived applicability of CA principles across different educational stages.

Benefits and Discrepancies of CONALI

The data indicate that prior to utilizing Constructive Alignment (CA), many teachers felt only moderately capable of designing an Individualized Education Plan (IEP) with aligned learning objectives, methods, and assessment modalities. Nursery and primary school teachers felt more confident compared to their secondary school counterparts, reflecting a potential discrepancy in familiarity or comfort with inclusive design tools across different educational levels.

This familiarity is likely attributable to the greater experience of nursery and primary school teachers compared to those in lower and upper secondary education. Additionally, teachers believed that using CA during the course enhanced their ability to align learning objectives with appropriate teaching methods and assessment modalities.

The practical examples provided and the support received during the course were unanimously appreciated by teachers across all educational levels. This underscores the importance of providing practical feedback on the educational theories and paradigms presented during lessons, enabling participants to immediately understand the procedures for their implementation and the corresponding benefits. Teachers also emphasized that CA would improve student learning outcomes and that they intended to apply its principles in the design of their future courses and educational interventions.

The support and resources provided during the course were deemed adequate by a significant majority, and the collaborative environment was positively received. This collective agreement highlights the perceived utility and effectiveness of the CONALI Ontology in promoting inclusive educational design.

4.2 Implementation of ChatGPT in IEP Design

The integration of ChatGPT into the design of Section 5 of the IEP has yielded various advantages and challenges. Despite a significant portion of teachers expressing neutrality, a considerable number of those who used ChatGPT felt that it helped them generate objectives, strategies, and systems congruent with the IEP. More than half of the participants completed the task in less than an hour, indicating the tool's efficiency in compiling the IEP.

However, the implementation encountered several issues. In nursery, primary, and lower secondary schools, many teachers did not use the AI system, citing difficulties in connecting to the interface. Additionally, there was considerable scepticism regarding the potential and reliability of ChatGPT, leading some teachers to avoid using it. This reluctance, possibly stemming from a lack of teacher training [22, 23], highlights the need for greater awareness and education on the benefits and practical applications of AI in educational contexts.

Despite these challenges, teachers who engaged with ChatGPT generally reported that it aided them in structuring their ideas and formulating more coherent learning objectives, strategies, and assessment criteria. By automating certain planning aspects, the tool enabled teachers to allocate more cognitive resources to refining the quality of IEP design. This finding is consistent with emerging research on AI-assisted educational planning, which suggests that AI can serve as a valuable cognitive support system rather than a replacement for teacher expertise.

4.3 Future Prospects and Critical Integration

Looking ahead, it is imperative to ensure a critical and reflective approach to integrating AI tools like ChatGPT into educational design. While the study demonstrates AI's potential to support personalized learning pathways, educators must remain vigilant regarding its limitations. AI-generated content may contain inaccuracies or fail to account for contextual nuances, necessitating continuous human oversight.

One promising direction is the integration of taxonomic tools within AI systems to enhance alignment between learning objectives and assessment methods. By incorporating structured classification frameworks, AI can provide more targeted and pedagogically sound recommendations, ensuring consistency in instructional design. Additionally, the development of AI literacy programs for educators will be crucial in fostering a nuanced understanding of both the benefits and risks associated with AI-based educational tools.

4.4 Answer to Research Question (RQ1)

The integration of AI, specifically ChatGPT, in designing Section 5 of the IEP and its interaction with the CONALI Ontology revealed significant insights into teachers' perceptions across different educational levels.

General Perceptions of AI in IEP Design

Overall, many teachers recognized ChatGPT's potential in generating instructional components aligned with the IEP, with more than half completing the task in under an hour. However, neutrality in responses suggests that skepticism and uncertainty remain prevalent, reinforcing the necessity for targeted training.

Technical barriers were a recurrent theme, with many teachers in nursery, primary, and lower secondary schools reporting connectivity issues and doubts regarding ChatGPT's reliability. However, post-course reflections indicated that previously skeptical teachers acknowledged the tool's benefits upon deeper engagement.

Differences Across Educational Levels

1. Nursery and primary school teachers felt more confident in using inclusive design tools compared to their secondary school counterparts.

This confidence likely stems from their greater experience and familiarity with teaching, positively impacting the implementation of these tools.

A significant number of nursery and primary school teachers regretted not using ChatGPT due to technical difficulties or initial skepticism but recognized its potential benefits after the course.

2. Lower secondary school teachers showed a higher level of neutrality in their responses, possibly indicating a lack of familiarity or comfort with AI tools or a more cautious approach to adopting new technologies.

   This group had a higher percentage of skepticism towards ChatGPT, reflecting the need for more targeted training and awareness programs.
3. Upper secondary school teachers displayed a balanced perception, with many acknowledging the tool's effectiveness and expressing willingness to adopt it in future IEP projects.

   This group particularly appreciated the system's ability to organize ideas and improve the planning process, despite initial skepticism.

Challenges and Recommendations

Technical and Training Issues

1. Connectivity problems and inadequate AI training emerged as key barriers to effective implementation. Addressing these issues through improved infrastructure and comprehensive training programs is essential.
2. Providing concrete examples of AI's pedagogical applications can reduce skepticism and enhance educators' confidence in leveraging AI tools effectively.

Future Prospects

- The study's findings suggest that ChatGPT and the CONALI Ontology have the potential to enhance inclusive educational planning. However, continuous refinement of AI systems and sustained professional development for educators will be critical to ensuring their long-term success.
- Further research should explore the longitudinal impact of AI integration in IEP design, examining whether sustained exposure leads to greater teacher confidence and improved student outcomes.

5 Conclusions

The investigation into teachers' perceptions regarding the use of AI in IEP design, supported by the CONALI Ontology, reveals a nuanced landscape of both enthusiasm and skepticism. Our findings suggest that AI, specifically ChatGPT, holds significant promise for enhancing the efficiency and effectiveness of IEP planning across various educational levels.

Teachers from all educational stages recognized the potential of AI tools in streamlining the design process for Section 5 of the IEP. Many reported that ChatGPT helped them generate well-aligned objectives, strategies, and assessment systems, which were more congruent with IEP requirements than those they might have developed independently.

The efficiency gains were notable, with over half of the participants completing the task in less than an hour, highlighting the potential time-saving benefits of AI in educational settings.

The CONALI Ontology was highly appreciated for its structured approach to aligning educational objectives, teaching strategies, and assessment methods. The practical examples provided during the course facilitated a clearer understanding of how to apply the ontology in IEP design, helping teachers at all levels feel more capable of creating cohesive and comprehensive IEPs.

However, the study also highlighted several challenges. Connectivity issues were a significant barrier, particularly for teachers in nursery, primary, and lower secondary schools, which prevented some from fully utilizing the AI system.

Additionally, a considerable degree of skepticism about the reliability and potential of AI tools persisted among teachers, especially those less familiar with such technology. This skepticism appears to be linked to a lack of comprehensive training and exposure, emphasizing the need for targeted professional development programs to build confidence and competence in using AI tools.

The differing levels of confidence and acceptance among teachers from various educational stages point to the importance of tailored support and resources. Nursery and primary school teachers felt more confident in using inclusive design tools, likely due to their greater familiarity and experience. In contrast, lower secondary school teachers exhibited more neutrality and skepticism, reflecting a need for more robust training and awareness initiatives in this group.

Despite these challenges, the overall feedback from teachers who used ChatGPT was positive. They found that the tool helped organize their ideas and manage less interesting aspects of planning, allowing them to focus on enhancing the quality of the IEP. This led to a more engaging and enjoyable planning process, as indicated by the participants' feedback.

In conclusion, while the integration of AI in IEP design is met with both enthusiasm and skepticism, the potential benefits are clear. The integration of AI tools with taxonomic frameworks like the CONALI Ontology can contribute positively to creating congruent and inclusive IEPs, improving teachers' efficiency and effectiveness in providing optimal educational pathways for their students.

To fully realize these benefits, it is crucial to address technical barriers, provide comprehensive training, and foster a critical but open-minded approach to AI in educational planning.

Future efforts should focus on continuous improvement and updates of AI systems, combined with ongoing professional development, to ensure that teachers are well-equipped to harness the full potential of AI tools in creating inclusive and effective educational plans.

Appendix A: Teacher Perception Questionnaires

Introduction

This appendix presents the questionnaires used to assess teachers' perceptions regarding the integration of ChatGPT and the CONALI Ontology in the design of Individualized Education Plans (IEPs).

The questionnaires were designed to evaluate:

- Teachers' confidence and satisfaction with IEP design.
- The perceived effectiveness of ChatGPT in supporting the IEP planning process.
- Potential limitations and challenges encountered while using AI in educational design.

The survey items included Likert-scale questions (1–5), multiple-choice items, and open-ended responses, ensuring a combination of quantitative and qualitative insights.

Questionnaire on IEP Design With ChatGPT (Experimental Group)

General Perception of the Task

1. To what extent did you understand the task? (1 = Strongly disagree; 5 = Strongly agree)
2. Are you satisfied with how you performed the task? (1 = Not satisfied at all; 5 = Very satisfied)
3. How much time did you spend designing the IEP? (Open-ended response)
4. Which version of ChatGPT did you use for IEP design? (Open-ended response)
5. Had you ever used ChatGPT before this activity? (Yes/No)

Effectiveness of ChatGPT in IEP Design

6. ChatGPT provided comprehensive answers, but it did not allow me to properly learn how to design an IEP. (1 = Strongly disagree; 5 = Strongly agree)
7. ChatGPT facilitated the generation of goals, strategies, and evaluation systems aligned with the IEP. (1 = Strongly disagree; 5 = Strongly agree)
8. ChatGPT facilitated the organization of my IEP design ideas. (1 = Strongly disagree; 5 = Strongly agree)
9. ChatGPT allowed me to find more appropriate goals, strategies, and evaluation systems than I would have found on my own. (1 = Strongly disagree; 5 = Strongly agree)
10. ChatGPT helped me with the less engaging aspects of planning, freeing up time to focus on the quality of goals and the search for evaluative strategies and systems to include in the IEP. (1 = Strongly disagree; 5 = Strongly agree)
11. ChatGPT helped me complete the IEP design process more quickly. (1 = Strongly disagree; 5 = Strongly agree)
12. ChatGPT made the IEP design process more enjoyable and interesting. (1 = Strongly disagree; 5 = Strongly agree)

Ease of Use and Technical Issues

13. How would you rate the ease of using ChatGPT for the IEP design task? (1 = Very difficult; 5 = Very easy)
14. List any technical issues encountered while using ChatGPT (e.g., slow interface, limited server availability for the free version, etc.). (Open-ended response)

Accuracy and Reliability of ChatGPT

15. How would you rate the accuracy of the feedback provided by ChatGPT? (1 = Not accurate at all; 5 = Very accurate)
16. Did you feel that ChatGPT understood your questions and provided relevant answers? (1 = Strongly disagree; 5 = Strongly agree)

Critical Thinking and AI Limitations

17. Do you think that, despite the use of ChatGPT, it is still necessary to apply one's own critical thinking while performing the task? (Yes/No)
18. Do you believe you would have found the same goals, methodological strategies, and evaluation systems without using ChatGPT? (Yes/No)

Overall Perception

19. Do you think ChatGPT is a useful tool for IEP design? (Yes/No)
20. Do you have any comments or feedback you would like to share? (Open-ended response)

Appendix B: Constructive Alignment and CONALI Ontology Questionnaire

Introduction

This questionnaire assesses teachers' perceptions of Constructive Alignment (CA) and the CONALI Ontology after attending the training course. The aim is to evaluate the effectiveness of the training, the clarity of the materials, and the perceived impact of Constructive Alignment on IEP design and teaching practices.

Most questions use a 5-point Likert scale ranging from:

1. Strongly Disagree
2. Disagree
3. Neutral
4. Agree
5. Strongly Agree

Additional open-ended questions allow teachers to elaborate on their experiences and insights.

Constructive Alignment and CONALI Ontology Questionnaire

Understanding and Application of Constructive Alignment

1. Before applying Constructive Alignment, I felt confident in my ability to design an IEP that aligned learning objectives with assessments and teaching methods. (1 = Strongly Disagree; 5 = Strongly Agree)
2. The principles of Constructive Alignment were explained effectively during the course, and the course materials were clear and easy to understand. (1 = Strongly Disagree; 5 = Strongly Agree)
3. After the course, I feel more capable of aligning IEP learning objectives with appropriate teaching and assessment methods. (1 = Strongly Disagree; 5 = Strongly Agree)
4. The course provided practical examples that I can apply to IEP design. (1 = Strongly Disagree; 5 = Strongly Agree)
5. Using Constructive Alignment will improve my students' learning outcomes. (1 = Strongly Disagree; 5 = Strongly Agree)
6. I intend to apply the principles of Constructive Alignment in the design of my future courses. (1 = Strongly Disagree; 5 = Strongly Agree).

Course Support and Collaboration

7. During the course, I received adequate support and resources to understand and apply the concepts. (1 = Strongly Disagree; 5 = Strongly Agree)
8. The course encouraged collaboration and the exchange of ideas among participants. (1 = Strongly Disagree; 5 = Strongly Agree)
9. Overall, I am satisfied with the Constructive Alignment lesson and its content. (1 = Strongly Disagree; 5 = Strongly Agree)
10. The course met my expectations in terms of learning and Constructive Alignment training. (1 = Strongly Disagree; 5 = Strongly Agree)

Course Support and Collaboration

11. Describe your experience in designing an IEP before and after learning about Constructive Alignment. What were the main differences? (Open-ended response)
12. How do you think applying Constructive Alignment principles will impact your teaching practice? (Open-ended response)
13. Share any personal insights or significant moments you experienced during the lesson. (Open-ended response)
14. How do you plan to integrate what you have learned about Constructive Alignment into your teaching practice? (Open-ended response)

Appendix C: Questionnaire for the NO ChatGPT Group

Introduction

For questions using a 5-point Likert scale, responses range from:

1. Strongly Disagree
2. Disagree
3. Neutral
4. Agree
5. Strongly Agree

Questionnaire for the NO ChatGPT Group

General Perception of the Task

1. To what extent did you understand the task? (1 = Strongly Disagree; 5 = Strongly Agree)
2. Are you satisfied with how you performed the task? (1 = Strongly Disagree; 5 = Strongly Agree)
3. How much time did you spend designing the IEP? (Less than 1 hour, 1 hour, Less than 2 hours, 2 hours, More than 2 hours, Other)

Reasons for Not Using ChatGPT

4. Why did you choose not to use ChatGPT? (Open-ended response)
5. Do you regret not using ChatGPT? (Yes/No)
6. Why? (Open-ended response)
7. Did you end up using ChatGPT anyway? (Yes/No)

Perceived Usefulness of ChatGPT

8. Do you think ChatGPT could be useful for IEP design? (1 = Strongly Disagree; 5 = Strongly Agree)
9. Do you think you will use ChatGPT for IEP design in the future? (Yes/No)

Overall Perception of the Activity

10. Do you think the activity was interesting and useful for IEP design? (1 = Strongly Disagree; 5 = Strongly Agree

References

1. Chan, K.S., Zary, N.: Applications and challenges of implementing artificial intelligence in medical education: integrative review. JMIR Med. Educ. **5**(1), e13930 (2019). https://doi.org/10.2196/13930
2. Bhimdiwala, A., Neri, R.C., Gomez, L.M.: Advancing the design and implementation of artificial intelligence in education through continuous improvement. Int. J. Artif. Intell. Educ. **32**, 756–782 (2022). https://doi.org/10.1007/s40593-021-00278-8
3. Pratama, M.P., Sampelolo, R., Lura, H.: Revolutionizing education: harnessing the power of artificial intelligence for personalized learning. Klasikal J. Educ. Lang. Teach. Sci. **5**(2), 350–357 (2023). https://doi.org/10.52208/klasikal.v5i2.877
4. Yiğitcanlar, T., Desouza, K.C., Butler, L., Roozkhosh, F.: Contributions and risks of artificial intelligence (AI) in building smarter cities: insights from a systematic review of the literature. Energies. **13**(6), 1473 (2020). https://doi.org/10.3390/en13061473

5. Maffei, A., Boffa, E., Lupi, F., Lanzetta, M.: On the design of constructively aligned educational unit. Educ. Sci. **12**(7), 438 (2022). https://doi.org/10.3390/educsci12070438
6. Maffei, A., Daghini, L., Archenti, A., Lohse, N.: CONALI ontology: a framework for design and evaluation of constructively aligned courses in higher education: putting in focus the educational goal verbs. Procedia CIRP. **50**, 765–772 (2016). https://doi.org/10.1016/j.procir.2016.06.004
7. Lupi, F., Maffei, A., Podržaj, P., Požrl, T., Stadnicka, D., Lanzetta, M.: Ontology for constructively aligned, collaborative, and evolving engineer knowledge-management platforms. In: HELMeTO 2023 - Conference Proceedings (2024, in press)
8. Samoili, S., Cobo, M. L., Gómez, E., De Prato, G., Martínez-Plumed, F., Delipetrev, B.: AI Watch. Defining artificial intelligence. Towards an operational definition and taxonomy of artificial intelligence. JRC Research Reports JRC118163, Joint Research Centre (2020)
9. Onesi-Ozigagun, O., Ololade, Y.J., Eyo-Udo, N.L., Ogundipe, D.O.: Revolutionizing education through AI: a comprehensive review of enhancing learning experiences. Int. J. Appl. Res. Soc. Sci. **6**(4), 589–607 (2024). https://doi.org/10.51594/ijarss.v6i4.1011
10. Meng, W., Sumettikoon, P.: The use of artificial intelligence to enhance teaching effectiveness in vocational education. Euras. J. Educ. Res. **98**(98), 266–283 (2022). https://doi.org/10.14689/ejer.2022.98.017
11. Chen, L., Chen, P., Lin, Z.: Artificial intelligence in education: a review. IEEE Access. **8**, 75264–75278 (2020). https://doi.org/10.1109/access.2020.2988510
12. Lin, H.: Influences of artificial intelligence in education on teaching effectiveness. Int. J. Emerg. Technol. Learn. **17**(24), 144–156 (2022). https://doi.org/10.3991/ijet.v17i24.36037
13. Chiu, T.K., Xia, Q., Zhou, X., Chai, C.S., Cheng, M.: Systematic literature review on opportunities, challenges, and future research recommendations of artificial intelligence in education. Comput. Educ. Artific. Intell. **4**, 100118 (2023). https://doi.org/10.1016/j.caeai.2022.100118
14. Kabudi, T., Pappas, I., Olsen, D.H.: AI-enabled adaptive learning systems: a systematic mapping of the literature. Comput. Educ. Artific. Intell. **2**, 100017 (2021). https://doi.org/10.1016/j.caeai.2021.100017
15. Muthmainnah, Ibna Seraj, P.M., Oteir, I.: Playing with AI to investigate human-computer interaction technology and improving critical thinking skills to pursue 21st century age. Educ. Res. Int. **1**, 6468995–6468917 (2022). https://doi.org/10.1155/2022/6468995
16. Salas-Pilco, S.Z., Xiao, K., Oshima, J.: Artificial intelligence and new technologies in inclusive education for minority students: a systematic review. Sustainability. **14**(20), 13572 (2022). https://doi.org/10.3390/su142013572
17. Pardamean, B., Suparyanto, T., Cenggoro, T.W., Sudigyo, D., Anugrahana, A.: AI-based learning style prediction in online learning for primary education. IEEE Access. **10**, 35725–35735 (2022). https://doi.org/10.1109/access.2022.3160177
18. Garg, S., Sharma, S.: Impact of artificial intelligence in special need education to promote inclusive pedagogy. Int. J. Inform. Educ. Technol. **10**(7), 523–527 (2020)
19. Zhang, L., Basham, J.D., Yang, S.: Understanding the implementation of personalized learning: a research synthesis. Educ. Res. Rev. **31**, 100339 (2020). https://doi.org/10.1016/j.edurev.2020.100339
20. Ogbeiwi, O.: Why written objectives need to be really SMART. Br. J. Healthc. Manag. **23**(7), 324–336 (2017). https://doi.org/10.12968/bjhc.2017.23.7.324
21. Diehm, E.: Writing measurable and academically relevant IEP goals with 80% accuracy over three consecutive trials. Perspect. ASHA Spec. Inter. Groups. **2**(16), 34–44 (2017). https://doi.org/10.1044/persp2.SIG16.34
22. Oran, B.B.: Correlation between artificial intelligence in education and teacher self-efficacy beliefs: a review. RumeliDE Dil ve Edebiyat Araştırmaları Dergisi. **34**, 1354–1365 (2023). https://doi.org/10.29000/rumelide.1316378

23. Zulkarnain, N.S., Yunus, M.M.: Primary teachers' perspectives on using artificial intelligence technology in English as a second language teaching and learning: a systematic review. Int. J. Acad. Res. Progr. Educ. Dev. **12**(2), 861–875 (2023). https://doi.org/10.6007/IJARPED/v12-i2/17119

AI-Personalized Mindfulness Sessions to Promote the Emotional Well-Being in Higher Education

Nadia Carlomagno[1](✉), Valeria Vadalà[2], and Maria Vittoria Battaglia[3]

[1] Suor Orsola Benincasa University, Naples, Italy
nadia.carlomagno@unisob.na.it
[2] Pegaso University, Naples, Italy
valeria.vadala@unipegaso.it
[3] Niccolò Cusano University, Rome, Italy
mariavittoria.battaglia@unicusano.it

Abstract. In relation to the continuous social challenges that characterise contemporary society, safeguarding mental health is an emergency to which we are all called to respond.

The role of political institutions in the promotion of mental health must not be limited to the provision of services, but must extend towards the creation of an environment conducive to the psychological well-being of the population, promoting a culture of well-being that starts as early as the educational cycle.

In several foreign countries, many educational institutions have introduced meditation practices, such as Mindfulness, within the higher education cycle to promote well-being in the lives of their students. The proposed exploratory-comparative research aims to assess whether integrating Mindfulness into educational contexts with the support of AI-based applications can reduce e feelings of stress, anxiety, boredom and inattention that increasingly characterise the everyday life of Italian students. This approach, by combining meditation practices with digital technology, aims to create learning experiences that promote the subject's physical and emotional well-being by providing generative settings for wellbeing and supporting mindful, embodied learning in the 'here and now'.

Keywords: Emotional Well-being · Artificial intelligence · Education

1 Introduction

In recent decades, well-being and mental health have been recognised as essential components of global health, with significant implications for health and education policies. According to the World Health Organisation [1] Mental health is defined not only as the absence of disease, but as a state of well-being in which the individual can develop his or her potential, manage daily challenges, maintain work productivity and contribute to society [2]. This definition expands the traditional conception of health, drawing attention to the importance of mental well-being as an integral part of general well-being.

P. Ardimento et al. (Eds.): HELMeTO 2024, CCIS 2468, pp. 28–44, 2025.
https://doi.org/10.1007/978-3-031-93999-0_2

In the educational context, recent studies [3] highlight how increasing pressures related to academic performance, personal and social expectations are perceived by students as a source of stress, negatively affecting their mental health. Increased stress and anxiety conditions are correlated with a decrease in motivation and concentration, impairing learning abilities and individual potential [4].

Other studies also show that school environments that promote psycho-physical well-being improve not only academic performance but also the quality of life of students, strengthening their resilience and self-esteem [5].

In this scenario, the integration of practices promoting mental wellbeing, such as mindfulness, a mindfulness practice based on conscious attention and aimed at developing the individual's ability to bring attention, intentionally and without judgement, to the present moment. Originating from ancient meditative traditions, mindfulness has been applied in psychological and scientific fields and is now used as a tool to improve mental wellbeing and reduce stress, assuming an increasingly relevant role in educational strategies to support students' mental health.

2 Theoretical Framework

2.1 Mindfulness Practice: Cultivating Awareness for Mental Well-Being

Mindfulness, a term derived from the concept of 'remembering' in the sense of 'keeping in mind' in a mindful manner [6] was originally conceptualised as a practice involving voluntary and sustained attention to one's mental and bodily states, has shown clear beneficial effects on both psychological and neurobiological levels. Recent studies [7] confirm that mindfulness promotes a significant reduction in perceived stress, improving emotion regulation and resilience to negative stimuli. On the neurophysiological level, it has been observed that the practice of mindfulness is associated with increased grey matter density in brain areas such as the anterior cingulate cortex and insula, structures involved in the processes of self-regulation and interoceptive awareness [8]. This supports the thesis that mindfulness acts not only as a relaxation strategy, but as a practice that profoundly modulates cognitive and affective processes, contributing to the reorganisation of neural functions related to psychophysical well-being.

In education, mindfulness is closely linked to the theory of Embodied Cognition [9] and supports the interaction between mind and body in information processing and emotional regulation [10]. Thus, it is an effective practice for reducing stress, improving emotional regulation and enhancing cognitive abilities. Learning in a mindful context, in fact, not only enhances cognitive skills, but also fully integrates the emotional and bodily dimensions, contributing to a holistic and potentially transformative educational experience [11] whereby the human mind cannot be considered as isolated from the body and emotions.

The way the subject perceives, interprets and responds to external stimuli is profoundly influenced by his or her bodily experiences [12]. In education, this translates into transformative learning that involves not only cognitive, but also bodily and emotional processes [13]. Indeed, mindfulness practices improve the subject's attention and cognitive control, characteristics that have been widely associated with increased learning efficacy and persistence [14]. Cognitive mechanisms enhanced by mindfulness, such as attention and awareness of internal processes, not only allow students to self-regulate more efficiently, but also facilitate a reduction in intrusive thoughts, a phenomenon that often compromises academic performance [15].

In a social context characterised by accelerated rhythms and the high performance expectations that schools demand from their students, resorting to mindfulness practices becomes a valid tool to promote a "slow temporality" and a stable awareness of the present moment one is living, embracing Kabat-Zinn's [16] and Csikszentmihalyi's [17] theories on flow, a psychological state that fosters engagement and personal satisfaction, promoting a feeling of greater well-being and personal fulfilment. The concept of *slow time* supports a more reflective and less reactive way of life, facilitating optimal states of immersion and engagement, essential conditions for a fulfilling and meaningful learning experience [18].

2.2 Meditation in the Age of Technology

Parallel to the spread of Mindfulness, technological innovation in higher education contexts has offered new opportunities to personalise and improve teaching-learning pathways.

The integration of digital technologies and artificial intelligence (AI) in higher education contexts is transforming the dynamics of teaching and learning, opening new perspectives to personalise learning pathways and improve students' psychological and physical well-being [19].

AI, in particular, represents a resource with the potential to experience advanced personalisation of the educational process according to individual needs, creating pathways that not only meet academic requirements but also take into account the emotional and psychological aspects of students. The AI-based approach allows the content and pace of learning to be adapted to each student's abilities, promoting an educational experience that integrates academic knowledge with direct support for emotional well-being [20]. Recent studies highlight how the use of AI-supported mindfulness applications are particularly effective in the educational context to enable everyone to develop greater self-awareness and the ability to regulate their emotions [11]. In this way, AI does not merely offer a simple didactic tool, but becomes a resource for improving students' well-being by generating positive learning settings [21] reducing anxiety and stress associated with the academic context and offering new opportunities for learning and innovation in educational processes [22].

The use of Information and Communication Technologies (ICT) is not limited to making educational content accessible, but supports the constructivist learning model, according to which technologies act as cognitive tools for knowledge construction [22]. Mindfulness applied through digital technologies facilitates a state of flow, a state of cognitive absorption that fosters deep and immersive learning, promoting a transformative learning experience that engages the individual in his or her physical, cognitive and emotional totality [17].

In this context, ICT is not merely a tool for transmitting knowledge, but become key elements in the development of critical and collaborative skills, promoting active and immersive learning modes [23] by enabling students to experience complex concepts in a more concrete and interactive way.

Through the personalisation of mindfulness pathways, AI can help students develop greater self-awareness, improving their physical and emotional wellbeing and enabling them to experience a teaching process based on moving from *an experience-of to an experience-with* an object [24].

In an age of rapid change and increased academic demands, offering students tools that promote mental well-being is not only desirable, but necessary to create more inclusive and positive educational environments [21]. This approach could not only reduce stress, anxiety, boredom and inattention by improving students' psycho-physical well-being, but by drawing students' attention to their bodily, performative and emotional presence, alive and active, in relation to themselves, to each other and to the context in which they are embedded, it could also create educational environments that promote conscious, embodied and transformative learning [25] in line with the new demands of contemporary society.

3 Research Design

The presented study is an exploratory research that adopts an Arts-Based Research (ABR) approach, a methodology that combines artistic practices with empirical research [26] to examine the effect of Mindfulness on students' mental health.

The aim of the proposed exploratory research is to examine digital tools and in particular the support of generative artificial intelligence, the effectiveness of mindfulness as a tool that can offer significant benefits to Italian students in order to improve their educational experience and general well-being. The research aims to promote the creation of positive educational environments that facilitate students' growth by reducing their feelings of stress, anxiety, boredom, and inattention while fostering optimal physical and emotional well-being. This work aims to further previous research that, through the analysis of quantitative data, has highlighted the importance of integrating Mindfulness into higher education contexts [21].

This practice recognises the individuality of each student and places personal well-being at the centre of the learning process, emphasising the importance of the body as a performing element. In this way, it encourages the creation of more intelligent and personalised learning environments.

Methodologically, the emphasis is on building customised learning paths, where adaptive artificial intelligence (AI) plays a key role. The AI monitors learners' progress and modifies Mindfulness content and practices according to their specific needs, providing real-time feedback to meet individual needs. Mindfulness can help individuals develop metacognitive skills, recognise and be more aware of themselves and their potential.

The research presented adopts a *Mixed Methods* design [27] with a focus on qualitative analysis of the logbooks completed by students at the end of each workshop lesson. This approach aims to enhance the contribution of Mindfulness, integrated with AI applications [28] in educational contexts.

4 Methodology

An Arts-Based Research approach, a methodology combining artistic practices and empirical research, was adopted for the proposed research. The integration of artistic practices into the Mindfulness experience, within this methodological framework, represents a significant opportunity to gain a deeper understanding of the students' personal experiences, fostering more profound reflection on their emotional and cognitive journey.

The proposed exploratory research specifically investigated the English meditation digital application 'Headspace' to explore students' emotions prior to the introduction of Mindfulness practice. The digital application, using AI, through precise prompting provided by the students, was able to offer a guided didactic meditation activity, characterised by three meditation paths, successfully customising the activity for the group of students involved by providing targeted meditations to reduce stress and improve concentration on the present moment.

The mindfulness experience, designed as a customised path, consisted of three guided meditation paths in English delivered via the Headspace app. To facilitate all students' understanding of the mindfulness experience, the paths were translated and recorded in Italian using a voice recorder. The programme included four weekly meetings lasting 4 h, for a total of 4 weeks.

For this research, an initial questionnaire was administered to the students involved before the mindfulness experience, which we will call Phase 0 (T0), at the end of the first meditation session, which we will call Phase 1 (T1), an intermediate questionnaire was administered instead. In Phase 2 and Phase 3, meditation sessions took place without any questionnaire being administered to the students. Finally, at the end of the last mindfulness session, which we will call Phase 4 (T2), an exit questionnaire was administered.

4.1 Data Analysis

The exploratory research involved 46 university students, with an average age of 21, mainly from the Campania Region. The students took part in the compulsory workshop *Giocando s'impara: tecniche per l'animazione e la comunicazione teatrale*, scheduled in the second year of the curriculum of the three-year degree course in Educational Sciences at the Suor Orsola Benincasa University of Naples, during the academic year 2023–2024. The workshop aimed to integrate theoretical-methodological knowledge with practical experience, offering students a learning opportunity that combines theory and experiential practice.

4.2 Procedures

The research consisted of three main stages (Fig. 1):

1. **Phase 0 (T0):** Initially, students were asked to complete a preliminary questionnaire to assess their mental and emotional state before embarking on any mindfulness experience. This phase, termed 'Phase 0', represented the starting point, as the students

had not yet had any contact with the practice of mindfulness. The answers provided in this questionnaire were also used as a prompt to customise the application used.

2. **Phase 1 (T1):** At the end of the first mindfulness session, a second questionnaire was administered to assess the changes in the students' mental and emotional state during the course. Although the experience was still incomplete, this moment allowed the impact of the practice to be monitored longitudinally. At this stage, the students also wrote a logbook, describing their emotions and the first perceived changes.
3. **Phase 2: The second mindfulness session characterised by the three customised meditation paths.** In this phase, the students continued to write a logbook, describing the emotions and sensations experienced during the practice; they did not, however, answer any questionnaires, either before or after the meditation experience.
4. **Phase 3: The Third mindfulness session characterised by the three customised meditation paths.** Also in this phase, the students continued writing a logbook and did not answer any questionnaires, either before or after the meditation experience.
5. **Phase 4 (T2):** At the end of the complete cycle of the four mindfulness sessions, the students answered a concluding questionnaire and updated their logbook. This final phase, referred to as 'Phase 4', made it possible to collect conclusive data on the entire course and to compare the results obtained with the previous phases.

In the proposed exploratory research, data from Phase 0 (T0), Phase 1(T1) and Phase 4 (T2) will be analysed.

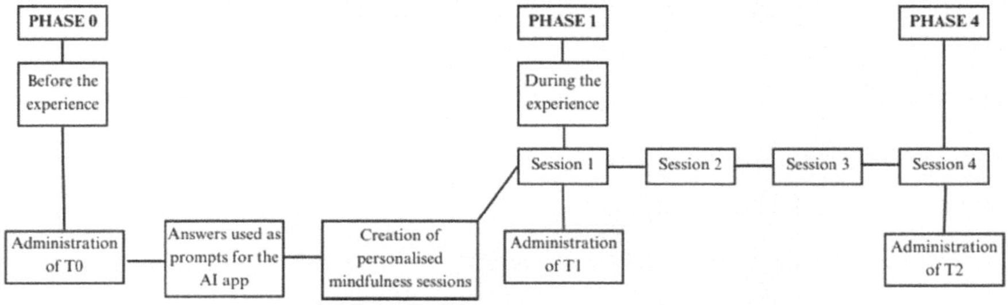

Fig. 1. Illustration of the research steps

4.3 Data Collection

In order to collect data, three questionnaires were administered anonymously to the students: an initial one, before the Mindfulness experience (T0; Phase 0); an intermediate one, administered after the first Mindfulness session (T1; Phase 1); and a final one, at the end of the four planned sessions (T2; Phase 4). Students were also asked to fill in logbooks, both during the course (Phase 1) and at its conclusion (Phase 4), offering a more detailed perspective on the development of their personal experience. In both the questionnaires and the logbooks, the participants were asked to reflect on their mental and emotional state, assess any changes, their level of connection with themselves, their ability to handle stress and the attainment of an optimal state of psycho-physical well-being, all with a view to greater awareness.

4.4 Intervention

In the entry questionnaire (T0) administered in PHASE 0, thus the preliminary phase preceding the mindfulness experience, the students were asked 10 questions structured on a 5-point Likert scale, with 1 indicating "very often" and 5 indicating "never".

The answers to the questions represented the prompts that were manually entered into the App's home screen. The questions posed to the students were aimed at detecting their level of stress (Graph. 1), coping with difficulties (Graph. 2), anxiety and nervousness (Graph. 3), and at assessing their ability to cope with issues such as worry (Graph. 4), difficulty in relaxing (Graph. 5), anger management (Graph. 6) and distress (Graph. 7).

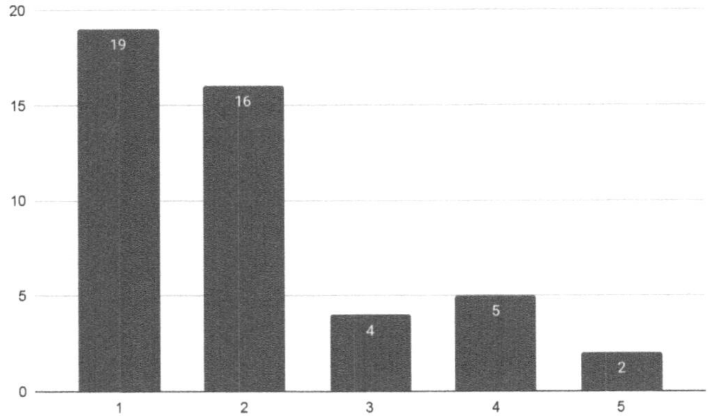

Graph. 1. In the past month, how often have you felt nervous and *'stressed'*?

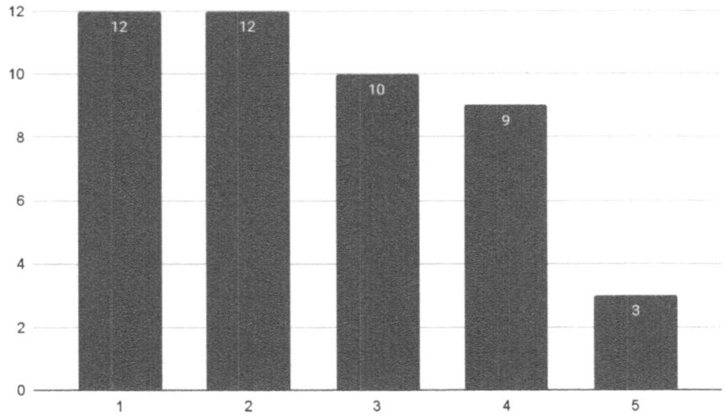

Graph. 2. In the last month, how often did you feel that difficulties were piling up to such an extent that you could not overcome them?

The students' answers were entered into the AI application, which generated a customised meditation path divided into 4 sessions. During Phase 1 and at the end of the course (Phase 4), the students were asked to reflect on their 'Mindfulness experience' and to observe any changes in their mental well-being in everyday life.

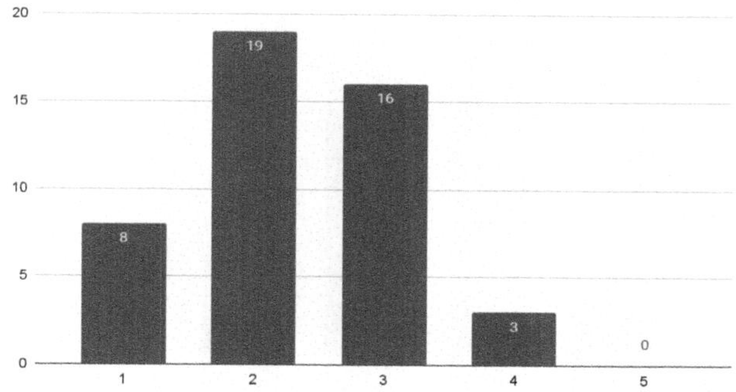

Graph. 3. In the last 2 weeks, how often have you been disturbed by one of the following problems? *Feeling nervous, anxious* or *on edge.*

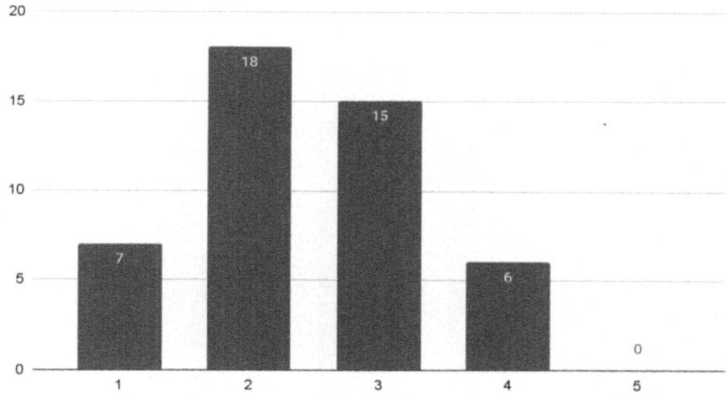

Graph. 4. In the last 2 weeks, how often have you been disturbed by one of the following problems? *Not being able to stop or control your worries?*

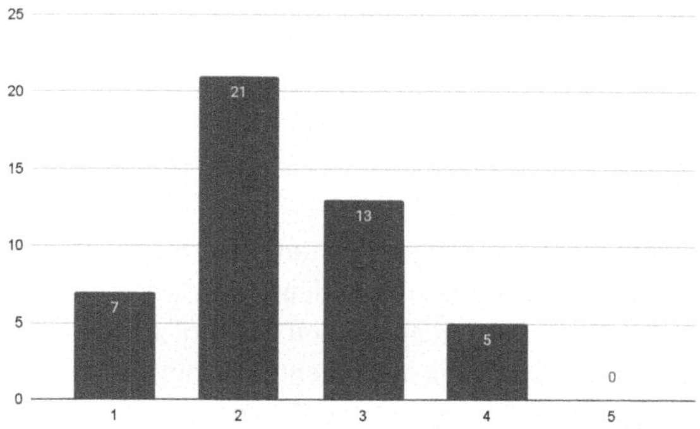

Graph. 5. In the last 2 weeks, how often have you been disturbed by one of the following problems? *Difficulty relaxing.*

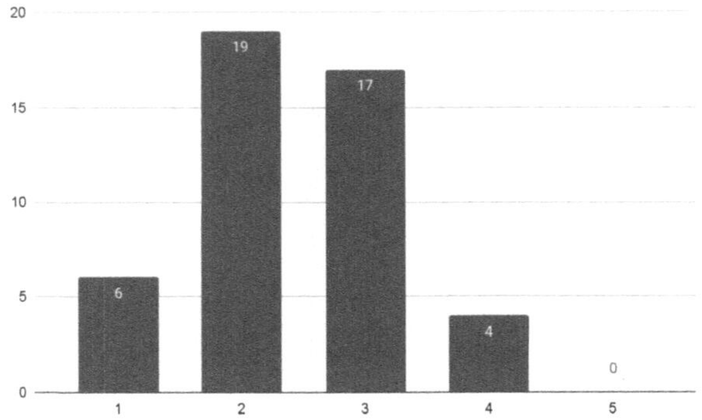

Graph. 6. In the last 2 weeks, how often have you been bothered by one of the following problems? *Becoming easily annoyed or irritable.*

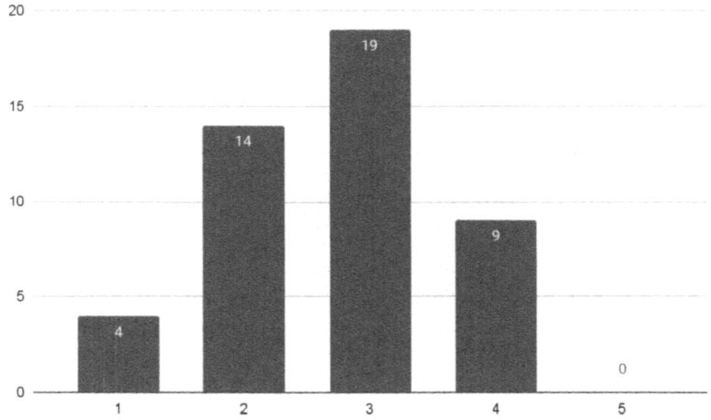

Graph. 7. In the last 2 weeks, how often have you been disturbed by any of the following? *Feeling of fear as if something terrible might happen.*

5 Results

5.1 Data Analysis

The data analysed were collected through the answers to questionnaires and thematic analysis of the logbooks. In both cases, the students were asked to reflect on their mental and emotional state, evaluate any changes, their level of connection with themselves, their ability to manage stress, and the achievement of an optimal state of psycho-physical well-being, all from the perspective of increased awareness.

In particular, three questionnaires were administered: an initial one, before the Mindfulness experience (Phase 0); an intermediate one, administered after the first Mindfulness session (Phase 1); and a final one, at the end of the four planned sessions (Phase 4).

Logbooks completed both during the course (Phase 1) and at its conclusion (Phase 4), offered a more detailed perspective on the development of the students' personal experience.

The research compared the results from the students' perceptions before the Mindfulness practice and at the end of the course, as well as between the intermediate (Phase 1) and final (Phase 4) phases, to monitor the evolution of their mental state over time (Fig. 2).

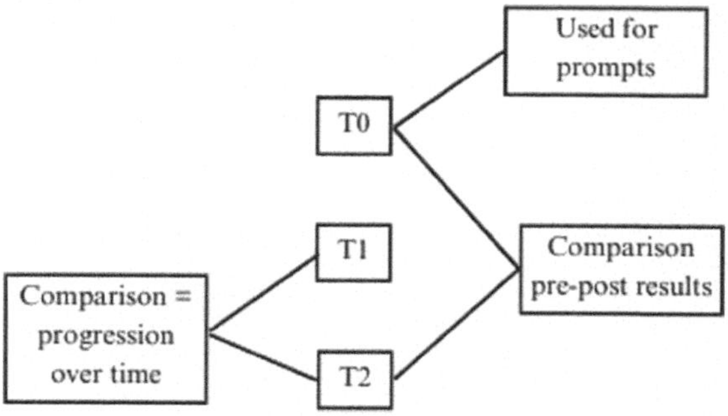

Fig. 2. Data analysis

Data collected from the questionnaires were subjected to descriptive statistical analysis, while data from the logbooks were subjected to thematic qualitative analysis.

5.2 Results

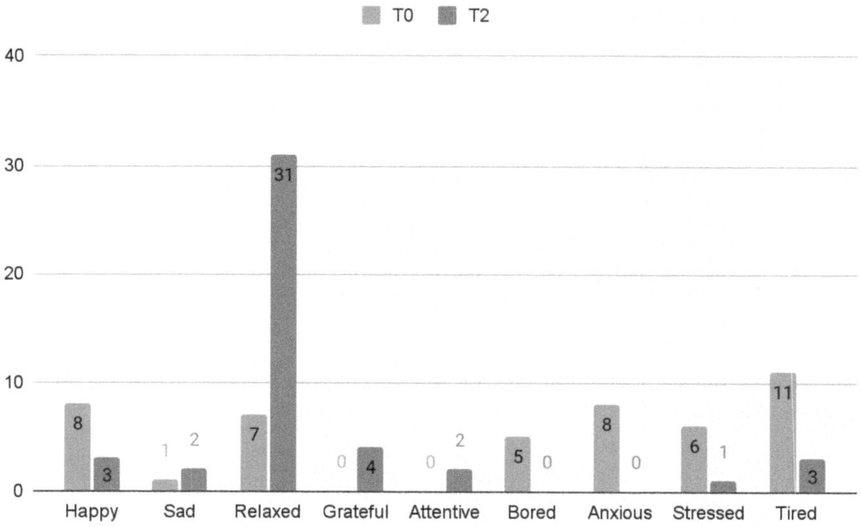

Graph. 8. *Select the word that best describes your mood.* Comparison of input (T0) and output (T2) questionnaire responses

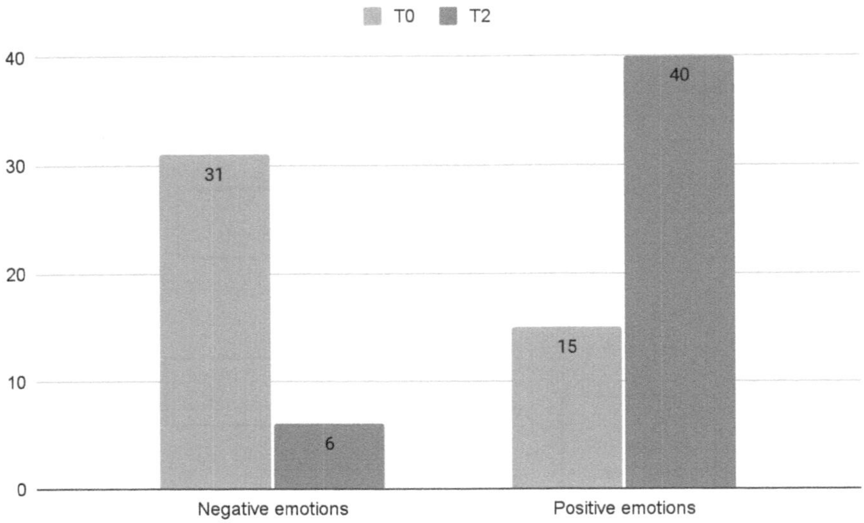

Graph. 9. *Select the word that best describes your mood.* Comparison of input (T0) and output (T2) questionnaire responses grouped into positive and negative emotions

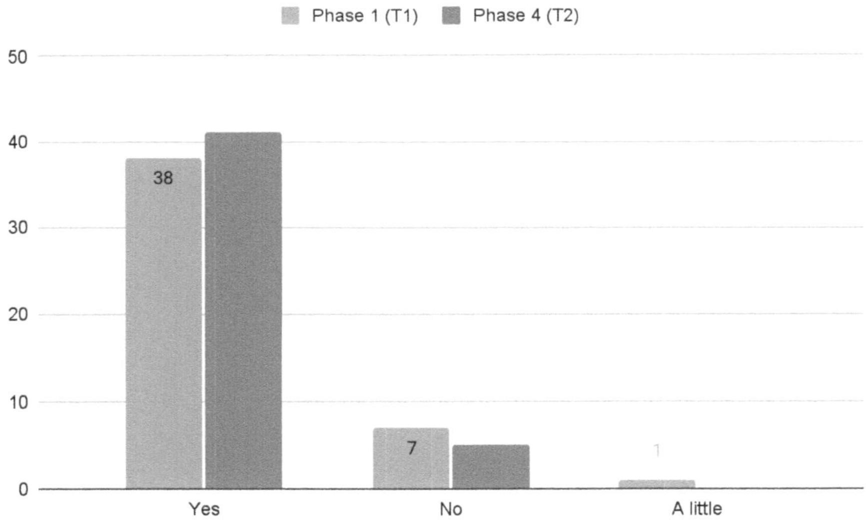

Graph. 10. *Did you get more in touch with yourself?* Answers during and at the end of the mindfulness experience

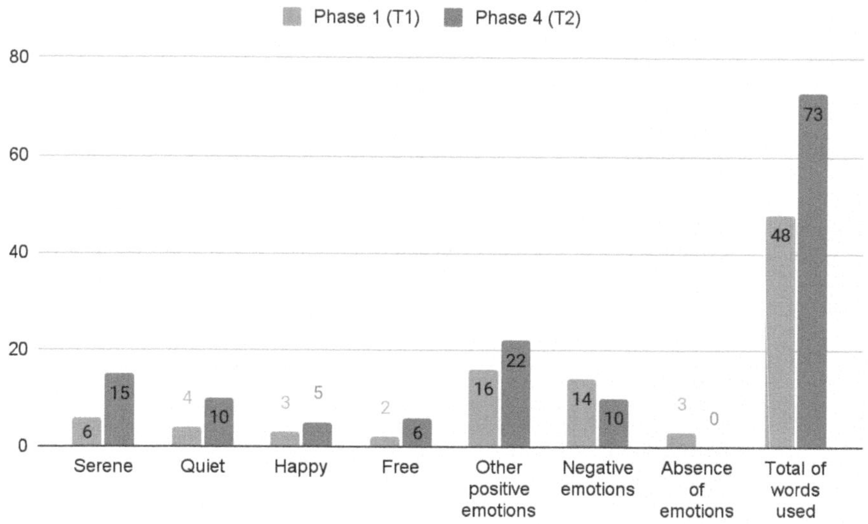

Graph. 11. Emotions felt during and at the end of the Mindfulness experience. Words extracted from the open-ended questions in questionnaires T1 and T2.

6 Discussion

Refer to Graphs. 8, 9, 10, 11, 12, 13 and Table 1 for a discussion of the results.

This study aims to promote positive educational environments that support students' growth, with a specific focus on reducing stress, anxiety, boredom and inattention, in order to improve their physical and emotional well-being. Using digital technologies, the research also explores the effectiveness of mindfulness as a tool potentially able to bring significant benefits to Italian students.

In order to answer these research questions, it is appropriate to compare data from the input and final questionnaires, but also to assess any changes in the emotional states of the students experienced as the Mindfulness experience progressed.

The first question in the questionnaires asked the students to select the word that best described their state of mind. Comparing the responses of the initial questionnaire of Phase 0, administered prior to the Mindfulness experience, with those of the final questionnaire of Phase 4 (Graphs. 8 and 9), a significant reduction in stress and fatigue was observed, which decrease from 14.9% and 31.9% to 2.2% and 6.5% respectively. Conversely, there is a significant increase in the feeling of relaxation, which rises from 10.6% to 67.4%. This seems to suggest that mindfulness can stimulate an emotional well-being in the students, who in fact stated that they were more in touch with themselves and their emotions from the very first mindfulness session, but with even greater intensity and awareness at the end of the whole course (Graph 10), demonstrating an increase in the benefits perceived for prolonged interventions over time; this is further evidenced by the open-ended questions in the questionnaires on what the students felt at the end of the session (Graph 11), from whose answers it emerges that the participants experienced a predominance of positive emotions. In fact, the most recurrent words are: serenity,

Table 1. Codes, themes and example sentences resulting from the thematic analysis of the logbooks.

Phase	Codes	Themes	Quotes
0 (before)	Tense; Pensive; Overthinking; Confused; Stressed; Agitated;	Tension	*I've been a little bit overthinking, but I was feeling pensive and tense*
	Boredom; Quiet; Apathy	Apathy	*I didn't feel any mood, neither relaxed nor agitated* *At the beginning only the idea of boredom persisted*
1 (during)	Relax; Calm; Lightness; Quiet	Relaxation	*I feel relaxed and at a peace with myself*
	Well-being; feeling well; Lightheartedness	Well-Being	*I feel very in touch with my emotions and I feel well* *I feel my mind is clearer and my body lighter*
4 (at the end)	Consciousness; Reflection; Connection; Self-reinforcement; Focused	Awareness and contact	*[The experience] allowed us to put in place some kind of positive self-reinforcement, compared to everything around us that we cannot control*
	Relaxation; Calm; Lightness; Tranquillity; Breath;	Relaxation and tranquillity	*Emotionally I feel free and light without thoughts*
	Gratitude; Grateful	Gratitude	*This mindfulness exercise reminds me to be grateful for life* *I realised that I am grateful to life for the little things it has given to me*
	Well-being; presence; Lightheartedness	Well-Being	*I feel very in touch with my emotions and I feel well*

tranquillity, happiness and freedom. This can be seen both following a single session (Phase 1-T1) and at the end of the whole course (Phase 4-T2).

It is interesting to note that the students, who were given the opportunity to choose more than one word, used a much greater number of words in Phase 4, a result that can be interpreted, when contextualised with other data, this suggests an increased awareness and deeper connection with their emotions, as evidence of an acquisition of greater awareness and contact with their emotions.

The progressive growth of the benefits of implementing mindfulness in an educational context is also visible in the qualitative analysis of the logbooks, in which the

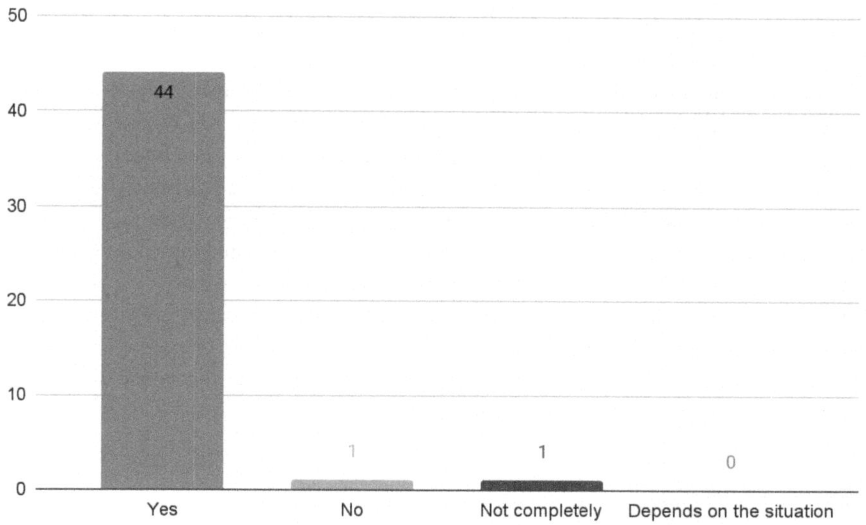

Graph. 12. *Is the Mindfulness experience beneficial to students' well-being?* Answers from the final questionnaire administered at the end of the course.

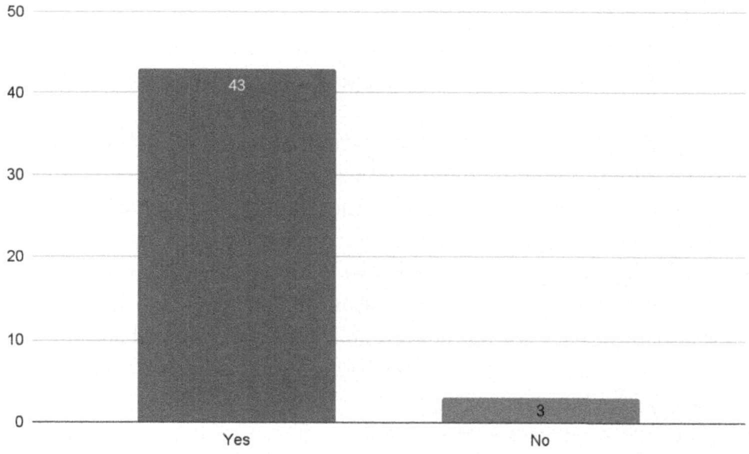

Graph. 13. *Do you feel that the mindfulness experience positively influences your emotional well-being?*

students state that they experienced a change in their emotional state. Analysing the differences in responses, we can hypothesise that the effect was greater when the course was prolonged in time (Phase 4): in fact the content analysis of the logbooks led to the identification of 4 thematic areas, related to what the students experienced (Table 1), namely: Relaxation and tranquillity, awareness and contact with oneself, gratitude and well-being. In line with what emerged from the analysis of the questionnaires, these emotional states, already perceived in phase 1, i.e. during the experience, were experienced in a deeper and more conscious way in Phase 4 (at the end of the course), when they also learnt to better manage negative feelings or discomfort with a focus on calm and emotional control.

The results show that the majority of the students rated the mindfulness experience positively with regard to the benefits to their well-being (Graph. 12). According to these students, the meditation exercises were helpful in managing stress and negative emotions in general, thanks to the concentration on breathing and self-reflection, which enabled connection with oneself, with the other person and with one's surroundings, thus promoting a general state of well-being. It is precisely for this reason that the students emphasised the crucial importance of this experience, highlighting how the personalisation of the pathway made it possible to respond to their specific needs, promoting optimal psycho-physical well-being within the educational environment (Graph 13) as well as, the promotion of a 'slow temporality' in instructional contexts that allows students to live a more meaningful and less stressful educational experience.

7 Conclusion

The research results support the effectiveness of personalised Mindfulness practice through Artificial Intelligence (AI)-based applications in improving the psycho-emotional well-being of university students.

Analysis of the data reveals a significant reduction in negative emotional states such as stress, anxiety and irritability, with a corresponding increase in positive emotions such as relaxation, serenity and self-awareness, suggesting a positive impact on mental health in general.

A relevant aspect that emerges from the research is the AI's ability to customise meditation paths according to specific individual needs. This made it possible to develop a tailor-made meditation practice, facilitating the attainment of greater emotional balance and better stress management, adapting exercises to meet the different needs of participants, and thus creating a more inclusive learning environment.

AI proves to be a valuable tool for monitoring student progress and adapting the content of meditation sessions based on the feedback gathered. Mindfulness practices could therefore be integrated into teacher training programmes to promote a more empathetic and person-centred teaching approach.

Furthermore, the comparison between the different phases of the course (Phase 0, Phase 1 and Phase 4) showed that the effectiveness of mindfulness progressively increases over time, with a more pronounced impact at the end of the full four-session cycle. This suggests that although even a single session can produce positive results, prolonged and continuous practice is essential for profound and lasting change. Further research developments require a longer duration than the four sessions planned in this pilot phase, in order to assess which time frame is best suited to maximise the effects of the intervention.

What emerges from this initial exploratory research is that Mindfulness, combined with AI technologies, offers significant potential to support students' emotional well-being, contributing to the creation of more inclusive and individual-centred educational environments. Mindful, embodied learning, based on mindfulness, fosters greater cognitive control and better emotional regulation, reducing intrusive thoughts that often impair students' academic performance. This suggests the need to extend the research to other educational and training contexts, hypothesising, from the findings, that this approach can foster more mindful learning and a better quality of life for students.

Acknowledgement. Nadia Carlomagno is the author of the paper. She is the main researcher of the project; she wrote the Sect. Theoretical framework 2.2 "Meditation in the age of technology" and 3. "Research design".

Valeria Vadalá is the co-author of the paper, she wrote the Sect. 1. "Introduction"; Theoretical framework 2.1 "Mindfulness practice: cultivating awareness for mental well-being"; 4. "Methodology"; 4.1 "Data Analysis"; 4.2 "Procedures"; 4.3 "Data collection" and 4.4 "Intervention".

Maria Vittoria Battaglia is the co-author of the paper, she wrote the Sect. 5. "Results" and 6. "Discussion".

Together they wrote the Sect. 7. "Conclusion".

References

1. World Health Organization: Comprehensive mental health action plan 2013–2030 (2021)
2. World Health Organization: Mental Health and Substance Use. (2021). www.who.int/teams/mental-health-and-substance-use
3. Pascoe, M.C., Hetrick, S.E., Parker, A.G.: The impact of stress on students in secondary school and higher education. Educ. Psychol. Rev. **32**(1), 147–175 (2020)
4. Galanti, M.A., Giaconi, C., Zappaterra, T.: Didattiche e progettazioni: storie e tracce evolutive verso l'inclusione. Ital. J. Spec. Educ. Incl. **9**(1) (2021)
5. Mace, C.: Mindfulness e salute mentale. Terapia, teoria e scienza. Astrolabio Ubaldini (2010)
6. Mele, S.: La relazione mente-corpo. Embodiment, mindfulness, neuro fenomenologia. Libreriauniversitaria.it. **66** (2010)
7. Hölzel, B.K., et al.: Mindfulness practice leads to increases in regional brain gray matter density. Psychiatry Res. Neuroimaging. **191**(1), 36–43 (2011)
8. Fox, K.C., et al.: Is meditation associated with altered brain structure? A systematic review and meta-analysis of morphometric neuroimaging in meditation practitioners. Neurosci. Biobehav. Rev. **43**, 48–73 (2014)
9. Caruana, F., Borghi, A.M.: Embodied Cognition. Una nuova psicologia. G. Ital. Psicol. **40**(1), 23–48 (2013)
10. Varela, F.J., Thompson, E., Rosch, E.: The Embodied Mind: Cognitive Science and Human Experience. MIT Press (1991)
11. Dahl, C.J., Wilson-Mendenhall, C.D., Davidson, R.J.: The plasticity of well-being: a training-based framework for the cultivation of human flourishing. Proc. Natl. Acad. Sci. **117**(51), 32197–32206 (2020)
12. Gallese, V., Lakoff, G.: The brain's concepts: the role of the sensory-motor system in conceptual knowledge. Cogn. Neuropsychol. **22**(3–4), 455–479 (2005)
13. Carlomagno, N.: La didattica performativa come modello di ibridazione formativa. In: Corbi, E., Frosini, T., Villani, P. (eds.) Parrhesia. In dialogo tra i saperi, Studi per Lucio d'Alessandro. Editoriale scientifica, Napoli (2023)
14. Chambers, R., Lo, B.C., Allen, N.B.: The impact of intensive mindfulness training on attentional control, cognitive style, and affect. Cogn. Ther. Res. **32**(3), 303–322 (2008)
15. Roeser, R.W., et al.: Mindfulness training and reductions in teacher stress and burnout: results from two randomized, waitlist-control field trials. J. Educ. Psychol. **105**(3), 787–804 (2013)

16. Kabat-Zinn, J.: Wherever you Go, there you Are: Mindfulness Meditation in Everyday Life. Hyperion (1994)
17. Csikszentmihalyi, M.: Flow: the Psychology of Optimal Experience. Harper & Row (1990)
18. Davidson, R.J., McEwen, B.S.: Social influences on neuroplasticity: stress and interventions to promote well-being. Nat. Neurosci. **15**(5), 689–695 (2012)
19. Esposito, E.: Comunicazione Artificiale. Come gli algoritmi producono intelligenza sociale, BUP (2022)
20. Holmes, W., Bialik, M., Fadel, C.: Artificial Intelligence in Education: Promises and Implications for Teaching and Learning. Center for Curriculum Redesign, Boston, MA (2019)
21. Vadalà, V., Meo, M., Fusco, M.S., Carlomagno, N.: AI and emotional well-being in teaching. Cultivating well-being through the use of Ai-based mindfulness for Italian students. Ital. J. Health Educ. Sport Inclus. Didact. **8**(2) (2024)
22. Laurillard, D.: Rethinking University Teaching: A Conversational Framework for the Effective Use of Learning Technologies. Routledge (2002)
23. Jonassen, D.H., Peck, K.L., Wilson, B.G.: Learning with Technology: A Constructivist Perspective. Prentice Hall (1999)
24. Matteucci, G.: Estetica e Natura Umana. La Mente Estesa tra Percezione, Emozione ed Espressione, Carocci, Roma (2019)
25. Carlomagno, N.: Le potenzialità didattiche delle arti sceniche. Education Sciences & Society (2020)
26. Leavy, P.: Research Design: Quantitative, Qualitative, Mixed Methods, Arts-Based and Community-Based, Participatory Reseaech Approaches. The Guilford Press (2022)
27. Creswell, J., Plano Clark, V.: Designing and Conducting Mixed Methods Research. Sage, Thousand Oaks (2018)
28. Finestronea, F., Limone, P., Peconioc, G.: Nuovi scenari di progetta-zione educativa: esperienze di didattica immersiva. Open J. IUL Univ. **4**(7), 190–203 (2023)

University Students with Special Educational Needs: An Assessment of Satisfaction and Perceptions of e-Learning and Services Provided

Venusia Covelli(✉), Laura Panizza, Miriam Trezzi, Elisa Zugno, and Alessandra Marelli

Department of Theoretical and Applied Sciences, eCampus University, Novedrate, Italy
venusia.covelli@uniecampus.it

Abstract. Students with special educational needs (SEN) encounter more substantial challenges in higher education compared to their peers, including physical, behavioral, technological, organizational, and financial barriers. Despite these difficulties, higher education can serve as a transformative experience, enhancing their quality of life, promoting well-being, supporting employability, fostering independence, and offering significant empowerment opportunities. To encourage academic success and social inclusion, it is essential to implement tailored support measures. E-learning represents a practical and effective educational strategy for students with SEN, serving as a platform for fostering self-determination and empowerment by enhancing access to and engagement in academic activities. After presenting the organizational model and services provided by the eCampus University Commission for students with SEN, the present contribution aims to explore student satisfaction through an online survey. Specifically, it investigates (1) students' levels of satisfaction with the available services, (2) their suggestions for service improvement, and (3) their evaluation of the suitability of an e-learning university for addressing their specific needs. The findings will provide insights into the experiences and perceptions of students regarding the support services offered to students with SEN.

Keywords: students with disability · special learning disorders · special educational needs · academic education · higher education · university · e-learning · inclusion

1 Introduction

1.1 Students with Special Educational Needs at University

Over the past few years, research has focused increasingly on college students with special educational needs (SEN), a definition by which we mean people with disabilities, with specific learning disorders, or with other educational needs [1].

P. Ardimento et al. (Eds.): HELMeTO 2024, CCIS 2468, pp. 45–58, 2025.
https://doi.org/10.1007/978-3-031-93999-0_3

As reported elsewhere [2], the expression "student with disability" referred to Article 3 of the Italian law number 104/92 ("Framework Law for assistance, social integration and rights of the handicapped"), which defined an "handicapped person" (the outdated term used to identify a person with disability) as someone "having a permanent or a progressive physical, mental or sensory impairment that determines difficulties in learning, social relations, and work integration, in such a way as to determine a process of social disadvantage or marginalization". It is only since the introduction of the UN Convention on the Rights of Persons with Disabilities, approved by the United Nations in 2006 and ratified in Italy in 2009 by law, that the expression "persons with disabilities" became mandatory. Instead, the expression "students with specific learning disorders" referred to the Italian Law number 170/2010 that has recognized dyslexia, dysgraphia, dysorthography, and dyscalculia as Specific Learning Disorders (SLD) (Disturbi Specifici dell'Apprendimento, DSA), which are associated to adequate learning abilities, without sensory or neurologic deficit [3]. Therefore, in the last few years, inclusive disability legislation has increased the number of students with disabilities entering higher education [4]. Despite this, much national and international research on students with special educational needs has explicitly examined the target population of childhood and adolescence [5]. At the same time, there is a lack of research exploring the correlations between students and SEN across their lifespans and among university students.

Specifically, the existing international literature that takes into consideration students with SEN in the university environment has focused on the study of the mechanisms that contribute to the permanence and successful completion of university studies, on how the university can be an experience that can help these students to improve their quality of life and well-being, maintain a job, lead an independent life and be an essential empowerment experience [6]. Other research, on the other hand, has examined the perceptions and experiences of students with SEN with the services adopted in support of disability, emphasizing how with greater awareness and accessibility to these services, students with disabilities in the university environment could improve their performance by achieving more fruitful academic results [7–9]. A study [10] investigated the motivation, emotions, and importance of relationships between teachers and students in the learning processes of students with disabilities. It showed that students with disabilities are more motivated than their classmates to achieve success and good results. However, additional actions are needed to involve them in the learning process.

Part of the Italian literature highlights the lack of inclusive accessibility standards and the lack of attention to specific tools to address the needs of students with SEN. This could lead to students developing high levels of stress, anxiety, depression, and emotional distress, as well as low levels of self-esteem and self-efficacy, with a consequent impact on well-being, quality of life, learning experiences, and university career [11–13]. Another field of study has focused on inclusive education policies for students with SEN, which has been seen to have positive effects on various dimensions of student well-being, not only in terms of academic achievement but also in terms of promoting the general development and quality of life of students [1]. Research studies have also explored how students with SEN can develop better levels of performance, self-regulation, emotional awareness, and high inclusion levels based on the measures used. Many researchers have emphasized the effectiveness of e-learning and the use of technological tools by professors as a means of consolidating professor-student relationships, as it can affect the student's well-being and learning outcomes, as a means of reducing emotional distress and promoting positive psychological factors and as a means of involving students in the learning process and improving their academic experience [14–17].

1.2 e-Campus Learning Environment

The transformation to Industry 4.0 depends not only on technology but also on people's skills. However, companies struggle to find candidates with up-to-date skills. To meet this need, eCampus University offers market-oriented bachelor's and master's degree programs, providing students with professional skills and personal growth. The goal is to train specialists to be ready for the world of work. eCampus courses are fully online, complemented by professional and in-person activities. The university also has an extensive network of tutors throughout Italy, offering personalized educational support. This is a significant advantage for students with SEN, who can access local support without traveling long distances to take exams.

The eCampus Virtual Learning Environment (VLE) platform offers numerous services to foster learning and support students with disabilities. Its features include tools for individualized learning support and course management. This integrated approach allows for responding to students' specific needs, improving educational processes and creating an inclusive and effective learning environment.

The architecture of VLE platforms described by Avgeriou and colleagues [18] identifies the application-specific layer at its highest level, which includes several key functions. These cover user profile management, encompassing the handling of students' portfolios, grades, system usage statistics, and coordination of working groups and assignments. Course administration involves creating, customizing, managing, and monitoring educational offerings. Educational resource delivery focuses on tracking the use of learning materials and evaluating assessment results. Administrative functions address student registrations, authentication processes, records management, access permissions, and usage logs. Furthermore, learner support services provide annotation spaces, bookmarks, notepads, statistics, personalized recommendations, and help-desk assistance. These components constitute the primary interface for learners and serve as a crucial context for integrating services that support students with disabilities.

The eCampus VLE offers a wide array of features, some of which are particularly valuable for adapting to the needs of learners with special requirements. These include software solutions for students with hearing and speech impairments, such as speech synthesis and recognition, along with browser extensions to enhance the platform's accessibility. The platform delivers educational content through lessons and study sessions using slides, digital documents, and videos, tracking all interactions between learners and resources in compliance with SCORM Runtime Environment standards. Evaluations are conducted through online tests for both formative and summative assessments, with results recorded in the learner's profile. Monitoring tools track all online activities, including platform access, document downloads, and interactions in asynchronous and synchronous communication channels. The platform also supports e-portfolios, which store exam results, essays, student-generated materials, and collaborative activities like concept mapping and wikis. All these features generate extensive data, which predictive and descriptive models can leverage to offer personalized suggestions and recommendations, particularly relevant for supporting learners with special needs.

1.3 Services Provided to Students with Special Educational Needs at e-Campus University

In the last decade, students accessing the e-Campus University Commission for Students with Special Needs (CABES)[1] service increased from 8 in 2014 to 870 during the 2023/2024 academic year. Over time, this required an increasingly articulated organization of services to provide the best possible response to the needs of these students. In 2021, the previous e-Campus University disability commission was transformed into the current CABES commission, with the appointment of a delegate by the Rector and a Professor representative for each faculty, as required by Italian law.[2] Specifically, the CABES commission has been formed to assess the needs of students with SEN and to plan helpful interventions to guarantee the right to study and inclusion of all enrolled students under current Italian legislation.

There are several objectives of the CABES commission. The commission aims to promote students' academic progress with SEN by providing the services and aids necessary to overcome the difficulties. For students with SLD, adopting dispensatory or compensatory measures. The commission also trains and updates staff on SEN and inclusive education issues. Finally, it defines methods for evaluating and monitoring services for students with a SEN. The primary services provided by the CABES commission are:

The Welcome Interview and Monitoring. After presenting the documentation, a psychologist will contact the student for a welcome interview. The aim is to assess and better understand the student's needs and to prepare valuable interventions to support the student's educational progress. An individual support plan is then agreed upon, monitored over time, and updated as necessary throughout the course.

Personalization of Examination Tests. Students may have access to individualized forms of assessment following the certificates presented, as detailed below:

- Practical assistance from a tutor, who will be present during the examination. Students will have the possibility, upon explicit request, to be assisted by a tutor in reading the examination paper and/or writing answers.
- Additional time to complete examinations. Following an explicit request, students will benefit from additional time during the performance of profit exams, equal to at least 30% more than the time generally granted for the test performance.
- Subdivision of the study plan of an exam into several partial examinations.
- Mode of examination most appropriate to one's learning characteristics (in written or oral form).
- Use of concept maps.

[1] Commissione di Ateneo per i Bisogni Educativi Speciali

[2] Ex L.17/1999; L. 170/2010

– Use a non-scientific calculator or other form approved by the course lecturer.

Accommodation Within the University Campus. Students will be allowed to be accompanied to exam accommodations upon explicit request.

Training on Concept Maps. Video tutorials, templates, and examples of structuring concept maps for independent study. Training and counselling sessions on concept maps: Students can attend regularly scheduled training group meetings and any specific consultation on structuring maps to support exams and study.

Books and Study Materials in Accessible Formats. Students can be assisted, upon explicit request, in finding textbooks and study materials in accessible formats.

CABES commission determines which interventions it will grant to the student based on the documentation submitted and drafts a formal resolution containing all directions for their proper implementation. If the initial conditions change, CABES can amend the resolution issued at the student's request, reserving the right to request any updated documentation.

2 The Survey

2.1 Research Aim

This study aims to investigate students' satisfaction with the service provided by the CABES commission and to collect students' suggestions about how to improve the service. The CABES activities target students with SEN with a flexible e-learning environment provided by the university (see Sect. 1.2) that promotes inclusion and supports self-determination and empowerment.

This exploratory study aims to describe the current state of the student support service and then reflect on how it can be improved. In detail, the primary study questions will be answered by a descriptive analysis of the answers to the following questions:

– how satisfied are our students with the services provided?
– to what extent have their special educational needs created difficulties while studying?
– to what extent does the online university meet their educational needs?
– what suggestions do students make to improve service?

2.2 Method and Participants

The study is an online survey conducted during May 2024 and aimed at exploring what e-Campus University students with SEN may have experienced during their academic year (2023–2024) regarding the CABES' services. The entire population of students registered with CABES services was involved in the survey ($N = 870$). The online questionnaire was administered through email dissemination by the CABES commission to all students. Participation was on a voluntary basis, and students were informed that their responses would be anonymous and confidential. Participants could leave the study at any time, they needed to indicate their preference.

2.3 Research Instruments and Data Analysis

This descriptive and exploratory study was a mixed-method survey design [19]. The data were collected using a structured online questionnaire to facilitate dissemination and data collection.

The questionnaire consisted of 35 open-ended and closed-ended questions. Students were asked to respond by thinking about their experiences with the services provided by the CABES commission for students with SEN. Specifically, they were asked to answer some socio-demographic questions; questions about the type of disability and/or the SLD or other SEN; the compensatory tools and dispensatory measures they had been assigned; their general level of satisfaction; their level of satisfaction with the services offered by CABES, and with the functionality of the online University. Finally, they were asked to make some suggestions for improving the service.

The data were analyzed using SPSS software (version 26.0) [20]. Descriptive statistics were computed to summarize the socio-demographic characteristics of the sample. We performed the analysis of variance (ANOVA) with LSD posthoc tests to analyze differences in the type of SEN and levels of satisfaction. Pearson correlation coefficients were employed to examine associations between variables. The level of statistical difference was set at $p < 0.05$. A thematic analysis followed Braun and Clarke's [21] methodological framework to explore the open-ended responses. This approach aimed to identify and interpret explicit and implicit themes emerging from participants' answers. Two independent researchers (VC, AM) analyzed the responses and separately identified recurring themes, ensuring a rigorous and comprehensive interpretation of the data.

3 Results

3.1 Sample Description

Table 1 presents the frequency distributions of the variables considered. In total, 227 university students completed the online survey. Most participants were female (71.4%). The mean age was 28.9 years (± 10.5), and most were enrolled in a bachelor's course (79.3%). Of 870 students contacted, 227 were retrieved, representing a response rate of 26%.

Based on their health status classification (see Sect. 1.1), students who responded to the survey are grouped as follows: 89% of students with disabilities, 44.5% of students with special learning disorders, and 5.7% of students with special educational needs (for example, attention-deficit hyperactivity disorder ADHD, or borderline intellectual functioning). Details on the type of SEN are shown in Table 2.

Regarding the type of compensatory tools and dispensatory measures, most students requested the use of concept maps (24.2%) and additional time for the performance of the written test (21.7%). In addition, students were asked to assess written exams without considering spelling and grammatical errors (10.8%).

Table 1. Demographic characteristics of the study participants

		N (%)
Gender	Male	65 (28.6)
	Female	162 (71.4)
Age (years)	*Mean (SD)*	28.9 (±9.5)
Degree program	Bachelor's degree	180 (79.3)
	Master's degree	47 (20.7)
Faculty	Economics	9 (4.0)
	Law	31 (13.7)
	Faculty of Arts and Humanities	33 (14.5)
	Psychology	132 (58.1)
	Engineering	22 (9.7)
Year of attendance	First-year bachelor' students	72 (31.7)
	Second-year bachelor' students	64 (28.2)
	Third-year bachelor' students	52 (22.9)
	First-year master' students	22 (9.7)
	Second-year master' students	17 (7.5)

3.2 Satisfaction and Suggestions for Service Improvement

Overall, most of the sample is satisfied with the service provided by the CABES commission (Table 3). The mean level of satisfaction was 3.7 (range 1–5). 59.5% declared that they were very or extremely satisfied, and only 4.8% said they were not at all satisfied. Results are in line with the previous survey [2]. Moreover, we asked students to evaluate two services, a concept map training and the welcome interview and monitoring service. In the case of the concept map service, most students did not use it (71.4%), and of those who did, only 7.9% were dissatisfied. Similarly, about half of the sample did not use the welcome interview, and of those who did, the evaluation was mostly positive (very and extremely satisfied 35.7%).

Regarding suggestions for improving the CABES' services, students reported the possibility of enabling training for tutors (33.8%) and professors (24.2%) and training for students about the compensatory tools and dispensatory measures. To better understand the students' responses, through open-ended questions, we asked them to explain and justify their answers regarding their overall satisfaction and how to improve the service.

In the first case, the answers of the students who expressed a high level of satisfaction with CABES (very and extremely satisfied, n = 135) were divided into two categories: the first (n = 49) related to the people of CABES and some of their characteristics (helpfulness, kindness, cordiality, competence, professionalism); the second (n = 61) related to organizational aspects and the utility of the service (efficiency and effectiveness of the service, suitability for taking exams, etc.). Twenty-five of the respondents were satisfied but did not have an answer. Those who are not at all or not very satisfied (n = 28)

Table 2. Type of special educational needs

	N (%)
Special educational needs	
Student with disability	89 (39.2)
Student with special learning disorder	101 (44.5)
Student with other educational special need	13 (5.7)
Student with disability and special learning disorder	24 (10.6)
Type of disability (N = 89) (multiple choice)	
Motor disability	35 (27.6)
Hearing sensory disability	4 (3.1)
Seeing sensory disability	16 (12.6)
Hearing and seeing sensory disability	7 (5.5)
Psychic disability	39 (30.7)
Rare syndrome	14 (11.0)
Disease-related disability	11 (8.7)
Mild intellectual disability	1 (0.8)
Type of special learning need (N = 101) (multiple choice)	
Specific learning disorder with impairment in reading	77 (28.2)
Specific learning disorder with impairment in written expression	54 (19.8)
Specific learning disorder with impairment in mathematics	61 (22.3)
Mixed specific developmental disorders	51 (18.7)
Specific developmental disorders of scholastic skills	21 (7.7)
Unspecified specific developmental disorders of scholastic skills	8 (2.9)
Other specific developmental disorder of motor function	1 (0.4)
Type of educational special need (N = 13) (multiple choice)	
Specific language disorder	16 (26.2)
Specific developmental disorder of motor function (i.e. dyspraxia)	3 (4.9)
Autism spectrum disorder	8 (13.1)
Attention-deficit/hyperactivity disorder	18 (29.5)
Borderline intellectual functioning	15 (24.6)
Nonverbal learning disorder	1 (1.7)
Compensatory tools and dispensatory measures (N = 227) (multiple choice)	
Conceptual maps	163 (24.2)
Increasing the size of written texts	44 (6.5)

(continued)

Table 2. (*continued*)

	N (%)
Support for reading the text	58 (8.6)
Assessing written exams without considering spelling and grammatical errors	73 (10.8)
Use of calculators and/or forms	101 (15)
30% extra time for written exams	146 (21.7)
Written assignment support	20 (4.7)
Written and oral examination only	53 (7.9)
Dividing the exam into several parts	4 (0.6)

and those who are quite satisfied (n = 64) sometimes complain about the Commission's long response times and the complexity of the service when it comes to requesting compensatory measures.

Finally, among the suggestions for improving the CABES service, the students most frequently mentioned training for tutors (41.9%) and lecturers (25.1%), followed by the possibility of opening a helpdesk that would always be available to students (14.5) and training for students on compensatory tools (11.5).

3.3 E-Learning Suitable for Inclusion

Students were asked whether they had encountered difficulties during their academic path due to their SEN. Most stated no difficulties (57.7%), 32.2% a little or quite, and 10.1% very or very much. On the other hand, regarding how functional they thought the online university was for their SEN, students mostly answered that it is very or very much functional (71.4%). Only 9.7% did not consider it so functional (Table 4).

Open-ended questions were also used to ask students to justify which difficulties or obstacles related to their health condition experienced during their academic path and why they considered the online university to be functional for their health condition.

Most of the students (57.7%) declared that they did not experience difficulties related to their health condition experience during their academic path. Among those who indicated a little/quite/very/very much difficulties during their undergraduate studies (42.3%, N = 96), 35.4% (N = 34) encountered personal difficulties in studying (of memorization, concentration, attention, anxiety); 26.1% (N = 25) report encountering organizational procedural obstacles (booking exams, missing speech synthesis, poor support); 38.5% (N = 37) encountered obstacles related to study material (using lectures or slides, preparing maps, complex e-same questions, high study volume).

When we asked them to explain why they were (very or extremely) satisfied with the University online mode, 98 did not answer, 38 referred to the possibility of managing their own time, personalizing their studies, or having constant access to the lectures, 14 referred to the convenience of not having to move because of their disability and 12 referred to the reduced anxiety and stress associated with the exam. Of the 22 who were not very satisfied or not at all satisfied, 14 did not give a reason, and eight referred to

Table 3. Satisfaction and suggestions for service improvement

	N (%)
Overall satisfaction of CABES' services (N = 227)	
Mean (SD) 3.7 (1.1) *(min-max 1–5)*	
Not at all satisfied	11 (4.8)
Not very satisfied	17 (7.5)
Quite satisfied	64 (28.2)
Very satisfied	72 (31.7)
Extremely satisfied	63 (27.8)
Satisfaction of concept mapping training (N = 227)	
Mean (SD) 2.94 (1.5) *(min-max 1–5)*	
Not at all satisfied	18 (7.9)
Not very satisfied	6 (2.6)
Quite satisfied	14 (6.2)
Very satisfied	16 (7.0)
Extremely satisfied	11 (4.9)
I didn't use the service	162 (71.4)
Satisfaction of welcome interview and monitoring of academic career (N = 227)	
Mean (SD) 3.9 (1.2) *(min-max 1–5)*	
Not at all satisfied	8 (3.5)
Not very satisfied	5 (2.2)
Quite satisfied	28 (12.3)
Very satisfied	31 (13.7)
Extremely satisfied	50 (22.0)
I didn't use the service	105 (46.3)
Satisfaction of compensatory tools and dispensatory measures (N = 227)	
Mean (SD) 3.63 (1.1) (min-max 1–5)	
Not at all	15 (6.6)
A little	11 (4.8)
Quite	71 (31.3)
Very	77 (33.9)
Very much	53 (23.4)
Suggestions for improving the CABES' services (multiple choice)	
Training for tutors	95 (33.8)

(*continued*)

Table 3. (*continued*)

	N (%)
Training for professors	68 (24.2)
Help desk for students	48 (17.1)
Help desk for professors	19 (6.8)
Training for students on compensatory tools and dispensatory measures	41 (14.6)
No suggestions, it's all right	2 (0.7)
I don't know	2 (0.7)
Other	6 (2.1)

Table 4. Difficulties and satisfaction with e-learning

	N (%)
Have you encountered or are you experiencing difficulties or obstacles related to your health condition during your academic experience?	
Mean (SD) 2,19 (1.2) (min-max 1–5)	
Not at all	131 (57.7)
A little	34 (15.0)
Quite	39 (17.2)
Very	11 (4.8)
Very much	12 (5.3)
How suitable is the online University for your health condition o[1]r SEN?	
Mean (SD) 3.97 (1.1) (min-max 1–5)	
Not at all	10 (4.4)
A little	12 (5.3)
Quite	43 (18.9)
Very	72 (31.8)
Very much	90 (39.6)

the fact that the platform was not always functional or that it was sometimes difficult to use the course materials produced by the lecturers.

3.4 Differences in Perceived Satisfaction

ANOVA analyses were conducted to examine potential differences in students' satisfaction levels across different types of SEN (students with disabilities, students with SLD, students with other SEN, and students with both disabilities and SLD). The analysis focused particularly on satisfaction with the overall educational experience, specific services offered, and the online learning modality of the e-Campus University. No significant differences were found, except for the question assessing the perceived suitability of the university's online format, where a statistically significant difference emerged among groups [$F(3,016) = 3.520$; $p = .031$]. Post hoc analyses using the LSD criterion for significance revealed that students with disabilities ($M = 4.20$; $SD = 1.036$) reported a significantly higher level of satisfaction compared to students with SLD ($M = 3.90$; $SD = 0.995$), students with SEN without disability ($M = 3.54$; $SD = 1.506$), and students with both disabilities and SLD ($M = 3.63$; $SD = 1.313$).

The correlations between age, the number of examinations taken, overall satisfaction levels, and various services revealed some significant associations. The results of the correlation analysis are presented in Table 5.

Table 5. Correlations analysis.

	1	2	3	4	5	6	7	8	9	10	11
1. Age	1										
2. Number of exams taken	0.227**	1									
3. Total of disabilities	0.405**	0.093	1								
4. Total of SLD	−0.330**	−0.146*	−0.491**	1							
5. Total of other SEN	0.076	−0.007	0.086	−0.024	1						
6. Total compensatory/dispensational tools used	−0.246**	−0.202**	−0.136*	0.502**	0.061	1					
7. Overall satisfaction with CABES services	0.245**	0.208**	0.074	−0.131*	−0.018	−0.008	1				
8. Satisfaction with concept maps service	0.214	0.414**	0.121	−0.177	0.062	−0.009	0.549**	1			
9. Satisfaction with welcome interview service	0.226*	0.073	0.089	−0.126	−0.142	0.050	0.713**	0.765**	1		
10. Satisfaction with compensatory/dispensatory measures	0.058	0.101	−0.023	0.015	−0.124	0.120	0.545**	0.363**	0.653**	1	
11. The online university is suitable for your health condition or SEN.	0.153*	0.242**	0.089	−0.097	−0.023	−0.003	0.485**	0.339**	0.455**	0.382**	1

*$P < 0.05$; **$P < 0.01$

A positive correlation was observed between students' age and the number of exams taken ($r = 0.227$, $p < 0.01$), the number of disabilities reported ($r = 0.405$, $p < 0.01$), overall satisfaction with CABES services ($r = 0.245$, $p < 0.01$), satisfaction with the welcome interview service ($r = 0.226$, $p < 0.01$), and the perceived suitability of the online university ($r = 0.153$, $p < 0.05$). Furthermore, the number of exams taken was positively correlated with overall satisfaction with CABES services ($r = 0.208$, $p < 0.01$), satisfaction with the concept map service ($r = 0.414$, $p < 0.01$), and the perceived suitability of the online university ($r = 0.242$, $p < 0.01$).

4 Final Remarks

The present contribution describes the eCampus University organizational model and Virtual Learning Environment, which offer various services and tools to support students with disabilities and special learning needs [2]. Then, an aggregate picture of eCampus students with SEN and the services provided is presented. The analyses consider various sample characteristics, such as gender, type of SEN, and degree of satisfaction. Particular attention is paid to personalized support measures, such as the different categories of tutoring, adaptation of examination formats, compensatory tools, and dispensatory measures.

Overall, a positive picture emerged, although survey responses did not cover the entire sample of students with SEN at our university. One possibility for future surveys will be to conduct recalls by inviting as many students as possible to respond to the questionnaire. Overall, students expressed satisfaction with the services they received and indicated some suggestions for improving the service. Most importantly, they reported that they did not encounter many difficulties in their academic journey due to their health condition, presumably mediated by the support they received. At the same time, they found the e-learning mode functional.

Future research may also consider possible academic careers by comparing the university system's different in-person or online modes. In addition, considering the literature described in the introduction, future research may explore how students with SEN may develop better levels of achievement, self-regulation, emotional awareness, and high levels of inclusion based on the measures used. Studies emphasized the effectiveness of e-learning and the use of technological tools by teachers as a means of strengthening the teacher-student relationship, as it can affect student well-being and learning outcomes, as a means of reducing emotional distress and promoting positive psychological factors, and as a means of engaging students in the learning process and enhancing their academic experience [15–17].

References

1. Brussino, O.: Mapping policy approaches and practices for the inclusion of students with special education needs. OECD Education Working Papers No. 227 (2020). https://doi.org/10.1787/600fbad5-en
2. Covelli, V., Mana, R., Panizza, L., Sarti, L., Zugno, E.: Higher education and students with disabilities: E-learning for inclusion at eCampus University, pp. 18–29 (2019). https://doi.org/10.1007/978-3-030-31284-8_2
3. Chieffo, D.P.R., Arcangeli, V., Moriconi, F., Marfoli, A., Lino, F., Vannuccini, S., Marconi, E., Turrini, I., Brogna, C., Veredice, C., et al.: Specific learning disorders (SLD) and behavior impairment: comorbidity or specific profile? Children. **10**, 1356 (2023). https://doi.org/10.3390/children10081356
4. Biggeri, M., Di Masi, D., Bellacicco, R.: Disability and higher education: assessing students' capabilities in two Italian universities using structured focus group discussions. Stud. High. Educ. **45**(4), 909–924 (2020). https://doi.org/10.1080/03075079.2019.1654448
5. Matteucci, M.C., Soncini, A.: Self-efficacy and psychological well-being in a sample of Italian university students with and without specific learning disorder. Res. Dev. Disabil. **110**, 103858 (2021). https://doi.org/10.1016/j.ridd.2021.103858
6. Melero, N., Moriña, A., López-Gavira, R.: In life-lines of Spanish students with disabilities during their university trajectory. Qual. Rep. **23**(5), 1127–1145 (2018). https://doi.org/10.46743/2160-3715/2018.3092
7. Abreu, M., Hillier, A., Frye, A., Goldstein, J.: Student experiences utilizing disability support services in a university setting. Coll. Stud. J. **50**(3), 323–328 (2017)

8. McGregor, K.K., Langenfeld, N., Van Horne, S., Oleson, J., Anson, M., Jacobson, W.: The university experiences of students with learning disabilities. Learn. Disabil. Res. Pract. **31**(2), 90–102 (2016). https://doi.org/10.1111/ldrp.12102
9. Aguirre, A., Carballo, R., Lopez-Gavira, R.: Improving the academic experience of students with disabilities in higher education: faculty members of social sciences and law speak out. Innovat. Eur. J. Soc. Sci. Res. **34**(3), 305–320 (2021). https://doi.org/10.1080/13511610.2020.1828047
10. Moriña, A.: The keys to learning for university students with disabilities: motivation, emotion and faculty-student relationships. PLoS One. **14**(5), e0215249 (2019). https://doi.org/10.1371/journal.pone.0215249
11. Iaia, M., Vizzi, F., Carlino, M.D., Turi, M., Marinelli, C.V., Angelelli, P.: Specific learning disabilities and associated emotional-motivational profiles: a study in Italian university students. Front. Psychol. **15** (2024). https://doi.org/10.3389/fpsyg.2024.1365980
12. Benedetti, I., Barone, M., Panetti, V., Taborri, J., Urbani, T., Zingoni, A., Calabrò, G.: Clustering analysis of factors affecting academic career of university students with dyslexia in Italy. Sci. Rep. **12**(1), 9010 (2022). https://doi.org/10.1038/s41598-022-12985-w
13. Donato, A., Muscolo, M., Arias Romero, M., Caprì, T., Calarese, T., Olmedo Moreno, E.M.: Students with dyslexia between school and university: post-diploma choices and the reasons that determine them. An Italian study. Dyslexia. **28**(1), 110–127 (2022). https://doi.org/10.1002/dys.1692
14. Cataudella, S., Carta, S., Mascia, M.L., Masala, C., Petretto, D.R., Penna, M.P.: Psychological aspects of students with learning disabilities in e-environments: a mini review and future research directions. Front. Psychol. **11**, 611818 (2021). https://doi.org/10.3389/fpsyg.2020.611818
15. Carpinelli, L., Bruno, G., Savarese, G.: A brief research report on the perception and satisfaction of Italian university students with disabilities and specific learning disabilities at the emergency remote teaching during the COVID-19 lockdown. In: Frontiers in Education, vol. 6, p. 680965. Frontiers Media SA (2021). https://doi.org/10.3389/feduc.2021.680965
16. Bellacicco, R.: Ripensare la disabilità in università: le voci di studenti e docenti. Ital. J. Spec. Educ. Incl. **5**(2), 25–42 (2018)
17. Bellacicco, R., Parisi, T.: Persistence and academic performance in higher education: a comparison between students with and without reported learning disabilities. Int. J. Incl. Educ. **28**(7), 1185–1204 (2024). https://doi.org/10.1080/13603116.2021.1988157
18. Avgeriou, P., Retalis, S., Skordalakis, M.: An architecture for open learning management systems. In: Advances in Informatics, pp. 183–200. Springer (2001). https://doi.org/10.1007/3-540-38076-0_13
19. Creswell, J.W., Tashakkori, A.: Differing perspectives on mixed methods research. J. Mixed Methods. **1**(4), 303–308 (2007). https://doi.org/10.1177/1558689807306132
20. IBM, C.: IBM SPSS Statistics for Windows. Version 24: Armonk. NY-IBM Corp (2016)
21. Braun, V., Clarke, V.: Using thematic analysis in psychology. Qual. Res. Psychol. **3**(2), 77–101 (2006). https://doi.org/10.1191/1478088706qp063oa

Play at First Sight: A Literature Review on the Integration of Eye-Tracking into Special Needs Education

Nadia Di Leo(✉), Martina Rossi, Anna Teresa Musicco, and Giusi Antonia Toto

Department of Humanities, University of Foggia, Foggia, Italy
{nadia.dileo,martina.rossi,anna.musicco,giusi.toto}@unifg.it

Abstract. This paper examines the integration of Eye-tracking technology with educational games in special education contexts, focusing on assessment and intervention applications. Through a literature review of recent research and implementations, the study analyzes how Eye-tracking technology enhances learning experiences and provides new forms of interaction for students with diverse needs. The research methodology involved analyzing papers from academic databases, categorizing them into five key themes: Eye-tracking as a tool to improve learning and training, Eye-tracking to improve diagnosis and medical training, Eye-tracking as a tool for diagnosing and studying clinical conditions, Eye-tracking in clinical and educational contexts related to autism spectrum disorders, Eye-tracking as a technology to develop or evaluate digital tools and interfaces. Results demonstrate that Eye-tracking technology has shown significant promise across multiple applications, from improving reading capabilities in dyslexia to enhancing emotional regulation in autism spectrum disorders. This technology enables precise measurement of visual attention and cognitive processing, while providing new interaction possibilities for students with physical limitations. Key findings highlight the importance of customization and adaptation to individual learner needs, the necessity of robust theoretical frameworks linking visual patterns to cognitive development, and critical ethical considerations in data collection and privacy protection. Future research directions include developing more affordable hardware solutions, integrating artificial intelligence for real-time adaptation, and creating sophisticated assessment tools. The paper concludes that successful implementation requires careful attention to both technical and pedagogical frameworks, while maintaining focus on ethical considerations. These developments contribute to creating more inclusive educational environments and making quality education accessible to all students regardless of their specific challenges or abilities.

Keywords: Game Based Learning · Eye-tracking · Special Needs Education

1 Introduction

The integration of technology in education has created new opportunities to support diverse learning needs through innovative tools and approaches.

P. Ardimento et al. (Eds.): HELMeTO 2024, CCIS 2468, pp. 59–75, 2025.
https://doi.org/10.1007/978-3-031-93999-0_4

The evolution of educational technology has been particularly significant in special education, where traditional teaching methods often face limitations in addressing the complex and varied needs of learners. Among these technological advances, Eye-tracking has emerged as a particularly promising tool for both assessment and intervention in special education contexts. By providing objective measurement of visual attention and cognitive processing, Eye-tracking offers unique insights into how learners interact with educational content while enabling new forms of interaction for those with physical limitations.

The significance of this technological integration extends beyond mere accessibility. While traditional assistive technologies have focused primarily on enabling basic access to educational content, modern Eye-tracking systems represent a paradigm shift toward more sophisticated understanding and support of learning processes. These systems not only facilitate interaction but also provide detailed data about how students engage with educational materials, offering unprecedented opportunities for personalizing instruction and measuring learning outcomes.

Furthermore, the convergence of Eye-tracking technology with educational gaming environments presents unique opportunities for creating engaging and effective learning experiences. The combination of game-based learning's motivational benefits with Eye-tracking's precise measurement capabilities offers potential solutions to longstanding challenges in special education, such as maintaining student engagement, providing appropriate levels of challenge, and offering immediate feedback.

The rapid advancement of Eye-tracking technology, coupled with decreasing costs and increasing accessibility, has created new possibilities for widespread implementation in educational settings. However, this potential can only be realized through careful consideration of both technical and pedagogical factors. Understanding how to effectively integrate these tools into educational practice requires a comprehensive examination of current research, successful implementations, and emerging best practices.

This paper examines the current state of Eye-tracking applications in special education, with a particular focus on its integration with educational games and learning platforms. Through a literature review of recent research and implementations, we analyze how this technology is being used to enhance learning experiences, support assessment, and provide new forms of interaction for students with diverse needs. We also consider the practical implications for educators and developers, including technical requirements, implementation challenges, and ethical considerations.

The review aims to synthesize current knowledge and best practices while identifying promising directions for future research and development. By examining both the potential and limitations of Eye-tracking in special education, we seek to provide valuable insights for researchers, educators, and developers working to create more effective and accessible learning experiences. This analysis is particularly timely given the increasing focus on inclusive education and the growing recognition of technology's role in supporting diverse learners.

Our examination encompasses multiple perspectives, including technological capabilities, pedagogical applications, and implementation considerations. Through this comprehensive approach, we aim to provide a foundation for understanding how Eye-tracking technology can be effectively utilized to support learning and development in special education contexts, while also identifying areas requiring further research and development.

2 Video Games and Special Needs Education: A Theoretical Exploration of Accessibility and Learning Innovations

Video games and gamification approaches have emerged as powerful educational tools, demonstrating remarkable potential in special education contexts through their ability to create engaging, adaptive, and personalized learning experiences [21, 57].

As di Furia et al. [14] emphasize, these digital environments enable users to actively manipulate and interact with information rather than passively absorbing content, resulting in more effective learning processes. Such digital environments serve multiple pedagogical purposes, offering immersive, interactive experiences that not only enhance student engagement and motivation but also provide structured opportunities for repetitive practice and systematic skill development across various cognitive, social, and motor domains [16, 67].

The implementation of serious games-digital games designed for purposes beyond entertainment-has shown particular promise in therapeutic and educational interventions for diverse special needs populations [57].

For children with Autism Spectrum Disorders (ASD), game-based interventions have effectively targeted core developmental areas, including social skills, emotional recognition, and communication [54, 67]. Both specially designed serious games and commercial off-the-shelf games have demonstrated success in improving facial recognition and social interactions [58].

Students with Attention Deficit Hyperactivity Disorder (ADHD) have shown significant improvements in executive functioning, attention span, and self-regulation through engagement with action and strategy games [16, 49]. Additionally, games incorporating biofeedback mechanisms have proven effective for developing self-regulation skills [45].

The integration of embodied cognition principles into educational games has yielded particularly noteworthy results, demonstrating positive impacts on children's short-term memory skills and emotional regulation [32], as well as motor performance [33]. These benefits have been observed in children with special educational needs [4, 17, 34, 41].

For individuals with severe motor control and communication challenges, such as those with Rett Syndrome, combining games with advanced eye-tracking technology has opened new avenues for assessment and interaction. Such combinations enable the evaluation of cognitive abilities that might otherwise remain hidden due to physical limitations [52, 62]. Eye-tracking has proven especially valuable for people with Rett syndrome, who exhibit intense eye gaze, offering crucial communication opportunities for individuals with limited expressive abilities [62].

Students with specific learning disabilities also benefit significantly from the multisensory and scaffolded learning environments that educational games provide [1]. Targeted interventions have shown marked efficacy in addressing challenges related to dyslexia and dyscalculia [61]. The immediate feedback mechanisms and self-paced nature embedded in many game-based learning platforms align closely with evidence-based practices for learning disabilities [16]. These approaches simultaneously support the development of twenty-first-century skills, including enhanced attention, memory, concentration, motor planning, and time management capabilities [8, 19, 50].

As Prensky [48] noted, this shift toward digital game-based learning represents a crucial evolution in educational methodology, offering more learner-centered formats that may be more effective for students who have grown up immersed in digital media. Ongoing advancements in game-based learning technologies, supported by increasing research, suggest that video games will play an even more significant role in special education. They offer innovative solutions for addressing various learning needs while maintaining high levels of engagement and motivation.

The evolution of adaptive hardware and assistive technologies has become paramount in ensuring video game accessibility across diverse user populations, particularly as games gain prominence in educational contexts [70]. A comprehensive array of input devices has emerged to accommodate players with physical disabilities, including sip-and-puff controllers, eye gaze tracking systems, single-switch interfaces, voice control systems, and customizable button mapping solutions [2, 70].

For visually impaired users, alternative means of interaction are enabled by auditory feedback systems, haptic controllers, text-to-speech technology, and high-contrast visual modes [66]. Players with hearing impairments, on the other hand, benefit from visual alternatives to audio cues, closed captioning, and sign language avatars [30, 70].

The integration of cognitive accessibility features, such as difficulty scaling and simplified controls, supports players with intellectual disabilities [2], while specialized hardware solutions like modified controllers and switch interfaces enhance gameplay accessibility [70].

Recent developments in haptic feedback devices have shown particular promise in post-stroke rehabilitation [5, 27], motor skills training [23, 40, 43], and handwriting assistance [23, 37].

The implementation of these adaptive technologies often relies on sophisticated calibration systems that match task difficulties to individual user capabilities [69], with real-time assessment of user engagement through attention tracking [37, 44].

The integration of robotics has further expanded accessibility options, with low-cost platforms being deployed across educational and therapeutic settings [23], while traditional adaptive hardware solutions such as braille displays, screen readers, and magnification systems continue to play crucial roles in ensuring comprehensive accessibility [11].

As game developers increasingly embrace universal design principles, many of these adaptive features are being incorporated into mainstream games rather than requiring specialized hardware [47], reflecting a growing commitment to creating inclusive gaming experiences that accommodate players with diverse abilities and needs.

Eye-tracking technology, which utilizes sophisticated infrared light reflection from the cornea and pupil to determine precise gaze direction and movement patterns, has emerged as a transformative tool in special education, offering both comprehensive assessment capabilities and interactive possibilities for students with diverse needs. Modern video-based eye trackers provide high-accuracy measurement of various eye movement parameters, including fixations (200-300 ms periods of stable gaze), saccades (rapid eye movements between fixation points), scan paths (sequential patterns of eye movements), dwell time, pupil dilation, and carefully defined Areas of Interest (AOIs) for detailed analysis [25, 35]. The technology's theoretical foundation rests on the extensively researched connection between eye movements and fundamental cognitive processes such as attention, working memory, visual processing speed, and inhibitory control [24, 51, 59], with numerous studies documenting distinct and often diagnostically relevant eye movement patterns in various neurodevelopmental conditions including Autism Spectrum Disorder, ADHD, and specific learning disabilities [7, 38].

In terms of practical applications, Eye-tracking has demonstrated significant utility across multiple educational domains: for students with ADHD, sophisticated gaze-based games have shown remarkable promise in training sustained attention, selective attention, and inhibitory control, with documented improvements in attention spans and behavioral regulation [20, 36]; for individuals with autism spectrum disorders, the technology has enabled the development of innovative gaze-contingent training programs targeting social attention, joint attention, emotion recognition, and face processing skills, leading to measurable improvements in social cognition [56]; for students with dyslexia and reading difficulties, specialized eye movement training games have contributed to significant improvements in reading speed, comprehension, and overall reading abilities through targeted oculomotor exercises [6, 7]; and for those with severe motor impairments, advanced eye-controlled communication systems have facilitated expressive language development and academic participation [39]. Recent research has also explored the integration of Eye-tracking with artificial intelligence and machine learning algorithms to create adaptive learning systems that automatically adjust to individual student needs and learning patterns [65].

The technology's implementation considerations encompass critical hardware specifications such as sampling rate (typically ranging from 60 to 2000 Hz), tracking accuracy (0.5 to 1.0 degrees of visual angle), head movement tolerance ranges, illumination requirements, and calibration procedures [63], while evidence-based design principles emphasize the importance of user-specific adaptability, real-time performance feedback, distraction-free interfaces, carefully calibrated progressive difficulty levels, and comprehensive objective performance metrics for progress monitoring [15].

Leading companies like Tobii [60], EyeTech [18], and SMI [55] have made technology increasingly accessible through both consumer-grade and research-grade systems, with recent innovations focusing on smooth pursuit-based interaction techniques that enable calibration-free gaze interaction [64], particularly beneficial for spontaneous use by individuals with motor impairments or limited understanding of traditional calibration procedures.

The integration of Eye-tracking in special education has also led to the development of specialized assessment protocols for visual attention patterns, cognitive processing speeds, and learning strategies, providing educators with objective data to inform individualized intervention planning and progress monitoring [22, 31].

Furthermore, research has demonstrated technology's potential in early identification of learning difficulties through the analysis of distinctive eye movement patterns associated with specific cognitive challenges [28], while also highlighting its role in supporting multimodal learning through the combination of Eye-tracking with other assistive technologies and traditional educational methods [11].

3 Research Methodology

The literature review was conducted through these steps: initially, relevant sources were gathered from academic databases, including ResearchGate, Web of Science (WOS), and Google Scholar, to ensure broad coverage of studies on video games into special needs education through the use of innovative software and hardware tools.

Next, a critical assessment was conducted to evaluate the quality and relevance of each source to the research topic. Subsequently, the selected studies were organized into key thematic categories based on the research objectives (table 1).

Table 1. Overview of the analyzed papers.

Paper name	Authors (year)	Objective	Eye-tracking role
Eye-tracking training improves the learning and memory of children with learning difficulty	Chan, A. S., Lee, T. L., Sze, S. L., Yang, N. S., & Han, Y. M. (2022)	To evaluate the effectiveness of eye-tracking-based training in improving learning and memory in children with learning difficulties	Eye-tracking as a tool to improve learning and training
Visual expertise in paediatric neurology	Balslev, T., Jarodzka, H., Holmqvist, K., de Grave, W., Muijtjens, A. M., Eika, B., ... & Scherpbier, A. J. (2012)	Investigating how doctors with different levels of experience use visual attention and cognitive processes to diagnose paediatric cases through authentic videos	Eye-tracking to improve diagnosis and medical training
Gaze tutor: A gaze-reactive intelligent tutoring system	D'Mello, S., Olney, A., Williams, C., & Hays, P. (2012)	Develop and evaluate an intelligent tutoring system that uses eye-tracking to detect boredom and disengagement in students, reacting dynamically to redirect their attention and improve learning, motivation and engagement	Eye-tracking as a tool to improve learning and training
A closer look at split visual attention in system- and self-paced instruction in multimedia learning	Schmidt-Weigand, F., Kohnert, A., & Glowalla, U. (2010)	Examine how visual attention is distributed during learning from text and images in multimedia instruction with self-imposed or system-controlled temporal modes, analysing the effect of learning pace and text mode (written or spoken)	Eye-tracking as a tool to improve learning and training

(*continued*)

Table 1. *(continued)*

Paper name	Authors (year)	Objective	Eye-tracking role
Eye-tracking studies of normative and atypical development	Karatekin, C. (2007)	Exploring the use of eye-tracking to study normative and atypical development in children and adolescents, focusing on oculomotor measures (saccades, fixations, pupil dilation) and their contribution to understanding cognitive and clinical development	Eye-tracking as a tool for diagnosing and studying clinical conditions
Eyes are the window to the mind: Eye-tracking technology as a novel approach to study clinical characteristics of ADHD	Levantini, V., Muratori, P., Inguaggiato, E., Masi, G., Milone, A., Valente, E., ... & Billeci, L. (2020)	To explore the potential of eye-tracking as a method to analyse neurological mechanisms related to attention disorders and inhibitory control in young people with ADHD, supporting diagnosis and treatment	Eye-tracking as a tool for diagnosing and studying clinical conditions
A pilot study on evaluating children with autism spectrum disorder using computer games	Chen, J., Wang, G., Zhang, K., Wang, G., & Liu, L. (2019)	To examine the effectiveness of computer games as an objective, motivating and safe method to assess developmental skills in children with autism spectrum disorders in comparison to typically developing peers	Eye-tracking in clinical and educational contexts related to autism spectrum disorders
Rett syndrome: An eye-tracking study of attention and recognition memory	Rose, S. A., Djukic, A., Jankowski, J. J., Feldman, J. F., Fishman, I., & Valicenti-Mcdermott, M. (2013)	Analysing attention and recognition memory in patients with Rett syndrome using eye-tracking, to characterise the cognitive phenotype of this neurodevelopmental disorder	Eye-tracking as a tool for diagnosing and studying clinical conditions
Visual training could be useful for improving reading capabilities in dyslexia	Bucci, M. P. (2021)	Examining visual and attentional deficits in children with dyslexia, exploring the use of eye-tracking and visual rehabilitation interventions to improve reading and oculomotor patterns	Eye-tracking as a tool for diagnosing and studying clinical conditions
Pursuits: Spontaneous interaction with displays based on smooth pursuit eye movement and moving targets	Vidal, M., Bulling, A., & Gellersen, H. (2013)	To present an innovative technique for spontaneous interactions with interfaces based on fluid pursuit eye movements, evaluating its effectiveness and proposing real-life usage scenarios	Eye-tracking as a technology to develop or evaluate digital tools and interfaces

(continued)

Table 1. *(continued)*

Paper name	Authors (year)	Objective	Eye-tracking role
Visual attentional training improves reading capabilities in children with dyslexia: An eye tracker study during a reading task	Caldani, S., Gerard, C. L., Peyre, H., & Bucci, M. P. (2020)	To explore whether brief visual attentional training can improve reading skills in children with dyslexia by improving oculomotor characteristics	Eye-tracking as a tool for diagnosing and studying clinical conditions
Eye movements and problem solving: Guiding attention guides thought	Grant, E. R., & Spivey, M. J. (2003)	Demonstrate how eye movements during diagram-based problem solving correlate with success in solving problems and how perceptual highlighting of critical elements can improve reasoning ability	Eye-tracking as a method for studying cognition and perception
Eye-tracking in educational games environment: Evaluating user interface design through eye-tracking patterns	Mat Zain, N. H., Abdul Razak, F. H., Jaafar, A., & Zulkipli, M. F. (2011)	Analysing eye-tracking models to evaluate user interface design in educational games and proposing design guidelines to improve usability and effectiveness	Eye-tracking as a technology to develop or evaluate digital tools and interfaces
Worth a glance: Using eye movements to investigate the cognitive neuroscience of memory	Hannula, D. E., Althoff, R. R., Warren, D. E., Riggs, L., Cohen, N. J., & Ryan, J. D. (2010)	Investigating how eye movements can reveal the memory of past experiences and how this methodology is useful for studying special populations and integrating different neuroscientific disciplines	Eye-tracking as a method for studying cognition and perception
Performing locomotion tasks in immersive computer games with an adapted eye-tracking interface	Vickers, S., Istance, H., & Hyrskykari, A. (2013)	To develop and adapt eye-tracking-based interaction techniques to enable young people with severe physical disabilities to control characters in immersive games	Eye-tracking as a technology to develop or evaluate digital tools and interfaces
Brief report: a novel digital therapeutic that combines applied behavior analysis with gaze-contingent eye-tracking to improve emotion recognition in children with autism spectrum disorder	Sosnowski, D. W., Stough, C. O., Weiss, M. J., Cessna, T., Casale, A., Foran, A., ... & Farber, M. A. (2022)	To evaluate the feasibility, acceptability and effectiveness of a therapeutic video game to improve emotion recognition in children with autism spectrum disorders using eye-tracking	Eye-tracking in clinical and educational contexts related to autism spectrum disorders
Development of eye movement games for students with low vision: Single-subject design research	Donmez, M., & Cagiltay, K. (2019)	Design and develop games based on eye movements to improve the visual skills of students with low vision through an iterative development process	Eye-tracking as a technology to develop or evaluate digital tools and interfaces

(continued)

Table 1. (*continued*)

Paper name	Authors (year)	Objective	Eye-tracking role
Eye-tracking in educational practice: Investigating visual perception underlying teaching and learning in the classroom	Jarodzka, H., Skuballa, I., & Gruber, H. (2021)	To study visual perception in authentic educational contexts in order to better understand the visual interaction between teachers and students and to propose new theoretical models on teachers' professional attention and vision	Eye-tracking as a tool to improve learning and training
Using eye-tracking in education: Review of empirical research and technology	Ke, F., Liu, R., Sokolikj, Z., Dahlstrom-Hakki, I., & Israel, M. (2024)	To provide a systematic review of eye-tracking studies in educational contexts and an overview of machine learning technologies and techniques used	Eye-tracking as a tool to improve learning and training
Using eye-tracking technology for communication in Rett syndrome: Perceptions of impact	Vessoyan, K., Steckle, G., Easton, B., Nichols, M., Mok Siu, V., & McDougall, J. (2018)	Exploring the impact of eye-tracking technology as a method of communication for people with Rett syndrome, including assessing parents' perceptions of psychological and social functioning	Eye-tracking as a tool for diagnosing and studying clinical conditions
Effects of a gaze-based 2D platform game on user enjoyment, perceived competence, and digital eye strain	Colley, M., Wanner, B., Rädler, M., Rötzer, M., Frommel, J., Hirzle, T., Jansen, P., & Rukzio, E. (2024)	Investigates how the inclusion of various gaze-based interactions in a platform game ("shed some fear") influences user enjoyment, perceived competence, and digital eye strain in a five-day study. Results highlight the trade-off between the fun/challenge of gaze interaction and increased DES	Eye-tracking as a technology to develop or evaluate digital tools and interfaces
A real-time camera-based gaze-tracking system involving dual interactive modes and its application in gaming	Zhang, H., Yin, L., & Zhang, H. (2024)	Presents a camera-based, real-time gaze-tracking system offering dual interactive modes (eye gaze and head gaze). Accuracy tests show results comparable to commercial trackers. The authors also integrate the system into a brick breaker–style game to examine feasibility, revealing different user experiences (challenge, tension, enjoyment) across modes	Eye-tracking as a technology to develop or evaluate digital tools and interfaces

These categories included: (1) Eye-tracking as a tool to improve learning and training.; (2) Eye-tracking to improve diagnosis and medical training; (3) Eye-tracking as a tool for diagnosing and studying clinical conditions; (4) Eye-tracking in clinical and educational contexts related to autism spectrum disorders; (5) Eye-tracking as a technology to develop or evaluate digital tools and interfaces; (6) Eye-tracking as a technology to develop or evaluate digital tools and interfaces.

4 Innovative Applications of Eye-Tracking: From Education to Therapy

From specialized gaming to educational tools, eye-tracking has revolutionized user interaction, offering unique capabilities that enhance more than just accessibility features.

The development of specialized games like "The Revenge of the Killer Penguins" and "Rabbit Run" has pioneered hands-free gaming interaction through features such as SmartText that adapts to players' reading patterns [68].

Notable implementations include sophisticated adaptive systems that combine eye-tracking with haptic feedback for visio-motor skills development, where "eye-tracking provides spatial information and haptic provides texture details" [13]. Systems like COGPACK demonstrate this technology's practical implementation, offering 64 different tasks for training visual attention, saccades, eye-hand coordination, and visual memory [46].

In specialized educational applications, groundbreaking research by Donmez and Cagiltay [15] has revealed significant improvements in visual focusing abilities and object manipulation skills among students with low vision through customizable eye-tracking games. Technology has shown particular promise in classroom implementations, where researchers have observed significant improvements in communication abilities.

Technology's impact extends significantly into professional training and educational design. Balslev et al. [3] demonstrated impressive results in developing visual expertise in pediatric neurology training, while Jarodzka et al. [26] found improved diagnostic performance when students could observe expert eye movement patterns. In educational design optimization, Schmidt-Weigand et al. [53] provided valuable insights into how students distribute attention between text and visualizations during instruction, contributing to more effective learning material design.

Recent innovations have focused on specialized applications and system refinements. D'Mello et al. [12] have demonstrated the effectiveness of gaze-reactive tutoring systems that adapt to students' attention patterns, while Chan et al. [9] have shown that children with learning difficulties who received eye-tracking training demonstrated significantly improved memory and learning capabilities compared to those in conventional remediation classes. Computer-guided reading systems now highlight text based on children's eye movements, resulting in improved reading comprehension [29]. The success of these implementations relies on specific design considerations, including sufficient contrasts, colorblindness considerations, adjustable object speeds, customizable background colors, brightness controls, and screen resolution options [29].

Another recent contribution highlights the broader range of interactive possibilities Eye-tracking can offer. Zhang et al. [72] proposed a real-time camera-based gaze-tracking system featuring two modes—eye gaze and head gaze—allowing users to interact without specialized hardware. Their approach uses a single standard camera to capture and map gaze directions (including head orientation) onto the screen after a brief calibration. Through user studies in a brick-breaker–style video game, they not only demonstrated accuracy comparable to certain commercial systems but also underscored how each gaze mode (eye vs. head) can yield distinct user experiences in terms of challenge, tension, and overall enjoyment.

Technology has also shown promise in specialized therapeutic contexts. Research has demonstrated enhanced control capabilities for students with cerebral palsy and muscular dystrophy through adapted eye-tracking interfaces [63]. These applications extend beyond direct interaction to include observational learning and performance analysis, contributing to both immediate educational outcomes and longer-term therapeutic goals. The evolving landscape of eye-tracking applications continues to expand, with new implementations regularly emerging in both educational and clinical settings, suggesting a rich future for this technology in specialized learning and therapeutic environments.

5 Results and Discussion

Research has revealed that eye movements reflect strategic problem-solving approaches [42] and can predict learning outcomes before conscious awareness [22, 24].

Visual expertise studies in pediatric neurology have demonstrated how eye-tracking reveals expert diagnostic patterns [3]. Recent research shows that specialized visual training can improve reading capabilities in dyslexia [6] and enhance learning and memory in children with learning difficulties [9]. Studies with Rett syndrome have revealed important insights about attention and recognition memory [52], with significant implications for communication support [62].

Several limitations must be acknowledged. The methodology's effectiveness depends on clear theoretical frameworks, as the relationship between cognitive processes and eye movements remains incompletely understood [28, 38]. Technical constraints are detailed in comprehensive methodological guides [25], including challenges with foveal vision recording. Recent innovations like smooth pursuit-based interaction techniques [64] and adapted interfaces [63] have attempted to address these technical challenges.

Individual differences significantly influence effectiveness. Studies in multimedia learning have revealed important insights about split visual attention [53]. Visual attentional training has shown improvements in reading capabilities for children with dyslexia [7] and requires validation across different settings to enhance ecological validity [10]. Novel digital therapeutics combining gaze-contingent tracking with behavioral analysis have improved emotion recognition in ASD [56]. Interactive eye-tracking games have demonstrated improvements for students with low vision [15] and attention training in ADHD [20].

Critical ethical and privacy considerations must be addressed, particularly given the vulnerable nature of special needs populations. Recent educational reviews emphasize ethical considerations in data collection [29], while studies of eye-tracking in educational practice highlight important classroom implementation factors [26]. The collection of eye-tracking data requires careful attention to data protection regulations and informed consent procedures, especially crucial when working with individuals who cannot verbally express preferences.

Some research has also examined how eye-tracking might be harnessed to both increase user enjoyment and systematically measure health-related outcomes. For instance, Colley et al. [71] developed a 2D platform game, "Shed Some Fear", embedding multiple gaze-driven interactions (e.g., fixations, smooth pursuits, and the use of peripheral vision). Their study not only demonstrated how such mechanics can enhance perceived competence and overall enjoyment but also revealed a trade-off with increased Digital Eye Strain (DES), especially when long periods of uninterrupted gaze input are required. This work underlines the importance of balancing engaging game design with careful consideration for potential strain on users' visual systems—further emphasizing the need for integrating targeted eye-exercise elements or other countermeasures.

Moving forward, successful implementation requires a balanced approach combining multiple assessment modalities and carefully designed screening protocols. Studies incorporating gaze-reactive tutoring systems show promise for adaptive learning [12]. Future implementations should consider developing standardized protocols that balance technological innovation with ethical considerations while ensuring interventions remain effective and accessible to diverse learner populations.

6 Charting the Future: Eye-Tracking Research and Development Pathways

Future research directions and applications of video games and adaptive technologies in special education present significant opportunities for developers, educators, and researchers.

Technological applications, such as video games and eye-tracking, offer promising avenues for assessment and intervention in children with Autism Spectrum Disorder (ASD).

As highlighted by Chen et al. [10], it is essential to develop more robust and valid screening tools that can be used not only for preliminary assessments but also to support targeted interventions. Therapeutic games like Lookware™ [56] illustrate the potential of digital technologies to enhance emotional regulation (ER) skills, positioning them as complementary interventions to traditional Applied Behavior Analysis (ABA) therapy, especially in resource-limited settings or where direct access to treatment is restricted.

The study by Vickers et al. [63] further emphasises the need to customise interaction techniques based on users' abilities. Automated system configurations tailored to individual performance can significantly enhance autonomy and self-confidence. This customisation, along with continuous adaptation algorithms, is a key step toward creating more inclusive and personalised learning and gaming experiences.

Additionally, advances in eye-tracking technologies, particularly more accessible and affordable solutions like spectacle-mounted devices, could broaden the dissemination of these tools. Their educational and therapeutic applications include the realisation of interactive tasks and missions in immersive environments, providing new learning opportunities for children with physical limitations. Beyond the technical aspects, these systems can have a profound impact on individuals.

As noted by Vickers et al. [63], the ability to control an avatar independently can boost self-esteem and a sense of empowerment, positively affecting various aspects of daily life. Looking forward, the integration of emerging technologies, such as AI-enhanced eye-tracking and virtual reality, shows promise for further improving the adaptability and personalisation of educational tools.

Moreover, implementing adaptive controllers and similar technologies that promote accessibility in classrooms should be encouraged. These tools can be utilised in game-based activities, fostering a more inclusive and participative educational environment. Finally, interdisciplinary collaboration among pedagogy, neuroscience, and engineering could lead to innovative and targeted solutions, solidifying the role of play-based and adaptive technologies as fundamental components of special education in the future.

7 Conclusions

The integration of Eye-tracking technology with educational games represents a significant advancement in special education, offering both innovative assessment capabilities and new intervention possibilities.

While research has demonstrated technology's effectiveness across various applications, from improving reading capabilities to enhancing emotional regulation, several key considerations emerge for future development and implementation.

First, the successful deployment of these technologies requires careful attention to both technical and pedagogical frameworks. While Eye-tracking offers powerful insights into learning processes, its effective implementation depends on robust theoretical models linking visual attention patterns to cognitive development. Future research should focus on strengthening these theoretical foundations while developing standardized protocols that can be readily implemented in educational settings.

Second, the customization and adaptation of these technologies to individual learner needs remains crucial. The development of systems that can automatically adjust to user capabilities while maintaining engagement presents both a challenge and an opportunity. This includes not only interface design considerations but also the integration of real-time adaptation mechanisms that can respond to learner progress and engagement levels.

Third, ethical considerations must remain at the forefront of future developments. As these technologies become more sophisticated and widely implemented, establishing clear guidelines for data collection, storage, and usage becomes increasingly important, particularly when working with vulnerable populations. This includes developing appropriate consent procedures and ensuring that privacy protections are built into system designs from the outset.

Looking forward, the continued evolution of Eye-tracking technology in educational settings will likely be shaped by several key factors: the development of more affordable and accessible hardware solutions, the integration of artificial intelligence for real-time adaptation, and the creation of more sophisticated assessment tools. Success in these areas will require ongoing collaboration between educators, researchers, and developers to ensure that technological innovations align with pedagogical needs and ethical considerations.

The potential impact of these developments extends beyond individual applications to the broader goal of creating more inclusive educational environments. By providing new ways to understand and support diverse learning needs, Eye-tracking technology contributes to the larger mission of making quality education accessible to all students, regardless of their specific challenges or abilities.

Disclosure of Interests. The authors have no competing interests to declare that are relevant to the content of this article.

References

1. Annetta, L.A.: The "i's" have it: a framework for serious educational game design. Rev. Gen. Psychol. **14**(2), 105–113 (2010)
2. Archambault, D., Gaudy, T., Miesenberger, K., Natkin, S., Ossmann, R.: Towards generalised accessibility of computer games. In: Pan, Z., Cheok, A.D., Müller, W., Lidar, X. (eds.) Technologies for E-Learning and Digital Entertainment: Edutainment 2008, LNCS, vol. 5093, pp. 518–527. Springer, Berlin Heidelberg (2008)
3. Balslev, T., Jarodzka, H., Holmqvist, K., de Grave, W., Muijtjens, A.M., Eika, B., Scherpbier, A.J.: Visual expertise in paediatric neurology. Eur. J. Paediatr. Neurol. **16**(2), 161–166 (2012)
4. Bartoli, L., Corradi, C., Garzotto, F., Valoriani, M.: Exploring motion-based touchless games for autistic children's learning. In: Proceedings of the 12th International Conference on Interaction Design and Children, pp. 102–111. ACM, New York, NY (2013)
5. Broeren, J., Claesson, L., Goude, D., Rydmark, M., Sunnerhagen, K.S.: Virtual rehabilitation in an activity Centre for community-dwelling persons with stroke: the possibilities of 3-dimensional computer games. Cerebrovasc. Dis. **26**(3), 289–296 (2008)
6. Bucci, M.P.: Visual training could be useful for improving reading capabilities in dyslexia. Appl. Neuropsychol. Child. **10**(3), 199–208 (2021)
7. Caldani, S., Gerard, C.L., Peyre, H., Bucci, M.P.: Visual attentional training improves reading capabilities in children with dyslexia: an eye tracker study during a reading task. Brain Sci. **10**(8), 558 (2020)
8. Cassar, A.G., Jang, E.E.: Investigating the effects of a game-based approach in teaching word recognition and spelling to students with reading disabilities and attention deficits. Aust. J. Learn. Diff. **15**(2), 193–211 (2010)
9. Chan, A.S., Lee, T.L., Sze, S.L., Yang, N.S., Han, Y.M.: Eye-tracking training improves the learning and memory of children with learning difficulty. Sci. Rep. **12**(1), 13974 (2022)
10. Chen, J., Wang, G., Zhang, K., Wang, G., Liu, L.: A pilot study on evaluating children with autism spectrum disorder using computer games. Comput. Hum. Behav. **90**, 204–214 (2019)
11. Cook, A.M., Polgar, J.M.: Assistive Technologies: Principles and Practice, 4th edn. Elsevier Health Sciences, St. Louis (2014)
12. D'Mello, S., Olney, A., Williams, C., Hays, P.: Gaze tutor: a gaze-reactive intelligent tutoring system. Int. J. Hum. Comp. Stud. **70**(5), 377–398 (2012)
13. Deng, R., Gao, Y.: A review of eye-tracking research on video-based learning. Educ. Inf. Technol. **28**(6), 7671–7702 (2023)
14. di Furia, M., Ciletti, M., Toto, G.A., Guarini, P.: Verso un'evoluzione pedagogica del videogioco: il caso del Massively Multiplayer Online Role-Playing Game (MMORPG). Nuova Secondaria Ricerca. **42**(2), 269–275 (2024)

15. Donmez, M., Cagiltay, K.: Development of eye movement games for students with low vision: single-subject design research. Educ. Inf. Technol. **24**, 295–305 (2019)
16. Durkin, K., Boyle, J., Hunter, S., Conti-Ramsden, G.: Video games for children and adolescents with special educational needs. Z. Psychol. **223**(2), 79–89 (2015)
17. Edwards, J., Jeffrey, S., May, T., Rinehart, N.J., Barnett, L.M.: Does playing a sports active video game improve object control skills of children with autism spectrum disorder? J. Sport Health Sci. **6**(1), 17–24 (2017)
18. Eye-Tech srl: https://www.eye-tech.it/, last accessed 27 Nov 2024
19. Frutos-Pascual, M., García-Zapirain, B., Méndez-Zorrilla, A.: Improvement in cognitive therapies aimed at the elderly using a mixed-reality tool based on tangram game. In: International Conference on Computer Graphics Animation and Games, pp. 68–75. Springer, Berlin Heidelberg (2012)
20. García-Baos, A., Tomas, D., Oliveira, I., Collins, P., Echevarria, C., Zapata, L.P., Super, H.: Novel interactive eye-tracking game for training attention in children with attention-deficit/hyperactivity disorder. Prima. Care Companion CNS Disord. **21**(4), 26348 (2019)
21. Granic, I., Lobel, A., Engels, R.C.: The benefits of playing video games. Am. Psychol. **69**(1), 66–78 (2014)
22. Grant, E.R., Spivey, M.J.: Eye movements and problem solving: guiding attention guides thought. Psychol. Sci. **14**(5), 462–466 (2003)
23. Guneysu Ozgur, A., Wessel, M.J., Olsen, J.K., Johal, W., Ozgur, A., Hummel, F.C., Dillenbourg, P.: Gamified motor training with tangible robots in older adults: a feasibility study and comparison with the young. Front. Aging Neurosci. **12**, 59 (2020)
24. Hannula, D.E., Althoff, R.R., Warren, D.E., Riggs, L., Cohen, N.J., Ryan, J.D.: Worth a glance: using eye movements to investigate the cognitive neuroscience of memory. Front. Hum. Neurosci. **4**, 166 (2010)
25. Holmqvist, K., Nyström, M., Andersson, R., Dewhurst, R., Jarodzka, H., Van de Weijer, J.: Eye-Tracking: A Comprehensive Guide to Methods and Measures. OUP, Oxford (2011)
26. Jarodzka, H., Skuballa, I., Gruber, H.: Eye-tracking in educational practice: investigating visual perception underlying teaching and learning in the classroom. Educ. Psychol. Rev. **33**(1), 1–10 (2021)
27. Joo, L.Y., Yin, T.S., Xu, D., Thia, E., Fen, C.P., Kuah, C.W.K., Kong, K.H.: A feasibility study using interactive commercial off-the-shelf computer gaming in upper limb rehabilitation in patients after stroke. J. Rehabil. Med. **42**(5), 437–441 (2010)
28. Karatekin, C.: Eye-tracking studies of normative and atypical development. Dev. Rev. **27**(3), 283–348 (2007)
29. Ke, F., Liu, R., Sokolikj, Z., Dahlstrom-Hakki, I., Israel, M.: Using eye-tracking in education: review of empirical research and technology. Educ. Technol. Res. Dev. **72**, 1383–1418 (2024)
30. Kipp, M., Dackweiler, T., Gebhard, P.: Designing emotions: an empirical approach to realistic affect simulation. KI-Künstliche Intelligenz. **25**, 205–211 (2011)
31. Knoblich, G., Flach, R.: Predicting the effects of actions: interactions of perception and action. Psychol. Sci. **12**(6), 467–472 (2001)
32. Kosmas, P., Ioannou, A., Retalis, S.: Moving bodies to moving minds: a study of the use of motion-based games in special education. TechTrends. **62**(6), 594–601 (2018)
33. Kosmas, P., Ioannou, A., Zaphiris, P.: Implementing embodied learning in the classroom: effects on children's memory and language skills. Educ. Media Int. **56**(1), 59–74 (2019)
34. Kourakli, M., Altanis, I., Retalis, S., Boloudakis, M., Zbainos, D., Antonopoulou, K.: Towards the improvement of the cognitive, motoric and academic skills of students with special educational needs using Kinect learning games. Int. J. Child Comput. Interact. **11**, 28–39 (2017)

35. Lai, M.L., Tsai, M.J., Yang, F.Y., Hsu, C.Y., Liu, T.C., Lee, S.W.Y., Tsai, C.C.: A review of using eye-tracking technology in exploring learning from 2000 to 2012. Educ. Res. Rev. **10**, 90–115 (2013)
36. Lee, E.J., Kim, H.S., Choi, S.: Violent video games and aggression: stimulation or catharsis or both? Cyberpsychol. Behav. Soc. Netw. **24**(1), 41–47 (2021)
37. Lemaignan, S., Garcia, F., Jacq, A., Dillenbourg, P.: From real-time attention assessment to “with-me-ness” in human-robot interaction. In: In: 2016 11th ACM/IEEE International Conference on Human-Robot Interaction (HRI), pp. 157–164. IEEE, New York, NY (2016)
38. Levantini, V., Muratori, P., Inguaggiato, E., Masi, G., Milone, A., Valente, E., Billeci, L.: Eyes are the window to the mind: eye-tracking technology as a novel approach to study clinical characteristics of ADHD. Psychiatry Res. **290**, 113135 (2020)
39. Light, J., McNaughton, D.: Communicative competence for individuals who require augmentative and alternative communication: a new definition for a new era of communication? Augment. Altern. Commun. **30**(1), 1–18 (2014)
40. Malik, M.M., Hachach-Haram, N., Tahir, M., Al-Musabi, M., Masud, D., Mohanna, P.N.: Acquisition of basic microsurgery skills using home-based simulation training: a randomised control study. J. Plast. Reconstr. Aesthet. Surg. **70**(4), 478–486 (2017)
41. Malinverni, L., Mora-Guiard, J., Padillo, V., Mairena, M., Hervás, A., Pares, N.: Participatory design strategies to enhance the creative contribution of children with special needs. In: Proceedings of the 2014 Conference on Interaction Design and Children, pp. 85–94. ACM, New York (2014)
42. Mat Zain, N.H., Abdul Razak, F.H., Jaafar, A., Zulkipli, M.F.: Eye-tracking in educational games environment: evaluating user interface design through eye-tracking patterns. In: Visual Informatics: Sustaining Research and Innovations: IVIC 2011 LNCS, vol. 7067, pp. 64–73. Springer, Berlin Heidelberg (2011)
43. Matarić, M.J., Eriksson, J., Feil-Seifer, D.J., Winstein, C.J.: Socially assistive robotics for post-stroke rehabilitation. J. Neuroeng. Rehabil. **4**, 1–9 (2007)
44. Olsen, J.K., Belenky, D.M., Aleven, V., Rummel, N.: Intelligent tutoring systems for collaborative learning: enhancements to authoring tools. In: Artificial Intelligence in Education: AIED 2013 LNCS, vol. 7926, pp. 900–903. Springer, Berlin Heidelberg (2013)
45. Parnandi, A., Gutierrez-Osuna, R.: Physiological modalities for relaxation skill transfer in biofeedback games. IEEE J. Biomed. Health Inform. **21**, 361–371 (2017)
46. Pettersen, H.H.: Design and Development of Game-Based Oculomotor Training Using Eye-Tracking. Master’s Thesis,. University of Bergen (2018)
47. Porter, J.R., Kientz, J.A.: An empirical study of issues and barriers to mainstream video game accessibility. In: Proceedings of the 15th International ACM SIGACCESS Conference on Computers and Accessibility, pp. 1–8. ACM, New York, NY (2013)
48. Prensky, M.: Digital game-based learning. Comput. Entertain. **1**(1), 21–21 (2003)
49. Prins, P.J., Dovis, S., Ponsioen, A., Ten Brink, E., Van Der Oord, S.: Does computerized working memory training with game elements enhance motivation and training efficacy in children with ADHD? Cyberpsychol. Behav. Soc. Netw. **14**(3), 115–122 (2011)
50. Qian, M., Clark, K.R.: Game-based learning and 21st-century skills: a review of recent research. Comput. Hum. Behav. **63**, 50–58 (2016)
51. Rayner, K.: Eye movements in reading: models and data. J. Eye Mov. Res. **2**(5), 1–10 (2009)
52. Rose, S.A., Djukic, A., Jankowski, J.J., Feldman, J.F., Fishman, I., Valicenti-McDermott, M.: Rett syndrome: an eye-tracking study of attention and recognition memory. Dev. Med. Child Neurol. **55**(4), 364–371 (2013)
53. Schmidt-Weigand, F., Kohnert, A., Glowalla, U.: A closer look at split visual attention in system-and self-paced instruction in multimedia learning. Learn. Instr. **20**(2), 100–110 (2010)

54. Serret, S., Hun, S., Iakimova, G., Lozada, J., Anastassova, M., Santos, A., Askenazy, F.: Facing the challenge of teaching emotions to individuals with low-and high-functioning autism using a new serious game: a pilot study. Mol. Autism. **5**, 1–17 (2014)
55. SMI S.p.A.: https://www.smigroup.it/profilo/AR-glasses, last accessed 27Nov 2024
56. Sosnowski, D.W., Stough, C.O., Weiss, M.J., Cessna, T., Casale, A., Foran, A., Farber, M.A.: Brief report: a novel digital therapeutic that combines applied behavior analysis with gaze-contingent eye-tracking to improve emotion recognition in children with autism spectrum disorder. J. Autism Dev. Disord. **1–10** (2022)
57. Susi, T., Johannesson, M., Backlund, P.: Serious Games: an Overview. Technical Report HS-IKI-TR-07-001, School of Humanities and Informatics, University of Skövde (2007)
58. Tanaka, J.W., Wolf, J.M., Klaiman, C., Koenig, K., Cockburn, J., Herlihy, L., Schultz, R.T.: Using computerized games to teach face recognition skills to children with autism spectrum disorder: The Let's Face It! program. J. Child Psychol. Psychiatry. **51**(8), 944–952 (2010)
59. Theeuwes, J., Belopolsky, A., Olivers, C.N.: Interactions between working memory, attention and eye movements. Acta Psychol. **132**(2), 106–114 (2009)
60. Tobii: Investor relations - Tobii Corporate. (2024). Retrieved November 27, 2024, from https://corporate.tobii.com/
61. Toffalini, E., Marsura, M., Garcia, R.B., Cornoldi, C.: A cross-modal working memory binding span deficit in reading disability. J. Learn. Disabil. **52**(2), 99–108 (2019)
62. Vessoyan, K., Steckle, G., Easton, B., Nichols, M., Mok Siu, V., McDougall, J.: Using eye-tracking technology for communication in Rett syndrome: perceptions of impact. Augment. Altern. Commun. **34**(3), 230–241 (2018)
63. Vickers, S., Istance, H., Hyrskykari, A.: Performing locomotion tasks in immersive computer games with an adapted eye-tracking interface. ACM Trans. Access. Comput. **5**(1), 1–33 (2013)
64. Vidal, M., Bulling, A., Gellersen, H.: Pursuits: Spontaneous interaction with displays based on smooth pursuit eye movement and moving targets. In: Proceedings of the 2013 ACM International Joint Conference on Pervasive and Ubiquitous Computing, pp. 439–448. ACM, New York, NY (2013)
65. Wang, W., Arora, R., Livescu, K., Bilmes, J.: On deep multi-view representation learning. In: International Conference on Machine Learning, pp. 1083–1092. PMLR (2015)
66. Westin, T., Bierre, K., Gramenos, D., Hinn, M.: Advances in game accessibility from 2005 to 2010. In: Stephanidis, C. (ed.) Universal Access in Human-Computer Interaction: UAHCI 2011, LNCS, vol. 6766, pp. 400–409. Springer, Berlin Heidelberg (2011)
67. Whyte, E.M., Smyth, J.M., Scherf, K.S.: Designing serious game interventions for individuals with autism. J. Autism Dev. Disord. **45**, 3820–3831 (2015)
68. Wilcox, T., Evans, M., Pearce, C., Pollard, N., Sundstedt, V.: Gaze and voice-based game interaction: the revenge of the killer penguins. SIGGRAPH Posters. **81**(10.1145), 1400885–1400972 (2008)
69. Yannakakis, G.N., Hallam, J.: Real-time game adaptation for optimizing player satisfaction. IEEE Trans. Comput. Intell. AI Games. **1**(2), 121–133 (2009)
70. Yuan, B., Folmer, E., Harris, F.C.: Game accessibility: a survey. Univ. Access Inf. Soc. **10**, 81–100 (2011)
71. Colley, M., Wanner, B., Rädler, M., Rötzer, M., Frommel, J., Hirzle, T., Jansen, P., Rukzio, E.: Effects of a gaze-based 2D platform game on user enjoyment, perceived competence, and digital eye strain. In: Proceedings of the CHI Conference on Human Factors in Computing Systems, pp. 1–14 (2024)
72. Zhang, H., Yin, L., Zhang, H.: A real-time camera-based gaze-tracking system involving dual interactive modes and its application in gaming. Multimedia Systems. **30**, 15 (2024)

Innovative Approaches in Teacher Education: Active Breaks and Technology Integration

Elif Gulbay, Alessandra La Marca, Giorgia Rita De Franches(✉), and Savannah Olivia Mercer

University of Palermo, Palermo, Italy
giorgiarita.defranches@unipa.it

Abstract. In today's so-called information society, teacher education must adapt to changing social dynamics. This requires initial training for future teachers to develop key competencies for teaching practice, including digital literacy and metacognitive skills, to make the transition from being mere transmitters of knowledge to facilitators of learning.

The challenges of the twenty-first century, dictate that teachers need to be familiar with educational technologies that enable them to design new learning experiences. Technologies are powerful tools that can also support teaching practices such as active breaks.

Active breaks are short physical or mental activities that take place during lessons, and they are effective tools that should be part of teacher training. These breaks not only improve physical and mental well-being, but also increase attention, engagement, and learning outcomes.

Active breaks can take place at different times during the school day. These variations offer flexibility and adaptability in the way active breaks are implemented, with benefits such as improved attention, motivation, and engagement.

This study analyzes the impact of active breaks on teacher education by assessing the attitudes of 1005 prospective secondary school teachers and the role of technology in facilitating breaks.

The findings aim to offer guidelines for incorporating active breaks into teaching practice, promoting a more dynamic and inclusive learning environment.

The integration of active breaks has not been given much attention in the Italian educational context, thus making this study particularly relevant to teacher training programs in Italy.

Incorporating active breaks enables the promotion of healthier routines that improve learning effectiveness, emphasizing the value of balanced, interactive and technological approaches in teacher education.

Keywords: Active breaks · Technologies · Initial teacher training

1 Introduction

The lack of physical activity among children is an increasingly concerning public health issue with significant implications for physical and mental well-being.

P. Ardimento et al. (Eds.): HELMeTO 2024, CCIS 2468, pp. 76–87, 2025.
https://doi.org/10.1007/978-3-031-93999-0_5

Physical activity (PA) is a key health factor [1] in children's physical and psychological development [2, 3], as it improves motor development [4], self-esteem [5] and cardiorespiratory fitness [6].

Movement breaks, classroom oxygenation through window opening, and drinking some water during the school morning seem to improve the classroom environment and, consequently, academic performance [7].

Active Breaks (AB) consist of short (5–15 min), moderate-to-vigorous physical activity (PA) in the classroom supervised while both prepared and supervised by a teacher trained for this purpose, performed during or between school-lesson blocks. They are a great tip to interrupt long sitting times at school [8].

Furthermore, the literature highlights that active breaks help students reconnect with the joy of movement and reach the minimum physical activity threshold for health indicated by the WHO [1].

ABs have also been shown to affect concentration, selective attention and classroom behavior [8].

Active break programs have been linked to benefits for students' psychophysical health and academic performance. Additionally, they have a positive impact on academic outcomes, particularly on students' behavior in the classroom [9].

Active breaks involve activities such as muscle stretching exercises, marching in place, muscle relaxation or breathing control techniques, joint mobility exercises, dancing, and more.

These activities activate fundamental motor skills (walking, running, jumping, balancing, pulling, pushing, lifting, throwing).

Indeed, their effectiveness in increasing students' physical activity levels and reducing school-related inactivity and sedentary behaviors has been demonstrated in several studies [10].

Active breaks offer significant logistical and organizational advantages for teachers [10]: the required execution space is minimal, as the exercises are designed to be performed in small spaces. They require neither large areas nor bulky equipment and are cost-free, making them feasible even in classrooms.

The presence of professionals or specialists is not necessary, as their simplicity makes them easy for teachers to manage.

Active breaks are short and can be repeated throughout the day, making them adaptable to the needs of children, teachers, and the educational context. Scheduling active breaks within the school day does not disrupt or interfere with curricular requirements; they align with the school's teaching schedule, especially when designed with flexibility and appropriate motivation by teachers [11]. Finally, active breaks help to relieve and declutter children's minds from the high cognitive effort required by academic activities, promoting better focus on subsequent tasks [12].

2 Active Breaks in Initial Teacher Training

Teacher training can be defined as a process aimed at improving the quality of teaching to maximize student learning [13].

In this way, teaching can ensure students the opportunity to enhance the skills required by the sociocultural context.

Avalos [14] argues that the training process is complex, as it demands significant commitment and participation from teachers in training, requiring the openness necessary to learn, reflect, and collaborate with colleagues in order to change their beliefs about teaching and their ability to implement teaching models different from traditional ones.

These dimensions, in fact, are central to influencing the teaching delivery methods adopted by educators.

To achieve a genuine change in the ways teachers implement their teaching, Darling-Hammond et al. [15] highlight the importance of specific characteristics that an effective training intervention must have: practical activities, content focus, collaboration, modelling, support, reflection, and the duration of the intervention.

The first key element of effective training is the implementation of practical activities, allowing teachers in training to apply and experiment, both individually and in groups.

This aspect is significant because it enables greater teacher engagement and participation, improving the quality of learning both theoretically and practically, as it allows them to experience the same learning processes they will implement with students.

The scientific literature presents a limited number of studies on how to adequately train teachers on the implementation of active breaks in the classroom.

Active breaks are also very flexible and adaptable to the school context and specific class needs because they allow teachers to design the breaks according to all these factors and situations.

There are several ways active breaks can be integrated into the school day [16, 17]:

- at the beginning of curricular lessons;
- as a break between two consecutive lessons;
- as a break within the same lesson, tied to the content being covered;
- as outdoor activities, such as walking for predetermined distances or times.

Their duration can range from 5 to 15–20 minutes, and while they are usually conducted in the classroom near students' desks, they have also expanded to outdoor environments, such as the schoolyard, where some teachers feel more confident in leading activities.

Active breaks, as any other sensory-motor activities, need to be within students' curricular experience and embraced by a pedagogical framework that defines teaching and learning experiences. They should be seen as a crucial, practical aspect in the healthy development of every person.

It is not about creating more time or room, but rather a daily school routine that reflects attention to the entirety of each student's academic experience, not simply bounded to content-specific assignments.

Within this educational complexity, active breaks need to find a proper space in the mosaic of teaching strategies [18].

It is therefore crucial to train teachers and future teachers in the use of active breaks so that they become teaching tools capable of promoting the optimal development of every individual, improving the learning environment, and fostering motivation toward educational pathways.

Active breaks represent an innovative educational strategy to integrate movement and learning in school contexts. These breaks, often consisting of short moments of physical activity or structured reflection, aim to improve not only students' physical and cognitive well-being but also to promote a dynamic teaching approach tailored to the needs of teachers in training. According to Watson et al. [19], teacher training on the use of active breaks is essential to enhance their confidence and competence in implementing these strategies in the classroom.

A crucial aspect of active breaks is their connection to experiential and motivational learning theories. Studies highlight how they can support a transition toward more participatory teaching methods, fostering autonomy among both students and teachers.

Ruiz-Hermosa et al. [20] claim that using real-time digital platforms for active breaks can increase the confidence of teachers and equip them with more effective tools of training.

Furthermore, active breaks end up working well in improving mental and physical well-being. Infantes-Paniagua et al. [21] state that universal active breaks in the learning environment enhance students' attention span, which can be easily delivered by teachers even with basic training.

Active breaks can also serve as professional development in initial teacher training. Examples of studies are McMullen et al. [22] such implementations have been previously proven to allow trainee teachers to experiment with new teaching approaches and increase engagement and adaptability in the classroom.

According to Jiménez-Parra et al. [23] implemented hybrid programs that combine active breaks with a program for teaching the development of personal responsibility in educational settings to increase both the effectiveness of teachers and teachers' overall well-being.

Integrating active breaks into teaching presents a major challenge for any teacher because it is a change from traditional teaching methods. The challenge is even more complicated when it is necessary to conduct active breaks outside the classroom.

Therefore, before we implement active breaks, we must always think through the challenges that may hinder the successful use of active breaks in the classroom. it is therefore important for teachers to be trained proficiently in the use of these practices in teaching.

Moving away from the traditional approach and towards methodologies based on active breaks, for example, constitutes a potential pathway for rethinking teaching practice but also involves a set of overlaps between pedagogical ideas and practicalities that must be planned. The biggest challenges include controlling noise that would disrupt the normal conduct of classes in nearby classrooms or make it difficult for teachers to communicate with students. To avoid this possibly problematic core value—set up an aversion to silence routines from the very beginning stages of adapting and try, when possible, to make rooms with access.

Another important consideration is the wide variation in students' needs. We should design activities for individuals, which constantly encourage diverse methods that allow everyone to participate equally without stalling the learning of those with higher levels of competence. This can include assigning roles, ensuring groups are mixed and balanced, and tasks that aim tasks that aim to promote peer interaction.

One major limitation is that teaching staff are not very experienced or specifically trained with these methodologies, reducing their confidence to apply them.

In this context, a phased rollout with sufficient training support is necessary to foster appropriate and proficient use of active breaks.

Also, inequities in student involvement based on unequal knowledge or skill levels can be minimized by using small group work and activities requiring all participants to work together.

Simultaneously another main challenge with limited classroom space becomes a serious concern in schools which have restricted infrastructure. In these instances, coordinating with colleagues (especially PE teachers) and arranging low-space-impact activities can be a good solution [20].

3 Integrating Active Breaks with Digital Technologies in Teacher Training

The use of technologies in the teaching and learning process represents an open issue in today's society.

Recent scientific literature states that most teachers do not adequately exploit technologies; rather, they use them only to support traditional teaching methods [24, 25].

Introducing technologies into teaching is not an immediate process and is not sufficient to positively impact educational practices or promote the development of the digital skills required of students [26].

Rather, technology should be used as a tool to mediate the building of collaborative knowledge creation experiences [27].

In a study by Sansone et al. [28] highlighted how in initial teacher training courses, technology is not placed at the center of the learning contents.

Prospective teachers attend classes in which they passively acquire information on a variety of software or applications through "how-to" lessons [29, 30].

As a result, teachers lack the opportunity to understand the implications that can arise from the use of technologies, such as when to introduce technology while considering students' needs and how it can foster active participation. To this end, Bautista and Ortega-Ruiz [31] emphasize the importance of implementing training programs aimed at developing in teachers the skills needed to effectively use technologies.

Technologies can be defined as innovative tools to encourage active breaks and consequently mental and physical well-being and productivity.

Indeed, today there are Apps and smartwatches that send push notifications to users to make movements after long sedentary moments are detected.

In addition, there are now virtual reality immersion experiences to relax the mind and practice yoga or meditation.

Movement practice during video tutorials and interactive games can be done in confined areas due to the lightweight nature of such activities.

With these solutions, active breaks become accessible to all and more effective, enabling stress reduction, improved concentration, and counteracting the negative effects of sedentariness in the workplace or during study.

The current generation of students has been labelled as digital natives. Technology has also been defined as a useful tool that can develop motivation in students.

Today many educational applications allow students to perform physical activities without moving from home.

These activities can also be experimented with in school environments and aim to foster the development of motor skills while also combining interdisciplinary and cross-curricular skills. These methodologies are particularly significant during developmental stages, as they enable teachers to train students in the appropriate and responsible use of technologies that promote physical activity in both real and virtual environments.

The use of technologies in teaching, particularly as support for active breaks, can enhance students' motivation, allowing teachers to personalize instruction [32].

4 Analyzing the Impact of Active Breaks on Teacher Training: A Survey-Based Approach

Active breaks represent an innovative approach in the context of initial teacher education.

This research investigates the positive impact of active breaks with the aim of improving metacognitive competence (sustained attention, focused attention, cognitive and emotional self-regulation skills) and consequently learning.

4.1 Structure of the Questionnaire

This quantitative study investigates the impact of active breaks in initial teacher education by using a survey. This study will attempt to measure the attitude towards active breaks by pre-service secondary school teachers, perceptions about the facilitation of benefits and challenges to implementing the strategies, as well as how technology can support their use.

This study was conducted between September–October 2024 and included a web-based survey of a large sample of teacher trainees.

The research involved a sample of 1005 teachers enrolled in university pathways for the training of secondary school teachers.

The questionnaire investigated participants' attitudes towards active breaks and explored the role of technology in facilitating these practices.

The latter consisted of questions on the frequency and duration of active breaks, preferences for certain types of activities and the effectiveness of the use of technology in supporting the implementation of these breaks.

The instrument developed by our research team for data collection is a questionnaire structured in 4 sections with a total of 15 items. The items use a 4-point Likert scale with the following response options: 1 ("Strongly disagree"), 2 ("Disagree"), 3 ("Agree") and 4 ("Strongly agree").

The questionnaire presented to the students, in the form of a Google Form, was not designed for future validation, as there is no intention to generalise the results. It was specifically adapted to the context in question.

4.2 Results

This is an exploratory study, and as such, no tests of inference were carried out, so interpretations remained purely descriptive in nature.

Results are presented as a narrative summary, highlighting key messages regarding teachers' perceptions of active breaks.

Section 1 of the questionnaire explores attitudes towards active breaks, collecting general information on the frequency, duration and preferences regarding activities performed during active breaks, as well as the benefits of using them.

Analysis of the data for this section reveals that 66% of teachers do not frequently incorporate active breaks in their teaching by selecting the 'Disagree' and 'Strongly Disagree' options more often.

This indicates a potential resistance or lack of awareness of the benefits of using active breaks in teaching.

72% of teachers prefer active breaks lasting less than 10 minutes, with a majority choosing the options 'Agree' and 'Strongly Agree'.

A significant proportion of teachers believe that shorter breaks can be more effective in maintaining attention and optimising classroom time.

Approximately 65 per cent of the teachers expressed a preference for active breaks in which physical activities are performed rather than mindfulness activities.

The majority of future teachers selected the answers 'Agree' or 'Strongly Agree', suggesting that physical movement is considered most effective in stimulating the regeneration of students' attention.

78% of teachers believe that active breaks significantly improve concentration, with a majority of responses 'Agree' and 'Strongly agree'.

Section 2 focuses on how technologies can facilitate the implementation of active breaks, investigating how technological tools can support these practices.

The data for this section, 'Role of technology in facilitating active breaks', reveal that a significant percentage of teachers, 70%, believe that using technology increases the effectiveness of active breaks.

This suggests a widespread belief among teachers about the benefits of technology in making active breaks more engaging.

A crucial aspect of this study is the incorporation of digital technology during active breaks through the Gamification, apps which delivered as planned strategies to boost engagement and get the students moving during lessons.

Pre-service teachers were further trained regarding the function of such interactive methods as active breaks to promote cognitive engagement and movement, as designed. The training sessions highlight the pedagogical aspects of these tools, with a view to instruct teachers to create gamified activities that are crafted that include short physical exercises, problem-solving tasks and movement-based challenges.

About 62% of teachers prefer to use educational applications to facilitate active breaks; in fact, the interactivity of applications is considered an effective method to stimulate interest by making breaks more dynamic.

55% of teachers identified limited access to technology as one of the main obstacles to the implementation of active breaks. Despite their appreciation for technology, many teachers face practical challenges related to the availability of technology resources.

Another interesting finding concerns the 68% of teachers who believe that technology fosters creativity during active breaks. This highlights how many teachers consider technology to be a useful element in stimulating the imagination, making breaks more stimulating.

The third section deals with the practical application of active breaks, examining how they can be integrated into teaching practice.

Analysis of the data shows that 68% of teachers customise active breaks based on students' needs. This suggests an awareness of students' needs.

74% of teachers believe that active breaks should be adaptable to specific classroom needs. This indicates a positive outlook towards the customisation of active breaks, which could make it possible to meet the needs of teachers and students.

Sixty-five per cent of teachers express disagreement with the effectiveness of using technology in active breaks; in fact, they dispute the fact that these are not necessarily accessible to all age groups. Many teachers see technological accessibility as a significant barrier, fearing that the use of technology is not suitable for all students, thus limiting the inclusiveness of active breaks.

A worrying figure comes from 70% of teachers, who believe that classroom space significantly limits their ability to implement effective active breaks. This is a concrete barrier related to insufficient classroom space, which may hinder the performance of physical activities, thus limiting the effectiveness of active breaks.

This analysis highlights the favourable disposition of teachers towards personalisation of active breaks while identifying practical obstacles, including technological accessibility and space concerns in the classroom.

Finally, the fourth section analyses the degree of adaptability of active breaks, assessing the ease with which they can be modified to different educational contexts and the specific needs of students.

An analysis of this data shows that 62% of teachers believe that technology-based active breaks are more effective than breaks based on traditional methods, with 'Agree' and 'Strongly Agree' options predominating. Teachers therefore recognise the added value of technology.

Some 58% of teachers indicated the need for specific training to effectively implement technology-based active breaks.

This reflects the awareness of the difficulties in integrating technology effectively and the demand for training to improve their skills in the use of these innovative active breaks.

Seventy-five per cent of teachers stated that they would integrate active breaks more frequently into their teaching practices in the future, with a predominance of 'Agree' and 'Strongly Agree' responses.

This highlights the willingness on the part of teachers for a long-term commitment to integrating active breaks as an integral part of teaching, suggesting motivation on the part of teachers to implement them more frequently in future lessons.

These results highlight a positive outlook for the use of technology-based active breaks, with a strong desire for training and a commitment to their future use in teaching practices.

In conclusion, the results of this survey provide precise indications of future teachers' perceptions and practices regarding active breaks.

The results show a recognition by teachers of the benefits of these breaks, especially in improving concentration, commitment and motivation.

Although most teachers recognise the positive aspect of using technology in facilitating the implementation of active breaks, they also recognise the challenges of these technology-integrating breaks, such as limited access to resources and the limitations of classroom space that remain significant obstacles.

However, the analysis demonstrates a growing interest in the integration of active breaks in teaching and the need for professional training and this indicates a promising prospect for the incorporation of active breaks in teaching-learning practice.

By addressing these obstacles and providing adequate training and resources, active breaks could become a powerful tool to promote more interactive and inclusive learning environments at school.

5 Conclusion

Teacher education should be conceived in the light of life-long learning, continuing education from the perspective of in-service training and ongoing professional development. In-service training is a fundamental device of teachers' professional development, particularly when conducted in a reflective manner.

Thus, one can distinguish the figures of the teacher in initial training, or pre-service teacher, the novice teacher, with little context awareness and little reflexivity, the expert teacher or master teacher (Snow, Griffin & Burns, 2005).

This study has highlighted how active breaks and technology integration can be two innovative approaches to promote teaching that is more dynamic, inclusive, and focused on improving the learning-teaching process.

Active breaks emerge as a versatile teaching strategy that can positively affect students' physical and mental well-being, improving their concentration, motivation and performance.

Analysis of the data showed that although there is high awareness among prospective teachers about the benefits of such breaks, barriers such as the lack of adequate space and technological resources persist. It is therefore essential to overcome these barriers by including strategies to adapt active breaks to the specifics of different school settings.

Technology integration offers further potential for making active breaks more accessible and engaging. However, for technologies to become effective tools in education, a paradigm shift in their use is needed: from support for traditional methods to a resource for building collaborative and motivational learning experiences.

A relevant finding of this research is the demand for more training support, both in the management of active breaks and in the use of technologies.

This points to the need for investments in professional development pathways, which would give teachers the opportunity to develop practical and theoretical skills to implement these innovations in daily teaching.

The future prospects as outlined by the results show a growth in interest and motivation among the teachers themselves to employ active breaks systematically as an instrument for education.

This willingness, when combined with adequate training support, leads to a big transformation in teaching practice that can respond to students' needs and be true to their psychological and physical well-being.

The integration of active breaks with technology during initial teacher education is one of the very fundamental steps toward innovative education.

For that matter, a necessary impulse must be given to cultural change so that flexibility, collaboration, and adaptability are considered part of teaching practice.

Only an integrated and participatory approach can ensure that teachers receive new tools to deal effectively with contemporary educational challenges within teaching.

The future prospects outlined by the results show a growing interest and motivation on the part of teachers to systematically use active breaks as an educational tool.

This willingness, combined with adequate training support, can lead to a significant transformation in teaching practice that can respond to students' needs and that is geared true to their psychological and physical well-being.

In conclusion, integrating active breaks with technology in initial teacher education is a key step toward more innovative education.

For this to happen, it is crucial to promote a cultural change that values flexibility, collaboration and adaptability as key elements of teaching practice.

Only through an integrated and participatory approach will it be possible to ensure that teachers have the tools they need to successfully address contemporary educational challenges.

References

1. World Health Organization: Physical activity. Key facts. (2020). http://www.who.int/en/news-room/fact-sheets/detail/physical-activity
2. Blanco, M., Veiga, O.L., Sepúlveda, A.R., Izquierdo-Gomez, R., Román, F.J., López, S., Rojo, M.: Ambiente familiar, actividad física y sedentarismo en preadolescentes con obesidad infantil: estudio *ANOBAS de casos-controles*. Atención Primaria. **52**(4), 250–257 (2020)
3. Strong, W.B., Malina, R.M., Blimkie, C.J., Daniels, S.R., Dishman, R., Gutin, B., Hergenroeder, A.C., Must, A., Nixon, P.A., Pivarnik, J.M., Rowland, T., Trost, S., Trudeau, F.: Evidence based physical activity for school-age youth. J. Pediatr. **146**(6), 732–737 (2005)
4. Williams, H., Pfeiffer, K., O'Neill, J., Dowda, M., Mclver, K., Brown, W., Pate, R.: Motor skill performance and physical activity in preschool children. Obesity. **16**(6), 1421–1426 (2008)
5. Ulrich, B.: Perceptions of physical competence, motor competence and participation in organized sport: their interrelationships in young children. Res. Q. Exerc. Sport. **58**(1), 57–67 (1997)
6. Okely, A.D., Booth, M.L., Patterson, J.W.: Relationship of cardiorespiratory endurance to fundamental movement skill proficiency among adolescents. Pediatr. Exerc. Sci. **13**(4), 380–391 (2001)
7. Mulato, R., Riegger, S.: Maestra facciamo una pausa? La Meridiana, Bari (2014)
8. Dallolio, L., Gallè, F., Masini, A., Valeriani, F., Ceciliani, A., di Cagno, A., et al.: Active breaks: a strategy to counteract sedentary behaviors for health promoting schools. A discussion on their implementation in Italy. Annali di Igiene Medicina Preventiva e di Comunità. **35**(2), 202–212 (2022)
9. Masini, A., M. S.: Active breaks: a pilot and feasibility study to evaluate the effectiveness of physical activity levels in a school based intervention in an Italian primary school. Int. J. Environ. Res. Public Health. **17**, 4351 (2020)

10. Casolo, F.: Scuola primaria: Spazi ambientali e temporali per l'educazione motoria. Pedagogia Oggi. **17**(1), 493–508 (2019)
11. Calella, P., Mancusi, C.: Classroom active breaks: a feasibility study, pp. 1–8. Health Promotion International (2019)
12. Kibbe, D.L., et al.: Ten years of TAKE 10: integrating physical activity with academic concepts in elementary school classrooms. Prev. Med. **52**, S43–S50 (2011)
13. Van der Klink, M., Kools, Q., Avissar, G., White, S., Sakata, T.: Professional development of teacher educators: what do they do? Findings from an explorative international study. Prof. Dev. Educ. **43**(2), 163–178 (2017)
14. Avalos, B.: Teacher professional development in teaching and teacher education over ten years. Teach. Teach. Educ. **27**(1), 10–20 (2011)
15. Darling-Hammond, L., Hyler, M.E., Gardner, M.: Effective Teacher Professional Development. Learning Policy Institute (2017)
16. Chesham, R.A., Booth, J.N., Sweeney, E.L., Ryde, G.C., Gorely, T., Brooks, N.E., Moran, C.N.: The daily mile makes primary school children more active, less sedentary and improves their fitness and body composition: a quasi-experimental pilot study. BMC Med. **16**(1), 64 (2018)
17. Marchant, E., Todd, C., Stratton, G., Brophy, S.: The daily mile: whole-school recommendations for implementation and sustainability. A mixed-methods study. PLoS One. **15**(2), e0228149 (2020)
18. Masini, A., Coco, D., Russo, G., Dallolio, L., Ceciliani, A.: Active breaks in primary school: teacher awareness. Formazione Insegnamento. **21**(1S), 107–113 (2023)
19. Watson, A.J., Timperio, A., Brown, H., Hesketh, K.D.: A pilot primary school active break program (ACTI-BREAK): effects on academic and physical activity outcomes for students in years 3 and 4. J. Sci. Med. Sport. **22**(4), 438–443 (2019)
20. Ruiz-Hermosa, A., Sánchez-Oliva, D., Sánchez-López, M.: Active classrooms in school curricula and active breaks. In: Promotion of Physical Activity and Health in the School Setting, pp. 233–250 (2024)
21. Infantes-Paniagua, Á., Silva, A.F., Ramirez-Campillo, R., Sarmento, H., González-Fernández, F.T., González-Víllora, S., Clemente, F.M.: Active school breaks and students' attention: a systematic review with meta-analysis. Brain Sci. **11**(6), 675 (2021)
22. McMullen, J., Kulinna, P., Cothran, D.: Physical activity opportunities during the school day: classroom teachers' perceptions of using activity breaks in the classroom. J. Teach. Phys. Educ. **33**(4), 511–527 (2014)
23. Jiménez-Parra, J.F., Manzano-Sánchez, D., Camerino, O., Prat, Q., Valero-Valenzuela, A.: Effects of a hybrid program of active breaks and responsibility on the behaviour of primary students: a mixed methods study. Behav. Sci. **12**(5), 153 (2022)
24. Petrucco, C., Grion, V.: An exploratory study on perceptions and use of technology by novice and future teachers: more information and less online collaboration? Int. J. Dig. Liter. Dig. Compet. **6**(3), 50–64 (2015). https://doi.org/10.4018/IJDLDC.2015070104
25. Sipilä, K.: Educational use of information and communications technology: teachers' perspective. Technol. Pedagog. Educ. **23**(2), 225–241 (2014)
26. Sansone, N., Ritella, G.: Formazione insegnanti "aumentata": integrazione di metodologie e tecnologie al servizio di una didattica sociocostruttivista. Qwerty. **15**(1), 70–88 (2020)
27. Scardamalia, M., Bereiter, C.: Knowledge building: Theory, pedagogy, and technology. In: Sawyer, K. (ed.) Cambridge Handbook of the Learning Sciences, pp. 97–118 (2006)
28. Sansone, N., Lattanzio, M.: Apprendimento collaborativo della matematica in una scuola secondaria di primo grado: l'impatto delle tecnologie. VII Congresso Nazionale Collaborative Knowledge Building Group, Padova, 18–20 Novembre 2019

29. Barton, R., Haydn, T.: Trainee teachers' views on what helps them to use information and communication technology effectively in their subject teaching. J. Comput. Assist. Learn. **22**(4), 257–272 (2006)
30. Tondeur, J., Pareja Roblin, N., van Braak, J., Voogt, J., Prestridge, S.: Preparing beginning teachers for technology integration in education: ready for take-off? Technol. Pedagog. Educ. **26**(2), 157–177 (2017)
31. Bautista, A., Ortega-Ruíz, R.: Desarrollo profesional docente: Perspectivas y enfoques internacionales. Psychol. Soc. Educ. **7**(3), 343–355 (2015)
32. Monacis, D., Colella, D., Scarinci, A.: Interventi di educazione alla salute nella scuola primaria: le pause attive per la promozione dell'attività motoria. Form@re. **20**(1), 336–355 (2020)

Development and Initial Validation of a Future Teacher Anxiety Questionnaire: A Pilot Study

Savannah Olivia Mercer(✉), Ylenia Falzone, Alessandra La Marca, Benedetta Miro, Giorgia Rita De Franches, and Mariagemma Pecoraro

University of Palermo, Palermo, Italy
savannaholivia.mercer@unipa.it

Abstract. The development of effective measures to understand anxiety in future teachers is essential. Research shows that the initial, training stages of a teacher's career are often accompanied by heightened anxiety, driven by the challenges of managing academic assessment demands, gaining confidence in classroom management skills, and facing new teaching environments. This study employed a two-phase, mixed-methods approach to develop and pilot a new questionnaire to measure stress and anxiety in future teachers. Phase 1 involved informal observations and interviews to identify markers of anxiety and inform questionnaire design. Phase 2 piloted the questionnaire with participants enrolled in a teacher training course at the University of Palermo, assessing the internal consistency and exploratory factor analysis to guide future item refinement and domain structure. Preliminary results demonstrated high reliability for the total scale (Cronbach's $\alpha = 0.966$) and individual subscales addressing Classroom Management and Student Engagement ($\alpha = 0.900$), Workload and Teaching Stress ($\alpha = 0.903$), Performance and Evaluation Anxiety ($\alpha = 0.895$), and Emotional and Physical Manifestations ($\alpha = 0.896$). Exploratory factor analysis then revealed three distinct factors, suggesting a need for revisions to improve alignment with theoretical constructs. Qualitative participant feedback highlighted opportunities to enhance the questionnaire by addressing areas not yet covered, such as systemic issues like precarious teaching conditions and bureaucratic stress, along with suggestions regarding scale length and item clarity. This initial analysis establishes the questionnaire as a foundation for future refinement and validation, essential for triangulating data with emerging technologies in subsequent research.

Keywords: future teachers · teacher anxiety · questionnaire development

1 Introduction

Teacher anxiety and stress are increasingly recognized as critical areas of research due to their profound influence not only on the teachers' well-being but also on the classroom environment and educational outcomes. Emotional well-being plays a pivotal role in shaping teachers' professional experiences, their ability to manage classroom dynamics, and their rapport with students. High levels of stress and anxiety among educators are associated with reduced teaching efficacy, adverse student outcomes, and increased

P. Ardimento et al. (Eds.): HELMeTO 2024, CCIS 2468, pp. 88–103, 2025.
https://doi.org/10.1007/978-3-031-93999-0_6

rates of burnout, which can ultimately lead to educators leaving the profession [1, 2]. Addressing teacher anxiety is, therefore, not only vital for improving teacher well-being but also for fostering positive, inclusive learning environments where all students can thrive [3].

While research has sought to understand and support teacher anxiety, less attention has been given to the emotional experiences of pre-service, future, teachers. Future teachers face unique challenges in managing the demands of their training and the emotional complexities of the teaching profession. For future teachers, mastering this is crucial to their long-term success and resilience in the profession.

Central to understanding and addressing teacher anxiety is the availability of valid and reliable tools to measure it. Existing measures tend to focus on in-service teachers, or have been developed in previous decades, thus lacking in encapsulating the stressors experienced by pre-service teachers within contemporary education systems. This study seeks to fill this gap through the development of a new questionnaire designed to assess anxiety among future teachers. By drawing on established concepts of teacher anxiety in existing measures, as well as observations and interviews with 62 pre-service teachers during simulated teaching activities, the questionnaire translates indicators such as body language and physical signs of discomfort into measurable items in order to capture the distinct ways in which anxiety manifests in educational contexts. This questionnaire was piloted on 88 in-training teachers at the University of Palermo in order to gain crucial preliminary insights into scale properties and factor structure, as well as participant feedback for future refinement and revision studies.

Recently, innovative and assistive technologies have moved to the forefront of educational research [4]. The development of a valid questionnaire represents a crucial foundational step within a broader goal of triangulating teacher emotional data through multiple methodologies, including subjective self-reports, observational studies, and emerging technologies. Integrating these technologies with subjective and contextual measures through triangulation can yield a richer and more accurate understanding of teacher well-being. However, for such triangulation to be effective, a robust foundation of valid self-report measures is essential and the present study's contribution, a questionnaire tailored to pre-service teachers, addresses this. By capturing the nuanced emotional experiences of future educators, this work not only addresses an existing gap in the literature but also lays the groundwork for integrating diverse data sources, derived from innovative technologies, in future studies to support teacher resilience and create inclusive educational environments.

2 Background

2.1 A Foundation for the Triangulation of Data for Measuring Teacher Emotion

The growing integration of innovative technologies in education provides new opportunities for studying teacher emotions and their impact on classrooms. While teacher emotions have traditionally been assessed through subjective methods like self-reports, interviews, and observations, these approaches are inherently limited due to their reliance on self-awareness or interpretation from external perspectives. Triangulation, a method that involves combining theories, methods, perspectives, or data sources within research

[5–7] can increase validity and credibility [8, 9]. Within the context of teacher emotions, combining subjective self-report questionnaire data, interview and observation data, with objective physiological measures can generate more valid findings, offering a more holistic approach to understanding teacher well-being. For instance, combining self-reports with physiological data can help validate subjective experiences of stress, while observations provide a contextual understanding of classroom interactions.

Wearable technologies such as electrodermal activity (EDA) sensors, which measure physiological markers of emotional arousal, offer valid, objective insights into stress and anxiety levels [10–12]. These tools are becoming increasingly accessible and have already been used within educational settings with student samples [13, 14], though their use with teacher samples remains scarce [15]. By incorporating innovative methods such as wearable sensors to measure biomarkers, future studies can better address the emotional complexities of teaching.

The lack of exploration into teacher emotions is an important gap to address. Negative teacher emotions have been found to have significant impacts on students' well-being and emotional regulation [16, 17]. Researchers in this area have highlighted the need to shift away from reliance solely on self-report measures [18], making a multidimensional approach to understanding teacher emotions with increased credibility crucial. Therefore, the questionnaire developed within this study serves as a key foundation for triangulation with other physiological biomarkers as data sources, promoting emotionally safe, inclusive classrooms where teachers are emotionally regulated.

2.2 Existing Measures of Teacher Emotion

Teacher anxiety has been acknowledged as a phenomenon in the field of education, and tools have been developed to measure and address this concept. Frequently used questionnaires and scales include: the Student Teacher Anxiety Scale (STAS) [19], the Teaching Anxiety Scale (TCHAS) [20], and the Teacher Stress Inventory (TSI) [21]. Most of the existing scales within the literature are generalized to serve teachers, as opposed to specifically addressing the anxieties of in-training teachers. Whilst the STAS was designed for student teachers, this along with the other often used scales, though providing valuable insights, were primarily designed within a different era, and thus cannot fully meet the specific needs of today's in-training teachers. Research has acknowledged that anxiety in teacher training stands as an issue throughout teachers' training journeys [22] yet the available tools are not fully aligned with the complex challenges and expectations faced by modern in-training teachers.

As educational practices evolve, there is a need for updated instruments that reflect contemporary realities. Factors such as inclusive education and accommodating the needs of diverse learners, the integration of modern technology into classrooms, and a struggle to advocate for a work-life balance present unique stressors for in-training teachers. The limitations of existing tools in addressing these modern challenges accentuate the need for a new, comprehensive questionnaire tailored to the realities of present-day teacher training. By incorporating updated terminology and capturing the experiences of in-training teachers, this new instrument aims to bridge the gap between past validated measures and present-day demands. A tool as such is crucial for the design and measure of the effectiveness of new interventions that seek to promote the mental well-being of future teachers as they navigate the multifaceted challenges of their profession.

2.3 Research Questions of the Present Study

1. What observable markers indicate anxiety in in-training teachers during simulated classroom activities?
2. How can insights from observations and interviews with in-training teachers inform the design of a questionnaire for assessing teaching-related anxiety?
3. What are the initial psychometric properties (internal consistency, factor structure) of the newly developed future teacher anxiety questionnaire?
4. What are suggestions for revisions and improvements based on pilot testing and analysis of respondent feedback?

3 Methodology

3.1 Phase 1: Questionnaire Item Development Through Observations and Interviews

During the development of the questionnaire items, existing tools and theories, such as the STAS and TCHAS measures, served as scientific references. These frameworks provided a foundation for identifying relevant items, which were then adapted to address the specific needs of pre-service, future teachers. It was also decided that it was important to include a section for the physical manifestations of anxiety and stress. Thus, identifications were needed of the behavioural and physical markers of anxiety within a teaching context. To achieve this, we conducted observations and interviews with in-training teachers, utilizing grids guided by existing references. However, some additional anxiety markers emerged organically during observations, thus also combining established theory with inductive Grounded Theory. This hybrid approach ensured that the study remained rooted in the established literature whilst also allowing for the identification of new, context-specific anxiety indicators.

Sample
The observations included 62 future teachers enrolled in a teacher training course. The sample was diverse in terms of age, gender, and teaching specialisation.

Procedure
Participants engaged in a simulated teaching activity in which each in-training teacher conducted a brief mock lesson in front of their peers, whilst observations were carried out using a structured observational grid. Researchers made note of items that tracked visible markers of anxiety, including physical discomfort (e.g., shaking, trembling), nervous gestures (e.g., fidgeting, tapping), and changes in speech patterns (e.g., hurried speech). To add context to the observed markers participants were invited to partake in informal interviews after being observed. The interviews used open-ended questions to explore their experiences during the mock lesson. Questions focused on identifying specific stressors and associated levels of anxiety. These interviews aimed to explore how

the participants perceived their anxiety during the activity and whether they were aware of the signs they displayed. Many participants recognized their own physical anxiety markers, which validated the initial observations and helped ensure that these markers were relevant to the teachers' lived experiences.

3.2 Phase 2: Piloting of the Newly Developed Questionnaire

Before utilizing or formally validating the questionnaire, a pilot study should be conducted [23] with a small sample of people similar to the intended group of interest [24], in this case, future teachers.

Sample

For the pilot testing of the newly developed questionnaire, a sample of in-training teachers was recruited ($N = 88$). The sample comprised 52.2% female and 47.8% male participants, all of whom were enrolled in teacher training programs at the University of Palermo. Participants were evenly distributed across training for primary school (49.5%) and secondary school (50.5%) education. The sample encompassed a broad age range, from 23 to 59 years ($M = 37$, $SD = 8.9$), ensuring diverse representation.

Instrument Description

The questionnaire was developed using the insights gained from Phase 1, alongside the constructs from the previously cited existing teacher anxiety measures. Items were adapted and expanded based on specific needs identified in the observations and interviews, including the incorporation of modern-day demands and concepts like technology use and work-life balance. During the item generation phase, inspiration was drawn from established scales, with modifications made to better reflect the specific context of pre-service teachers and contemporary challenges. Consistent with best practices in scale development [25, 26], new items were developed based on existing frameworks. The existing instruments such as the TCHAS and TSI informed thematic areas like teaching-related anxiety and stress, but the new items were adapted to address the unique challenges encountered by pre-service teachers during their training. This approach allowed for a more targeted and contextually relevant questionnaire.

The final questionnaire consisted of 30 items divided into four subscales: Classroom Management and Student Engagement (CMSE), Workload and Teaching Stress (WTS), Performance and Evaluation Anxiety (PA), and Emotional and Physical Manifestations (EPM). The CMSE subscale relates to classroom management and student rapport, including items such as "I am afraid I won't be able to build a good relationship with my students". The WTS subscale relates to workload and work-life balance, including items such as "I feel overwhelmed thinking about how I will balance lesson planning, grading, and other tasks" and "I feel stressed thinking about how I will balance my teaching responsibilities with my personal life". The PA subscale relates to performance and assessment anxiety and includes items such as "I feel anxious about being observed by supervisors or colleagues while teaching." and "I feel less confident than other teachers in my training program". Finally, the EPM subscale relates to the physical markers of anxiety as identified in Phase 1 and includes items such as "I often experience physical symptoms (e.g., sweating, trembling, fast heartbeat) while preparing for or teaching lessons" and "My speech becomes faster or less clear when I am nervous during teaching-related activities". Each item is rated on a 5-point Likert scale (1 = strongly disagree; 5 = strongly agree), with higher scores relating to increased anxiety.

Procedure

The present study was conducted as an open pilot study, in that the participants were made aware that the study was a pilot study to gain their feedback. The questionnaire was distributed to the Phase 2 sample online through Google Forms. Consent was gained and a disclaimer regarding the sensitive nature of the questionnaire items was disseminated at the beginning of the questionnaire. At the end of the questionnaire, there were additional questions in which participants were asked to evaluate the questionnaire's design and content using a combination of closed-ended and open-ended questions. Participants were encouraged to provide feedback on clarity, length, ease of answering, relevance to their experience, and aspects not covered. Closed-ended questions (e.g., Yes, Partly, No) provided structured feedback, while open-ended questions allowed participants to elaborate on their answers and suggest improvements. This approach ensured a comprehensive assessment of the questionnaire's effectiveness and usability. An Italian translation of the questionnaire was conducted by a native Italian speaker, and thus disseminated to the Italian participants.

Data Analysis

Statistical data analysis was conducted using Jamovi 2.2.5. Quantitative analysis was performed on the pilot study data to assess the questionnaire's internal consistency, item-rest and inter-item correlations, and factor structure [27]. Following data collection, raw data was cleaned, and assumption checks for the analyses were carried out and considered prior to statistical analysis. Qualitative analysis was conducted on the written feedback from participants in order to identify key themes within the dataset.

4 Results

4.1 Reliability and Factor Structure Analysis

Reliability Analysis

To evaluate the internal consistency of the newly developed questionnaire, Cronbach's alpha coefficients for each of the four subscales were calculated. Table 1 represents the descriptive statistics of the items along with the Cronbach's alpha coefficients for each of the four subscales, demonstrating high reliability.

Table 1. Descriptives and Cronbach's alpha of total and subscales

Scale	No. Items	Mean	SD	Minimum	Maximum*	Cronbach's alpha
Class management and student engagement	9	2.34	0.694	1.00	4.11	0.900
Workload and teaching stress	8	2.49	0.810	1.00	4.38	0.903
Performance and evaluation anxiety	6	2.24	0.809	1.00	4.17	0.895
Emotional and physical manifestation	7	1.85	0.727	1.00	3.71	0.896
Total scale mean	30	2.25	0.672	1.00	4.00	0.966

*Note: Theoretical minimum and maximum values for all subscales and the total scale are 1 and 5.

To further refine the questionnaire, both inter-item and item-rest correlation analyses were conducted. Within the CMSE subscale, item-rest correlations ranged from $r = .533$ (CMSE7) to $r = .753$ (CMSE1), thus, it can be concluded that all items contributed positively to the scale, meeting the rule of thumb of minimally required value [28]. Whilst the removal of any item only affected reliability minimally, CMSE7 had the lowest item-rest correlation, and the highest potential increase in if item dropped Cronbach's alpha, suggesting it is the least consistent item within the subscale. As demonstrated in Fig. 1, the inter-item correlations ranged from $r = .26$ to $r = .71$, with the lowest correlations seen between CMSE7 and the other items, supporting the item-rest correlations findings.

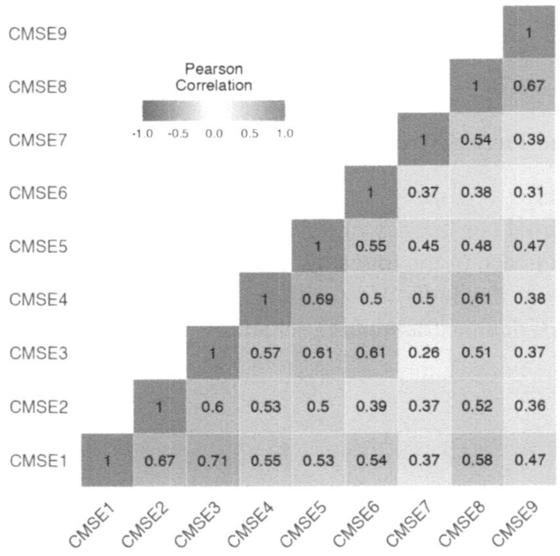

Fig. 1. Correlation heatmap for the Classroom Management and Student Engagement subscale.

Within the WTS subscale, all item-rest correlations were between $r = .666$ and $r = .797$, except from item WTS8 ($r = .438$), which if removed affects the overall subscale reliability the most (Cronbach's $\alpha = 0.918$). The inter-item correlations supported these findings, whilst correlations amongst other items were moderate to high. WTS8 had the lowest correlations, ranging between $r = .29$ and $r = .41$.

For the PA subscale, item-rest correlations for individual items ranged from $r = .571$ (PA6) to $r = .846$ (PA4), suggesting that all items are moderately to highly correlated with the total score. If individual items were dropped, Cronbach's alpha values ranged between $\alpha = .855$ (PA4 dropped) and $\alpha = .898$ (PA6 dropped), suggesting that removing any item would not substantially improve the overall reliability. The correlation heatmap overall demonstrated moderate to high inter-item correlations ($r = .43$ to $r = .81$), demonstrating acceptable coherence among the items whilst highlighting PA6 for its consistently lower intercorrelations with the other items.

Finally, for the EPM subscale, whilst item-rest correlations for EM1, EM2, EM3, EM4, and EM7 were high (between $r = .739$ to $r = .792$), EM5 ($r = .588$) and EM6 ($r = .520$), produced lower correlations and higher increases in Cronbach's α if removed ($\alpha = .894$ and $\alpha = .901$, respectively). The correlation heatmap also indicated EM6 as having the lowest correlations with other items, ranging from $r = .32$ to $r = .45$.

Exploratory Factor Analysis

An exploratory factor analysis (EFA) was conducted to investigate the questionnaire's underlying domain structure and to inform potential item removal [29]. Assumptions of linearity were met as correlation coefficients among all items were over .30 [30–32]. Given that this factor analysis was conducted on a preliminary dataset derived from a pilot study with a modest sample (N = 88) intending to inform future refinement of the questionnaire rather than to draw definitive conclusions, certain assumption checks were not fully performed or interpreted. Thus, while multivariate normality, sampling adequacy, and sphericity were considered, the results should be interpreted cautiously. Future analyses, conducted with larger and more diverse samples, will include a more thorough examination of these assumptions to ensure the validity of the factor structure through confirmatory factor analysis, thus offering greater reliability and applicability to wider contexts.

We used a principal axis extraction due to its well-suitedness for data that are not normally distributed [33]. Given the hypothesised interrelationships between factors, which aligns with expectations within the social sciences in that attitudes are rarely considered independent [34] an oblique, Oblimin rotation was applied to allow factors to correlate. The number of factors to retain was determined through parallel analysis [35], which indicated the retention of 3 distinct factors. Full factor loading and uniqueness values output can be seen in Table 2.Factor 1 consisted of all WTS items (WTS1-WTS7) with high loadings, except WTS8, which did not load significantly. It also consisted of four out of the six PA items (PA1-PA4) with small to moderate loadings, as well as one item from the EPM subscale (EPM6) with a loading of 0.672.

Factor 2 consisted of CMSE items (CMSE1-CMSE8) with moderate to high loadings ranging from 0.406 to 0.785. CMSE9 did not load significantly onto this factor, or any factor, suggesting it may not align with the intended construct of the CMSE subscale. It also consisted of four items from the PA subscale (PA1, PA3, PA4, PA5), and one item from the WTS subscale (WTS8). While most CMSE items exhibited moderate to high loadings, CMSE7 loaded less highly (0.406), supported by the higher uniqueness value of 0.639, suggesting this item has a potential for removal. Items from the PA subscale also had relatively smaller loadings, suggesting that although the factor analysis suggested a merging of items from two of the putative subscales, the loadings indicate that Factor 2 is still more strongly characterised by CMSE items.

Factor 3 consisted of six out of the original seven items from the EPM subscale with moderate to high loadings, along with one item from the PA subscale (PA6) with a particularly high loading (0.933).

4.2 Participant Feedback Analysis

Quantitative Feedback

Table 3 represents the quantitative feedback gathered at the end of the questionnaire from participants. Most participants felt the questionnaire was clear and easy to understand and had little difficulty answering the questions. However, approximately 18% of participants felt that a 30-item questionnaire was too long and that the questionnaire did not fully capture all stressors related to being an in-training teacher.

Qualitative Feedback

The qualitative feedback from participants highlighted several areas for improvement. Participants provided detailed and constructive feedback on both the teaching-related content and the design of the questionnaire. Table 4 represents the themes identified and the frequencies mentioned. The themes included: job insecurity, and the unique pressures faced by precarious or temporary teachers, including challenges with substitute roles, ranking systems, and temporary contracts. Bureaucratic burdens, such as administrative tasks, class coordination, and mandatory training, were also identified as significant sources of stress that detract from teaching. Classroom-specific challenges were highlighted, particularly managing challenging students and maintaining continuity in lessons. Regarding the questionnaire, participants suggested improvements such as shortening it and including additional items to reflect their lived experiences. Specific suggestions included adding questions about extracurricular preparation time, bureaucratic pressures, interactions with colleagues, and job instability. Feedback also pointed to systemic issues, with participants critiquing aspects of teacher recruitment, such as oral exam preparation and constantly changing regulations. Comments on socio-environmental factors emphasized the impact of under-resourced schools and inadequate teaching infrastructures on their experiences. Several participants expressed satisfaction with the questionnaire, describing it as complete or adequate.

5 Discussion

The reliability and factor structure analysis offered important insights into which items did not contribute to the subscales or which needed to be reconsidered. Cronbach's alpha coefficients revealed excellent internal consistency for the subscales and the overall scale. This high reliability suggests that the questionnaire items effectively captured the

Table 2. Factor Loadings

	Factor			
	1	2	3	Uniqueness
CMSE1		0.718		0.383
CMSE2		0.602		0.538
CMSE3		0.783		0.413
CMSE4		0.785		0.389
CMSE5		0.753		0.385
CMSE6		0.588		0.510
CMSE7		0.406		0.639
CMSE8		0.647		0.498
CMSE9				0.593
WTS1	0.788			0.312
WTS2	0.790			0.367
WTS3	0.807			0.400
WTS4	0.663			0.383
WTS5	0.634			0.361
WTS6	0.744			0.457
WTS7	0.650			0.290
WTS8		0.517		0.657
PA1	0.504	0.359		0.355
PA2	0.494			0.451
PA3	0.338	0.414		0.471
PA4	0.352	0.486		0.294
PA5		0.474		0.378
PA6			0.933	0.138
EM1			0.755	0.304
EM2			0.933	0.138
EM3			0.746	0.368
EM4			0.728	0.434
EM5			0.506	0.629
EM6	0.672			0.432
EM7			0.702	0.352

Note. 'Principal axis factoring' extraction method was used in combination with an 'oblimin' rotation

Table 3. Participant responses to questions

Question	Yes %	Partly %	No %
Did the questionnaire seem too long to you?	3.4	14.8	81.8
Did you find the questions clear and easy to understand?	95.5	3.4	1.1
Did the questions reflect your experience?	81.8	–	18.2
Did you have difficulty answering the questions?	1.1	–	98.9

Table 4. Themes within open-ended responses

Theme	Frequency
Interpersonal relationships with colleagues	3
Precarious/temporary teaching concerns	7
Bureaucratic workload	5
Systemic issues in teacher recruitment	4
Extracurricular preparation time	3
Social and environmental factors	3
Issues with length or term clarity	6

nuances of teaching anxiety, from classroom management to emotional and physical manifestations of anxiety. The Cronbach's alpha values for the subscales suggest that the constructs are internally cohesive and reflect well-defined aspects of in-training teacher anxiety. The factor analysis revealed 3 distinct factors as opposed to the original 4: a combined Workload and Performance Anxiety subscale, a combined Classroom Confidence and Student Engagement subscale, and the original Emotional and Physical Manifestations (EPM) subscale.

The Workload and Performance Anxiety factor (1) is comprised mostly of items relating to workload stress from the original WTS subscale, strongly characterized by WTS3 (loading = .807) "The pace of the school day seems too fast for me to manage everything" and WTS2 (loading = .790) "I am afraid that I will have too much work to do as a teacher". This is combined with items reflecting anxiety regarding observations and evaluations such as PA1 (loading = .503) "I feel anxious about being observed by supervisors or colleagues while teaching" and PA2 (loading = .494) "I am afraid I won't meet the expectations of my mentor teachers, supervisors, or students". This could be explained by the fact that these items share the same focus on external pressures of workload, teaching responsibilities and evaluations from supervisors and colleagues. This suggests that the originally theorized Performance and Evaluation Anxiety items are interlinked with workload and expectations pressures.

The Classroom Confidence and Student Engagement factor (2) consists mostly of items regarding classroom management and student engagement from the original

CMSE, most strongly characterized by CMSE3 (loading = .783) “I feel nervous thinking about how I will respond when students challenge my instructions” and CMSE4 (loading = .785) “I feel stressed about finding effective strategies to actively engage all my students during lessons”. However, the factor also consists of items relating to adaptability in the classroom, such as PA3 (loading = .414) “I feel nervous at the thought of trying new teaching strategies or technologies” and confidence in teaching abilities, such as (PA5 = .474) “I worry about making mistakes or not being able to answer students’ questions in class”. Furthermore, the factor consists of an item regarding concerns over not receiving appropriate recognition (WTS8 = .517) “I worry about not receiving proper recognition or appreciation for the hard work I will put in as a teacher”, suggesting that anxieties relating to teaching abilities are also entwined with a recognition (or lack of) of ability and efforts from others. The item-rest and inter-item correlation values highlighted that the CMSE subscale may benefit from revision or removal of CMSE7 “I am afraid I won’t be able to build a good relationship with my students”, and this was supported by the factor analysis, which demonstrated CMSE7 as having the lowest loading (.406) onto factor 2.

The third and last factor consisted of all items from the putative Emotional and Physical Manifestations of anxiety, with moderate to high loadings ranging from .506 to .933, except EM6 (“I feel tired or fatigued quickly after teaching or planning a lesson”) which did not load, suggesting a potential redundancy of the item also supported by the inter-item and item-rest correlation analyses. This finding supports our theorized subscale as a solid, definitive subscale worthy of inclusion. Interestingly, there was one additional item from a different subscale, PA6 (loading = .933) “I feel less confident than other teachers in my training program”. This could point to the importance of considering comparison to others as a key component within the emotional manifestation of anxiety.

The preliminary analysis will ultimately guide revision and refinement of the questionnaire to streamline the instrument, addressing feedback from the pilot study participants, some of whom indicated that the current 30-item version was too long, thus supporting considerations for item elimination based on the reliability, inter-item relations, and factor structure findings. In doing so, we aim to address potential respondent fatigue, which may compromise the quality of the data. The written feedback was crucial for identifying potential problems with the questionnaire and highlighting areas of improvement and suggestions for new dimensions and items not already covered. Analysis of the themes within the written feedback revealed key factors of anxiety inclusive of precarious stress, bureaucratic stress, and school environmental factors. Notably, precarious teacher stress emerged as a prominent factor in future teacher anxiety, participants frequently cited job instability and administrative burdens as sources of anxiety. This aligns with broader research indicating that early-career teachers often deal with a lack of institutional support [36]. As well as this, the high number of responses relating to bureaucratic stress also reflects the increasing administrative pressures placed on teachers in modern educational systems, particularly in Italy, as was highlighted by researchers exploring stress factors in Italian teachers [37]. By integrating such themes into the questionnaire in future revisions, items will be able to capture dimensions of anxiety that may otherwise go unnoticed in existing measures like the TCHAS or the TSI, which were developed in markedly different educational contexts.

Ultimately, this research aims to contribute to the development of evidence-based strategies for supporting pre-service teachers in managing anxiety, thereby promoting their emotional well-being and professional development. By equipping teacher training programs with tools to better measure and address anxiety, this research has the potential to inform targeted interventions that support future educators in navigating the challenges of their profession. In doing so, it contributes to the broader goal of fostering a sustainable and resilient teaching body who are prepared to create positive and inclusive learning environments for all students.

6 Limitations and Future Research Directions

The present study, being a pilot, has presented some limitations and several opportunities for future research. While the observations and interviews in Phase 1 provided rich qualitative insights, they were subject to observer bias as well as confined to a single teacher training course, potentially limiting the generalizability of findings to broader cultural or institutional contexts. The small sample size, while necessary for initial validation, limits the generalizability of the findings. As a pilot study, the aim was to refine the research instrument and gather preliminary data, so the results should be interpreted with caution. A larger, more diverse sample is the next step required for further validation of the findings.

Future research should focus on testing the refined questionnaire on a broader and more diverse sample to enhance the generalizability and robustness of the results. Longitudinal studies could also provide insights into how teacher anxiety evolves over time, both during training and throughout their careers. As mentioned, incorporating mixed methods and data sources, such as physiological measures of stress or peer evaluations, could provide a more comprehensive understanding of teacher anxiety. These directions will enhance the robustness and applicability of the tool, enabling its use in diverse educational contexts to inform targeted interventions and support systems for teacher well-being.

7 Conclusion

The present study developed and piloted a questionnaire to assess anxiety among in-training teachers, addressing stressors specific to future, in-training teachers. High internal consistency and reliability were observed across the questionnaire's subscales, suggesting the tool effectively captures anxiety markers in teaching contexts. An exploratory factor analysis indicated potential overlaps in the original constructs, leading to three refined factors: Workload and Performance Anxiety, Classroom Confidence and Student Engagement, and Emotional and Physical Manifestations. Participant feedback highlighted systemic stressors such as job instability, bureaucratic demands, and under-resourced schools as significant contributors to anxiety, emphasizing areas for further scale enhancement. While preliminary results are promising, further refinement and validation with larger, diverse samples are essential to ensure the questionnaire's reliability, validity, and relevance. The developed questionnaire stands as an important foundational step for future triangulation of data alongside technological-based objective measures of teacher anxiety in order to holistically address anxiety within the digital era. The refined tool holds the potential for aiding teacher training programs by identifying stress factors and fostering targeted interventions to enhance teacher preparedness and well-being.

Author Contributions. This article is the result of the joint work of the authors. S.O. Mercer wrote sections 2.1, 3.2, 4.1 and 5, Y. Falzone wrote sections 1 and 4.2, A. La Marca wrote section 7, B. Miro wrote sections 2.3 and 3.1, G.R. De Franches wrote section 2.2, and M. Pecoraro wrote section 6.

Funding. This research is funded by "SiciliAn MicronanOTecH Research and Innovation CEnter "SAMOTHRACE"" (MUR, PNRR-M4C2, ECS_00000022), spoke 3 - Università degli Studi di Palermo "S2-COMMs - Micro and Nanotechnologies for Smart & Sustainable Communities".

References

1. Madigan, D.J., Kim, L.E.: Does teacher burnout affect students? A systematic review of its association with academic achievement and student-reported outcomes. Int. J. Educ. Res. **105**, 101714 (2021). https://doi.org/10.1016/j.ijer.2020.101714
2. Turner, K., Garvis, S.: Teacher educator wellbeing, stress and burnout: a scoping review. Educ. Sci. **13**(4), Article 4 (2023). https://doi.org/10.3390/educsci13040351
3. Burić, I., Slišković, A., Sorić, I.: Teachers' emotions and self-efficacy: a test of reciprocal relations. Front. Psychol. **11**, 1650 (2020). https://doi.org/10.3389/fpsyg.2020.01650
4. Moraes, E.B., et al.: Integration of industry 4.0 technologies with education 4.0: advantages for improvements in learning. Interact. Technol. Smart Educ. **20**(2), 271–287 (2023). https://doi.org/10.1108/ITSE-11-2021-0201
5. Denzin, N.: The Research Act, 2nd edn. Aldine, Chicago (1978)
6. Patton, M.Q.: Enhancing the quality and credibility of qualitative analysis. Health Serv. Res. **34**(5 Pt 2), 1189–1208 (1999)
7. Noble, H., Heale, R.: Triangulation in research, with examples. Evid. Based Nurs. **22**(3), 67–68 (2019). https://doi.org/10.1136/ebnurs-2019-103145
8. Guion, L., Diehl, D., McDonald, D.: Triangulation: establishing the validity of qualitative studies. EDIS. **3** (2011). https://doi.org/10.32473/edis-fy394-2011
9. Sciberras, M., Dingli, A.: Research analysis—triangulation approach. In: Sciberras, M., Dingli, A. (eds.) Investigating AI Readiness in the Maltese Public Administration, pp. 31–32. Springer, Cham (2023). https://doi.org/10.1007/978-3-031-19900-4_9
10. Tronstad, C., et al.: Current trends and opportunities in the methodology of electrodermal activity measurement. Physiol. Meas. **43**(2), 02TR01 (2022). https://doi.org/10.1088/1361-6579/ac5007
11. Li, S., et al.: Electrodermal activity measure: a methodological review. Ann. Tour. Res. **96**, 103460 (2022). https://doi.org/10.1016/j.annals.2022.103460
12. Meijer, A.L., et al.: Electrodermal activity: a continuous monitor of Well-being. J. Smart Cities Soc. **2**(4), 193–207 (2023). https://doi.org/10.3233/SCS-230021
13. Betancourt, M.A., et al.: Skin conductance as an in situ marker for emotional arousal in children with neurodevelopmental communication impairments. ACM Trans. Access. Comput. **9**(3), 1–8 (2017). https://doi.org/10.1145/3035536
14. Disalvo, B., et al.: Reading the room—automated, momentary assessment of student engagement in the classroom. Proc. ACM Interact. Mobile Wearab. Ubiquit. Technol. **6**(3) (2022). https://doi.org/10.1145/3550328

15. Bower, J.M., Carroll, A.: Capturing real-time emotional states and triggers for teachers through the teacher wellbeing web-based application. Teach. Teach. Educ. **65**, 183–191 (2017). https://doi.org/10.1016/j.tate.2017.03.015
16. Braun, S.S., et al.: Effects of teachers' emotion regulation, burnout, and life satisfaction on student well-being. J. Appl. Dev. Psychol. **69**, 101151 (2020). https://doi.org/10.1016/j.appdev.2020.101151
17. Sáez-Delgado, F., et al.: Teacher self-regulation and its relationship with student self-regulation in secondary education. Sustain. For. **14**, 16863 (2022). https://doi.org/10.3390/su142416863
18. Frenzel, A.C., et al.: Teacher emotions in the classroom and their implications for students. Educ. Psychol. **56**(4), 250–264 (2021). https://doi.org/10.1080/00461520.2021.1985501
19. Hart, N.I.: Student teachers' anxieties: four measured factors and their relationships to pupil disruption in class. Educ. Res. **29**(1), 12–18 (1987). https://doi.org/10.1080/0013188870290102
20. Parsons, J.S.: Assessment of anxiety about teaching using the Teaching Anxiety Scale. In: The Annual Meeting of American Educational Research Association. ERIC, Louisiana (1973) https://eric.ed.gov/?id=ED079330
21. Fimian, M.J.: The development of an instrument to measure occupational stress in teachers: the Teacher Stress Inventory. J. Occup. Psychol. **57**(4), 277–293 (1984)
22. Gorospe, J.D.: Pre-service teachers' teaching anxiety, teaching self-efficacy, and problems encountered during the practice teaching course. J. Educ. Learn. **11**(4), 84–91 (2022)
23. Oppenheim, A.N.: Questionnaire Design, Interviewing and Attitude Measurement. Pinter Publishers, London (1992)
24. Holmes, A.: The design and use of questionnaires in educational research: a new (student) researcher guide. Innov. J. Educ., 1–5 (2023). https://doi.org/10.22159/ijoe.2023v11i3.47599
25. DeVellis, R.F.: Scale Development: Theory and Applications, 2nd edn. Sage, Thousand Oaks (2016)
26. Boateng, G.O., et al.: Best practices for developing and validating scales for health, social, and behavioral research. Front. Public Health. **6** (2018). https://doi.org/10.3389/fpubh.2018.00149
27. Rattray, J., Jones, M.C.: Essential elements of questionnaire design and development. J. Clin. Nurs. **16**(2), 234–243 (2007). https://doi.org/10.1111/j.1365-2702.2006.01573.x
28. Zijlmans, E.A.O., et al.: Item-score reliability in empirical-data sets. Educ. Psychol. Meas. **78**(6), 998–1020 (2018). https://doi.org/10.1177/0013164417728358
29. Worthington, R.L., Whittaker, T.A.: Scale development research: a content analysis and recommendations for best practices. Couns. Psychol. **34**(6), 806–838 (2006)
30. Hair, J.F., et al.: Multivariate data analysis. Prentice-Hall, Englewood Cliffs (1995)
31. Hair, J.F., et al.: Multivariate Data Analysis, 6th edn. Pearson Prentice Hall, New Jersey (2006)
32. Tabachnick, B.G., Fidell, L.S.: Using Multivariate Statistics, 4th edn. Allyn and Bacon, Boston (2001)
33. Taherdoost, H., et al.: Exploratory factor analysis; concepts and theory. In: Balicki, J. (ed.) Advances in Applied and Pure Mathematics, vol. 27, pp. 375–382. WSEAS (2014) https://hal.science/hal-02557344
34. Costello, A.B., Osborne, J.: Best practices in exploratory factor analysis: four recommendations. Pract. Assess. Res. Eval. **10**(1), Article 1 (2005). https://doi.org/10.7275/jyj1-4868
35. Field, A.: Discovering Statistics Using SPSS, 3rd edn. Sage, Thousand Oaks (2009)

36. Napanoy, J.B., et al.: Difficulties encountered by pre-service teachers. Univ. J. Educ. Res. **9**(2), 342–349 (2021). https://doi.org/10.13189/ujer.2021.090210
37. Conte, E., et al.: Exploring stress factors and coping strategies in Italian teachers after COVID-19: evidence from qualitative data. Educ. Sci. **14**, 152 (2024). https://doi.org/10.3390/educsci14020152

Stress in the University Population: A Literature Review of the Positive Role of Physical Activity to Improve the Wellbeing of Students

Mariasole Antonietta Guerriero[1,2](✉), Marilena di Padova[1], Fiorenzo Moscatelli[3], Sergio Bellantonio[4], Anna Dipace[3], and Angelo Basta[1]

[1] Department of Humanistic Studies, University of Foggia, Foggia, Italy
{mariasole.guerriero,marilena.dipadova,angelo.basta}@unifg.it
[2] Department of Human Sciences, IUL Telematic University, Florence, Italy
[3] Department of Education and Sport Sciences, Pegaso Telematic University, Naples, Italy
{fiorenzo.moscatelli,anna.dipace}@unipegaso.it
[4] Department of Clinical and Experimental Medicine, University of Foggia, Foggia, Italy
sergio.bellantonio@unifg.it

Abstract. Physical activity plays a vital role in maintaining both physical and mental health, yet many university students adopt sedentary lifestyles, which contribute to stress and anxiety that can impair academic performance. Exercise is known to reduce anxiety, depression, and stress, while also improving sleep quality and cognitive abilities. Despite these benefits, physical inactivity remains common during stressful times, such as exam periods. AI-driven tools, such as chatbots and wearable devices, offer personalized support to encourage regular exercise and enhance overall well-being. A review of the literature, focusing only on reviews published in recent years, highlights the positive impact of regular physical activity on students' mental and physical health. However, there is a need for more focus on the quality and consistency of exercise, particularly during high-stress periods. Accurate methods for measuring activity and stress, along with timely data collection, are essential for better understanding and addressing peak stress times. Physical activity interventions, supported by AI tools like chatbots and wearable devices, could significantly improve students' well-being and academic outcomes by offering tailored support and maintaining motivation. By considering individual factors such as gender, habits, and motivation, these interventions could provide effective strategies to combat sedentary behavior and promote exercise within this population, helping to build healthier, more resilient adults and reduce future pressures on healthcare systems.

Keywords: Physical activity · Stress · University student

M. A. Guerriero and M. di Padova—Have contributed equally to this work.

P. Ardimento et al. (Eds.): HELMeTO 2024, CCIS 2468, pp. 104–119, 2025.
https://doi.org/10.1007/978-3-031-93999-0_7

1 Introduction

Physical activity is widely acknowledged as an essential factor in enhancing both physical and mental health. The World Health Organization (WHO) suggests engaging in a minimum of 150 minutes of moderate exercise or 75 minutes of vigorous exercise per week [4]. This level of activity is linked to a lower risk of several chronic diseases and considerable improvements in psychological well-being. Sedentary lifestyle is now a global pandemic, and, despite the well-established benefits, sedentary lifestyles continue to be widespread, particularly among college students and young adults that represent a significant portion of the affected population.

Globally, 1 in 4 adults do not meet the recommendations on physical activity for health, and in the case of college students, the reasons include academic commitments, changing habits, required study and lecture hours, financial management and facility costs, or lack of adequate facilities [26]. In addition, students facing high-stress situations tend to be more sedentary, especially if in tandem with this there is an overuse of technological devices between study and leisure [6, 14, 26]. These sedentary behaviors are closely linked to elevated levels of stress and anxiety and time spent sitting, between studying and using technological devices, increases the metabolic health risk for students.

This group represents the future adult population, with university years laying the foundation for life habits that will solidify in adulthood [18], and addressing their needs is crucial given the strain it places on healthcare systems.

In addition to metabolic and cardiovascular risks, university students face stressful daily challenges such as examinations and the volume of academic material to be studied, the cognitive demands of learning, managing one's finances, being away from one's family and dealing with academic demands and pressure [6, 16, 18]. Many students experience both physical and psychological health challenges due to stress, which can negatively affect their academic performance [28].

The university period, especially during exam seasons, is marked by heightened stress and anxiety levels. Stress is described as the result of interactions between the person and external events that stress them, so-called stressors, which produce a physiological organic response [5]. When these exceed the person's ability to handle the stress load, it becomes a negative response that undermines their psychological well-being. Academic stress, therefore, refers to any pressure related to the educational environment, such as examinations, assignments, external expectations that may overwhelm the ability to handle such demands [5].

This condition is often worsened by inactivity and insufficient physical exercise [14]. Research indicates that during these high-stress cognitive periods, perceived stress can significantly impair cognitive functions and academic outcomes [21, 22]. Anxiety, depression and stress are negative emotional symptoms that emerge in response to difficult situations and, if not managed properly, can increase the risk of mental health problems. According to the two-continuum model, mental health and mental illness are distinct but interconnected concepts, which means that a person may experience high levels of these symptoms but not necessarily develop a mental illness [16].

University students who, therefore, are already a highly vulnerable and proven population have since 2020 experienced the devastating effects of the measures taken for the covid-19 pandemic. Many universities have adopted online teaching, cancelling practical activities, leading to significant changes in the study environment. As a result, students have lost not only the social sphere, but also the habit of movement or structured physical activity [16], becoming more sedentary and losing spaces and opportunities for movement.

Numerous studies reinforce the notion that physical activity can serve as a protective buffer against stress, helping to alleviate the adverse effects of stress on health.

Regular physical exercise is linked to reduced symptoms of anxiety and depression, as well as better sleep quality and overall well-being [10, 28]. Moreover, physical activity has been significantly associated with improved academic performance and reduced stress, particularly among students with initially low levels of physical activity [6, 10].

Physical activity is not to be understood only as exercise or sport, but as anything that in the context of life involves energy expenditure; if this is then planned and organised with a physical well-being objective in mind, it becomes exercise [5]. The aim is therefore to offer as many opportunities for students to be active as possible and educate and motivate them towards a healthy lifestyle.

One promising approach to encouraging physical activity is the use of digital tools and artificial intelligence (AI)-driven training, which has shown positive outcomes [3, 6, 15]. For instance, virtual chatbots, wearable devices that provide auditory feedback, as well as message and reminder services, not only help monitor daily physical activity and overall lifestyle but often tailor feedback and activities based on the data collected from individuals [6]. The use of AI, through personalized interventions and verbal or visual feedback on exercise performance, along with chatbots and messages to sustain daily motivation, can serve as an effective tool for improving students' well-being by addressing their specific needs.

This study aims to review the existing literature on the relationship between physical activity and stress among university students as a review of reviews, considering the body of evidence highlighting the benefits of exercise and its impact on stress. Furthermore, the integration of artificial intelligence has been considered as a means of promoting physical activity and the existing findings in the literature in this regard. The research is intended as an initial exploratory effort to provide a comprehensive overview of this topic and lay the groundwork for future experimental studies.

2 Materials and Methods

A literature review was conducted on Scopus and PubMed including studies between 2021 and 2024. The choice of 2021 as the extreme lower end of the range was dictated by the need to analyse the existing literature from the pandemic period to the current year. The search query included the terms: university student AND physical activity AND stress. The inclusion and exclusion criteria were review only, English language only, open access only. Each term had to be present in the title and/or abstract. Scopus provided 2,855 results and PubMed 11 results. In the initial phase of selection, which involved analyzing titles and abstracts and removing duplicates, 126 results were retained. Of these 126 results, 90 were reviews that initially met the eligibility criteria. In the screening phase, the results were significantly reduced, and 18 reviews were included in this study at the final stage of selection and inclusion. The reasons for exclusion were target population not meeting the criteria, publication year not meeting the criteria, the paper not being a review, not all the considered variables were in the studies, lack of thematic relevance or research scope, the focus of the contribution being more on diseases or mental disorders than on stress. The selection also included contributions related to the COVID-19 pandemic period.

Zotero software was used for the collection of results and their selection. In addition, the software was used for the removal of duplicates and for the proper management of the bibliography in APA format.

3 Results

The results of the selection process were 18. The two identifiable areas of research that relate to the macro-theme of this study, namely the correlation between physical activity and stress in the university population, are physical activity interventions of different types and the use of technology and virtual reality or artificial intelligence devices.

What emerges is the lack of specific physical activity protocols and a multitude of different types of intervention, with different applications of intensity and volume. What clearly emerges is the centrality of the concept of physical activity and exercise over modalities, showing a positivity of movement, regardless of administration, quantity and method, on stress. The studies analyzed and their objectives are summarized in Table 1.

Assessment of Quality of Reviews
An analysis was conducted to assess the methodological quality of the reviews and possible risks of bias. The AMSTAR 2 review-specific tool was used for this purpose, using 10 items of the checklist that are specific for reviews. Table 2 shows the details of the 10 item in respect of each of the studies analysed.

4 Discussion and Conclusions

The university population represents a particular population subject to decisive changes in their lives. From the transition from adolescence to adulthood, through the educational transition from institutionalized schooling to the academic world, the changes, especially related to university life, are radical and often stressful.

Life habits change, responsibilities for managing oneself and one's finances increase, students often have to live away from their family and social relationships. Academic commitments, between exams, assignments, lecturers' expectations added to university life made up of changes in relationships and one's own independence in life can be particularly stressful external events.

Increased sitting hours to study and attend lectures, decreased time devoted to physical activity for reasons of time, money and motivation, and the prolonged use and abuse of technological devices lead to a significant increase in sedentariness among university students. Sedentariness and low levels of physical activity place this already highly vulnerable and fragile population at risk of developing problems such as diabetes, obesity and cardiovascular disease. In the university population, perceived stress levels can reach very high values, often leading to a high risk of compromising the health and

Table 1. Summary of the results analyzed in this study

Author	Study design	Studies included	Objectives	Main Outcomes
Abd-Alrazaq et al.	Systematic review and meta-analysis	19	Assess the performance of wearable AI in detecting and predicting stress among students.	Wearable AI demonstrated an average accuracy of 85.6% in detecting stress among students, yet its performance remains suboptimal, requiring further studies to enhance reliability and clinical applicability.
Al Mamun et al.	Systematic review	7	Examines the prevalence of depression, anxiety and stress among Bangladeshi students during the COVID-19 pandemic.	Bangladeshi students faced high rates of depression (46.92% - 82.94%), anxiety (26.6% - 96.82%) and stress (28.5% - 70.1%) during COVID-19. Key risk factors include young age, female gender, low income, poor sleep and fear of infection.
Chong et al.	Systematic review	51	Identify well-being issues in undergraduate clinical students.	Undergraduate clinical students0 face significant wellbeing challenges, including stress, burnout, anxiety, depression and mistreatment, especially emotional wellbeing.

(*continued*)

Table 1. (*continued*)

Author	Study design	Studies included	Objectives	Main Outcomes
Salazar de Pablo et al.	Systematic review and meta-analysis	276	Review the consistency and magnitude of the efficacy of universal and selective interventions to promote good mental health in young people	Universal and selective interventions improve mental health outcomes, notably mental health literacy, emotional wellbeing and quality of life and exercise benefits physical health.
Gardani et al.	Systematic review and meta-analysis	34	Relationship between sleep quality and/or insomnia with stress in students.	Moderate association between stress and poor sleep quality and insomnia. Stress and sleep disturbances were bidirectionally linked, influenced by academic and lifestyle factors.
Guerriero et al.	Literature review	72	Investigate the use of current AI in physical activity focusing on the findings related to the use of physical activity interventions via AI, the lifestyles and wellbeing of university students and correlations between academic performance and physical activity.	AI powered interventions can enhance PA levels, reduce sedentary behavior and improve mental wellbeing by providing personalized recommendations and real time feedback. Increased PA levels are associated with lower stress, anxiety and depression.

(*continued*)

Table 1. (*continued*)

Author	Study design	Studies included	Objectives	Main Outcomes
Harris et al.	Scoping review	23	Identify the effectiveness of strategies implemented by pharmacy schools to improve the wellbeing of pharmacy students.	Interventions such as yoga, mindfulness courses and digital wellbeing apps can reduce stress and burnout while improving resilience and engagement.
Hickey et al.	Systematic review	17	Identify and critically appraise the most recent smart and wearable devices used to identify depression, anxiety and stress and the physiological process linked to that.	HRV, EDA, and respiratory rate are the most accurate wearable metrics for detecting stress and anxiety, while EEG based devices are best for depression but lack commercial availability.
Huang et al.	Systematic review and meta-analysis	59	Effectiveness of physical activity interventions on undergraduate students' mental health	Physical activity interventions significantly reduce anxiety, depression and stress in undergraduate students.
Manchia et al.	Critical review	145	Investigate how the pandemic has affected mental health in general and how human stress resilience has shaped its impact on the sorter and longer term	University students faced increased stress, anxiety and depression due to academic disruptions, social isolation and financial concerns during COVID-19 with online learning and uncertainty as key stressors.

(*continued*)

Table 1. (*continued*)

Author	Study design	Studies included	Objectives	Main Outcomes
Oliveira Carvalho et al.	Systematic review and meta-analysis	13	Determine the prevalence of anxiety, depression and stress during the coronavirus lockdown.	High prevalence rates of anxiety (55%), depression (63%) and stress (62%) among European university students during COVID-19 lockdowns.
Pascoe et al.	Scoping review	14	Provide an overview of controlled trial testing the effect of short-term exercise across mental health domains in tertiary students.	Short-term exercise reduces anxiety symptoms and anxiety sensitivity and helps buffer against mood declines following stress exposure. Importance of increasing student awareness and access to exercise facilities.
Puente—Hidalgo et al.	Literature review	32 articles and 6 web pages	Describe the benefits of promoting healthy habits at university, highlighting the role of prevention and the creation of healthy routines.	University students face poor diets, low physical activity levels, and high stress highlighting the need for preventive health strategies.
Qi et al.	Systematic review	22	Evaluate the current literature surrounding the effects of Taichi on physical and phychological health health among college students and establish future guidelines.	Taichi improves balance, flexibility and mental health but its less effective than Pilates, yoga and mindfulness.

(*continued*)

Table 1. *(continued)*

Author	Study design	Studies included	Objectives	Main Outcomes
Špiljak et al.	Narrative review	15	Present current data on psychological stress among university students and the possibilities for its assessment using salivary biomarkers.	Impact of academic stress on students and the use of salivary biomarkers (cortisol alpha amylase) for stress assessment.
Strehli et al.	Systematic review and meta-analysis	26	Investigate the effects of MBPA on stress related physiological health markers in primary, secondary and higher education students.	Mind-body physical activity interventions (yoga, Taichi, qigong) significantly reduce the health rate, cortisol and blood pressure especially in older students.
Wang and Bíró	Literature review	112	Review the various determinants of sleep quality among college students.	Physical activity and social relationships improve sleep quality. Mental health issues and academic pressure also impact sleep.
Wunsch et al.	Systematic review and meta-analysis	4	Summarize evidence for the tridimensional construct of physical activity, stress and academic performance and their relationship.	Physical activity reduces stress but its effect is unclear on academic performance.

mental well-being of students. Academic demands and life away from home represent lifestyle changes that involve radical instability and external stressors. If these external stressors become unmanageable for students, stress is no longer a physiological response but an element of risk for compromising students' psychological well-being. Increased perceived stress increases the use of technological devices and time spent sitting, decreasing opportunities for activity and exercise. Decreased physical activity

Table 2. AMSTAR 2 analysis of studies.

Study	1	2	3	4	5	6	7	8	9	10
Abd-Alrazaq	Yes	Yes	Yes	Yes	Partial	Yes	Yes	Yes	Partial	Yes
Al Mamun	No	Yes	Yes	Partial	No	Partial	Yes	No	No	No
Chong	Partial	Yes	Yes	Yes	No	Partial	Yes	Yes	No	Yes
Salazar de Pablo	Yes	Yes	Yes	Yes	Yes	Yes	Yes	Yes	Yes	Yes
Gardani	Yes	Yes	Yes	Yes	Partial	Yes	Yes	Yes	Yes	Yes
Guerriero	No	Yes	Partial	No	No	No	Partial	No	No	Partial
Harris	Partial	Yes	Yes	Yes	No	Partial	Yes	Yes	No	Yes
Hickey	Yes	Yes	Yes	Partial	Partial	Yes	Yes	Yes	Partial	Yes
Huang	Yes	Yes	Yes	Yes	Yes	Yes	Yes	Yes	Yes	Yes
Manchia	Partial	Yes	Yes	Partial	No	Partial	Yes	Partial	No	Yes
Oliveira-Carvalho	Yes	Yes	Yes	Yes	Partial	Yes	Yes	Yes	Partial	No
Pascoe	Partial	Yes	Yes	Yes	No	Partial	Yes	Yes	No	Yes
Puente-Hidalgo	Yes	Yes	Yes	Partial	Partial	Yes	Yes	Yes	Partial	Yes
Qi	Yes	Yes	Yes	Yes	Yes	Yes	Yes	Yes	Yes	Yes
Spiljak	Partial	Yes	Yes	Partial	No	Partial	Yes	Partial	No	Yes
Strehli	Yes	Yes	Yes	Yes	Partial	Yes	Yes	Yes	Partial	Yes
Wang	Yes	Yes	Yes	Partial	Partial	Yes	Yes	Yes	Partial	Yes

Legend of items: 1 = Protocol registration (e.g., PROSPERO); 2 = Clearly defined inclusion criteria; 3 = Comprehensive literature search; 4 = Duplicate study selection; 5 = Provision of excluded studies list; 6 = Adequate risk of bias assessment in primary studies; 7 = Appropriate statistical methods for meta-analysis; 8 = Consideration of risk of bias in results; 9 = Assessment of selective outcome reporting; 10 = Transparency in conflict-of-interest disclosure

and increased sedentariness in turn increase levels of perceived stress or decrease its tolerance.

In addition, the increasing focus on wellness and care among university students has started to explore other innovative and effective solutions including not only physical activity in all its forms but also advanced technologies such as artificial intelligence, wearable devices and mobile applications.

In the following study, we therefore questioned the state of the literature about the effects of the use of physical activity interventions in university students with particular reference to and correlation with stress. Furthermore, as part of this study, we analysed the presence of research frameworks in the literature regarding the role of technologies and new frontiers of artificial intelligence in promoting physical activity and healthy lifestyles in students and the motivation to maintain them.

Physical Activity and Physical Exercise: Effects on Stress

Reviews were analyzed about the effects of different physical activity and exercise protocols on the stress of university students. The studies reviewed used a variety of methodologies to analyze the effectiveness of PA, from structured exercises to brief interventions, providing a holistic perspective on the benefits of this practice. The studies used heterogeneous methodologies, including randomized controlled trials (RCTs), meta-analyses and qualitative approaches. The most frequently used outcome measures included perceived stress scales (PSS), sleep quality tests (PSQI) and specific mental health indicators but also analysis of biomarkers such as cortisol and heart rate. This methodological variety allowed for a broader understanding of the effects of PA, although it limited comparability between studies.

Huang et al. [9] demonstrated that regular AP interventions significantly reduce stress levels with a quantified mean effect (SMD = −0.61).

Pascoe et al. [17] observed that short, intensive exercises can act as a 'buffer' against mood decline in acute stressful situations, such as examination periods. Same results emerged from Wunsch et al. [28] that identified a negative correlation between regular AF and perceived stress, supporting the thesis that AF may act as a 'buffer' against the negative effects of stress.

Some studies analyzed the combined effects on anxiety and stress, such as Oliveira-Carvalho et al. [16] that showed a combined prevalence of anxiety (55%) and stress (62%) during lockdown, significantly mitigated by regular AP programs.

Qi et al. [20] highlighted those disciplines such as Tai Chi, although less effective than aerobic practices or yoga, offer specific benefits in reducing stress and improving alertness.

Studies on the hypothalamic-pituitary-adrenal (HPA) axis, as the one of Špiljak et al. [24] have shown that regular AF reduces chronic activation of the axis, lowering glucocorticoid levels and promoting better resilience to stress.

Furthermore, AF contributes to better regulation of the autonomic nervous system by lowering resting heart rate and blood pressure.

Furthermore, analyzing studies it emerged that many indirect benefits are derived from the use of physical activity. PA indirectly contributes to improved sleep, an essential aspect of mental well-being, as highlighted by Gardani et al. [13], who observed that stress is closely linked to sleep quality as it has observed by Wang and Bíró [27] too.

It also promotes the adoption of other healthy habits, as evidenced by Puente-Hidalgo et al. [19], encouraging a holistic approach to stress management.

The studies by Huang et al. [9] and Pascoe et al. [17] adopted strict inclusion criteria to examine structured and brief interventions, respectively, while Qi et al. [20] explored specific practices such as Tai Chi. Interventions that integrate mind-body activities (MBPA), such as yoga and Tai Chi, have shown significant effects in reducing cortisol levels and improving physiological markers of stress as emerged from the studies of Strehli et al. [25] and Qi et al. [20]. The effects are more pronounced during periods of high stress, such as during examinations, demonstrating the potential of AF to mitigate acute stress. However, some methodological limitations emerge, such as high heterogeneity and the risk of bias in observational studies and such as the difference of intensity, frequency and type of physical activity intervention; this demonstrates that, even if all the interventions have positive, some are more significant than others. Tai Chi is effective but not as much as dynamic or intensive activities.

Regarding the duration of the interventions Pascoe et al. [17] suggest that short-term interventions can also be effective, but in literature there isn't an evaluation of long-term effects.

Physical Activity Intervention and Digital Tools

The literature also revealed a body of research focusing on the use and integration of technologies to monitor and promote physical activity as well as to increase motivation and adherence to active living habits.

The studies analyzed considered systematic and literature reviews. In the systematic review by Abd-alrazaq et al. [1], 19 studies concerning the use of wearable devices based on artificial intelligence to detect the stress levels in students, were analyzed; the wearable devices considered in the studies were smartwatches, smart bracelets and sensors; biomarkers such as heart rate (HR), heart rate variability (HRV), and electrodermal activity (EDA) were analyzed. The study found that AI-enhanced wearable technologies offer a non-invasive solution to monitor stress in real time. The average measured accuracy was 85.6% in detecting stress based on biomarkers such as variable heart rate (HRV) and electrodermal activity (EDA). However, the effectiveness varied depending on the type of device and the methodology used to validate the data.

Hickey et al. [8] conducted a systematic review on the use of wearable technologies to monitor stress. Their work showed that HRV-based devices combined with EEG offer 87.5% accuracy in stress detection.

Electrodermal activity was particularly useful for identifying changes in acute stress, but its reliability varies depending on the context of use.

Hickey et al. also identified a common problem: users prefer non-invasive devices that are comfortable to wear, which limits the adoption of more advanced technologies. However, combining different physiological measurements offers a promising avenue for improving reliability and accuracy.

Referring more specifically to physical activity, the literature review by Guerriero et al. [6] found that the integration of physical activity and advanced technologies creates a synergistic approach for stress management in university students. The study emphasises that mobile applications and wearable devices, including chatbots and virtual conversation agents, can not only promote an active lifestyle, but also provide motivational and personalized support. in fact, the ability to provide feedback and the ability to tailor AF programs to students' needs is a key factor in increasing participation and improving long-term outcomes. This is especially important not only to promote physical activity but also to maintain adherence to the practice that is often abandoned due to lack of motivation.

Abd-alrazaq et al. and Hickey et al. demonstrated that wearable devices are not only tools to monitor stress, but also powerful means to intervene in real time. Their ability to detect physiological changes associated with acute stress situations provides students with immediate feedback, giving them a signal of the need to make lifestyle changes by, for example, increasing movement and motor engagement time.

Sociodemographic Factors and Correlation with Stress and Sedentariness

Ultimately, a possible correlation between stress, sedentariness and socio-demographic factors in the university population was investigated in the reviews. It emerged that few studies directly analysed the correlation between sedentariness and sociodemographic factors among the studies analysed. There is a lack of insight into the differences between groups by age, gender and socioeconomic status in sedentariness. The literature analysed shows that sedentariness is influenced by academic habits and the transition to university and that students far from family or with socio-economic disadvantages tend to be more sedentary due to the lack of an affective network and financial pressure [6, 12, 13, 16]. Students under greater academic pressure and with roles of academic responsibility report higher levels of sedentariness [17]. Furthermore, a gender difference emerges, with female students being more vulnerable to stress than men, a phenomenon that could be explained by greater social and academic pressure or differences in coping mechanisms [7, 11, 19, 27]. Age also seems to be a relevant factor, with younger students exhibiting higher levels of stress, probably due to less experience in dealing with academic pressures and the transition to university [24]. In parallel, physical activity and sedentariness also appear to be associated with socio-demographic factors. Women are more sedentary than men, indicating possible gender barriers in physical activity adherence or differences in leisure time preferences [9, 20]. Furthermore, students with high levels of stress and greater academic responsibilities tend to reduce the time spent on physical activity, establishing a vicious cycle between stress and sedentariness [17, 28]. Finally, it appears that older students benefit more from interventions based on mind-body activities such as yoga and tai chi, suggesting that perceptions of and adherence to physical activity may vary with age [25].

However, there are still limitations to such evidence as the number of studies that have directly analysed such correlations is small.

The university population represents a group that is particularly vulnerable to life changes and increasing academic demands, often with significant consequences on psychological and physical wellbeing. This study seems to show that physical activity and advanced technologies could be powerful tools for dealing with stress and improving students' quality of life. However, methodological limitations and practical challenges also emerge that require further investigation and targeted interventions. Positive results report direct effects on improved stress and thus also on academic performance; indirect effects include improved sleep quality and cardiovascular parameters. Technologies fit in as an excellent and advantageous means of monitoring stress and physical activity, customizing interventions and providing feedback that can guide and motivate students.

Limitations and Future Directions

This contribution shows some methodological limitations that do not allow the results to be generalised or reliable. The heterogeneity of the studies analysed, reviews, systematic reviews and meta-analyses, makes comparability complex since there is a vast difference and variability in the protocols in terms of intensity, duration and mode of delivery as well as the activity proposed. Many studies are methodologically flawed, in their inclusion criteria or due to the absence of certain data, making it impossible to draw conclusions or observe significant correlations. Furthermore, most protocols are short-term, limiting the possibility of a prediction on the long-term effects of physical activity and the use of digital devices on stress and increased well-being. Accessibility to wearable devices and AI-based tools also remains an obstacle due to financial and technological constraints. Future research should focus on standardised, long-term protocols that are replicable and comparable. Longitudinal studies are needed to evaluate long-term benefits, overcoming the limitations of short-term protocols. Within universities, more emphasis should be placed on structuring targeted physical activity programmes with the integration of digital health tools and providing programmes and strategies for stress management and mental well-being. Universities should ensure accessible and user-friendly solutions, improve awareness and education on body and mental health care and active lifestyles. Furthermore, implementation in the use of digital monitoring and motivation tools can be a turning point and facilitator to achieve these goals. Addressing these issues will not only improve student well-being and thus academic performance but can also help prevent the burden and future burdens on public health systems by taking care of university students who represent the adults of tomorrow.

References

1. Abd-Alrazaq, A., Alajlani, M., Ahmad, R., AlSaad, R., Aziz, S., Ahmed, A., Alsahli, M., Damseh, R., Sheikh, J.: The performance of wearable AI in detecting stress among students: systematic review and meta-analysis. J. Med. Internet Res. **26**(1) (2024)
2. Al Mamun, F., Hosen, I., Misti, J.M., Kaggwa, M.M., Mamun, M.A.: Mental disorders of Bangladeshi students during the covid-19 pandemic: a systematic review. Psychol. Res. Behav. Manag. **14**, 645–654 (2021)
3. An, R., Shen, J., Wang, J., Yang, Y.: A scoping review of methodologies for applying artificial intelligence to physical activity interventions. J. Sport Health Sci. **13**(3), 428–441 (2024)
4. Bull, F.C., Al-Ansari, S.S., Biddle, S., Borodulin, K., Buman, M.P., Cardon, G., Carty, C., Chaput, J.-P., Chastin, S., Chou, R., Dempsey, P.C., DiPietro, L., Ekelund, U., Firth, J., Friedenreich, C.M., Garcia, L., Gichu, M., Jago, R., Katzmarzyk, P.T., et al.: World Health Organization 2020 guidelines on physical activity and sedentary be haviour. Brit. J. Sports. (2020)
5. Chacón-Cuberos, R., Zurita-Ortega, F., Olmedo-Moreno, E.M., Castro-Sánchez, M.: Relationship between academic stress, physical activity and diet in university students of education. Behav. Sci. (Basel, Switzerland). **9**(6), 59 (2019)
6. Guerriero, M.A., Moscatelli, F., di Padova, M.: Integrating the use of artificial intelligence (AI) to promote physical activity: the effects on lifestyle and academic performance of university students. A literature review. Ital. J. Heal. Educ. Sport Inclu. Didact. **8**(2) (2024)
7. Harris, S.C., Gandavarapu, S., Zeeman, J.M.: Scoping review of programmatic well-being interventions and outcomes to support pharmacy students. Am. J. Pharm. Educ. **88**(2), 100638 (2024)
8. Hickey, B.A., Chalmers, T., Newton, P., Lin, C.-T., Sibbritt, D., McLachlan, C.S., Clifton-Bligh, R., Morley, J., Lal, S.: Smart devices and wearable technologies to detect and monitor mental health conditions and stress: a systematic review. Sensors. **21**(10) (2021)
9. Huang, K., Beckman, E.M., Ng, N., Dingle, G.A., Han, R., James, K., Winkler, E., Stylianou, M., Gomersall, S.R.: Effectiveness of physical activity interventions on undergraduate students' mental health: systematic review and meta-analysis. Health Promot. Int. **39**(3) (2024)
10. Kayani, S., Kiyani, T., Wang, J., Sánchez, M.L., Kayani, S.A., Qurban, H.: Physical activity and academic performance: the mediating effect of self-esteem and depression. Sustainability. (2018)
11. Chong, T.L., Lau, W.M., Tha, K.K.: Contemporary issues in the well-being of undergraduate clinical students: a systematic review. Educ. Med. J. **13**(1), 3–16 (2021)

12. Manchia, M., Gathier, A.W., Yapici-Eser, H., Schmidt, M.V., de Quervain, D., van Amelsvoort, T., Bisson, J.I., Cryan, J.F., Howes, O.D., Pinto, L., van der Wee, N.J., Domschke, K., Branchi, I., Vinkers, C.H.: The impact of the prolonged COVID-19 pandemic on stress resilience and mental health: a critical review across waves. Eur. Neuropsychopharmacol. **55**, 22–83 (2022)
13. Gardani, M., Bradford, D.R.R., Russell, K., Allan, S., Beattie, L., Ellis, J.G., Akram, U.: A systematic review and meta-analysis of poor sleep, insomnia symptoms and stress in undergraduate students. Sleep Med. Rev. **61**, 101565 (2022)
14. Moscatelli, F., De Maria, A., Marinaccio, L.A., Monda, V., Messina, A., Monacis, D., Toto, G., Limone, P., Monda, M., Messina, G., Monda, A., Polito, R.: Assessment of lifestyle, eating habits and the effect of nutritional education among undergraduate students in Southern Italy. Nutrients. **15**(13) (2023)
15. Oh, Y.J., Zhang, J., Fang, M.L., et al.: A systematic review of artificial intelligence chatbots for promoting physical activity, healthy diet, and weight loss. Int. J. Behav. Nutr. Phys. Act. **18**, 160 (2021)
16. Oliveira Carvalho, P., Hülsdünker, T., Carson, F.: The impact of the COVID-19 lockdown on European students' negative emotional symptoms: a systematic review and meta-analysis. Behav. Sci. (Basel, Switzerland). **12**(1), 3 (2021)
17. Pascoe, M.C., Bailey, A.P., Craike, M., Carter, T., Patten, R.K., Stepto, N.K., Parker, A.G.: Single session and short-term exercise for mental health promotion in tertiary students: a scoping review. Sports Med. Open. **7**(1), 72 (2021)
18. Peng, S., Yuan, F., Othman, A.T., Zhou, X., Shen, G., Liang, J.: The effectiveness of E-health interventions promoting physical activity and reducing sedentary behavior in college students: a systematic review and meta-analysis of randomized controlled trials. Int. J. Environ. Res. Public Health. **20**(1) (2022)
19. Puente-Hidalgo, S., Prada-García, C., Benítez-Andrades, J.A., Fernández-Martínez, E.: Promotion of healthy habits in university students: literature review. Healthcare (Switzerland). **12**(10) (2024)
20. Qi, F., Soh, K.G., Mohd Nasirudddin, N.J., Mai, Y.: Effects of taichi on physical and psychological health of college students: a systematic review. Front. Physiol. **13** (2022)
21. Rettinger, V. The Relationship Between Physical Activity, Stress, and Academic Performance (2011)
22. Ruthig, J.C., Marrone, S., Hladkyj, S., Robinson-Epp, N.: Changes in college student health: implications for academic performance. J. Coll. Stud. Dev. **52**(3), 307–332 (2011)
23. Salazar de Pablo, G., De Micheli, A., Solmi, M., Oliver, D., Catalan, A., Verdino, V., Di Maggio, L., Bonoldi, I., Radua, J., Baccaredda Boy, O., Provenzani, U., Ruzzi, F., Calorio, F., Nosari, G., Di Marco, B., Famularo, I., Montealegre, I., Signorini, L., Molteni, S., Filosi, E., et al.: Universal and selective interventions to prevent poor mental health outcomes in young people. Syst. Rev. Meta-Analy. Harvard Rev. Psych. **29**(3), 196–215 (2021)
24. Špiljak, B., Vilibić, M., Glavina, A., Crnković, M., Šešerko, A., Lugović-Mihić, L.: A review of psychological stress among students and its assessment using salivary biomarkers. Behav. Sci. (Basel, Switzerland). **12**(10), 400 (2022)
25. Strehli, I., Burns, R.D., Bai, Y., Ziegenfuss, D.H., Block, M.E., Brusseau, T.A.: Mind–body physical activity interventions and stress-related physiological markers in educational settings: a systematic review and meta-analysis. Int. J. Environ. Res. Public Health. **18**(1), 1–24 (2021)
26. Tan, S.L., Jetzke, M., Vergeld, V., Müller, C.: Independent and combined associations of physical activity, sedentary time, and activity intensities with perceived stress among university students: internet-based cross-sectional study. JMIR Public Health Surveill. **6**(4), e20119 (2020)
27. Wang, F., Bíró, É.: Determinants of sleep quality in college students: a literature review. Explore (NY). **17**(2), 170–177 (2021)

28. Wunsch, K., Fiedler, J., Bachert, P., Woll, A.: The tridirectional relationship among physical activity, stress, and academic performance in university students: a systematic review and meta-analysis. Int. J. Environ. Res. Public Health. **18**(2) (2021)

Pre-service Teachers and Public Speaking Anxiety. Insights and Possible Interventions through AI and IoT

Lorella Giannandrea[1], Lorenza Maria Capolla[1], Francesca Gratani[1](✉), Giacomo Nalli[2], and Stylianos Kapetanakis[2]

[1] Department of Education, Cultural Heritage and Tourism, University of Macerata, Macerata, Italy
{lorella.giannandrea,l.capolla,f.gratani}@unimc.it

[2] Computer Science, Science and Technology, Middlesex University, London, UK
{g.nalli,s.x.kapetanakis}@mdx.ac.uk

Abstract. Public speaking is an essential skill for pre-service teachers as it plays a critical role in both professional success and the teaching-learning process. Despite its importance, many individuals, particularly students, experience public speaking anxiety, which can affect their performance. This paper explores the intersection of self-assessed public speaking anxiety levels and biometric data collected through stress tracker devices and AI-based emotion detection tools, aiming to investigate students' awareness of their anxiety during public speaking. Data were collected from 257 students enrolled in a first-year course at the University of Macerata (2023/24). Students were asked to complete a survey and give an oral presentation in groups. A subset of 25 student responses were compared with biometric data, including heart rate measurements and data obtained by an AI emotion recognition system. Cross-referencing self-reported anxiety levels with heart rate data showed varying degrees of convergence, suggesting that students often misperceived their emotional state. In some cases, their self-assessments did not align with the biometric indicators of stress, suggesting a lack of self-awareness regarding their anxiety levels. These findings highlight the potential for AI and IoT technologies to provide useful data that can help teachers identify and support students who are not aware of their emotional state and who also have anxiety management issues. By incorporating these tools, university teachers can develop optimized and tailored interventions aimed at improving students' public speaking skills and emotional regulation. Further research should explore the effectiveness of these tools across different courses and sample sizes.

Keywords: Public Speaking Anxiety · Pre-service Teachers · AI · IoT

1 Introduction

Public Speaking (PS) is the ability to speak effectively in front of an audience [1]. PS falls under the broader category of oracy [2], which represents the essential set of oral communication skills, including coherent speaking, active listening, and effective

P. Ardimento et al. (Eds.): HELMeTO 2024, CCIS 2468, pp. 120–133, 2025.
https://doi.org/10.1007/978-3-031-93999-0_8

participation in discussions. It is a crucial skill for both professionals and university students. Parvis [3] emphasizes that PS is a key skill for professional success, as it allows individuals to present their ideas and persuade the audience, thereby facilitating the achievement of shared goals. Specifically, the ability to speak in public is an essential skill for pre-service teachers who must master it to avoid compromising effectiveness and to enhance the teaching-learning process [4]. To improve one's PS skills, it is important for the speaker to use intonation, rhythm, cadence, and volume effectively [5]. Non-verbal language also plays a central role during PS, as eye contact and facial and body movements can establish a connection with the audience and help maintain attention levels [6]. This is also crucial for teachers who, through verbal and non-verbal language, can capture and sustain their students' attention [7].

One of the main challenges people face when approaching PS is related to anxiety. Anxiety can be seen as a feeling of unease and heightened arousal that a person encounters in response to a situation perceived as broadly threatening. Karakaya [8] characterizes it as an excessive and irrational condition marked by intense fear and excitement, accompanied by a reaction to the perceived threat. More specifically, Public Speaking Anxiety (PSA) is defined as "a specific social anxiety occurring during or in anticipation of an oral presentation" [9], representing a common experience for most people, with affected individuals exceeding half of the population [10, 11]. Indeed, pre-service teachers often mention anxiety as a concern related to teaching experiences [12].

Obtaining data regarding PSA is not simple and remains an area of ongoing exploration in the literature. One of the main limitations is that it is not an easy phenomenon to capture, as some of the most commonly used tools, such as interviews and self-assessments, do not always present objective data and are often closely tied to the individual's perception of themselves and the anxiety-inducing situation. Some opportunities to explore PSA in a more systematic and less subjective way involve measuring cardiovascular responses, such as blood pressure and Heart Rate (HR), as well as electrodermal activity measurements [13]. Specifically, a high HR variability during PS is correlated with lower stress levels and a greater ability to regulate emotions [14]. Although not yet widely present in the literature, research combining HR data collected during PS with self-assessment data on PSA could provide an interesting framework to initiate a discussion on PSA prevalence, its effects on affected individuals, and possible improvement interventions. Given that PS is currently one of the key skills for nearly all professions, it is crucial that frequency monitoring, reflection, and possible interventions are considered starting from school, with particular attention in the university setting.

This contribution presents data from an experiment conducted with 25 students enrolled in the first year 'Foundations of Teaching and Learning' course of the Master's Degree in Primary Education at the University of Macerata in the 2023/24 academic year. Nevertheless, it is useful to report the data from the PSA survey administered to all 257 students in the course.

The data (Fig. 1) indeed show that the majority of students closely associate the idea of PS with feelings of anxiety. As shown in the pie charts, over 25% of the students find "giving a speech terrifying," while more than 50% of the total report feeling tense before speaking in public.

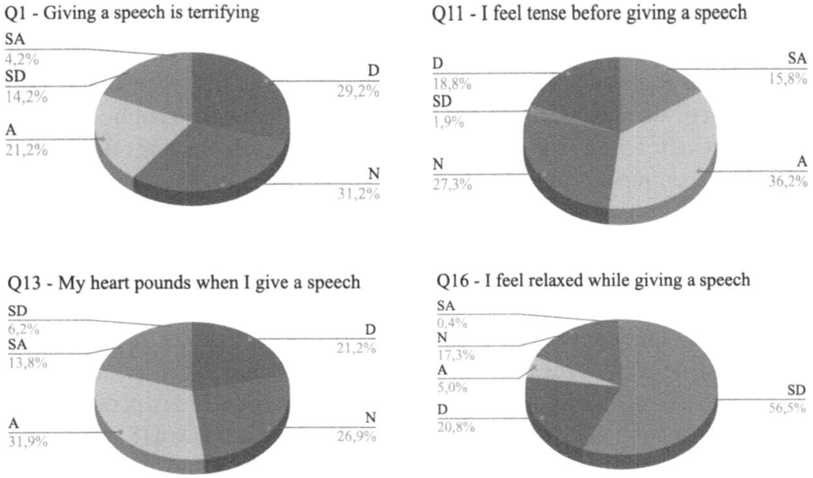

Fig. 1. Some PSAS answers returned by the 257 students before the PS activity.

It should be noted, however, that most of the stress and anxiety we encounter daily are psychological in nature and particularly related to our interpretation of events [15]. For this reason, self-assessing one's level of anxiety, especially if done prior to an event, cannot serve as an effective measure in itself. Therefore, it is important to pair qualitative investigation methods with quantitative methods that can both provide feedback to the initial self-assessment and offer objective data on the stress felt by those facing PS.

The proliferation of AI solutions has led several researchers to develop new models in education aimed at helping students improve their knowledge and skills and helping teachers develop strategies to improve the quality of teaching. AI solutions have not only been adopted to assist students during the learning journey but can also be used to detect the emotions felt during learning activities [16], facilitating the instructor's identification of potential issues in students that can negatively impact performance. Another aspect that can affect student performance is the level of stress perceived, which can influence memory and prevent from achieving learning outcomes [17]. Several researchers have identified the increase in HR during classroom activities as a sign of stress [18]. The collection of this data through stress tracker devices could be particularly beneficial to teachers during the feedback process [19].

From these premises, two research questions were formulated:

1. Are pre-service teachers aware of their anxiety levels related to PS?
2. Is there a convergence between the self-assessment data of students regarding their PSA levels and the quantitative data obtained through an IoT device designed to capture biometric stress data and an AI software?

This paper investigates students' awareness of their emotional states during PS, offering insights to help university educators develop impactful training programs and empower students to navigate their emotions effectively.

2 Methods

2.1 The Context

The research was carried out in the academic year 2023/24 and involved students enrolled in the first-year course 'Foundations of Teaching and Learning' of the Master's Degree in Primary Education at the University of Macerata.

The course aimed to provide the theoretical foundations of didactics focusing on the learning and teaching processes, and on the knowledge, skills and competences that underpin teaching professionalism. It consisted of 48 hours of lectures (with free attendance) and 20 hours of workshops (with compulsory attendance), which took place during the second semester.

The compulsory workshop was designed to deepen the core concepts covered in the lectures through a series of group activities led by a tutor. During the final session, we asked the students to give an oral presentation in groups (two or three students per group). Specifically, each group had to rethink and revise the metaphor, related to the teacher's role, which they had formulated in the first workshop session and then present its evolution orally to their colleagues.

In this study we discuss the results of the presentations held by 9 groups of students for a total of 25 students who were selected on a voluntary basis.

2.2 Data Collection and Design Process

Before the presentation, each student was asked to complete the PSA survey [20]. The survey was designed to measure students' perceptions of anxiety, focusing in particular on how they perceive their own anxiety when they have to give a public oral presentation. It consisted of 17 items with a 5-point Likert response scale: 1- Strongly Disagree (SD); 2- Disagree (D); 3- Neutral (N); 4- Agree (A); 5- Strongly Agree (SA).

Group presentations were not graded but were monitored by video recording for up to 3–5 minutes (approximately 1 minute for each speaker) and each student was required to wear a portable stress tracker device in order to extract the HR data needed to predict students' stress perceptions.

A Polar OH1+, an optical HR monitor connected to the online application 'Polar Flow' was used as it allows the accurate collection of 60 HR records per minute and the download of a csv file [21].

The data was then collected and pre-processed into a unique excel file (dataset) containing the following fields (features): ID device, heartbeat min, heartbeat max, heartbeat avg. and heartbeat standard deviation.

A clustering technique was then applied to this dataset in order to find similarities between the student and grouping together in homogeneous clusters to identify different stress levels during the PS. The clustering technique is indeed a machine learning technique that allow to detect data similarity in the dataset with several fields. It then creates groups (clusters) containing the elements (students in this paper) based on their similarity. Students who have similar characteristics will belong to the same group (cluster) [22].

Specifically, three different clustering algorithms (K-means [23], Mean Shift [24] and Gaussian Mixture Model [25]) have been implemented and compared the performance using the Silhouette Analysis [26] in order to identify the most performant which it will be selected for the data processing. Using this approach, each cluster could be represented by a silhouette index based on the comparison of its cohesion and separation. The Silhouette Coefficient is measured using the formula:

$$S(i) = \frac{b(i) - a(i)}{\max\{a, b(i)\}}$$

In this formula, *a(i)* is the average distance of the point *i* from all other points in the same cluster, while *b(i)* is the smallest average distance of the point *i* from all points in the nearest cluster. Specifically, the range of the silhouette score *s(i)* is $[-1, 1]$. If the silhouette index is close to 1, the sample is well-clustered and assigned to an appropriate cluster. Based on this method *s(i)* needs to be closer to 1 to have good clusters [27].

The subsequent study analyzed the video presentation of the students' public speaking in order to extract the main emotions felt during the activity. An AI detection model previously developed and tested during a group presentation activity, was adopted for this scope [28] (Fig. 2).

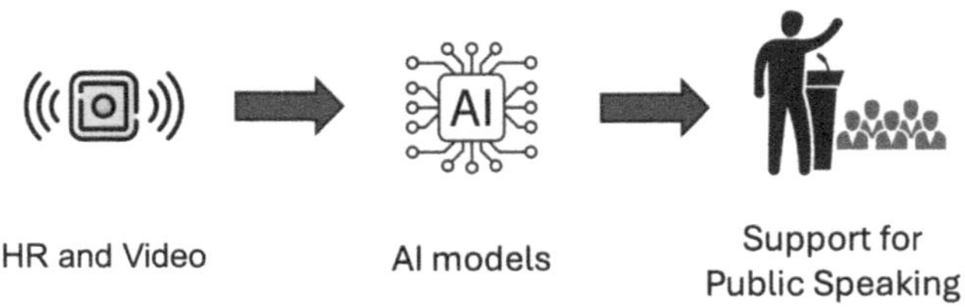

Fig. 2. The flow diagram of the data collection and data analysis involved in the research.

This model consists of a combination of several AI techniques, such as deep learning and convolutional neural networks, which thanks to the use of the OpenCV framework they can extract emotions from facial expressions. Emotion analysis was achieved based on symmetric filter characterization. Face key attributes were digitized and combined to facial landmarks. Based on the initial classification, emotions were mapped as landmark combinations that can classify emotions further down the line. A custom implementation of Python Keras and Tensorflow [29] was used to detect emotions. Detected landmarks were filtered to maximize model efficiency and classification since some emotions were hard to classify e.g. Anger vs Fear. A similar technique, focusing on recognizing facial landmarks over frames was used to monitor changes in predominant facial landmark positions. This technique was scored across several frames achieving change monitoring. This technique was able to calculate face movement via optical flow. These movements were determined across several videos and resulted in being able to understand head nodding, turn, and angle of view across multi participants across video feeds. All the above filters were combined to be able to annotate videos by ingesting face recognition labels, emotion labels and head movement indicators. A final post-processing component was developed to be able to persist changes across frames and generate an annotated version of the original video.

The model thus returns 7 main emotions and a list of body movements made by the students during the presentation.

Thanks to these data, it was possible to check potential changes in the emotional states of the students by monitoring the increase in HR during the video or the HR variability, which can be influenced by the stress condition [30]. Collected data were then processed and cross-referenced for analysis.

3 Results

3.1 Cluster Analysis

The identification of the different students' emotional changes during the PS required the application of clustering techniques aimed to discover the different levels of stress.

Once the necessary data had been collected during the student presentations using the stress tracker device and merged into a unique dataset, various clustering algorithms were applied.

Specifically, the following algorithms have been implemented to this scope: Gaussian Mixture Model, Mean Shift and K-means.

The clustering models have been developed in Python using the Scikit learn libraries using a pre-processed and normalized dataset. The results returned by the different models were then compared using silhouette analysis to identify the most powerful models able to produce the most consistent clusters.

Table 1 shows the silhouette index obtained for each model and shows that, according to the silhouette analysis, K-means is the best performing model because its silhouette analysis is higher compared to Mean Shift and Gaussian Mixture Model and closer to 1 (which is the maximum value for the silhouette index). K-means returned 3 different clusters, each one identifying different levels of stress perceived by the students during the PS. The levels were identified taking into account previous research in this area, which identified a normal resting HR for adults as a range between 60 and 90 beats per minute (bpm) [31].

Table 1. Comparison of the performance of the different models.

Clustering algorithms	Silhouette score
K-means	0.5519
Mean Shift	0.5291
Gaussian Mixture Model	0.531

Specifically, Cluster 1 consists of 8 students, all female, with an average HR of 101.2 and a standard deviation of 3.5, Cluster 2 consists of 11 students, 9 female and 2 male, with an average HR of 124.5 and a standard deviation of 5.1 and Cluster 3 consists of 6 students, 5 female and 1 male, with values of average HR of 149.8 and standard deviation 6.6. Each cluster shows a small value of standard deviation, which indicates that the data points are close to the mean [32], so the value of the average HR was crucial in identifying stress levels. Cluster 1 was identified as "Stress", Cluster 2 as "High stress" and Cluster 3 as "Very high stress" (Table 2).

Table 2. Features values associated with distinct clusters.

Clusters	N.	Sex	MIN	MAX	AVG	ST. DEV
1. Stress	8	0% M 100% F	94.5	107.5	**101.2**	3.5
2. High Stress	11	18% M 82% F	115.3	131.3	**124.5**	5.1
3. Very High Stress	6	17% M 83% F	137.8	158.33	**149.8**	6.6

3.2 AI Emotion Recognition

The AI emotion recognition using the video analysis, instead, was performed on a 32GB Intel X2 Intel E5-2660v4 3.2GHz, and the workflow was deemed successful over more than 1400 processing turns, achieving an overall efficiency of 92.37%, and at the same time with an achieved rate of 96.74% face recognition (Fig. 3).

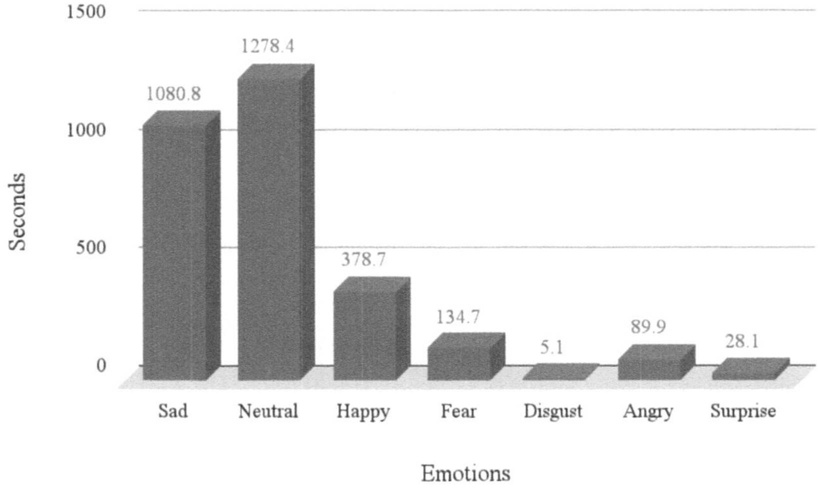

Fig. 3. Emotions felt by the 257 students during the PS activity.

The results obtained by the AI emotion recognition confirmed the stress perceived by students returning mainly negative and neutral emotions. In particular, Cluster 1 returned as main emotions 50% sad, 37% neutral and 13% happy, Cluster 2 82% neutral and 18% sad and Cluster 3 33% sad, 33% neutral and 33% happy (see Table 3).

Table 3. Features values and main emotions associated with distinct clusters.

Clusters	N.	Sex	AVG	ST. DEV	Main emotions
1. Stress	8	0% M 100% F	101.2	3.5	50% Sad 37% Neutral 13% Happy
2. High Stress	11	18% 82% F	124.5	5.1	82% Neutral 18% Sad
3. Very High Stress	6	17% M 83% F	149.8	6.6	33.3% Sad 33.3% Neutral 33.3% Happy

The distribution of emotions in the three clusters does not seem particularly significant, but we believe that these results are influenced by some contextual conditions that may have negatively affected the analysis. During the presentation, the students tended to frequently consult the notes on their devices (mobile phone and tablet). As a result, their gaze was directed downwards towards the screen, which may have made the task of detecting movement and facial expressions more difficult. We also believe that the AI emotion recognition system may have identified 'happy' expressions that were not actually happy, such as a pulled smile, an expression of nervousness.

3.3 PSA Survey

We examined the students' perceptions within the sample and whether their perceptions matched their actual state, as measured by the stress tracker device, to determine the level of self-awareness of their emotional state. We report the questions that matched the stress levels measured by the stress tracker device and the questions that didn't match.

As can be seen from Table 4, the response to Q4, which indicates the difficulty of refocusing on the speech after making a mistake, shows a 37% neutral and 12% agreement rate in Cluster 1 - stress, which rises to 40% in Cluster 3 - very high stress.

Similarly, Q6, where students are asked whether they concentrate on what they are saying during the speech, shows a percentage of around 50% agreement (A+SA) in Cluster 1, a percentage that reaches 90% in Cluster 2 and even 100% in Cluster 3. This can be explained by the assumption that those who are more confident in PS can control the reactions of the audience and the context, whereas those who are very anxious tend to focus exclusively on the content of the speech and what they have to say. Also, with regard to Q11 and 12, the percentages of A and SA with regard to feeling tense and trembling are significantly higher in Clusters 2 and 3 than in Cluster 1.

Table 4. PSAS results (Q4, Q6, Q11 and Q12) based on the clusters.

Clusters	Q4 - If I make a mistake in my speech, I am unable to re-focus	Q6 - I am focused on what I am saying during my speech	Q11 - I feel tense before giving a speech	Q12 - I fidget before speaking
1. Stress	25% SD 25% D **37% N** **12% A** **0% SA**	0% SD 0% D **50% N** **37% A** **12% SA**	12% SD 25% D **25% N** **37% A** **0% SA**	12% SD 25% D **37% N** **25% A** **0% SA**
2. High Stress	30% SD 10% D **50% N** **10% A** **0% SA**	0% SD 10% D **0% N** **90% A** **0% SA**	0% SD 50% D **10% N** **30% A** **10% SA**	0% SD 60% D **10% N** **20% A** **10% SA**
3. Very High Stress	20% SD 20% D **20% N** **40% A** **0% SA**	0% SD 0% D **0% N** **60% A** **40% SA**	20% SD 0% D **0% N** **40% A** **40% SA**	20% SD 0% D **20% N** **40% A** **20% SA**

On the other hand, it should be noted that other questions (see Table 5) produce data that do not match the clustering, showing that personal perceptions are not always fully in line with what is perceived by sensors attached to the body. The most obvious example of this divergence is Q13, where only 40% of the Very High Stress group admit that their heart beats fast when they have to give a speech, while the percentages of agreement with Q1 and Q10, which should have been predictably high, are actually 0% for the SA score and around 20% for the A score.

4 Discussion of Results

The results highlight an important divergence between self-reported anxiety levels and biometric data collected through sensors and AI emotion recognition. This misalignment across different stress clusters suggests that students' subjective perceptions of stress and anxiety may not always correspond to measurable biometric data.

Participants in the Very High Stress cluster showed the highest stress markers, while their self-reported anxiety did not always align with these measures. For instance, in Q13 ('*My heart pounds when I give a speech*'), only 40% of the Very High Stress cluster admitted to experiencing a rapid heartbeat before speaking, despite the expectation that biometric data would be higher in this group. Similarly, in Q1 ('*Public speaking is terrifying*') and Q10 ('*I feel bad before public speaking*') the Very High Stress cluster demonstrated very low percentages of agreement, with 20% A and 0% SA. In

Table 5. PSAS results (Q1, Q7, Q10 and Q13) based on the clusters.

Clusters	Q1 - Giving a speech is terrifying	Q7 - I am confident when I give a speech	Q10 - I feel sick before speaking in front of a group	Q13 - My heart pounds when I give a speech
1. Stress	25% SD 37% D **25% N** **12% A** **0% SA**	12% SD 25% D **50% N** **12% A** **0% SA**	50% SD 37% D **12% N** **0% A** **0% SA**	12% SD 25% D **50% N** **12% A** **0% SA**
2. High Stress	40% SD 20% D **10% N** **30% A** **0% SA**	0% SD 30% D **50% N** **20% A** **0% SA**	20% SD 30% D **40% N** **0% A** **10% SA**	10% SD 30% D **20% N** **20% A** **20% SA**
3. Very High Stress	40% SD 0% D **40% N** **20% A** **0% SA**	20% SD 0% D **40% N** **40% A** **0% SA**	20% SD 0% D **60% N** **20% A** **0% SA**	0% SD 40% D **20% N** **0% A** **40% SA**

other words, although the body shows an increased HR, students may not consciously recognize these signals or interpret them as indicators of anxiety.

A further interesting aspect emerges from the answers to Q4 ('*If I make a mistake in my speech, I cannot regain my concentration*') and Q6 ('*I am focused on what I am saying during my speech*'). In the clusters with higher stress levels, the proportion of students claiming to maintain concentration during the speech increases, with the Very High Stress cluster reporting 60% A and 40% SA and the High Stress cluster reporting 90% A and 0% SA. At the same time, the proportion of those claiming to lose concentration in case of a mistake decreases, with the Very High Stress cluster reporting 40% A and 0% SA and the High Stress cluster reporting 10% A and 0% SA. This could indicate an adaptation or rationalization effect: students with higher stress, while showing an increased HR, may have developed coping strategies that help them to concentrate and manage anxiety during a performance.

The answers to Q11 ('*I feel tense before speaking in public*') and Q12 ('*I get tense before speaking*') showed a distribution that more closely follows the expected trend: in the Very High Stress cluster, 40% of students agree or strongly agree with both statements, in line with the increase in HR. However, even in these cases, there is still a significant number of students who do not report high levels of anxiety, despite their placement in the Very High Stress cluster. These discrepancies may be related to individual factors such as a tendency to minimize anxiety, a lack of connection to one's bodily responses, or the adoption of emotional management strategies.

Correct discrimination of the signals coming from the body and the ability to manage emotions and stress are significant skills for pre-service teachers, especially since stress and anxiety are omnipresent in educational settings. Anxiety management should be pursued and built through specific pathways designed and implemented to train not only pre-service teachers but students in general since it is a necessary skill for active participation in social life [33, 34].

5 Conclusions

The analysis of the 257 answers gathered from the PSA survey shows that most students report high levels of PSA, as already stated in the introduction.

To answer the research questions, we cross-referenced survey responses from the 25 selected students with HR data collected from the stress tracker device and AI-based emotion detection tools. In some cases, we found a convergence between PSA data and the HR values, while in other cases substantial differences emerged. Indeed, students' considerations on their PSA, excerpted from the survey, were not consistently reflected in the emotional state detected by stress tracker devices and AI tools. While it is important to consider some limitations inherent in our video-recording process, which affected the AI-based analysis, the discrepancy between students' self-assessments and the data gathered from the tools mentioned above could stem from a lack of self-awareness among students, as well as their generally negative perception of PS. These findings revealed that students were not always able to correctly self-assess their PSA, underestimating or overestimating it.

This data analysis shows that AI-based emotion recognition software and stress tracker tools can help teachers identify and support students who are not aware of their emotional state and who also have anxiety management issues as well as students with high levels of PSA. Research has identified a significant impact of teachers' emotional state on the learning and teaching process. Teachers' emotions are linked to various classroom aspects such as students' well-being [35], motivation [36], and academic outcomes [37]. Various researchers have shown that more positive emotions lead to more innovative ideas and strategies [38], while a prevalence of negative emotions decreases motivation [39]. Furthermore, teachers' emotions have an impact on their personal and professional lives [40], and negative emotions, depending on anxiety and stress, could affect teachers' effectiveness [41].

Finally, collecting students' perceptions of their emotional states and PSA and biometric data can assist university teachers in designing targeted training on PS and in enhancing personalized and inclusive learning paths.

Future developments should include some key issues. First, it would be beneficial to test these tools in a broader range of courses and with a larger sample size to gain more comprehensive insights. Additionally, refining the video detection conditions to enhance the quality of video recordings could lead to more accurate responses from the AI emotion recognition system. Finally, the results of this research could be leveraged to identify students who experience higher levels of PSA, allowing for the implementation of targeted training programs, and potentially incorporating VR experiments or mindfulness-based paths to improve both emotional regulation and resilience.

Author Contributions. This paper stems from the collaborative work of the authors. Specifically, Lorella Giannandrea is the author of Sect. 3.3; Lorenza Maria Capolla is the author of Sect. 2.1;

Francesca Gratani is the author of Sects. 4 and 5; Giacomo Nalli is the author of Sects. 2.2 (early stress detection) and 3.1 and Stylianos Kapetanakis is the author of Sects. 2.2 (AI emotion detection) and 3.2. Abstract and references have been written collaboratively.

Disclosure of Interests. The authors have no competing interests to declare that are relevant to the content of this article.

References

1. Aqeel, Z.A., Chung, K.C.: Strategies to improve public speaking skills. Plast. Reconstr. Surg. **153**(2), 273–276 (2024)
2. Mercer, N., Warwick, P., Ahmed, A.: An oracy assessment toolkit: linking research and development in the assessment of students' spoken language skills at age 11–12. Learn. Instr. **48**, 51–60 (2017)
3. Parvis, L.F.: The importance of communication and public-speaking skills. J. Environ. Health. **63**(9), 44–44 (2001)
4. Kenoh, A.R.I.: A qualitative study on speaking anxiety among pre-service teachers. J. Learn. Dev. Stud. **1**(1), 34–39 (2021)
5. Gola, E., Mottola, P.: Public speaking: Il ritorno della comunicazione vocale nell'era della comunicazione digitale. Mimesis, Milano (2019)
6. Bolzan, N.: Public speaking e presentazioni efficaci-Organizzare speech di successo grazie a parole, emozioni e comunicazione non verbale. Dario Flaccovio Editore, Milano (2021)
7. Iftakhar, S.: Teaching speaking through public speaking course. Stamford J. English. **7**, 183–203 (2012)
8. Karakaya, F., Avgın, S.S., Gömlek, E., Balık, M.: Examination of pre-service teachers' anxiety levels about teaching profession. Int. Online J. Educ. Teach. **4**(2), 162–172 (2017)
9. Bodie, G.D.: A racing heart, rattling knees, and ruminative thoughts: defining, explaining, and treating public speaking anxiety. Commun. Educ. **59**(1), 70–105 (2010)
10. Burnley, M.C.E., Cross, P.A., Spanos, N.P.: The effects of stress inoculation training and skills training on the treatment of speech anxiety. Imagin. Cogn. Pers. **12**(4), 355–366 (1993)
11. Ferreira, A.C., Mesquita, A., Côrtes, A.C., Caldas, L.: Fear of public speaking: perception of college students and correlates. J. Voice. **31**(1), 7–11 (2017)
12. Pentucci, M., Rossi, P.G., Capolla, L.: Designing regulation in action to manage the unforeseen in teaching-learning contexts. In: EDULEARN23 Proceedings, IATED, pp. 1151–1158 (2023)
13. Weinberger, D.A., Schwartz, G.E., Davidson, R.J.: Low-anxious, high-anxious, and repressive coping styles: psychometric patterns and behavioral and physiological responses to stress. J. Abnorm. Psychol. **88**(4), 369–380 (1979)
14. Appelhans, B.M., Luecken, L.J.: Heart rate variability as an index of regulated emotional responding. Rev. Gen. Psychol. **10**(3), 229–240 (2006)
15. Lupien, S.J., Maheu, F., Tu, M., Fiocco, A., Schramek, T.E.: The effects of stress and stress hormones on human cognition: implications for the field of brain and cognition. Brain Cogn. **65**(3), 209–237 (2007)
16. Ye, F.: Emotion recognition of online education learners by convolutional neural networks. Comput. Intell. Neurosci. **2022**(1), 4316812 (2022)
17. Mizoguchi, K., Yuzurihara, M., Ishige, A., Sasaki, H., Chui, D.H., Tabira, T.: Chronic stress induces impairment of spatial working memory because of prefrontal dopaminergic dysfunction. J. Neurosci. **20**(4), 1568–1574 (2000)

18. Elwess, N.L., Vogt, F.D.: Heart rate and stress in a college setting. Bioscene J College Biol. Teach. **31**(4), 20–23 (2005)
19. Nalli, G., Dafoulas, G., Tsiakara, A., Langari, B., Mistry, K., Aria, F.T.: Hybrid Educational Environments–Using IoT to detect emotion changes during student interactions. Interact. Design Archit. IxD&A J. **58**, 39–52 (2023)
20. Bartholomay, E.M., Houlihan, D.D.: Public speaking anxiety scale: preliminary psychometric data and scale validation. Personal. Individ. Differ. **94**, 211–215 (2016)
21. Mandal, S., Ghosh, B., Naskar, R.: A Photoplethysmography (PPG) sensor based stress level monitoring system for undergraduate students of technical education. In: 2023 IEEE 20th India Council International Conference (INDICON), pp. 197–202. IEEE (2023)
22. Nalli, G., Culmone, R., Perali, A., Amendola, D.: Online tutoring system for programming courses to improve exam pass rate. J. e-Learn. Knowl. Soc. **19**(1), 27–35 (2023)
23. Liu, R.: Data analysis of educational evaluation using K-means clustering method. Comput. Intell. Neurosci. **2022**(1), 3762431–3762410 (2022)
24. Chau, V.T.N., Loc, P.H., Tran, V.T.N.: A robust mean shift-based approach to effectively clustering incomplete educational data. In: 2015 International Conference on Advanced Computing and Applications (ACOMP), pp. 12–19. IEEE (2015)
25. Alshabandar, R., Hussain, A., Keight, R., Laws, A., Baker, T.: The application of Gaussian mixture models for the identification of at-risk learners in massive open online courses. In: 2018 IEEE Congress on Evolutionary Computation (CEC), IEEE, pp. 1–8 (2018)
26. Shutaywi, M., Kachouie, N.N.: Silhouette analysis for performance evaluation in machine learning with applications to clustering. Entropy. **23**(6), 759 (2021)
27. Rousseeuw, P.J.: Silhouettes: a graphical aid to the interpretation and validation of cluster analysis. J. Comput. Appl. Math. **20**, 53–65 (1987)
28. Fekry, A., Dafoulas, G., Ismail, M.: Automatic detection for students behaviors in a group presentation. In: 2019 14th International Conference on Computer Engineering and Systems (ICCES), pp. 11–15. IEEE (2019)
29. Abadi, M., Agarwal, A., Barham, P., et al.: Tensorflow: Large-scale machine learning on heterogeneous distributed systems. arXiv preprint arXiv:1603.04467 (2016)
30. Schubert, C., Lambertz, M., Nelesen, R.A., et al.: Effects of stress on heart rate complexity - a comparison between short-term and chronic stress. Biol. Psychol. **80**(3), 325–332 (2009)
31. Mason, J.W., Ramseth, D.J., Chanter, D.O., et al.: Electrocardiographic reference ranges derived from 79,743 ambulatory subjects. J. Electrocardiol. **40**(3), 228–234 (2007)
32. Andrade, C.: Understanding the difference between standard deviation and standard error of the mean, and knowing when to use which. Indian J. Psychol. Med. **42**(4), 409–410 (2020)
33. Uitto, M., Jokikokko, K., Estola, E.: Virtual special issue on teachers and emotions in Teaching and Teacher Education (TATE) in 1985–2014. Teach. Teach. Educ. **50**, 124–135 (2015)
34. Chen, J.: Teacher emotions in their professional lives: implications for teacher development. Asia Pac. J. Teach. Educ. **48**(5), 491–507 (2020)
35. van Uden, J.M., Ritzen, H., Pieters, J.M.: Engaging students: the role of teacher beliefs and interpersonal teacher behavior in fostering student engagement in vocational education. Teach. Teach. Educ. **37**, 21–32 (2014)
36. Becker, E.S., Goetz, T., Morger, V., Ranellucci, J.: The importance of teachers' emotions and instructional behaviour for their students' emotions—an experience sampling analysis. Teach. Teach. Educ. **43**, 15–26 (2014)
37. Fried, L., Mansfield, C., Dobozy, E.: Teacher emotion research: introducing a conceptual model to guide future research. Issue. Educ. Res. **25**(4), 415–441 (2015)
38. Chen, J.: Exploring the impact of teacher emotions on their approaches to teaching: a structural equation modeling approach. Br. J. Educ. Psychol. **89**, 57–74 (2019)
39. Sutton, R.E., Wheatley, K.F.: Teachers' emotions and teaching: a review of the literature and directions for future research. Educ. Psychol. Rev. **15**, 327–358 (2003)

40. Schutz, P.A., Zembylas, M.: Advances in Teacher Emotion Research: The Impact on Teachers' Lives. Springer, Dordrecht (2009)
41. Day, C.: New Understandings of Teacher's Work: Emotions and Educational Change. Springer, New York (2011)

Enhancing Social Presence Through Art: A Study on the Intersection of Emotions and Class Engagement

Barpi Fabrizio[1], Cereda Ambrogia[2(✉)], De Blasio Antonella[2], and Vinci Fiorella[2]

[1] Politecnico di Torino, Turin, Italy
[2] Università eCampus, Novedrate, Italy
ambrogia.cereda@uniecampus.it

Abstract. This study examines the role of emotions in educational relationships and the impact of artistic texts in fostering student engagement. Using a socio-cognitive perspective, it explores how artistic practices create shared emotional worlds, enabling students to critically redefine their identities. A comparative analysis between the Politecnico di Torino and eCampus Telematic University, based on an online questionnaire, highlights the role of *social presence* — a participatory climate shaped by shared emotions. The findings emphasize the transformative potential of artistic texts in creating a shared emotional framework, stimulating deeper engagement, and fostering a sense of community in diverse educational settings.

Keywords: Learning · Emotion · Social Presence

1 Introduction

In recent years, the integration of artistic practices into numerous educational programs, including those related to higher distance education, has become increasingly common. As highlighted by proponents of the Frankfurt School and subsequently theorized by Dewey, the relationship between art and educational practices holds enormous emancipatory potential, making individuals aware of their historical condition and eliciting needs and projects for social change. In particular, it seems that artistic texts primarily serve the function of creating common emotional worlds, where individuals can critically observe their identity affiliations and redefine them in a more universal sense.

Building upon these premises and adopting a socio-cognitive research perspective, this article presents the results of a comparative study between the Politecnico di Torino and the eCampus Telematic University. The study aimed to understand how emotions shape educational relationships and how they can be elicited through the didactic use of artistic texts. The research moves beyond the dichotomy between cognition and affectivity, delving into the social construction of emotions with the objective of understanding their role in two different university contexts and the unique functions of introducing and sharing artistic texts in teaching practices.

P. Ardimento et al. (Eds.): HELMeTO 2024, CCIS 2468, pp. 134–146, 2025.
https://doi.org/10.1007/978-3-031-93999-0_9

The hypothesis explored in this study is the formation, in both academic contexts, of a *social presence* – a participatory educational climate based on the construction and sharing of a common emotional world, whose generative processes are stimulated by the use of artistic texts.

The study was conducted using a quantitative methodology (an online questionnaire) administered to a sample of students who attended university courses at the Politecnico di Torino and the eCampus Telematic University during the same period. The research seeks to investigate which teaching techniques most effectively promote active student engagement and how their involvement varies with the use of artistic texts. Specifically, the students were presented with excerpts from literary texts and visual texts (works of art and architectural works).

2 Theoretical Framework and Research Objectives

2.1 Cognitive and Affective Studies

Cognitive models of learning, such as the cognitive theory of multimedia learning proposed by Mayer [1, 2], emphasize that when a learner is presented with instructional information, it triggers cognitive processing, leading to a learning outcome. However, other studies suggest the need to broaden these models to include the impact of emotional processing on learning, as cognitive processing alone does not fully capture the learner's internal activities during learning [3–6].

Several studies have examined the emotional impact of specific teaching practices and their influence on students' educational experiences starting with the pivotal role of the educational experience and delving into traditional studies of a socio-cognitive and pragmatic-cognitive approach.

According to these studies, emotions are generated by teaching techniques, vary with them, and have specific consequences on learning. Therefore, emotions, far from being confined to the affective sphere of individuals, influence their way of perceiving the educational experience and themselves within it, shaping whether they experience it passively or, conversely, as active protagonists. Emotion, in this context, refers to short-term, intense affects induced by specific objects or events [7].

According to an affective-cognitive model, the academic learning integrates both affective and cognitive processing: the learning episode triggers an emotional reaction in the learner, which influences cognitive processing during learning and contributes to the learning outcome. These studies highlight the relationship between emotions and learning, emphasizing the role of memory and the individual's motivation to engage in a specific learning process.

Every moment of our lives is accompanied by an emotion, which allows us to imprint pleasant or unpleasant experiences in our memory and communicate our moods to others and ourselves. Emotions are an essential element in every learning process; they represent a way through which we understand the world and an extraordinary driving force that motivates participation in it.

Although the world of emotions might seem distant from the educational domain, particularly in online learning, emotionally engaging students is crucial. This is because human memory is strongly influenced by emotional connections, which help us remember concepts or situations by associating them with an emotion. Consequently, even in e-learning, learning will be more effective if it can evoke positive emotions in users, fostering their engagement in lessons. Linking the information learned during an in-person lesson or an online course to positive emotions facilitates the recall of the concepts covered. As highlighted by numerous studies, an emotion-based approach directly impacts the level of learning and, consequently, participants' ability to apply or use the acquired information [8, 9]. For this reason, working on emotional engagement is essential to improve students' experience and increase their motivation. The emotional factor becomes crucial in the context of distance learning. Research on emotions in learning, both online and offline, focuses on affective and cognitive processes during learning and how these processes interact to produce learning outcomes.

Several studies demonstrate progress in identifying which emotions to study and how to measure them using self-assessment tests. However, systematic experimental research is needed to establish causal links between affective and cognitive processing during learning, as well as between cognitive processing and learning outcomes. These studies have theoretical implications for developing a more comprehensive theory of e-learning and practical implications for selecting emotional stimuli that enable deep cognitive processing, fostering solid learning outcomes [2, 5, 10].

Among the stimuli that activate forms of emotional intelligence, art holds a prominent place, as it fosters emotional connections, allowing us to remember concepts by linking them to an emotion. It captures the student's attention by creating the memory of a pleasant moment, thus facilitating learning while also stimulating expressiveness and creativity.

2.2 Social Presence

Supported by extensive research on the pedagogical benefits of both emotion elicitation and arts-integrated practices for student engagement in learning contexts, the study has aimed to explore the question: How does the integration of artistic texts influence student engagement with knowledge? The investigation is focused on how prompting students to confront themselves with artistic works, which include eminently visual but also literary texts, affects their engagement.

Fundamentally, the learning outcomes and skills the classroom aimed to generate/enhance are ascribable to the concept of "social presence", understood as that level of trust and respect that can motivate participants to take an active role in their own and their peers' construction of knowledge. This concept emerged in the late 1960s and 1970s, when telecommunication started to flourish and to raise questions about the deficiencies of remote communication experiences [11]. While the following decades witnessed the development of interactive media (i.e. interactive television, videoconferencing, and online learning environments), the concept of social presence became more complex, nuanced, and significant [12]. Indeed, the research on the topic has evolved from an initial phase in which social presence was investigated as a "property of a medium in mediated communication," to a second phase in which the focus has shifted to the "perceptions, behaviors, or attitudes of participants in a mediated interaction" [13].

Even if undoubtedly valuable, the definition of the concept remains debatable, difficult to operationalize, and uncertain to measure. Nonetheless, departing from the technological determinism of many interpretations, and insisting on the category of "realness", the review of the debate about social presence has lead to identify an interrelation with two other constructs, such as sociability and social space. The latter being defined as:

> the network of interpersonal relationships embedded in group structures of norms and values, rules and roles, and beliefs and ideals. A sound social space is manifested by a sense of community, group climate, mutual trust, social identity, and group cohesion. As such, social space can be seen as a group attribute. [...] Thus, apart from the spatial structure, social space also has a cultural structure because norms and values, rules and roles, and beliefs and ideals are cultural artifacts developed and maintained by the group members. [...] communicating persons may experience a shared social identity, group cohesiveness, connectedness with others, mutual trust, a sense of belonging, a sense of community, a social climate, and an open atmosphere. Hence, we speak of a *social* space ([14]: 159).

The former is referred to:

> the capacity of CMC tools and electronic platforms to allow for the expression of social presence, the experience of it, as well as for the emergence of a social space. As such, sociability is a medium attribute. [...] Sociability as a capacity of CMC tools and electronic platforms is considered an attribute of these and, therefore, can be designed ([14]: 160–161).

This triangulation is subsumed in the sphere of *social interaction* (see Fig. 1), which results in a combination of all the aspects that characterize the three components. In particular, social space is not to be understood only as the place—virtual or physical—in which the process of learning happens but it represents the foundation of productive social interaction for collaborative learning; as well, sociability does not refer to the mere capability of media to foster sociality and the exchange of verbal/nonverbal clues among students, but includes a certain degree of hedonicity, thus supporting pleasure and enjoyment experiences during working on group tasks.

In this scenario, when social interaction occurs, the role of emotions becomes crucial in deeply influencing the experience of learning. Indeed, as Whiteside and Garrett Dikkers have pointed out:

> Moreover, our key finding over the years is that social presence embodies an essential literacy for cultivating emotions and relationships that enhance the overall learning experience. [...] Social presence through the SPM represents an emotive quality that is essential to successful, meaningful online or blended learning experiences ([15]: 238–239).

Given the importance of emotions in learning experiences, the researchers have been directed to identify appropriate strategies for emotion elicitation in class. The choice has been to use artistic texts for class engagement, as Dewey's theory on aesthetic experience also suggests: "[W]orks of art are the most intimate and energetic means of

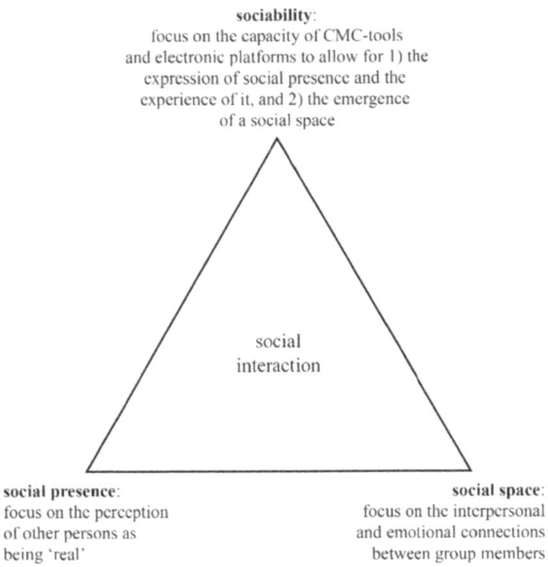

Fig. 1. The social presence, sociability, and social space triangle.

aiding individuals to share in the arts of living. Civilization is uncivil because human beings are divided into non-communicating sects, races, nations, classes and cliques" ([16]: 326).

Artistic texts have, indeed, a particular capability to connect the receivers to their emotional sphere. Appraisal theories of emotion have shown how even the study of aesthetics is enhanced by novel predictions about emotional responses to art, and the understanding of aesthetic emotions has expanded beyond just positive feelings like interest and enjoyment [17].

The relationship between emotions, artistic texts, and learning processes is a widely studied topic in academia, with significant implications for education. Emotions play a crucial role in learning, influencing students' motivation, memory, and engagement [18]. Artistic texts, such as literary, visual, or musical works, deeply stimulate emotions, creating a context that facilitates the understanding and retention of complex concepts [19]. Moreover, the use of artistic texts in teaching can foster empathy and critical thinking, enriching the educational experience [20]. Recent neuro-educational studies have demonstrated that the interaction between positive emotions and artistic content can activate neural networks related to reward and learning, enhancing knowledge acquisition [21]. These findings underscore the importance of integrating artistic tools into the educational process to promote students' emotional and cognitive engagement.

As to our case, the integration of arts for class engagement was based on preexisting evidence about the fruitfulness of the approach in teaching and learning: it enables students to develop and showcase their understanding through an art form as well as confronting themselves with the arts while learning other subjects. Students participate in a creative process that links an art form with another subject while achieving evolving objectives in both areas.

> Arts integration focuses on a process of learning by engaging arts-based strategies to integrate learning in the arts with other subjects. [...] What is unique to arts integration is the attention on the process of learning in the arts to engage discipline learning outside of the arts, such as literacy, math, science, or social studies. In this category the phrases "learning through the arts," and "learning with the arts" are common-place ([22]: 153).

3 Research Design and Methodology

The data collection of our research was thus aimed at investigating emotions as the root of social interaction and the base of the learning experience in class by integrating the role of artistic texts in different subject matters.

The research was conducted in the autumn 2023 at two Italian universities – a traditional university and an online university, specifically Politecnico di Torino and e-Campus Online University (Novedrate). Data were gathered from various courses, in which the researchers are also teachers.

The study was divided into two phases. In the first phase, artistic texts were presented as part of class instruction, and in the second phase, an online survey was conducted among the students.

The first phase of the research was conducted in two specific settings: the face-to-face environment of the traditional university lecture (45 min.) and the virtual classroom of the online university course (45 min.). Different from the traditional university in which students are physically present in the same classroom with the teacher and interact in immediate manners, the online setting implied a variable of mediation in the interaction that was taken into account, but that resulted in a typical element of a familiar setting for the students who have chosen distance learning as a privileged form of education and are accustomed to that typology of class experience.

The artistic texts selected to reach the above-mentioned purpose ranged from eminently visual (pictures of works of art, monuments, and interiors) to eminently textual forms (excerpts of novels, poems), including textual narration of visual forms.

The texts were administered during the lecture time and used as a stimulus for discussion, reflection, and confrontation among students and with the instructors in a conclusive session about the main topics of the class (15 min.). Teachers' interaction with students was aimed at creating a positive classroom emotional climate, that the teachers promoted by consistently showing a warm, respectful, and interested approach to their students' opinions and to their comfort and enjoyment in class, while also facilitating cooperation among them.

Teachers have encouraged students to construct meaning through reflection, cooperative learning, reciprocal teaching, and writing, applying an approach that can be largely related to the instructional method of "constructivist activity" as defined by Wiggins and McTighe [23]. The operation was conceived on three major components: 1. Identification of the desired results (What should students know, understand, and be able to do?); 2. Determination of acceptable levels of evidence that demonstrate the desired results (What constitutes acceptable evidence of student understanding?); 3. Design of activities that will encourage the achievement of the learning objectives (Considering teaching methods, the sequence of lessons, and resource materials).

The second phase of the research involved administering an online questionnaire, in order to be aware of both the emotional and academic needs of the students, and to select age-appropriate activities that can foster self-expression and align with students' interests and perspectives. The results could then serve as the foundation for future steps of inquiry.

The survey included an invitation message detailing the research's purpose. It assured students that their participation was voluntary, and that their information would be kept confidential and anonymous. Students had therefore the option to self-select for participation in the survey, resulting in 73 students accepting to take part in the study. This group included 37 online university students (from courses in Urban Sociology, Literary Criticism and Comparative Literature, and Sociology of Cultural Processes), comprising 86.5% female and 13.5% male, with ages ranging from 20 to 59. In addition, there were 36 traditional university students (from courses in Structural Mechanics and Construction Science), with a composition of 66.7% female and 33.3% male, and ages ranging from 20 to 45.

The questionnaire focused on exploring emotions aroused in class through the integration of artistic texts and their relation to social interaction as a complex construct.

The items were thus articulated into 3 sections, that investigated the presence of emotions as related to different aspects of the lecture/seminar as a type of social interaction, in which *social space*, *sociability* and *social presence* are intertwined. Each aspect was investigated through specific questions, with a conclusive explicit focus on the role of artistic texts.

Aspects considered through questionnaire can be schematized as follows (see Fig. 2).

The analysis reveals that *social space*, *sociability*, and *social presence* are interdependent and correlated factors that outline a generative framework for emotions in the context of educational experiences. These three components, which have distinct yet complementary functions, delineate a sort of generative schema of emotions during the educational experience.

The development of sociability constitutes the initial social environment, from which emotions emerge based on social interactions, their frequency, and their quality. *Social space* – the ability to feel more or less actively part of the class, to perceive the class as a shared, familiar, and safe place – circulates and develops emotions. This occurs because, within this space, it is possible to participate and receive feedback from peers and teachers.

Finally, the third component, *social presence*, is a transformative function: it is the ability to perceive a social community as a meaningful one, a community that is not only welcoming but also where individuals can discover their human nature and the possibility of being there for others [24]. This final stage is the one most influenced by the use of artistic texts, enabling the expression of personal thoughts, opinions, and beliefs, as well as fostering meaningful encounters with others. It facilitates the discovery of one's individual value in relation to a shared, evolving narrative.

Components	Questions	Possible answers
Sociability	In a learning community, what emotions does the possibility of being able to use a social group with my classmates evoke in me?	a. Anxiety
		b. Indifference
		c. Satisfaction
		d. Happiness
Social space	During a lesson or seminar, what emotions does the repetition of a topic I introduced by my classmates/the teacher arouse in me?	a. Anxiety
		b. Indifference
		c. Satisfaction
		d. Happiness
Social presence	During a lesson or seminar, what emotions does the possibility of participating in a collective discussion by freely expressing personal opinions and beliefs arouse in me?	a. Anxiety
		b. Indifference
		c. Satisfaction
		d. Happiness

Fig. 2. Questionnaire sample.

4 Results

The key findings regarding student experiences in online and traditional learning environments outline specific features of the interaction aimed at enhancing class engagement via artistic texts. They can be summarized as follows (see Fig. 3):

1. Promptness not only presence: a notable interest and happiness are associated with the possibility of prompt interaction via social media. This includes 47.2% of online students and 52% of traditional students expressing this sentiment. Additionally, a swift response from instructors is highly valued, with 69.4% of online learners and 72.2% of traditional learners emphasizing this need.

This result highlights how social interactions form the foundation for the emergence of social emotions. The data demonstrates that this is true for both in-person and online students, but also that the different nature of emotions is correlated with different types of social interactions. Among the various interactions, those with teachers hold a particularly significant weight: 72.2% of in-person students associate positive emotions with interactions with their teachers, revealing a genuine social need.

This data is quite intriguing in relation to the online context and its socio-didactic structure. It offers valuable insights into how to effectively structure courses with both synchronous and asynchronous activities. While the flexibility of online courses is a major draw for students, allowing them to attend at their convenience, the ability to

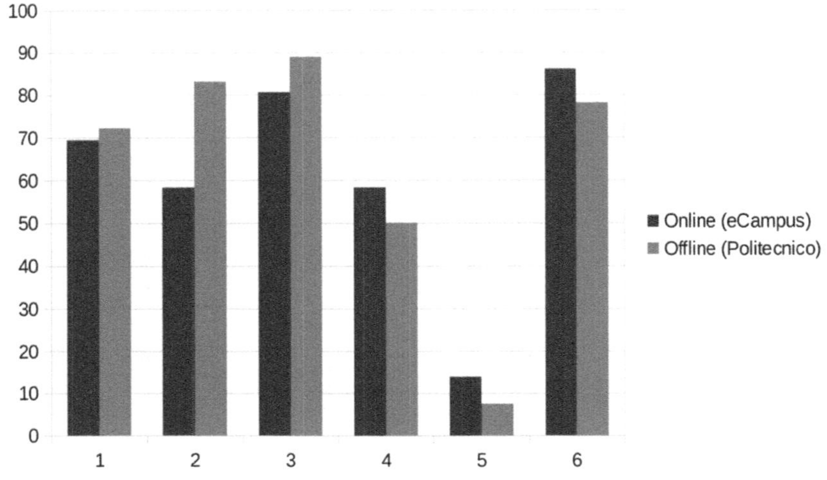

Fig. 3. Data comparison

interact with instructors in real time remains an essential aspect of the teaching process, even in an online setting.

As indicated by responses to the open-ended questions in the questionnaire, students at online universities – like their counterparts at traditional universities – highly value interactive teaching activities, such as virtual labs and synchronous webinars. These formats provide them with the chance to connect with their instructors and establish a more personal relationship before their final exams.

2. Being protagonist: students derive satisfaction from being involved in the learning process, with 58.3% of online students and 83% of traditional students feeling this way. Acknowledgment is also crucial, as 80.6% of online students and 88.9% of traditional students appreciate being recognized for their efforts.

Data reveal that the opportunity to participate in a lecture or seminar, and especially the possibility of receiving appreciation for one's contribution, either from peers or instructors, serves as a lever for generating positive emotions. These emotions shape a new social space, transforming a standardized and potentially anxiety-inducing environment into one perceived as safe and as a source of well-being. Once again, it is surprising how this data shows the same dynamic in both traditional and online academic contexts.

The comparison of answers to the open-ended questions from questionnaires administered at online and traditional universities provides important insights into the quality of social interactions with teachers. In both settings, students emphasize the significance of these interactions, highlighting how personal acknowledgment from teachers during discussions – both in-person and online – as well as appreciation for their work on individual or group exercises and projects, plays a crucial role.

This recurring theme in both contexts suggests a widespread desire for personal attention from teachers. It prompts us to consider the institutional and organizational conditions that enable teachers to focus on personal interactions with students, including the teachers' workloads and the teaching methods they employ.

Importantly, interactions with teachers in both universities do not solely generate positive feelings; they can also lead to anxiety. This anxiety often arises when interactions are perceived as strictly related to the evaluation of students, rather than being part of a broader knowledge-building process that encompasses not only course content but also students' motivations and personal learning goals.

The identification of anxiety and the students' reflections on its significance indicate a potential avenue for further investigation in future studies.

3. To be (or not to be) real: While having the opportunity to listen to other students' or professors' personal experiences and their reactions to artistic texts is perceived as a precious way of engagement and purveyor of realness as a fundamental feature of social presence, anxiety is a common emotional state experienced during (self) presentations/expression. This concerns 27% of online students and 33.3% of traditional students. Notably, this anxiety can co-occur with feelings of satisfaction (58.3% online and 50% traditional) and even happiness (13.9% online and 7.5% traditional).

This data is particularly interesting as it reveals how the use of artistic texts introduces a demand for authenticity into lessons and group dynamics—a kind of unmasking, a critical potential that not only influences how the world is observed but also reshapes the experience of the educational relationship, personal expectations (both of students and instructors), and the possibility of these expectations being fulfilled. However, this data also highlights that social presence and the techniques for fostering it are far from straightforward. The anxiety often generated by participation indicates the need for learning how to participate (e.g., respecting speaking turns, ensuring everyone can contribute, and instructors learning how to value each participant's contributions).

This summary reflects the complex emotional responses and preferences of students in both online and traditional education settings. More in detail, we can identify the prominence of specific emotions for the components highlighted above.

As to the social space, we need to remember that apart from its spatial structure, it also has a cultural structure because norms and values, rules and roles, and beliefs and ideals are cultural artifacts developed and maintained by the group members. In this perspective, the survey has revealed the relevance of satisfaction as a key feeling to create a shared social identity, foster group cohesiveness, enhance connectedness with others, build mutual trust, cultivate a sense of belonging, promote a sense of community, develop a positive social climate, and encourage an open atmosphere.

As to sociability, interest seems to dominate the scene: even engaging in small talk, often about everyday occurrences outside class, plays an important role in building trustworthy interpersonal relationships. While small talk may not directly contribute to formal communication or learning, it helps create a social environment that can be beneficial when class-related discussions are necessary or when collaboration in group projects is required.

Social presence, instead, seems a subjugated by a contradictory emotional condition, satisfaction for the possibility to empathize with others during the lecture and anxiety for the potentiality of misunderstanding, which seem at this point the to faced nature of the contingency of "going real".

The results of this research reveal its nature and the potential directions for future exploration. This study was designed as exploratory research, primarily focused on examining the social foundations of emotions and their connection to specific teaching methods. The small sample size is consistent with the type of research conducted. Additionally, the choice of an analysis method based on action research necessitated the inclusion of a control group of teachers who were not directly involved in the research's conception, particularly during the result analysis phase.

Regarding future research directions, the role of artistic texts in generating positive emotions and fostering attentive relationships with teachers has been noted but warrants further investigation. The results obtained clearly indicate the importance of a more thorough investigation of the typologies of artistic texts employed, which can be the aim of an upcoming phase of research, in which the recurring artistic elements identified in the questionnaires will be connected with the findings from the section that analyzed social interaction. It will focus on the creative forms that emerged from responses related to various aspects of the artistic text, such as enjoyment, involvement in its production, and design. The goal is to highlight the social space where social interaction is intended to elicit positive emotions.

5 Conclusions

This study investigates the correlation between affective processing – specifically the emotions experienced during learning – and cognitive processing, meaning the level of engagement during learning, as well as between affective processing and learning outcomes. The affective-cognitive pathway can be positive if the learning episode generates pleasure and engagement, leading to a good learning outcome, or negative if it generates emotions ranging from anxiety to disengagement, resulting in a poor learning outcome.

The research conducted through the administration of online questionnaires in two different academic contexts – the first being traditional, the Polytechnic University of Turin, and the second being online, eCampus University – highlights the relationship between emotions and artistic texts during the learning experience.

This research provides evidence on the types of emotions that can be activated in e-learning contexts and, based on the interviewees' responses, highlights the crucial role of artistic expression and emotional intelligence in capturing students' attention, facilitating comprehension, and promoting creativity.

The results of the questionnaires reveal a very similar social dynamic in both traditional and online contexts. Artistic texts help activate personal and meaningful educational relationships, and their use during a course contributes to transforming the social space into a vibrant and authentic environment. This potential seems particularly connected to two key aspects of artistic texts. The first lies in their ability to stimulate critical thinking not only about the world but also about one's way of living in it. The second relates to the fact that artistic texts facilitate the discovery of one's similarity with others and the realization of the possibility of feeling the emotions experienced by others as shared emotions.

Given the limited scope of the study, the results cannot be considered generalizable. The representativity of the sample is also limited, due to the process of self-selection of the participants in the online survey. However, the findings can contribute to future research, as representational language is rarely prioritized in the overall course design process, whether online or offline. Nevertheless, this study highlights that, when thoughtfully integrated into course design, artistic texts can significantly impact students' experiences and performance in such contexts.

Author Contributions. Although this article is the result of a common reflection, paragraphs 1 and 5 are attributable to Fiorella Vinci; paragraph 2.1 is attributable to Antonella De Blasio; paragraph 2.2 and 3. are attributable to Ambrogia Cereda; paragraph 4 is attributable to Fiorella Vinci and Fabrizio Barpi.

References

1. Mayer, R.E.: Multimedia Learning, 2nd edn. Cambridge University Press, New York (2009)
2. Mayer, R.E., Estrella, G.: Benefits of emotional design in multimedia instruction. Learn. Instr. **33**, 12–18 (2014)
3. Lajoie, S.P.: Multimedia learning of cognitive processes. In: Mayer, R.E. (ed.) The Cambridge Handbook of Multimedia Learning, pp. 623–646. Cambridge University Press, New York (2014)
4. Moreno, R., Mayer, R.E.: Interactive multimodal learning environments. Educ. Psychol. Rev. **19**, 309–326 (2007)
5. Pekrun, R., Perry, R.P.: Control-value theory of achievement emotions. In: Pekrun, R., Linnenbrink-Garcia, L. (eds.) International Handbook of Emotions in Education, pp. 120–141. Taylor & Francis, New York (2014)
6. Plass, J.L., Kaplan, U.: Emotional design in digital media. In: Tettegah, S., Gartmeier, M. (eds.) Emotion, Technology, Design, and Learning, pp. 131–161. Elsevier, New York (2016)
7. Duffy, M.C., Lajoie, S.P., Pekrun, R., Lachapelle, K.: Emotions in medical education: examining the validity of the Medical Emotion Scale (MES) across authentic medical learning environments. Learn. Instr. **70**, 101150 (2018)
8. Calvo, R., D'Mello, S.: New Perspectives on Affect and Learning Technologies. Springer Publishing Company, New York (2011)
9. Wang, Y., Gong, S., Cao, Y., Lang, Y., Xu, X.: The effects of affective pedagogical agent in multimedia learning environments: a meta-analysis. Educ. Res. Rev. **38**, 100506 (2023)
10. Um, E., Plass, J.L., Hayward, E.O., Homer, B.D.: Emotional design in multimedia learning. J. Educ. Psychol. **104**, 485–498 (2012)
11. Short, J., William, E., Christie, B.: The Social Psychology of Telecommunications. Wiley, Toronto (1976)
12. Tammelin, M.: From telepresence to social presence: the role of presence in a network-based learning environment. In: Tella, S. (ed.) Aspects of Media Education: Strategic Imperatives in the Information Age. Media Education Publications, Helsinki (1998)
13. Rettie, R.: Connectedness, awareness, and social presence. In: 6th International Presence Workshop. Aalborg University, Copenaghen (2003)
14. Kreijns, K., Xu, K., Weidlich, J.: Social presence: conceptualization and measurement. Educ. Psychol. Rev. **34**, 139–170 (2022)
15. Whiteside, A.L., Garrett Dikkers, A., Swan, K. (eds.): Social Presence in Online Learning: Multiple Perspectives on Practice and Research. Taylor & Francis, London (2023)
16. Dewey, J.: Art as Experience. New York, Minton, Balch & Co (1934)
17. Silvia, P.J.: Emotional responses to art: from collation and arousal to cognition and emotion. Rev. Gen. Psychol. **9**(4), 342–357 (2005)

18. Immordino-Yang, M.H., Damasio, A.: We feel, therefore we learn: the relevance of affective and social neuroscience to education. Mind Brain Educ. **1**(1), 3–10 (2007)
19. Robinson, K.: Out of Our Minds: Learning to Be Creative. Capstone, Mankato (2005)
20. Zull, J.E.: The Art of Changing the Brain: Enriching the Practice of Teaching by Exploring the Biology of Learning. Stylus Publishing, Sterling (2011)
21. Immordino-Yang, M.H., Damasio, A., Gardner, H.: Emotions, learning, and the brain: exploring the educational implications of affective neuroscience. Mind Brain Educ. **13**(2), 89–103 (2019)
22. Goldberg, M.: Arts Integration: Teaching Subject Matter through the Arts in Multicultural Settings. Routledge, London (2021)
23. Wiggins, G., McTighe, J.: Understanding by Design, Association for Supervision and Curriculum Development. Pearson, Upper Saddle River (1998)
24. Donati, P.P.: Sociologia della riflessività. Come si entra nel dopo-moderno. Il Mulino, Bologna (2011)

Enhancing Educational Inclusion Through Advanced Assistive Technologies: Impact of AR, VR and AI Integration in Supporting Students with Motor and Communication Impairments

Fabrizio Corradi[1,2(✉)], Cristiana Cardinali[1], and Maria Cinque[1]

[1] LUMSA University, Rome, Italy
f.corradi1@lumsa.it
[2] Foggia University, Foggia, Italy

Abstract. The integration of students with motor and communication disabilities represents a significant challenge within the educational context. The International Classification of Functioning, Disability and Health (ICF) defines disability as the result of the interaction between an individual's health and contextual factors. This underscores the importance of appropriate technological tools to facilitate cognitive, emotional, and social-relational development of students with disabilities. In this context, assistive technologies emerge as pivotal instruments to facilitate school, social, and work inclusion, markedly enhancing students' quality of life. The advent of innovative technologies, including augmented reality (AR), virtual reality (VR), and generative artificial intelligence (AI), presents potential for enhancing the effectiveness of traditional assistive technologies, such as eye tracking. These technologies have the potential to eliminate temporal and spatial barriers to learning, thereby enhancing student autonomy and accessibility to educational resources. Through systematic review methodology, this study evaluates the impact of AI-supported AR/VR applications on educational methods for students with motor and communication disabilities, compared to traditional approaches. The findings suggest that emerging technologies have the potential to facilitate greater inclusion and academic achievement than established assistive technologies alone. This is of particular significance for higher education contexts, where complex academic demands require sophisticated technological support.

Keywords: Assistive Technology · Educational Inclusion · Augmented Reality · Virtual Reality · Artificial Intelligence · Special Education

1 Introduction

Assistive technologies are emerging as crucial tools for improving inclusion and teaching effectiveness for students with motor and communication disabilities. The evolving landscape of educational technology has created new possibilities for supporting these students, particularly through the increasing role of assistive technologies in academic and social inclusion, the emergence of AR, VR, and AI as potential educational tools, and the growing recognition of the need for personalized technological solutions.

P. Ardimento et al. (Eds.): HELMeTO 2024, CCIS 2468, pp. 147–165, 2025.
https://doi.org/10.1007/978-3-031-93999-0_10

The evolving landscape of educational technology has given rise to new opportunities and challenges for higher education institutions. Empirical research has demonstrated that the effective integration of assistive technologies necessitates systematic evaluation processes and person-centred approaches [1, 2]. This approach is crucial for optimising technology adoption and reducing abandonment risk, particularly in higher education settings where students with disabilities face unique challenges [3–5].

The case of Arianna, a 23-year-old woman who has been routinely using eye tracking to communicate and interact in her daily life since age 8, illustrates the transformative potential of these technologies. Despite her academic success, graduating from high school with honours, Arianna now faces new challenges in the workplace, highlighting the need to explore long-term effectiveness of assistive technologies beyond the school context and the importance of proper training and support systems.

Research on assistive technologies has demonstrated the importance of a person-centered approach to optimize the effectiveness of these tools. A systematic and personalized evaluation process can lead to positive outcomes in assistive technology adoption [1, 6]. This approach not only improves user satisfaction but also reduces technology abandonment risk, a significant problem highlighted in literature [2], particularly when addressing the challenge of integrating new technologies with existing educational frameworks.

The ICF [7] defines disability as the result of interaction between individual health and contextual factors, emphasizing the importance of appropriate technological tools in facilitating cognitive, emotional, and social-relational development for students with disabilities [3]. Research has gained considerable attention in recent years, highlighting how new technologies can play crucial roles not only in enablement and rehabilitation but also in developing essential soft skills for academic and professional success [4, 8].

The integration of these technologies into the school curriculum and adoption of personalized approaches is fundamental for maximizing their effectiveness [8]. Cross-disciplinary skills and interdisciplinary training of education professionals [9] offer valuable insights into how assistive technologies can promote both disciplinary learning and broader transferable skills development. Media education represents a crucial challenge for contemporary schools, which must train students to use technological tools critically and consciously [10].

To address these emerging challenges and opportunities, we formulated specific research objectives focused on:

1. Examining current assistive technologies for motor and communication disabilities, with particular attention to AR, VR, and generative AI applications [11].
2. Evaluating inclusive effectiveness of existing technologies and identifying improvement areas through emerging technology integration [12].
3. Analyzing student satisfaction and expectations regarding assistive technologies, particularly concerning AR, VR, and AI integration [13].
4. Exploring implementation benefits and challenges through expert consultation using the DELPHI method [14].
5. Investigating eye tracking integration with emerging technologies for reducing learning barriers [15].

6. Developing guidelines for inclusive learning environments that integrate traditional and emerging technologies [17].
7. Identifying research priorities for technology development aimed at improving student autonomy and academic success [16].

Using the PRISMA model and PICOC method, we examine these objectives through systematic review of existing literature, comparing traditional and emerging assistive technologies in secondary education contexts [18, 19]. This approach enables evaluation of both current implementation status and potential impact of emerging technologies on educational outcomes.

2 Methodology

2.1 Research Design

The study adopted a comprehensive systematic review approach to evaluate the effectiveness of assistive technologies in educational settings. To ensure methodological rigor and comprehensive coverage, we employed the PRISMA guidelines [18] alongside the PICOC framework [20], which allowed for a structured examination of the existing literature.

Framework components included:

- Population: Students with motor and communication disabilities, focusing on those with adequate cognitive abilities
- Intervention: Use of assistive technologies, including AR, VR, and AI
- Comparison: Traditional teaching methods or alternative educational approaches
- Outcomes: Educational effectiveness (academic results, school inclusion, socio-emotional development)
- Context: Secondary school educational settings

2.2 Search Strategy

To capture the breadth of available research [19], we conducted an extensive search across major academic databases. This comprehensive approach ensured coverage of both established research and emerging studies in the field of assistive technologies. Databases consulted:

- Scopus
- PubMed
- Web of Science
- ProQuest
- Google Scholar.

Search string development focused on combining relevant terms related to assistive technologies, disabilities, and educational contexts: ((“assistive technology” OR “assistive technologies”) AND (“motor disability” AND (“communication disability” OR “AAC” OR “communication disorder” OR “speech disorder” OR “language disorder”)) AND (education OR school OR "child development" OR "developmental age" OR childhood OR adolescence OR pediatric OR youth) AND (effectiveness OR efficacy) AND ("virtual reality" OR "augmented reality" OR "mixed reality" OR "generative artificial intelligence")).

2.3 Selection Criteria

The selection process was guided by clearly defined criteria to ensure the relevance and quality of included studies (Table 2). These criteria were established prior to the search to minimize selection bias and ensure alignment with research objectives.

Inclusion criteria:

- Studies published between 2013–2024 (Table 1)
- Focus on motor and communication impairments
- Educational context
- Implementation of AR, VR, or AI technologies
- Empirical research or systematic reviews

Exclusion criteria:

- Studies focusing solely on traditional assistive technologies
- Studies set in non-educational settings
- Theoretical papers without empirical evidence
- Clinical cases differing from motor and communication disabilities.

2.4 Quality Assessment

To ensure the robustness of our findings, we implemented a comprehensive quality assessment process using validated tools appropriate for different study designs. This multi-tool approach allowed for appropriate evaluation of diverse research methodologies.

Assessment tools utilized:

- AMSTAR-2 for systematic reviews and meta-analyses [21]
- Cochrane Risk of Bias Tool for experimental studies [22]
- Newcastle-Ottawa Scale for observational studies [23]
- Mixed Methods Appraisal Tool (MMAT) for mixed-methods studies [24]
- Critical Appraisal Skills Programme for qualitative studies [25]
- JBI Critical Appraisal Checklist for scoping reviews [26].

The quality of the included studies was variable, with the majority demonstrating medium to high quality. Systematic reviews and meta-analyses typically demonstrated a medium to high rating on the AMSTAR-2 scale. Experimental studies exhibited a low to moderate risk of bias in accordance with the Cochrane Risk of Bias Tool. Observational studies attained a medium to high rating on the Newcastle-Ottawa Scale. Mixed-methods studies generally exhibited good quality in accordance with the MMAT. Qualitative studies received a medium to high rating using the CASP.

2.5 Data Extraction and Analysis

The data extraction and analysis process followed a systematic approach to ensure comprehensive capture of relevant information while maintaining methodological rigor. The process involved multiple stages of review and refinement.

Systematic review process steps (Fig. 1):

1. Initial identification: 66 publications
2. Duplicate removal: 60 unique articles
3. Title/abstract screening using PICOC criteria
4. Full-text review: 33 articles
5. Final analysis: 30 articles (3 articles unavailable for full review)

Data extraction elements:

- Author information and publication year
- Study design and methodology
- Population characteristics
- Intervention details
- Outcome measures
- Key findings

3 Results

3.1 Study Selection

The systematic review process yielded a comprehensive dataset through multiple screening stages. From an initial pool of 66 publications identified through database searches, 60 unique articles remained after duplicate removal. Following rigorous screening using the PICOC criteria, 33 articles qualified for full-text review, with 30 ultimately being accessible and included in the final analysis (Table 3).

3.2 Key Areas of Improvement

The analysis revealed five primary areas where assistive technologies demonstrated significant impact on educational outcomes and student development (Table 4).

- Communication: various technologies, such as augmentative and alternative communication (AAC) systems, brain-computer interfaces (BCIs) and eye-tracking devices, have been shown to significantly improve the communication skills of students with severe disabilities [15, 16, 27, 28, 35, 53].
- Access to learning: the use of assistive technologies has facilitated access to educational content and increased students' participation and independence in school activities [17, 29–31, 42].
- Cognitive development: multimedia applications and programmes based on assistive technologies have shown positive effects on the development of cognitive processes, including working memory, perceptual reasoning and verbal comprehension [32–34].

Table 1. Analysis of the timing of papers

Year	Number of Items
2013	1
2014	2
2016	3
2017	1
2018	4
2019	3
2020	1
2021	1
2022	2
2023	4
2024	8

- Social inclusion: Assistive technologies have contributed to improving the social inclusion and participation of students with disabilities in school and leisure activities [12, 35–37].
- Autonomy: Several studies have shown that assistive technologies increase students' independence in daily activities and access to information [35, 41, 52, 53].

3.3 Common Themes

The studies share the following common themes:

(a) Adaptation: some studies highlight the importance of adapting assistive technologies to the specific needs of each student [13, 31, 35, 38, 40].
(b) Training and support: a recurring theme is the need for appropriate training for students, teachers and carers to maximise the effectiveness of assistive technologies [41, 43].
(c) Curriculum integration: the importance of integrating assistive technologies into the regular school curriculum is highlighted in several studies [17, 30, 34, 35].
(d) Multidisciplinary approach: collaboration between educators, therapists and technicians is considered crucial for the effective implementation of assistive technologies [29, 38].
(e) Technological evolution: Recent studies highlight the emergence of advanced technologies such as virtual reality, augmented reality and artificial intelligence in the field of assistive technologies [11, 14, 35, 42, 52].

3.4 Differences or Weaknesses in Results

Despite the overall positive trend in the use of assistive technologies, analysis of studies revealed some discrepancies and weaknesses in the results:

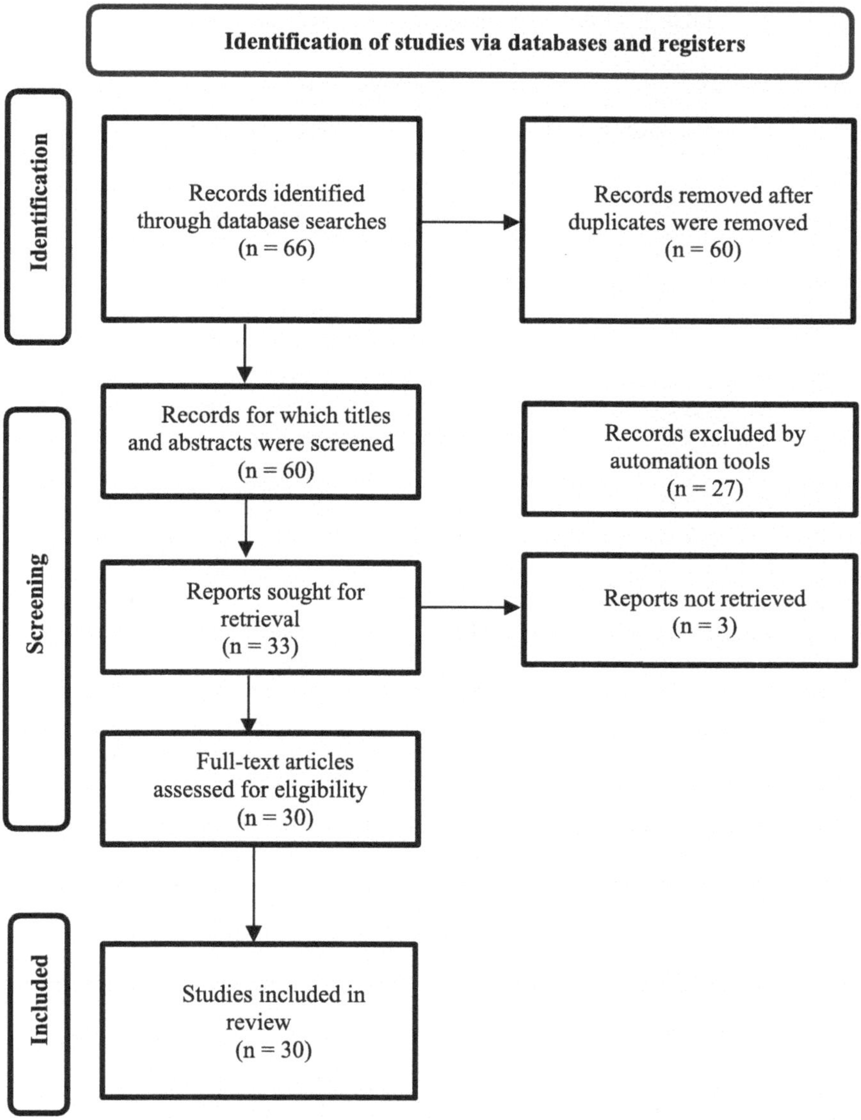

Fig. 1. PRISMA flow diagram of study selection process

(a) Long-term efficacy: While most studies report short-term benefits, the long-term efficacy of assistive technologies is not always clearly demonstrated [16, 41].
(b) Individual variability: some studies report significant variability in individual response to assistive technologies, suggesting that not all solutions are equally effective for all students [32, 38].
(c) Cost and accessibility: While some studies emphasize the benefits of advanced and expensive technologies, others emphasize the importance of low-cost and easily accessible solutions [12, 44].

Table 2. Overview of included studies *reference number

Id	No.*	Authors	Year	Title
1	5	Abbott, C., Brown, D., Evett, L., & Standen, P.	2013	Emerging issues and current trends in assistive technology use 2007–2010: Practising, assisting and enabling learning for all
2	11	Dudley, J., Yin, L., Garaj, V., & Kristensson, P. O.	2023	Inclusive Immersion: A review of efforts to improve accessibility in virtual reality, augmented reality and the metaverse
3	12	Domínguez González, M. Á., Hervás Gómez, C., & Román Graván, P.	2023	Technologies as a support resource for people with disabilities: A systematic review
4	13	Yu, L., Feng, H., Alghofaili, R., Byun, B., O'Neal, T., Rampalli, S., Chung, Y., Genaro Motti, V., & Yu, L. F.	2024	HoloAAC: A Mixed Reality AAC Application for People with Expressive Language Difficulties
5	14	Mott, M., Tang, J., Kane, S., Cutrell, E., & Ringel Morris, M.	2020	"I just went into it assuming that I wouldn't be able to have the full experience"
6	15	Passaro, A., Zullo, A., Di Gioia, M., Curcio, E., & Stasolla, F.	2024	A Narrative Review on the Use of Eye-Tracking in Rett Syndrome: Implications for Diagnosis and Treatment
7	16	Peters, B., Eddy, B., Galvin-McLaughlin, D., Betz, G., Oken, B., & Fried-Oken, M.	2022	A systematic review of research on augmentative and alternative communication brain-computer interface systems for individuals with disabilities
8	17	Istenic Starcic, A., & Bagon, S.	2014	ICT-supported learning for inclusion of people with special needs: Review of seven educational technology journals, 1970–2011
9	27	Lazarou, I., Nikolopoulos, S., Petrantonakis, P. C., Kompatsiaris, I., & Tsolaki, M.	2018	EEG-based brain–computer interfaces for communication and rehabilitation of people with motor impairment: A novel approach of the twenty-first century
10	28	Orlandi, S., House, S. C., Karlsson, P., Saab, R., & Chau, T.	2021	Brain-computer interfaces for children with complex communication needs and limited mobility: A systematic review

(continued)

Table 2. (*continued*)

Id	No.*	Authors	Year	Title
11	29	Bianquin, N., Sacchi, F., & Besio, S.	2018	Enhancing communication and participation using AAC technologies for children with motor impairments: A systematic review
12	30	Dessemontet, R. S., Geyer, M., Linder, A. L., Atzemian, M., Martinet, C., Meuli, N., Audrin, C., & de Chambrier, A. F.	2024	Effects of Shared Text Reading for Students With Intellectual Disability: A Meta-analytical Review of Instructional Strategies
13	31	Taheri, A., Gomez-Monroy, C. G., Borja, V., & Sra, M.	2024	MouseClicker: Exploring Tactile Feedback and Physical Agency for People with Hand Motor Impairments
14	32	Lancioni, G. E., Singh, N. N., O'Reilly, M. F., Alberti, G., Chiariello, V., Campanella, C., Grillo, G., & Tagliente, V.	2019	A Program Based on Common Technology to Support Communication Exchanges and Leisure in People With Intellectual and Other Disabilities
15	33	Derbissalova, G., Shayakhmetova, A., Avagimyan, A., & Pyanova, E.	2024	Multimedia applications in special education: New opportunities for the developing of cognitive processes of children with intellectual disabilities
16	34	Stasolla, F., Boccasini, A., & Perilli, V.	2016	Assistive technology-based programs to support adaptive behaviors by children with autism spectrum disorders: A literature overview
17	35	Ciarmoli, D., & Stasolla, F.	2023	New Technologies to Support People with Neurodevelopmental Disorders: A Selective Review
18	36	Dabiri Golchin, M., Ripat, J., & Verdonck, M.	2023	Assistive technology to facilitate children's play: A scoping review
19	37	Lancioni, G. E., Singh, N. N., O'Reilly, M. F., Sigafoos, J., Alberti, G., & Fiore, A.	2022	People with intellectual and multiple disabilities access leisure, communication, and daily activities via a new technology-aided program
20	38	Erdem, R.	2017	Students with special educational needs and assistive technologies: A literature review

(*continued*)

(d) Outcome measures: There is some variability in the *outcome* measures used between studies, sometimes making it difficult to compare outcomes directly [37, 38].

Table 2. *(continued)*

Id	No.*	Authors	Year	Title
21	39	Fager, S. K., & Burnfield, J. M.	2013	Patients' experiences with technology during inpatient rehabilitation: Opportunities to support independence and therapeutic engagement
22	40	Gomide, R. S., Loja, L. F. B., Lemos, R. P., Flôres, E. L., Melo, F. R., & Teixeira, R. A. G.	2016	A new concept of assistive virtual keyboards based on a systematic review of text entry optimization techniques
23	41	Oliver, M.	2019	Communication devices and electronic aids to activities of daily living
24	42	Gao, J., Song, W., Zhong, Y., Huang, D., Wang, J., Zhang, A., & Ke, X.	2024	Children with developmental coordination disorders: A review of approaches to assessment and intervention
25	43	Roulstone, A.	2016	Disability and technology: An interdisciplinary and international approach
26	44	Koester, H. H., & Arthanat, S.	2018	Text entry rate of access interfaces used by people with physical disabilities: A systematic review
27	45	Piekema, L., Ten Brug, A., Waninge, A., & van Der Putten, A.	2024	From assistive to inclusive? A systematic review of the uses and effects of technology to support people with pervasive support needs
28	46	Perilli, V., Stasolla, F., & Laporta, D.	2019	Enhancing Academic Performance of Children with Cerebral Palsy through Technological Aids: A Mini Review
29	52	Sahoo, S., & Choudhury, B.	2024	Exploring the use of computer vision in assistive technologies for individuals with disabilities: A review
30	53	Lancioni G.E.; Singh N.N.; O'Reilly M.F.; Sigafoos J.; Alberti G.; Perilli V.; Chiariello V.; Grillo G.; Turi C.	2018	Case series of technology-aided interventions to support leisure and communication in extensive disabilities

3.5 Overall Quality of Evidence

The quality of the evidence varies from Medium to High among the studies examined. Strengths include:

Table 3. Distribution of authors by geographical area (Co-authors indicates how many articles include at least one author affiliated with that area. Some articles appear in more than one area if they have co-authors from different countries. Corresponding author means the first author or corresponding author - when explicit - affiliated with that area).

Region	Co-authors	Corresponding author
Italy	8	8
Rest of Europe (United Kingdom, Greece, Spain, Netherlands, Slovenia, Switzerland, etc. except Italy	8	8
USA	8	7
Latin America (Brazil, Mexico)	2	1
Asia (China, India, Kazakhstan, Russia, Turkey)	4	4
Australia/New Zealand	3	0

Table 4. Summary table of the main results

Impact Area	Technologies	Main results	Quality of evidence
Communication	AAC, BCI, Eye-tracking	Significant improvement in communication skills	Loud
Access to learning	Adaptive devices, specialized software	Increased participation and independence in school activities	Medium-High
Cognitive development	Multimedia applications, interactive programs	Positive effects on working memory, perceptual reasoning, verbal comprehension	Medium
Social inclusion	Various assistive technologies	Improved social inclusion and participation	Medium
Autonomy	Environmental control devices, apps for everyday tasks	Increased independence in daily activities	Medium-High

1. Several well-designed studies, including randomized trials and systematic reviews [12, 33].
2. Use of standardized *outcome* measures in many studies [16, 37].
3. Inclusion of diverse populations with various types of disabilities [37, 38].

This quality assessment provided a solid basis for interpreting the results of the systematic review, allowing the evidence provided by each included study to be given due weight.

4 Discussion

The studies reviewed show a generally positive impact of assistive technologies on the teaching effectiveness and quality of life of students with motor and communication disabilities. The analysis also includes emerging findings on the use of advanced technologies such as AR, VR, and AI. There are also, however, some limitations.

A significant limitation emerges from the considerable heterogeneity of the studies included. The diversity in research designs, populations studied, and interventions analyzed, as highlighted by Bianquin et al. [29], made direct comparison between results particularly complex. This variability, while reflecting the richness of the field of study, poses considerable challenges in extrapolating generalizable conclusions about the effectiveness of assistive technologies in specific educational settings.

The rapid evolution of technologies, especially the emergence of AR, VR, and AI, has introduced a new dimension of complexity to our analysis. Studies by Dudley et al. [11] and Mott et al. [14] have begun to explore these emerging technologies, but the paucity of in-depth research in this area limits our ability to fully assess their potential impact in the educational context for students with motor and communication disabilities. This gap in the literature underscores the need for further targeted research exploring the integration of AR, VR, and AI into assistive educational practices.

Another significant limitation concerns the temporality of the studies included. The rapid evolution of technologies means that some of the results may not fully reflect the latest capabilities of these technologies. This time is particularly relevant when considering emerging technologies, the development of which is proceeding at an accelerated pace.

The variability in the methodological quality of the included studies is an additional challenge. Despite our efforts to rigorously assess the quality of each study, methodological limitations in some studies may affect the reliability of the overall results. As highlighted by Koester & Arthanat [44], the lack of standardization in *outcome* measures between studies makes it difficult to synthesize and compare results.

It is also important to note the potential for publication bias. Studies with positive results are more likely to be published, which could lead to an overestimation of the effectiveness of assistive technologies. This bias could be particularly pronounced in the case of emerging technologies, where enthusiasm for innovation could influence the publication of results.

Finally, our review focused mainly on *outcomes* related to teaching effectiveness and school inclusion. This focus, while important, may have led to the neglect of other significant aspects of the use of assistive technologies, such as the long-term impact on students' quality of life or career prospects, an aspect emphasized by Perilli et al. [46].

Acknowledging these limitations does not diminish the value of the results obtained but rather highlights the need to interpret them with caution and in the appropriate context. These limitations also offer valuable insights for future research in the field of assistive technologies for education, emphasizing the importance of longitudinal studies, more rigorous and standardized research methodologies, and a deeper exploration of emerging technologies in the educational context.

These limitations do not invalidate the results of the review, but they do emphasize the need to interpret the results with caution. They also provide guidance for future research in this field, highlighting areas that need further investigation and methodological improvements [5].

4.1 Impact on Educational Practice

The results of this review underscore the importance of tailoring assistive technologies to meet the individual needs of students. The effectiveness of assistive technologies increases significantly when they are tailored to the specific abilities and limitations of each student [29]. Educators should therefore collaborate closely with assistive technology professionals to ensure optimal personalization, adopting a user-centered approach in the design and implementation of assistive technologies [13, 38].

The need for continuous training for teachers on the use of assistive technologies is clear. Teachers' competence in implementing these technologies is crucial to their success [17]. Educational institutions should prioritize professional development programs in this area, including training on emerging technologies such as AR, VR, and AI.

The integration of assistive technologies within higher education settings necessitates a systematic incorporation within the prevailing educational frameworks [8, 9]. A significant body of research has indicated that members of academic staff frequently encounter difficulties in implementing reasonable adjustments, primarily due to their limited understanding of disability support [48]. This challenge is particularly pronounced in the context of emerging technologies such as augmented reality (AR), virtual reality (VR), and artificial intelligence (AI). Moreover, research has underscored that faculty attitudes towards students with disabilities have a substantial impact on the efficacy of inclusive practices [12, 49]. Consequently, educational institutions must prioritize the provision of comprehensive training programmes that address both technical competencies and disability awareness, thereby fostering inclusive learning environments [17].

Effective implementation of assistive technologies requires a multidisciplinary approach. Some studies have highlighted the benefits of collaboration between educators, therapists and technicians [37]. Schools should foster multidisciplinary teams to support the use of assistive technologies, including experts in emerging technologies.

Assistive technologies should be used not only to enhance academic learning, but also to promote social inclusion and active participation of students. These technologies can significantly improve social interaction and classroom participation [12].

It is important to consider integrating emerging technologies such as AR, VR, and AI into the design of inclusive learning environments. These tools offer new opportunities to create immersive and personalized educational experiences [11, 42].

4.2 Future Directions

There is a clear need for longitudinal studies to assess the long-term impact of assistive technologies. Future research should follow students for longer periods to better understand the long-term effects on learning and development [41].

The rapid evolution of technologies requires continuous research into emerging applications. It is critical to explore the use of virtual and augmented reality and AI with respect to the inclusion of students with disabilities [11]. Future studies should focus on these innovative technologies and their potential impact.

More in-depth research is needed on the effectiveness of assistive technologies in different educational and cultural contexts. The results are still highly variable in different survey environments [16]. Future studies should aim to better understand how the effectiveness of assistive technologies may vary by context.

Research in higher education settings has highlighted the importance of involving students with disabilities in the evaluation of educational technologies [29, 50]. This participatory approach ensures that technological implementations meet the specific needs of students with disabilities while addressing potential barriers to access and participation. Additionally, institutions must carefully consider the ethical implications of AI implementation, particularly regarding data security and algorithmic bias that might affect students with disabilities [37, 38, 51, 52]. This consideration assumes particular significance in the context of educational institutions' increasing reliance on advanced technologies for the purpose of inclusive education.

There is a need to improve the methodological quality of studies in this field [37]. Future research should focus on more rigorous study designs, including randomized controlled trials when possible, and the use of standardized *outcome* measures. Standardized research methodologies need to be developed to assess the effectiveness of assistive technologies, considering variability in *outcome measures* [38].

While many studies have focused on academic *outcomes*, some studies have emphasized the importance of also examining the social-emotional impacts of assistive technologies [34]. Future research should explore how these technologies affect students' self-esteem, motivation, and overall well-being.

The review highlighted the need for studies evaluating the cost-effectiveness of assistive technologies [38]. Future research should include economic analysis to help school agencies and school administrations make more informed decisions about the implementation of these technologies.

It is crucial to systematically include the voices of students, families, and teachers in future research. Understanding the lived experiences of end-users and their advocates can provide valuable insights to improve the design and implementation of assistive technologies [14, 38]. In addition, the inclusion of teachers' and caregivers' perspectives can offer a more comprehensive view of the effectiveness of these technologies in different settings [29].

It is essential to conduct longitudinal studies that assess the degree of student satisfaction with the use of assistive technologies and their impact on quality of life in the long term. Understanding the lived experiences of end-users and their supporters can provide valuable insights to improve the design and implementation of assistive technologies [34]. Future research should therefore prioritise the systematic integration of these voices, using qualitative and quantitative methods to capture the richness and complexity of users' experiences with assistive technologies in the educational context.

Future studies should explore the integration of assistive technologies with eye tracking, AR, VR and generative AI, in line with research objectives and building on the insights provided by recent studies [15, 16].

Guidelines need to be developed for the design of inclusive learning environments that integrate traditional assistive technologies with emerging ones. These guidelines should be based on the best practices identified in existing studies and consider the ongoing technological evolution [17, 34].

These implications underscore the importance of a continuous and multifaceted approach to researching and implementing assistive technologies in education and in general in everyday life. As technological advances continue to provide new opportunities, it is critical that research and practice go hand in hand to ensure that these technologies are used as effectively as possible to support the learning and inclusion of students with disabilities.

5 Conclusions

In conclusion, while evidence suggests a generally positive impact of assistive technologies on teaching effectiveness for students with motor and communication disabilities, more research is needed to confirm the long-term effectiveness and to optimize the implementation of these technologies in educational settings [15, 38]. Only a few partial answers to the research objectives formulated can be provided. The available data does not fully cover all aspects of the lenses, especially those related to the specific use of AR, VR and generative AI:

1. Current state of assistive technologies: The data show a wide range of assistive technologies in use, including augmentative and alternative communication (AAC) systems, brain-computer interfaces (BCIs), eye-tracking devices, and multimedia applications. However, the specific use of AR, VR, and generative AI is not widely documented in the included studies.
2. Teaching effectiveness and inclusion: Studies generally report a positive impact of assistive technologies on teaching effectiveness and inclusion. For example, Bianquin et al. [29] and Peters et al. [16] highlighted significant improvements in students' communication skills with the use of technologies from AAC and BCI.
3. Student satisfaction and experience: Some studies, such as Yu et al. [13], have looked at user satisfaction with assistive technologies, generally reporting positive feedback. However, specific data on student expectations regarding emerging technologies such as AR and VR is lacking.
4. Integration with eye-tracking: Studies such as Passaro et al. [15] have explored the use of eye-tracking, but specific integration with AR, VR, or generative AI has not been widely documented in the data collected.
5. Potential benefits and challenges: Several studies, such as Dudley et al. [11], have discussed the potential benefits of emerging technologies, but the specific challenges of implementing AR, VR, and generative AI have not been extensively explored in the available data.
6. Guidelines for immersive learning environments: While some studies (e.g., [17]) have discussed the integration of technologies into the curriculum, specific guidelines for AR, VR, and AI-based immersive environments are lacking.

7. Priority research areas: The review highlighted the need for further research in several areas, including longitudinal studies and research on the long-term effectiveness of assistive technologies [16, 41].

In conclusion, while the data collected provides valuable insights into assistive technologies in general, there are significant gaps regarding the specific use of AR, VR, and generative AI in the educational setting for students with motor and communication disabilities. This suggests the need for further targeted research in these emerging areas.

Disclosure of Interests. The authors have no competing interests to declare that are relevant to the content of this article.

References

1. Corradi, F., Scherer, M.J., Lo Presti, A.: Measuring the assistive technology MATCH. In: Federici, S., Scherer, M.J. (eds.) Assistive Technology Assessment Handbook, 2nd edn, pp. 53–69. CRC Press, Boca Raton, FL (2018) ISBN: 9781351228416
2. Federici, S., Borsci, S.: Providing assistive technology in Italy: The perceived delivery process quality as affecting abandonment. Disabil. Rehabil. Assist. Technol. **11**(1), 22–31 (2016). https://doi.org/10.3109/17483107.2014.930191
3. Federici, S., Scherer, M.J. (eds.): Assistive Technology Assessment Handbook, 2nd edn. CRC Press, Boca Raton, FL (2018) ISBN: 9781351228416
4. Cinque, M.: Le nuove tecnologie tra abilitazione e riabilitazione nei soggetti autistici. In: Binetti, P. (ed.) Lo spettro autistico. La legge n. 134/15 e i suoi risvolti clinici e sociali, pp. 303–324 (2016) MaGi. ISBN-10: 8874873603
5. Abbott, C., Brown, D., Evett, L., Standen, P.: Emerging issues and current trends in assistive technology use 2007-2010: Practising, assisting and enabling learning for all. Disabil. Rehabil. Assist. Technol. **9**(6), 453–462 (2013). https://doi.org/10.3109/17483107.2013.840862
6. Federici, S., Corradi, F., Meloni, F., Borsci, S., Mele, M.L., De Sylva, S.D., Scherer, M.J.: Successful assistive technology service delivery outcomes from applying a person-centered systematic assessment process: A case study. Life Span Disab. **18**(1), 41–74 (2015) Retrieved July 10, 2024, from https://lifespanjournal.oasi.en.it/client/abstract/ENG290_2.%20Federici.pdf
7. World Health Organization: International classification of functioning, disability and health (ICF). World Health Organization (2001) ISBN 9241545429
8. Cinque, M.: Valorizzare il talento a scuola. Processi di riconoscimento e accompagnamento. In: Sartori, L., Cinque, M. (eds.) Gifted. Conoscere, individuare e valorizzare i bambini plusdotati e di talento dentro e fuori la scuola, pp. 187–204. MaGi (2020) ISBN 8874874286
9. Cinque, M., Dessardo, A.: Competenze trasversali e interdisciplinarità come contenuti core per la formazione dei professionisti dell'educazione. Form@re - Open Journal Per La Formazione in Rete. **20**(2), 169–185 (2020). https://doi.org/10.13128/form-9056
10. Rivoltella, P.C.: Media education. Idea, metodo, ricerca. Scholè (2019) ISBN 8828401419
11. Dudley, J., Yin, L., Garaj, V., Kristensson, P.O.: Inclusive immersion: a review of efforts to improve accessibility in virtual reality, augmented reality and the metaverse. Virtual Reality. **27**, 2989–3020 (2023). https://doi.org/10.1007/s10055-023-00850-8
12. Domínguez-González, M.Á., Hervás-Gómez, C., Román-Graván, P.: Technologies as a support resource for people with disabilities: a systematic review. J. Turkish Sci. Educ. **20**(1), 23–42 (2023). https://doi.org/10.36681/tused.2023.035

13. Yu, L., et al.: HoloAAC: a mixed reality AAC application for people with expressive language difficulties. George Mason University Technical Reports, TR-2023-1 (2023). https://doi.org/10.1007/978-3-031-61047-9_20
14. Mott, M., Tang, J., Kane, S., Cutrell, E., Ringel Morris, M.: "I just went into it assuming that I wouldn't be able to have the full experience": Understanding the accessibility of virtual reality for people with limited mobility. In: Proceedings of the 22nd International ACM SIGACCESS Conference on Computers and Accessibility, pp. 1–13 (2020). https://doi.org/10.1145/3373625.3416998
15. Passaro, A., Zullo, A., Di Gioia, M., Curcio, E., Stasolla, F.: A narrative review on the use of eye-tracking in Rett syndrome: Implications for diagnosis and treatment. OBM Genet. **8**(1), 1–15 (2024). https://doi.org/10.21926/obm.genet.2403250
16. Peters, B., Eddy, B., Galvin-McLaughlin, D., Betz, G., Oken, B., Fried-Oken, M.: A systematic review of research on augmentative and alternative communication brain-computer interface systems for individuals with disabilities. Front. Hum. Neurosci. **16**, 952460 (2022). https://doi.org/10.3389/fnhum.2022.952380
17. Istenic Starcic, A., Bagon, S.: ICT-supported learning for inclusion of people with special needs: Review of seven educational technology journals, 1970–2011. Br. J. Educ. Technol. **45**(2), 202–230 (2014). https://doi.org/10.1111/bjet.12086
18. Page, M.J., McKenzie, J.E., Bossuyt, P.M., Boutron, I., Hoffmann, T.C., Mulrow, C.D., et al.: The PRISMA 2020 statement: An updated guideline for reporting systematic reviews. BMJ. **372**, n.71 (2021). https://doi.org/10.1136/bmj.n71
19. Petticrew, M., Roberts, H.: Systematic Reviews in the Social Sciences: A Practical Guide. Blackwell Publishing (2006). https://doi.org/10.1002/9780470754887
20. Richardson, W.S., Wilson, M.C., Nishikawa, J., Hayward, R.S.A.: The well-built clinical question: A key to evidence-based decisions. ACP J. Club. **123**(3), A12–A13 (1995). https://doi.org/10.7326/acpjc-1995-123-3-a12
21. Shea, B.J., Reeves, B.C., Wells, G., Thuku, M., Hamel, C., Moran, J., et al.: AMSTAR 2: a critical appraisal tool for systematic reviews that include randomized or non-randomized studies of healthcare interventions, or both. BMJ. **358**, j4008 (2017). https://doi.org/10.1136/bmj.j4008
22. Higgins, J.P.T., Altman, D.G., Gøtzsche, P.C., Jüni, P., Moher, D., Oxman, A.D., et al.: The Cochrane Collaboration's tool for assessing risk of bias in randomised trials. BMJ. **343**, d5928 (2011). https://doi.org/10.1136/bmj.d5928
23. Wells, G. A., Shea, B., O'Connell, D., Peterson, J., Welch, V., Losos, M., & Tugwell, P.: The Newcastle-Ottawa Scale (NOS) for assessing the quality of nonrandomized studies in meta-analyses. University of Ottawa (n.d.). Retrieved July 10, 2024, from http://www.ohri.ca/programs/clinical_epidemiology/oxford.asp
24. Hong, Q.N., Fàbregues, S., Bartlett, G., Boardman, F., Cargo, M., Dagenais, P., Gagnon, M.-P., Griffiths, F., Nicolau, B., O'Cathain, A., Rousseau, M.-C., Vedel, I., Pluye, P.: The Mixed Methods Appraisal Tool (MMAT), version 2018, for information professionals and researchers. Educ. Inf. **34**(4), 285–291 (2018). https://doi.org/10.3233/EFI-180221
25. Critical Appraisal Skills Programme: CASP qualitative checklist. CASP (2018). Retrieved July 10, 2024, from https://casp-uk.net/casp-tools-checklists/
26. Aromataris, E., Munn, Z. (eds.): JBI Manual for Evidence Synthesis. Joanna Briggs Institute (2024). https://doi.org/10.46658/JBIMES-20-12
27. Lazarou, I., Nikolopoulos, S., Petrantonakis, P.C., Kompatsiaris, I., Tsolaki, M.: EEG-based brain–computer interfaces for communication and rehabilitation of people with motor impairment: a novel approach of the 21st century. Front. Hum. Neurosci. **12**, 14 (2018). https://doi.org/10.3389/fnhum.2018.00014

28. Orlandi, S., House, S.C., Karlsson, P., Saab, R., Chau, T.: Brain-computer interfaces for children with complex communication needs and limited mobility: a systematic review. Front. Hum. Neurosci. **15**, 643294 (2021). https://doi.org/10.3389/fnhum.2021.643294
29. Bianquin, N., Sacchi, F., Besio, S.: Enhancing communication and participation using AAC technologies for children with motor impairments: a systematic review. Educ. Sci. Soc. **9**(2), 58–82 (2018). https://doi.org/10.3280/ess1-2018oa6012
30. Dessemontet, R.S., Geyer, M., Linder, A.L., Atzemian, M., Martinet, C., Meuli, N., Audrin, C., de Chambrier, A.F.: Effects of shared text reading for students with intellectual disability: a meta-analytical review of instructional strategies. Educ. Res. Rev. **41**, 100503 (2024). https://doi.org/10.1016/j.edurev.2024.100615
31. Taheri, A., Gomez-Monroy, C.G., Borja, V., Sra, M.: MouseClicker: Exploring tactile feedback and physical agency for people with hand motor impairments. ACM Trans. Access. Comput. **17**(1), 1–28 (2024). https://doi.org/10.1145/3648685
32. Lancioni, G.E., Singh, N.N., O'Reilly, M.F., Alberti, G., Chiariello, V., Campanella, C., Grillo, G., Tagliente, V.: A program based on common technology to support communication exchanges and leisure in people with intellectual and other disabilities. Behav. Modif. **43**(5), 639–659 (2019). https://doi.org/10.1177/0145445519850747
33. Derbissalova, G., Shayakhmetova, A., Avagimyan, A., Pyanova, E.: Multimedia applications in special education: new opportunities for the developing of cognitive processes of children with intellectual disabilities. Multimed. Tools Appl. **83**(5), 6789–6805 (2023). https://doi.org/10.1007/s11042-023-17512-1
34. Stasolla, F., Boccasini, A., Perilli, V.: Assistive technology-based programs to support adaptive behaviors by children with autism spectrum disorders: a literature overview. In: Kats, Y. (ed.) Supporting the Education of Children with Autism Spectrum Disorders, pp. 191–212). IGI Global (2016). https://doi.org/10.4018/978-1-5225-0816-8.ch008
35. Ciarmoli, D., Stasolla, F.: New technologies to support people with neurodevelopmental disorders: a selective review. OBM Neurobiol. **7**(1) (2023, 2023). https://doi.org/10.21926/obm.neurobiol.2301163
36. Dabiri Golchin, M., Ripat, J., Verdonck, M.: Assistive technology to facilitate children's play: a scoping review. Disabil. Rehabil. Assist. Technol. **19**(1), 1–12 (2024). https://doi.org/10.1080/17483107.2023.2298825
37. Lancioni, G.E., Singh, N.N., O'Reilly, M.F., Sigafoos, J., Alberti, G., Fiore, A.: People with intellectual and multiple disabilities access leisure, communication, and daily activities via a new technology-aided program. Front. Psychol. **13** (2022). https://doi.org/10.3389/fpsyg.2022.994416
38. Erdem, R.: Students with special educational needs and assistive technologies: A literature review. Turkish Online J. Educ. Technol. **16**(1), 128–146 (2017) Retrieved July 10, 2024, from https://files.eric.ed.gov/fulltext/EJ1124910.pdf
39. Fager, S.K., Burnfield, J.M.: Patients' experiences with technology during inpatient rehabilitation: Opportunities to support independence and therapeutic engagement. Disabil. Rehabil. Assist. Technol. **9**(2), 121–127 (2013). https://doi.org/10.3109/17483107.2013.787124
40. Gomide, R.S., Loja, L.F.B., Lemos, R.P., Flôres, E.L., Melo, F.R., Teixeira, R.A.G.: A new concept of assistive virtual keyboards based on a systematic review of text entry optimization techniques. Res. Biomed. Eng. **32**(2), 176–198 (2016). https://doi.org/10.1590/2446-4740.01715
41. Oliver, M.: Communication devices and electronic aids to activities of daily living. In: Atlas of Orthoses and Assistive Devices, pp. 543–556. Elsevier (2017). https://doi.org/10.1016/B978-0-323-48323-0.00040-8
42. Gao, J., Song, W., Zhong, Y., Huang, D., Wang, J., Zhang, A., Ke, X.: Children with developmental coordination disorders: a review of approaches to assessment and intervention. Front. Neurol. **15** (2024). https://doi.org/10.3389/fneur.2024.1359955

43. Roulstone, A.: Disability and Technology: An Interdisciplinary and International Approach. Palgrave Macmillan UK (2016). https://doi.org/10.1057/978-1-137-45042-5
44. Koester, H.H., Arthanat, S.: Text entry rate of access interfaces used by people with physical disabilities: A systematic review. Assist. Technol. **30**(3), 151–163 (2018). https://doi.org/10.1080/10400435.2017.1291544
45. Piekema, L., Ten Brug, A., Waninge, A., van Der Putten, A.: From assistive to inclusive? A systematic review of the uses and effects of technology to support people with pervasive support needs. J. Appl. Res. Intellect. Disabil. **37**(1), 3–18 (2024). https://doi.org/10.1111/jar.13181
46. Perilli, V., Stasolla, F., Laporta, D.: Enhancing academic performance of children with cerebral palsy through technological aids: A mini review. Arch. Neurol. Neurosci. **3**(3), 1–3 (2019). https://doi.org/10.33552/ANN.2019.02.000537
47. Bunbury, S.: Disability in higher education—do reasonable adjustments contribute to an inclusive curriculum? Int. J. Incl. Educ. **24**(9), 964–979 (2018). https://doi.org/10.1080/13603116.2018.1503347
48. López-Gavira, R., Moriña, A., Camacho, B.M.: Challenges to inclusive education at the university: The perspective of students and disability support service staff. Innov. Eur. J. Social Sci. Res. **34**(3), 292–304 (2019). https://doi.org/10.1080/13511610.2019.1578198
49. Fernández-Cerero, J., Cabero-Almenara, J., Montenegro-Rueda, M.: Technological tools in higher education: A qualitative analysis from the perspective of students with disabilities. Educ. Sci. **14**(3), 310 (2024). https://doi.org/10.3390/educsci14030310
50. Lin, M.P., Liu, A.L., Poitras, E., Chang, M., Chang, D.H.: An exploratory study on the efficacy and inclusivity of AI technologies in diverse learning environments. Sustain. For. **16**(20), 8992 (2024). https://doi.org/10.3390/su16208992
51. Robinson, D.: Effective inclusive teacher education for special educational needs and disabilities: Some more thoughts on the way forward. Teach. Teach. Educ. **61**, 164–178 (2017). https://doi.org/10.1016/j.tate.2016.09.007
52. Sahoo, S., Choudhury, B.: Exploring the use of computer vision in assistive technologies for individuals with disabilities: A review. J. Future Sustain. **4**(2024), 133–148 (2024). https://doi.org/10.5267/j.jfs.2024.7.002
53. Lancioni, G.E., Singh, N.N., O'Reilly, M.F., Sigafoos, J., Alberti, G., Perilli, V., Chiariello, V., Grillo, G., Turi, C.: Case series of technology-aided interventions to support leisure and communication in extensive disabilities. Int. J. Dev. Disab. **66**, 180–189 (2018). https://doi.org/10.1080/20473869.2018.1533062

Educational Policy, Ethics, and Teacher Professional Development

The Role of Universities in Teachers' Professional Development: A Model Proposal

Arianna Giuliani, Elisa Mazzella, and Serena Triacca(✉)

eCampus University, Novedrate, Italy
{arianna.giuliani1,elisa.mazzella,serena.triacca}@uniecampus.it

Abstract. Teacher training is a critical investment area in Italy, aimed at fostering equitable, high-quality education nationwide. Recent regulations have established Multidisciplinary Centers for Teacher Training to promote collaboration between schools and universities, enhancing both initial and in-service training as avenues for educational research and best practices. The 30 and 60 CFU Qualifying Pathways pose significant challenges for Italian universities, necessitating the careful design and management of training programs for a large number of secondary school teachers. This paper examines the training plan developed by *eCampus Telematic University* for the inaugural *30 CFU Qualifying Pathway*, which engaged approximately 14,000 teachers across Italy. The primary objective was to establish a model for managing large-scale teacher training that would be effective in both in-person and online environments. The study was structured in three phases: analyzing the CEMFI training offer and the methodological choices assumed by trainers; detecting if and how Padlet boards can be effective partners for Course designing and lecture managing; and collecting trainee feedback. Key findings reveal that the flexible design of the training program successfully engaged participants, despite challenges inherent in a fully online format. The shared Padlet platform proved invaluable for organizing content and facilitating interaction. *eCampus* tested a sustainable and adaptable model suitable for other academic contexts. The results highlight the role of universities as strategic hubs in teacher training and underscore the need for enhanced collaboration among universities to strengthen national teacher training initiatives and to share training models.

Keywords: Teacher Professional Development · Online Learning · Training Model

1 Introduction

1.1 Teacher Training and Professional Development

Teacher training is a key issue on the agenda of Italian academic pedagogy [1–4]. Recently, the Italian scientific community re-launched the need to deal with training of future and existing teachers, working at several levels and from many disciplinary perspectives [5]. Within the various scientific-disciplinary sectors of the pedagogical

P. Ardimento et al. (Eds.): HELMeTO 2024, CCIS 2468, pp. 169–185, 2025.
https://doi.org/10.1007/978-3-031-93999-0_11

field, the history of education and pedagogy also responded to this call, not with the intent of conforming to present-day demands, but rather to illuminate the processes, variables, and dimensions that have shaped the foundations of today's educational system. The focus is on addressing critical issues and longstanding challenges in Italian schools, particularly concerning the training and historical development of secondary school teachers. Studies indicate that the training of secondary school teachers remains an open field, requiring further exploration and analysis through the diverse perspectives that pedagogy can offer. It is also an issue that calls for urgent reflection and intervention [6–8].

It is widely recognized that the redefinition of the school's role, function, and mission in recent years has imposed new demands on both administrators and educators. In particular, teachers have been increasingly required to update their competencies and, not without difficulty—especially for those with greater seniority—rethink their teaching methodologies. This process has entailed the adoption of more advanced approaches in general pedagogy, special education, and the integration of insights from experimental pedagogy.

The most advanced educational research, both in Italy and internationally, has identified three key aspects that shape the teacher's profile: pedagogical knowledge of the subject taught and the socio-cultural dimensions of education [9, 10], reflective and self-regulatory competencies in professional learning [11] and relational and ethical competence [12–16]. It is also important to note that the student profile has evolved significantly over the past two decades, leading to an increased need for more complex and multifaceted teacher training. Such training equips educators to design teaching practices grounded in deep content knowledge, the promotion of critical thinking, and the development of advanced communication skills.

Numerous researchers have highlighted that the professional development of teachers has become a central focus of European education policies. Teachers are viewed as the pivotal element in all strategies aimed at fostering societal, knowledge, and economic development [17]. Critically reflecting on this issue, which underpins the pedagogical and cultural quality of the teaching profession, is, as previously noted, an increasingly urgent task. This reflection must also incorporate a comparison with theories and training practices developed in other European countries and beyond, fostering a dialogue that can lead to the development of a shared theoretical and operational model, adaptable to diverse socio-political and cultural contexts.

1.2 The Role of the Universities in Italy

Recent regulations connected to the National Recovery and Resilience Plan have confirmed this direction, particularly through the set up of Multidisciplinary Centers for Teacher Training (DPCM August 4, 2023). These Centers are strategic in strengthening the synergy between schools and universities [18–20], making both initial and in-service training an opportunity for educational research and for the promotion of best practices in teaching.

The *30 and 60 CFU Qualifying Pathways*, as outlined in the aforementioned DPCM, represent a significant challenge for Italian Universities. These *Pathways* have been recently implemented and will continue to require considerable effort in the design and management of training programs for a huge number of current and future secondary school teachers.

Literature has consistently highlighted the significance of managing educational practices with an understanding that existing methodological and didactic models are varied and must be tailored to specific contexts [21–23]. Similarly, in teacher training, it may be useful to define organizational and instructional models that the Centers can tailor to the specific needs of their target audience. In view of the high number of Italian teachers and future teachers currently involved in initial and in-service training policies, it may be useful to benefit from the experience gained by University contexts that by their nature systematically work with large audiences.

Furthermore, the *30 and 60 CFU Qualifying Pathways* offer a promising opportunity to reestablish a productive dialogue between the various dimensions of psycho-pedagogical, sociological, and methodological teaching practices and disciplinary content, which have been under scrutiny for several years. By drawing on the foundational principles of the previous Italian teacher training systems, these programs aim to foster a renewed understanding of the teaching profession. This is crucial for revitalizing the professional profile, intrinsic motivation, and mission of teachers. This commitment is a sign of the vitality of an academic community that every day is committed to promoting and ensuring quality teacher training, based on values such as justice, equality, freedom for a truly democratic and inclusive school.

2 Methodology

2.1 Context and Unit of Analysis

This paper examines the training plan designed by *eCampus Telematic University* (Italy) for the first edition of the *30 CFU Qualifying Pathway (ex art. 13).*

The Athenaeum was among the first in the country to have activated this training initiative, foreseen by DPCM August 4, 2023 ("Definition of the university and academic path of initial training for teachers of lower and upper secondary schools, for the purposes of complying with the objectives of the National Recovery and Resilience Plan").

The Pathway was designed and managed by the Multidisciplinary Center for Teacher Training (CEMFI) of *eCampus University* and engaged approximately 14,000 teachers from all over Italy. The *30 CFU Qualifying Pathway (ex art. 13)* took place between March and May 2024, totaling 180 hours of teaching activities, consisting of six courses in the pedagogical area and one course specific to the disciplinary field relevant to the future teaching qualification.

Also to respond to the complexity associated with such a large number of trainees, as an institutional choice, an online video conferencing system (OVS) was used in the pathway to manage the synchronous meetings. These meetings included both lectures and workshops.

Leading figures at CEMFI recommended the use of a Padlet board to enhance the teaching-learning experience for both trainers and trainees during synchronous online meetings. The primary motivation behind this choice was that Padlet allows for the sharing of various types of content (text, audio, video, images), as well as polls, links to external apps and resources, while also enabling comments and reactions. Given the large number of trainees, alternative methods of synchronous interaction were deemed impractical. Nonetheless, each trainer retained the autonomy to select specific methods and tools for designing the Padlet boards, conducting activities, and managing communication.

2.2 Main Objectives

The main objective of the study is to propose a model that could be useful to manage large-scale teacher training processes, by analyzing the experience of a telematic Atheneum who works systematically on this theme.

The perspective is to detect strategies that can be effective both in presential and in online professional development pathways.

To do that, some second-level objectives were defined. The study allowed to:

- detect the organizational and instructional choices assumed by an expert Center for Teacher Training for large-scale audience, that is the CEMFI;
- deepen Padlet in its technical and didactical functions, also designing a specific grid to analyze its structuring and openness to active learning;
- collect teachers' feedback about the methodological-didactic strategies used in a fully online training path.

2.3 Phases and Research Tools

The study was articulated in three phases. Data collection and analysis were mainly managed with a qualitative approach (e.g. analysis of pedagogical area team meetings' documents, of comments on Padlet, and of open-reply to questionnaires and forms). Quantitative data were collected through a semi-structured grid used to analyze the Padlets and, indirectly, by taking up the trainees' answers provided to instruments (e.g. questionnaires) administered within specific courses of the Qualifying Pathway. Specific features of QuestionPro and Google Forms were used to manage the quantitative analysis.

Phase 1. In the initial phase, an analysis of the training program offered by the Qualifying Pathway was conducted.

The *eCampus* team of the pedagogical area was involved by CEMFI in many coordination activities aimed at defining an homogeneous methodological-didactic approach, including the recommendation to use Padlet. Everyone was autonomous in adopting additional strategies or tools. The staff meetings were accompanied by the drafting of supporting documentation keeping track of the agreed policy lines.

For this study, the attention was on the choices that teachers declared to be adopted to design them individual Courses.

Data was collected discussing with CEMFI pedagogical staff and analyzing team meetings' documents. It was possible to define an overview about the overall training offer, specifying didactical strategies and tools that would be used in each Course.

Phase 2. In the second phase, further deepening the instructional designing of the trainers, each Padlet produced was analyzed. Being the main tool shared by the team, it seemed strategic to understand its specific use made by teachers.

Padlet boards were analyzed using a semi-structured grid. It was implemented on QuestionPro and used for the six Courses of the pedagogical area.

The grid was structured as follows:

- General information (e.g. Course; Lecturer);
- Methodological and didactical choices (e.g. Presentation of course objectives; Active learning inputs; Feedback);
- Layout and content (e.g. Colored posts; Types of resources; Objective of each resources);
- Interactions (e.g. Internal or external spaces for comments; Type of interactions).

For many sections was provided an open-annotation space.

Data collected allowed better focus on the coherence of the individual choices compared to the overall Qualifying Pathway coordinated by CEMFI. Everyone should have used Padlet as a resource to encourage trainees' engagement, using it as a space to share didactical materials and spaces for discussion.

Analyzed together with the feedback provided by the trainees, the information collected with the grid were also useful to reflect on the effectiveness of some strategies adopted.

Phase 3. In the last phase, the study gathered participants' perspectives on the organizational and instructional strategies used by the trainers. The analysis of their feedback was based on comments posted on the Padlets and on findings that emerged from Questionnaires and Questions Boxes used in some of the six Courses.

Trainees' feedback was gathered from Excel files linked to Google Forms or extracted from Padlet. This data was used to identify the most frequent keywords and thematic trends. In some cases, the volume of feedback provided enabled a direct analysis of all comments made by the trainees.

Reflecting on the feedback provided by the trainees was useful for evaluating the perceived effectiveness of the organizational and instructional strategies adopted by each teacher involved in CEMFI activities.

In developing a large-scale teacher training model, it was possible to identify best practices to enhance and critical issues to address, both for managing synchronous meetings and using Padlet.

Data collected was also important to detect strategies useful to redesign the further editions of the *eCampus 30 CFU Qualifying Pathway*.

3 Results

3.1 The Instructional Choices of the Pedagogical Team

Among the active instructors in the six courses within the pedagogical area, four primarily contributed during the initial planning phase.

In line with the basic guidelines set by CEMFI, the instructor who first introduced the course on *Competency-Based Teaching* was invited to elaborate on the methodological, didactic, and organizational decisions.

In terms of content, in addition to disciplinary elements, the instructor focused on launching workshops for the design of Learning Units. All colleagues from the pedagogical and disciplinary areas would continue this process, enriching it with their respective fields of expertise (e.g., methodologies, assessment, technologies, disciplinary thematic units).

During the initial meeting, the group agreed that interaction would be essential for managing the allocated time and ensuring instructional effectiveness. Given the technical limitations (no audio or video, no Zoom chat), it was decided to establish an external communication channel to supplement Zoom. The group reached a consensus on the potential applications to be utilized (e.g., Mentimeter, Google Forms). Each instructor applied these tools differently, based on their approach to structuring and conducting the synchronous sessions.

Following CEMFI's guideline to use Padlet, the instructor of *Competency-Based Teaching* opted to set up a board for each lesson and to enable comments, allowing participants to read and respond to each other's posts. Small time slots were dedicated for live reading and responses, giving trainees the opportunity to interact directly with the instructor's remarks. This choice was technically feasible by using the "Canvas" layout, which neatly organizes comments. Additional applications were integrated to support collaborative identification of nodes of a concept map (Mentimeter) and to facilitate various individual activities (Google Forms).

While most colleagues agreed with the overall course design, the use of applications, and the task proposals, the two colleagues of *Disciplinary Educational Technologies* and *Innovative Teaching Methodologies*, for example, while understanding the rationale behind the choices made in *Competency-Based Teaching*, opted to create a single Padlet with external question boxes. Their primary concern was to avoid communicative clutter within the Padlet board, given the large number of participants and the potential for off-topic messages. From a technical standpoint, it is also worth noting that enabling the comments feature is ineffective when using the "Wall" layout with sections. The system continuously refreshes, making it impossible to read the comments. The layout was chosen to guide participants step by step through the course timeline, with a new section activated for each training session or phase.

Based on the suggestions from the two instructors, several Padlets incorporated a scheduled posting strategy to avoid information overload.

Another colleague (*Disciplinary assessment elements*) found an effective strategy for the course by combining elements of the two approaches previously mentioned: a Padlet for each lesson to ensure greater organization and ease of access, allowing comments and questions to be posted on a platform external to Padlet to reduce communication clutter.

In the course of *Disciplinary Laboratory Teaching Methodologies*, the instructors adopted a single Padlet for the entire course, creating specialized Padlet boards facilitating task completion. In this instance, participants were invited to contribute as editors.

Overall, the group reached a consensus on adopting an active methodological approach. Despite variations in individual management strategies, all participants sought to maintain a balanced integration of lectures, reflective prompts, exercises, and feedback.

3.2 Courses Analysis: Focus on Padlet

The analysis of the data collected through the grid allowed the identification of key choices adopted, in line with what was previously agreed upon in CEMFI coordination, for instance, the decision to leave a written and/or graphical representation of the course structure and objectives.

All courses have set up easy-to-navigate Padlets. Each Padlet includes organizational information, learning materials to support the lesson (primarily slides) and assigned tasks.

With respect to organization and layout, a quite homogeneous situation emerged in Padlet implementation methods (Table 1).

Table 1. Padlet organization and layout.

Course	Set up		Layout	Sections	Colored posts
	one board for the whole course	*one board per session*			
Competency-based Teaching	–	X	canvas	–	X
Disciplinary Educational Technologies	X	–	wall	X	X
Innovative Teaching Methodologies	X	–	wall	X	X
Disciplinary Assessment Elements	–	X	wall	X	–
Disciplinary Laboratory Teaching Methodologies	X	–	wall	X	X
Design & Management of the Disciplinary Laboratory	X	–	wall	X	–
Inclusive Teaching for the Discipline	X	–	wall	X	X

Regarding the active learning inputs, individual tasks were assigned in all courses ($n = 7$), while group activities were proposed in two of the courses ($N = 2$). Nearly all Padlets included questionnaires/surveys ($n = 6$) and Q&A boxes ($n = 6$), only two adopted the Padlet integrated pools ($N = 2$). The use of audio-visuals has been proposed in most of the courses ($N = 5$). In three courses, specifically, it was proposed to work on the development of a Learning Unit ($N = 3$).

The matrix (Fig. 1) provides an overview of the types of resources and their respective goals within the courses' Padlets. All the courses included simple text posts for conveying information, attachments for tasks, and external links to provide additional content.

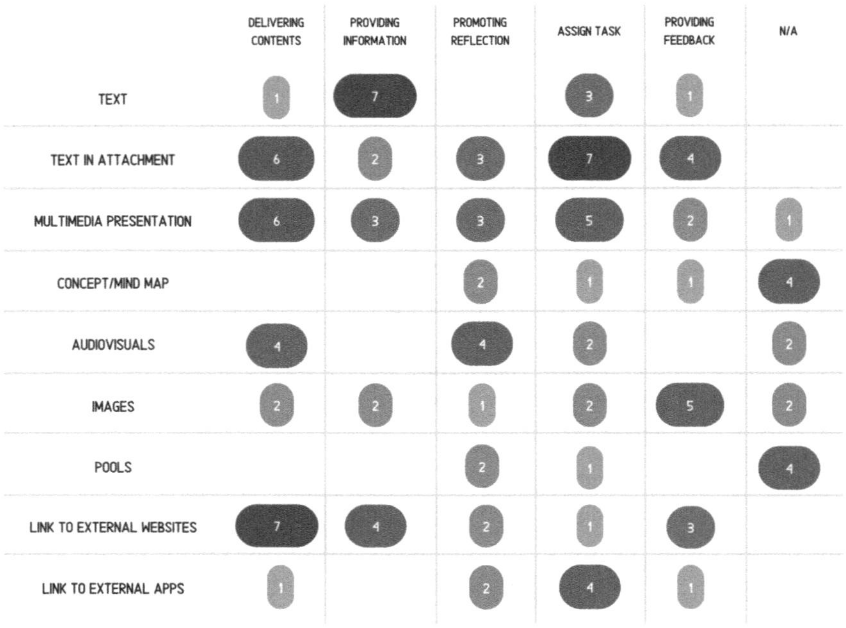

Fig. 1. Type of resources used in Padlet and goals.

It is evident that text in attachment, multimedia presentations, images and links were used in a variety of modality, according to all mapped features.

For example, in the *Disciplinary Educational Technologies* course, images were used to share session's storyboard and color legend of the posts, provide a job aid as a guide for completing a task, and convey a useful infographic to provide feedback on a task.

The CEMFI group has been active in both identifying applications to support synchronous teaching (e.g., Padlet, Google Forms, AnswerGarden, Mentimeter, Digisteps) and facilitating task completion (e.g., Cmap, Algor Education, Meme Generator, Canva, Google Forms).

Trainers expressed a strong interest in helping participants learn how to use these applications, which benefit them as trainees and future educators. In particular, within the *Disciplinary Educational Technologies* course, various applications were employed to familiarize participants with their strengths and limitations.

3.3 Trainees' Feedback

The feedback collected throughout the course was generally positive.

The critical elements reported were primarily related to the organizational challenges of the program itself, rather than the methodological and didactical choices made by the training instructors. In the comments shared by participants, there is clear recognition of the efforts made to manage the large number of trainees and the limitations imposed by the inability to implement synchronous audio-video communication.

For example, some observations found online include: «There was a functional and accessible working environment, despite the high number of participants. This was made possible by the instructors' competence and their ability to convey content and tools clearly and coherently» (id. DET-01, Disciplinary Educational Technologies Course); «The teaching was excellent, given the circumstances. The instructor did her best to engage and create a meaningful learning opportunity for such a large audience» (id. CT-01, Competency-based Teaching Course).

The development of a word cloud (Fig. 2) allowed for the identification of the most frequently used keywords and thematic trends.

Fig. 2. Most frequent keywords and thematic trends.

Participants particularly appreciated the effectiveness of instructors in mediating disciplinary content and providing alternative channels for communication in place of audio-video interaction. From their perspective, this approach fostered a supportive learning environment and enhanced motivation to engage in the proposed workshop activities. In the comments on the Padlet for the Competency-Based Teaching Course, one participant noted: «The interactive, participatory, and collaborative approach of the instructor enabled the development of new and deeper competencies in the educational field» (id. CT-02).

The accessibility of the provided materials and the clarity of the lessons were among the most appreciated aspects, along with the opportunity to leave comments on Padlet. This feature allowed participants to engage with the instructor and interact with fellow participants. As one participant commented: «The possibility to communicate with other participants was beneficial for collaborating on workshop activities and for building relationships that may serve future professional purposes» (id. CT-03).

The methodological choice to implement a Google Form titled "Backpack" (designed to prompt participants to reflect on what they "carry" from the course, whether tangible or intangible, at its conclusion) in the Disciplinary Educational Technologies course (DET) facilitated the collection of participants' reflections on the strengths and weaknesses of the training experience. A particularly significant reflection is the following: «Beyond the interesting content proposed by the instructor and her clear eloquence, observing the teaching choices made has allowed me to learn useful strategies to reuse in the future. These include the importance of structuring a lesson with progressive steps, balancing theory, practice, and feedback, and paying attention to the verbal and paraverbal aspects of communication» (id. DET-02).

In summarizing some reflections shared by participants during the early stages of the training program, it is notable that Padlet was initially perceived as an obstacle. Participants found it challenging to manage multiple devices or navigate between the meeting and the external environment. However, they soon recognized Padlet's role as a supportive and guiding tool for the internal structure of individual courses. One participant remarked: «Thanks to this program and to this course, I had the opportunity to deepen my understanding of how to use Padlet, which I was familiar with but had never tried as a useful tool for designing and managing teaching» (id. DET-03).

The use of a Padlet board connected to each specific lesson was seen as effective for focusing on lesson content. However, it was also considered somewhat dispersive, as a new link was required for each session, which meant participants had to save the old links independently. In contrast, using a single Padlet was viewed as very effective, as it allowed all materials and assignments to be consolidated in one location. To prevent information overload for some participants, a few instructors chose to schedule the publication of posts gradually, in line with their course storyboard.

Many participants found it was beneficial to have materials (e.g., slides) that reviewed content and assignments presented during synchronous sessions. Repetition was highlighted as a supportive element in the fully online format, facilitating access to materials asynchronously or enabling participants to catch up if they missed a synchronous session.

Participants also appreciated the analysis and reflective tasks, which were presented through various media in different courses (e.g., videos, forms for reworking personal experiences, texts, etc.). A particularly well-received approach was employed in the Disciplinary Assessment Elements course (DAE), where one participant stated: «Despite the challenging and technical nature of the topics covered in the course, the instructor was effective in making them relevant by selecting accessible stimuli that could also be reused in the classroom with high school students» (id. DAE-01).

In the Innovative Teaching Methodologies course (ITM), the feedback was also very positive, particularly regarding the systematic use of Mentimeter to integrate presentations with requests for feedback and critical analysis from participants. This feedback was reflected in the responses to one of the prompts provided by the instructor. A total of 4159 participants expressed their level of agreement or disagreement with certain statements (5-point Likert scale) revealing the following results: «The contents were clearly presented» ($\bar{x}$ 4.6); «The course content and activities helped me reflect on teaching practices» ($\bar{x}$ 4.4).

Among the teaching methods used by the *eCampus* teachers feedback emerged as particularly significant. Whether provided by the instructor during the same session or in a subsequent meeting after task submission, feedback was described as «an extremely important tool for individuals training in a specific context, entirely online and with limited channels for interaction» (id. DAE-02). However, across all courses, participants expressed dissatisfaction regarding the fact that feedback was based on a sample analysis of various submitted works; the highlighted need was for individual feedback on their own work.

The study also identified best practices that could be useful for managing large-scale teacher training processes. The training model used for sharing highlights what has proven effective in the methodological and didactical framework employed by CEMFI instructors. Additionally, the ongoing collection of participant feedback helped identify strengths and weaknesses in the program. The insights gathered allowed for a clearer focus on elements that could help reorient the internal organization of courses that had not yet started.

The feedback collected from the questionnaire administered at the end of the Competency-Based Teaching course (CBT) provided an initial overview of participant experiences. A total of 5449 trainees responded, with a majority expressing satisfaction with the course: 35.1% rated it as "very satisfied" and 59.1% as "satisfied". The use of Padlet and the incorporation of various engaging tasks were also highly appreciated, receiving average scores of 4.1 and 3.8, respectively, on a scale from 1 to 5. Even considering the perceived effectiveness of these methodological choices, the training program continued to focus on enhancing these dimensions.

4 Model Proposal for Teachers' Professional Development

4.1 Designing and Teaching for a Large-Scale Audience

The proposed model builds on the findings of the conducted study, focusing on a fully online training program. However, the identified best practices are equally effective in blended learning contexts.

Training large groups requires special attention from those responsible for managing the educational infrastructure, as well as designing and overseeing the teaching process. For very large groups, predominantly or entirely online pathways can be advantageous, optimizing resources and facilitating participation for trainees regardless of their geographic location. For a fully online program to be effective, it must ensure that trainees can still interact with instructors and peers and have access to support throughout the course. If face-to-face sessions are feasible, they should offer opportunities for shared reflection and discussion, extending beyond the presentation of disciplinary topics.

When organizing training for a large-scale audience, educators must consider the group's internal diversity, including entry profiles, dispositions, prior knowledge, expectations, and learning needs, which are likely to be varied. Two key factors to address are accessibility (of the program, study materials, tasks, etc.) and flexibility, including the ability to adjust the course in response to challenges encountered during the program, such as learning difficulties or participant feedback.

Just as in small group or face-to-face training, the instructor's approach remains essential: it should be open, flexible, and supportive. In a fully online context, providing written responses to frequently asked questions (FAQs) that are easily accessible to participants can be highly beneficial. Despite having these support materials in place, it is crucial to remain available to address recurring questions, especially when working with large groups.

In large-scale training, it can be challenging to have a detailed understanding of each participant's profile in advance. Therefore, it's important to design a gradual progression through the study materials and laboratory activities, with increasing complexity over time.

The following guidelines can be effective in addressing the challenges mentioned above:

1. In organizational terms, it's important to plan the use of user-friendly tools and applications and to prepare study materials in formats that are easily transferable. In a fully online program, even less experienced participants should be able to fully engage with the educational experience;
2. Regarding the content, the focus should be on the key topics of the discipline without assuming prior knowledge. It is essential to provide basic definitions, references to relevant authors or regulations, and links to external resources for further exploration, along with practical examples;
3. From a session management perspective, the structure and objectives of both the overall course and individual lessons should be clearly outlined from the outset. A clear, coherent, and linear Course Plan and Lesson Plan are valuable tools for keeping participants oriented, regardless of the logistical format of the training program;
4. On the communication front, strategies and channels should be established to ensure continuous communication. Even when live audio-video interactions are limited due to technical constraints, every participant must be able to share questions or observations, which should receive timely responses from the instructor and, when possible, be discussed with the group.

With the aim of promoting meaningful learning experiences, even in online and large-scale training contexts, it's essential to design and manage lessons in a way that encourages the active participation of trainees. Among the engaging tasks that can be proposed in online training, and for which it is feasible to manage the instructional side and provide feedback, are: guided analysis of textual and multimedia resources; prompts to express personal viewpoints on a given topic or critically reflect on related personal experiences; participation in brainstorming sessions; the creation of concept maps; the design and development of educational or assessment materials and tools; more generally, activities that require learners to actively engage in re-elaborative, critical, or creative processes.

The goal of such tasks should not be limited to engaging trainees in key dimensions relevant for those working in education and training, but also to introduce—following a modeling approach—content, strategies, and tools that can be leveraged in their professional practice. Furthermore, the feedback provided should serve a formative function and aim to enhance trainees' motivation to continue learning about the topics under discussion, encouraging further study and personal research.

The ability of the trainers must also be to prevent and counteract critical issues that may be related to infrastructural and organizational elements. For example, in the study conducted there was the need to manage a large lecture schedule totally online and without the possibility to activate the audio-video of trainees. In a similar scenario, an effective lesson should have a clear internal articulation, alternating face-to-face moments and moments of activation, discussion and feedback.

Table 2 presents an example of a Lesson Plan designed for a 5-hour academic session. Timing is approximate and varies based on the type of content and tasks planned; what is essential is that the instructor maintains a balanced approach among engaging activities, interactive sessions, and direct teaching, while also considering observations made during the lesson or feedback from participants. In the provided example (Table 2), the instructor reviews trainees' outputs during the break, enabling immediate feedback to be given afterward; for more complex tasks, however, this review can be deferred, with feedback provided in the following session.

Table 2. Example of Lesson Plan (lecture of academic hours).

Timing	Activities
30 min	Introduction to the Course (in the first lesson) *or* Feedback on previous tasks or topics focused
60 min	Focus on disciplinary themes; Conceptual framework
30 min	Presentation of Task 1, timing and guidelines for the replies
15 min	Pause
45 min	Feedback on Task 1; Continuation on disciplinary themes
30 min	Presentation of Task 2, timing and guidelines for the replies
15 min	Feedback on Task 2; Follow-up and lecture closing

Feedback is a strategic tool for sustaining learners' attention and engagement, particularly in training contexts where they may experience isolation and a lack of direct interaction with instructors and peers. To ensure effective communication, feedback should be provided not only in written form but also through supplementary channels for interaction and resource sharing. Whenever possible, it is recommended to create "templates of ideal responses" for submitted tasks, along with emphasizing the strengths and areas for improvement in the submitted work during synchronous sessions; this approach facilitates self-assessment.

To make feedback sustainable for the instructor, especially with large groups, it is advisable to prepare these supporting materials (e.g., "template responses") during the course design phase. The feedback provided during class should be formulated based on sample analyses that highlight common errors and exemplary work.

4.2 Padlet as an Integrative Resource

In a fully or predominantly online large-scale training scenario, Padlet has proven to be an effective teaching support application.

The study's analysis highlights various ways in which Padlet can be utilized by instructors. A consistent quality element—regardless of the approach taken—is the creation of an accessible and user-friendly environment, capable of guiding trainees in their learning and self-study even outside of synchronous class sessions.

To achieve this, careful content management design is essential:

- facilitating access to information by organizing it into sections and associating specific objectives with different post colors (e.g., informing, presenting disciplinary content, or summarizing workshop tasks);
- mitigating information overload by scheduling post publications to ensure participants access content according to the instructor's timeline, which should align with the pace of the lesson and the overall program;
- finally, enabling independent access to course materials by keeping the Padlet environment and resources available even after the official conclusion of the training program.

When used strategically, Padlet can serve as an effective communication resource, particularly in training courses where the large number of trainees makes synchronous audio-video interactions impractical. This can be achieved by allowing trainees to leave comments or by incorporating links to external tools if the commenting function is disabled (e.g., Google Forms with a "Question Box" feature).

There are currently two critical issues related to Padlet comments that warrant attention. First, the system does not support partial activation of the commenting function; participants can either comment on all posts or none at all. Second, the chosen board layout affects the visual accessibility of comments. For example, in the "Canvas" layout, comments are grouped together, maintaining the overall appearance of the Padlet as new comments are added. Conversely, the "Wall" layout expands the corresponding post's box with each new comment, which can reduce the platform's graphical and communicative effectiveness and increase the risk of system crashes.

The choice of the preferred mode ultimately rests with the instructors, depending on their pedagogical vision for structuring the lesson:

- Activating the comments function can encourage reciprocal reading and engagement among participants. However, this approach also requires the instructor to allocate time systematically to read and reply to comments. Moreover, for the reasons previously discussed, if comments are enabled, it is advisable to avoid certain layouts available on Padlet;
- Implementing an external space for comment storage facilitates direct communication between trainees and the instructor, free from layout constraints or potential disorganization within the shared environment. However, this method limits opportunities for meaningful interaction among participants unless the instructor provides alternative channels for engagement.

Figure 3 illustrates two examples of Padlet configurations: the first one is a Padlet board (one for each lesson) that use the Canvas layout with active comments for each post; the

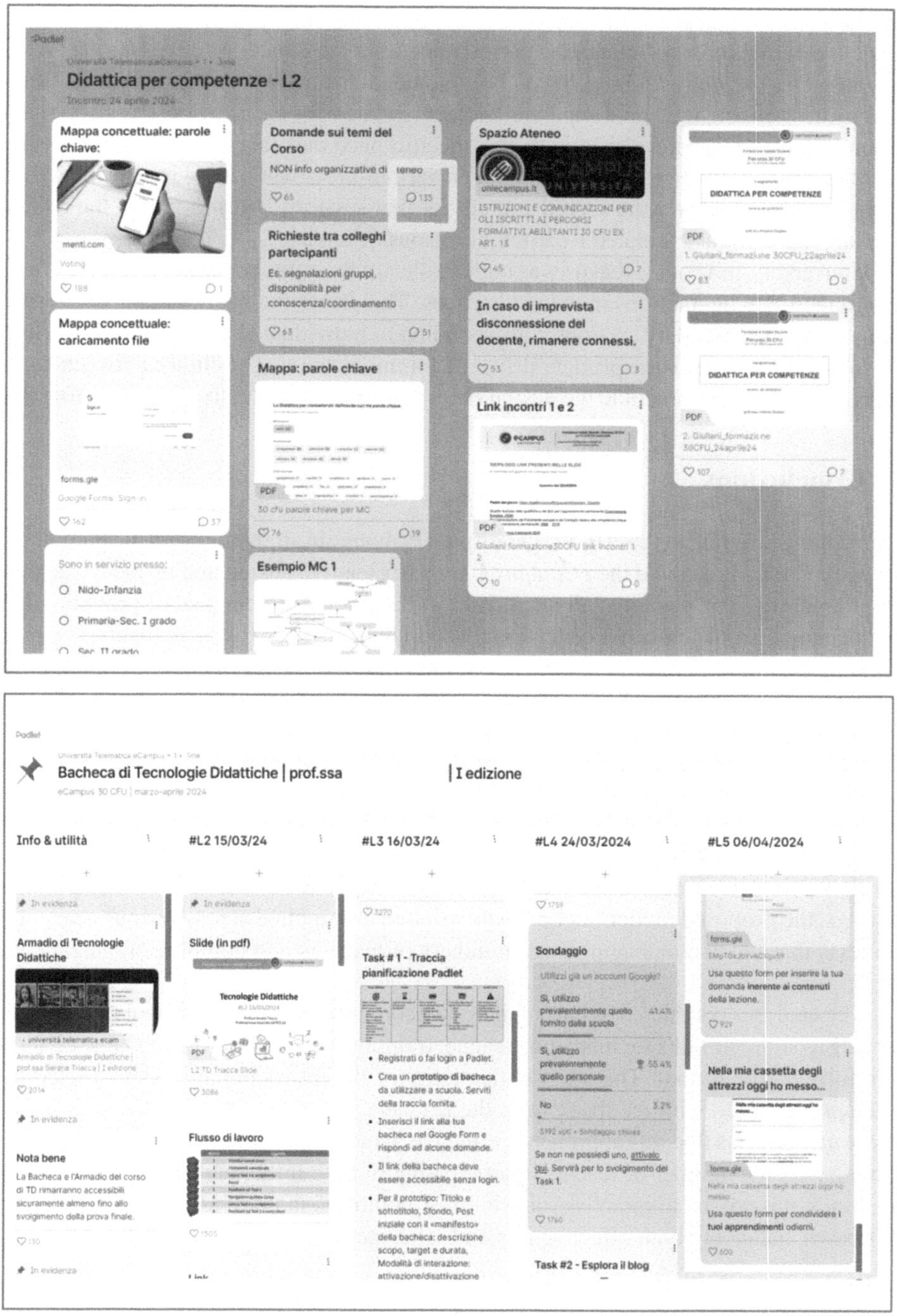

Fig. 3. Examples of Padlet configuration.

second one is a Padlet board (one for the entire course) that use the Wall layout, with links to external tools for managing communication.

Based on the study findings, it can be concluded that activating the comments function is most effective when a separate Padlet is created for each lesson. This approach ensures that each board aligns with the specific pace and themes of a given lesson, enabling trainees to interact and comment on various posts while allowing the instructor to maintain control over the shared content for that session. This minimizes the risk of overlapping comments related to different lessons or topics.

Conversely, in a course that uses a single Padlet for the entire program, it is more effective to facilitate interactions in external spaces. This keeps the board organized—especially when structured by sections corresponding to individual lessons—while enabling the instructor to remain the primary driver of communication. The choice between these approaches does not preclude the design of an engaging and effective training program.

5 Conclusions

The training program of the 30 CFU Qualifying Pathway, in alignment with the guidelines set by the DPCM, enabled the *eCampus University* team to design and manage teaching with flexibility. The pedagogical team, led by CEMFI, shared the goal of providing the most engaging and activating educational experience possible for participants.

Despite the challenge of addressing a large number of teachers and operating in a fully online environment where audio-video interaction was not feasible, CEMFI's decision to use a shared Padlet environment proved effective. This tool allowed trainers to organize teaching materials and workshop outputs in an accessible manner, even with varied approaches to setting up the environment. Participants provided positive feedback regarding the perceived effectiveness of the strategies, particularly in courses that integrated workshops and assignments alongside the core content delivery.

By relying on strategies and integrative tools adaptable to both in-person and online settings, the proposed model can be flexibly shared and applied across various academic contexts that involve managing large numbers of teachers and complex organizational processes.

The analyses conducted as part of the study confirmed the importance of universities serving as strategic hubs for managing teacher training, even when targeting large cohorts in a fully online format. The internal flexibility of the instructional model adopted by *eCampus*, coupled with feedback from the teachers who participated in the *Qualifying Pathway*, suggests that this approach is effective in defining universities' roles in teacher training. As the number of teachers participating in both initial and in-service training increases, it is crucial to establish robust infrastructures to manage teaching and learning processes, balancing both effectiveness and efficiency.

Authors' Contributions This article has been developed jointly by the authors. Arianna Giuliani wrote 'Methodology' (Sect. 2) and 'Model Proposal for Teachers' Professional Development' (Sect. 4); Elisa Mazzella wrote 'Introduction' (Sect. 1); Serena Triacca wrote 'Results' (Sect. 3) and 'Conclusions' (Sect. 5).

References

1. Earley, P., Bubb, S.: Leading & Managing Continuing Professional Development: Developing People, Developing Schools. SAGE, London (2007)
2. Magnoler, P., Notti, A.M., Perla, L. (eds.): La professionalità degli insegnanti. La ricerca e le pratiche. Pensa Multimedia, Lecce (2017)
3. Aglieri, M.: La formazione degli insegnanti e con gli insegnanti. Contesti, scenari, percorsi, messaggi. Pensa MultiMedia, Lecce (2020)
4. Baldacci, M., Riva, M.G., Nigris, E. (eds.): Idee per la formazione degli insegnanti. Franco Angeli, Milano (2020)
5. Fiorucci, M., Zizioli, E. (eds.): La formazione degli insegnanti: problemi, prospettive e proposte per una scuola di qualità aperta a tutti e a tutte. Pensa Multimedia, Lecce (2022)
6. Depaepe, M.: A professionally relevant history of education for teachers: does it exist? Reply to Jurgen Herbst's State of the Art Article. Paedagog. Hist. **37**, 631–640 (2001). https://doi.org/10.1080/0030923010370305
7. Becchi, E., Ferrari, M.: Professioni, professionisti, professionalizzare: storie di formazione. In: Becchi, E., Ferrari, M. (eds.) Formare alle professioni. Sacerdoti, principi, educatori, pp. 7–27. FrancoAngeli, Milano (2009)
8. Morandi, M.: La fucina dei professori. Storia della formazione docente in Italia dal Risorgimento a oggi. Scholé, Brescia (2021)
9. Shulman, L.S.: Those who understand: knowledge growth in teaching. Educ. Res. **15**, 4–14 (1986). https://doi.org/10.3102/0013189X015002004
10. Shulman, L.S.: Knowledge and teaching: foundations of the new reform. Harv. Educ. Rev. **57**(1), 1–22 (1987). https://doi.org/10.17763/haer.57.1.j463w79r56455411
11. Schön, D.: Formare il professionista riflessivo. Per una nuova prospettiva della formazione e dell'apprendimento nelle professioni. Franco Angeli, Milano (2006)
12. Campbell, E.: The Ethical Teacher. Open University Press, Maidenhead (2003)
13. Valica, R. T., Rohn, T.: Development of the professional competence in the ethics teachers. Procedia. Soc. Behav. Sci. **106**, 865–872 (2013). https://doi.org/10.1016/j.sbspro.2013.12.099
14. Déirdre, M.S.: A dialogic construction of ethical standards for the teaching profession. Issue Teach Educ. **22**(1), 49–62 (2013)
15. Damiano, E.: L'insegnante etico. Saggio sull'insegnamento come dimensione morale. Cittadella, Assisi (2007)
16. Perla, L. (ed.): Valutare per valorizzare. La documentazione per il miglioramento di scuola, insegnanti studenti. Morcelliana, Brescia (2019)
17. Perla, L.: Il modello DidaSCo per lo sviluppo professionale dell'insegnante in servizio. In: Tempesta, I. (ed.) Imparare a insegnare. Formazione e didattica per la scuola, pp. 89–97. Università del Salento, Lecce (2020)
18. Messina, L., Zambelli, F.: Formazione degli insegnanti e ricerca didattica universitaria. In: Biasin, C. (ed.) La responsabilità sociale dell'Università per le professioni, pp. 207–230. Pensa Multimedia, Lecce (2008)
19. Magnoler, P., Sorzio, P.: Didattica e competenze. Pratiche per una nuova alleanza tra ricercatori e insegnanti. EUM, Macerata (2012)
20. Sarmiento-Márquez, E.M., Pishtari, G., Prieto, L.P., Poom-Valickis, K.: The evaluation of school-university partnerships that improve teaching and learning practices: a systematic review. Educ. Res. Rev. **39**, 100509 (2023). https://doi.org/10.1016/j.edurev.2023.100509
21. Rivoltella, P.C., Rossi, P.G. (eds.): L'agire didattico. Manuale per l'insegnante. Scholé, Brescia (2017)
22. Perla, L., Martini, B. (eds.): Professione insegnante. Idee e modelli di formazione. Franco Angeli, Milano (2020)
23. Nigris, E.: Didattica generale. Edizioni Angelo Guerini e Associati, Milano (2020)

AI Act: A Quanti-qualitative Analysis

Delio De Martino[1(✉)], Marilena di Padova[2], Maria Clara Dicataldo[2], and Anna Dipace[1]

[1] Università Telematica Pegaso, Naples, Italy
{delio.demartino,anna.dipace}@unipegaso.it
[2] Università di Foggia, Foggia, Italy
{marilena.dipadova,mariaclara.dicataldo}@unifg.it

Abstract. In a context where the AI is changing the word of education, of work and of global and social powers, the Europe with the recent AI Act is trying to mark the boundaries of the use of a such disruptive and divisive technology.

This quantitative and qualitative analysis from a specific pedagogical point of view tries to verify if and how the education issues have been considered.

The first results show that educational issues are poor present in the text and that, despite an explicit appeal to the "anthropocentric perspective", real innovative AI educational paradigms are not yet implemented. The main focus remains the risk-benefit worry.

But in the future the framework of the AI Act could lead to a real innovation in the methodology and in the practices of educational use of AI.

Keywords: AI · Act · quantitative-qualitative analysis

1 The AI Act in the Global Scenario

The Artificial Intelligence is right now the most divisive technology the social and academic world is dealing with, polarizing the public opinion between apocalyptic and integrated ones. This distinction, that recalls the Italian title of the famous Umberto Eco's book "Apocalittici e integrati" [1], describes the two main attitudes toward digital technologies and describes the tendency to demonize new technologies and its risks.

In fact when a new disruptive technology is introduced in the global scenario the reactions are usually as intense as the capacity of the technology to change the socio-economic rules and the social balance of powers.

The need of a legal regulation has been a consequence of a divisive vision of this technology that quickly caught the social and educational attention in the place of other technologies that previously seemed about to emerge (as Augmented reality, Metaverse, etc.).

This article has been developed jointly. Delio De Martino wrote paragraph 3, Marilena di Padova paragraph 2, 2.2, Maria Clara Dicataldo paragraph 2, 2.1, Anna Dipace paragraphs 1 and 4.

P. Ardimento et al. (Eds.): HELMeTO 2024, CCIS 2468, pp. 186–198, 2025.
https://doi.org/10.1007/978-3-031-93999-0_12

In the case of Artificial Intelligence, the adoption and use are being so quick and unruly that the entire world just now is looking for a new legal and social frame that could trace the boundaries of a social and educational acceptable use of this technology.

The need of new rules is perceived more and more urgent because, as a look at the history of Artificial intelligence makes clear [2], the rise of AI in language and image recognition and production is evolving faster every year.

A milestone in this process has been the launch of the free version of ChatGPT in 2022 that has shown that the AI would change the world and that new rules were required. Also, in the specific field of education the need of a regulamentation has come out soon to mitigate the disruptive effects by "developing clear policies and guidelines" [3, p. 6159].

In 2022, when Open AI globally launched ChatGPT, the first AI chatbot, forefather of a large number of generative AI tools, the entire world expressed enthusiasm for the new capabilities but at the same time the society started to express its concerns about it [4]. The potential fearful consequences of this new special medium, accused of putting human life at risk, generated new concerns.

In this context some recent assertions of the multimillionaire businessman Elon Musk are paradigmatic of the global mood about the menace of the AI. Indeed, he warned about the catastrophic danger of AI and his potential of civilization destruction [5]. In the same way, many researchers have expressed worries about the extinction of humans because of AI [6]. The fear of the transgression of the famous ethic Asimov laws (and above all the first one "A robot may not injure a human being" [7]) awakened the most ancestral fears and the deepest technophobia.

In Italy the worries about this technology have been so strong that the measure has been adopted to contrast the most immediate law-infraction of the new technologies.

Indeed, Italian Data Protection Authority decided to temporarily block it on March 30th 2023. The reasons for this stop were two. The first one is "processing data in breach of data law". The second reason is more specifically related to the pedagogical field and to the concerns about the use of technology by children and fragile people. Indeed the authority "emphasizes in its order that the lack of whatever age verification mechanism exposes children to receiving responses that are absolutely inappropriate to their age and awareness, even though the service is allegedly addressed to users aged above 13 according to OpenAI's terms of service" [8].

This block has probably been in Europe the most evident sign of an urgent need for a new law that could precise how to use this technology in an appropriate way also from the pedagogical point of view.

Moreover, even from a legal perspective, a new technology often forces the legislator to change the legislation under social pressure. It is actually also a semiotic question because the previous laws often suddenly appear unable to interpret the new reality. That's because ancient law loses the referent to the current social context where the technology has modified the modus operandi.

In Europe the current arrival point of this social process, animated by fears but also by hopes of a bright future, is the AI European Act, approved on March 13th 2024 and entered into force on August first 2024 [9, 10].

It is a large text many pages long, where the general social new AI needs to converge to be regulated. The AI Act is globally a wide net aimed to circumscribe an enormous social context and to give the paths to use a continuously updated technology [11]. So it is a law that tries to set limits and offers rules of conduct for the future use and tries to reassure all the implicated stakeholders [12, 13].

From a pedagogical perspective nowadays it is very important to analyze this text, also from a different perspective in a transdisciplinary approach, to understand if and how the European commission proves to be able to focus on the most important education-related issues. Indeed, the pedagogical point of view is generally not sufficiently deep in a global context in which economical and working values are on the top of the world political agenda. The doubt emerges that in the AI act text in some way pedagogical and educational issues could be considered less crucial than economical and ones.

The present study intends to define, through a textual analysis, the presence, relevance and frequency of the Education theme in the AI European Act.

2 The Quantitative Analysis

The analysis proposed in this paper is a multiperspective textual analysis that has the objective to offer a first interpretation of the law based on a quantitative and qualitative analysis from a pedagogical point of view. The final aim is to identify pros and cons of this law in the specific field of education.

The first part of the analysis is a quantitative analysis. It aims to individuate the pedagogical lexicon in the global text of the law. The aim is to verify which are the specific pedagogical words the legislator has chosen, if they are sufficient to describe and offer guidance to the huge number of European citizens and to the different European states. The AI law is not specifically related to the educational legislation, but it is important to understand how much and how the legislator has taken into account the educational issues.

For the textual analysis has been used the Voyant tool (Fig. 1), a web-based text reading and analysis environment designed to facilitate reading and interpretive practices for digital humanities students and scholars as well as for the general public.

In order to put emphasis on the relevance of the theme of education in the discussed document, its word frequency and relevance has been compared to that of the theme of economy. For both themes, which is Education and Economy, have been selected keywords and reported their count and word frequency found in the document.

2.1 Economy Themes

The document has been thoughtfully read through first, and then according to a first analysis and screening the related keywords for the textual analysis have been defined in order to cover all the possible parts of interest of the text in relation to the research objective. The text has been read and analysed by two independent reviewers and then the keywords decided accordingly based on the reviewers' degree of agreement on the chosen terms and a peer debriefing process.

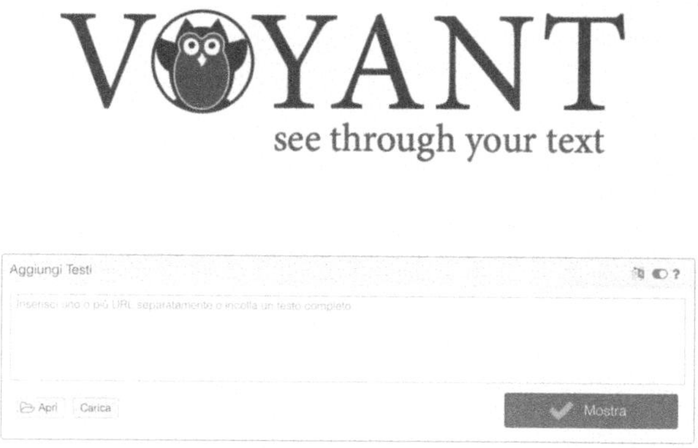

Fig. 1. Voyant tool: homepage of the web-tool (from https://voyant-tools.org).

It has been performed a word frequency analysis first and then a contextual analysis aimed at framing the specific contextual meaning of the keywords in the text.

Table 1 reports the count of the keywords found in the text regarding the analysis of the theme of Economy, while Fig. 2 represents the frequency of the keywords over the document segments.

Table 1. Results for the Economy theme: the keywords.

Keywords	Count
Economic*	15
Economy	3
Business*	22
Enterprise*	10
Firm*	5
Compan*	4
Management*	99

While carrying out the contextual analysis, it has been possible to define the main context of occurrence of the given keywords.

As far as the "Economic*" word is concerned, the most recurrent context is that referred to: the economic and financial risks, harms and security in relation to the use of AI systems; the economic situation and its relation to the vulnerability of a person or specific group of persons in terms of status, authority, knowledge, age and disability; the inclusion for persons with disabilities and to tackle socio-economic inequalities; the use of AI systems intended to be used as safety components in the management and operation of critical digital infrastructure; the use of AI systems for economic benefits; the procedural rights of economic operators of the general-purpose AI model.

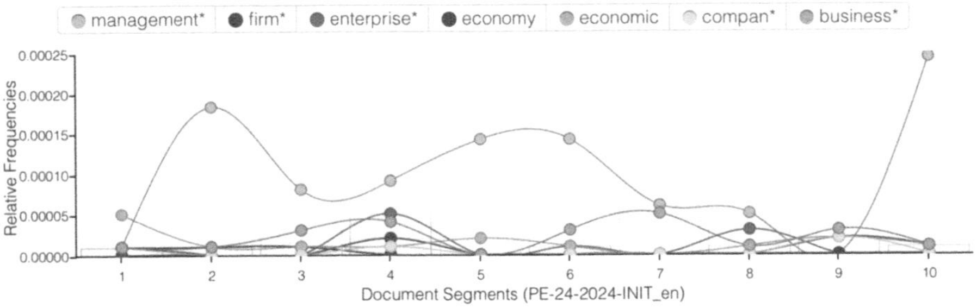

Fig. 2. Word frequency in the text for Economic themes.

The use of the word "Economy" mainly refers to: the large variety of sectors of the economy in which AI systems can be easily deployed; the deployment of AI systems in education is important to promote high-quality digital education and training and to allow all learners and teachers to take an active part in the economy, society, and in democratic processes; the growth opportunities for the Union Economy.

The word "Business*" is used with regards to: data protection of confidential business information; innovative business models embedding AI technologies; systematic risk for the designation of a general purpose AI model such as number of business and end users; development of AI systems paying attention to the themes of vulnerability and inclusion through the involvement of relevant stakeholders such as business organizations; facilitation of data sharing between businesses and with government in the public interest; promotion of business models embedding AI technologies.

The keyword "Enterprise*" mainly refers to the application of the present regulation to small-medium enterprises (SMEs) and support for their innovation; while the keyword "Compan*" and "Firm*" mainly refers to the application of the present regulation to companies or firms.

Finally, the word "Management*" is the most recurrent one and it makes reference to the application of the regulation in respect to: infrastructure and digital management; workers management; border control management; risk-management systems/measures/framework/procedures/processes/practices/policies/framework/rules; implementation of appropriate data governance and management practices; sound quality management system; quality management system; data management.

2.2 Educational Themes

The second reviewer dealt with the identification and analysis of keywords more specific to the educational context. Table 2 reports the count of the keywords found in the text regarding the analysis of the theme of Education, while Fig. 3 represents the frequency of the keywords over the document segments.

The word Education* appears in the text as a potentially transformative factor for the accessibility of education, respecting fundamental rights, and to indicate the potential benefits of AI in education and training for the personalisation of the educational activities of individuals and organizations. There is concern about the ethical principles and

Table 2. Results for the Education theme: the keywords.

Keywords	Count
Education*	22
Training*	99
Universit*	0
School*	0
"Higher education"	0

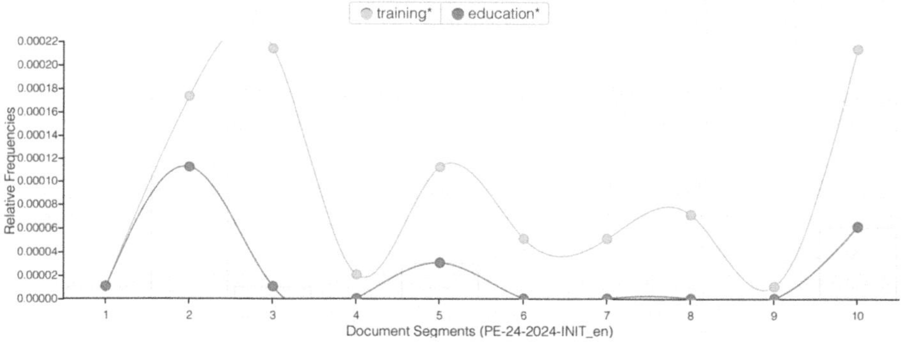

Fig. 3. Word frequency in the text for Education themes.

values to be respected in order to integrate such technology in educational contexts, with particular attention to the rights of children in the digital environment. Finally, concern is highlighted towards the identification of emotions in educational and work contexts, a use considered intrusive and potentially harmful, if not for medical and safety purposes.

The term Training* occurs 99 times in the document and is mainly used in training-related contexts, often in connection with the use and development of AI systems. There is mention of training of AI systems, ethical and legal implications related to the use of data for training systems, and test environments.

AI is also mentioned as a tool to improve human training, e.g. through advanced simulations or customisation of learning paths. A more training-related use relates to the demand for specific training for operators and users of AI systems, to mitigate possible risks, characterized by continuous updating in response to technological and regulatory changes, with due differences between the public and private sectors. Training is also mentioned on compliance with regulations on the use of AI, fundamental rights and the importance of ethics in the use of AI, and on improving the decision-making capabilities of individuals and organizations.

The words Universit*, School*, Higher education*, are not present in the text. This is also a significant fact.

Although the topic of education has been covered, the main focus of the paper is on the economic and social aspects of society in change, demonstrating an increased interest in the impact that Artificial Intelligence (AI) can have on industry, the market and technological innovation. Terms related to the field of education and training are often subordinated to the economic and social applications of the use of AI. The role of education is treated marginally, as an area in which AI can be applied or needs to be regulated, rather than as a tool for social transformation. The occurrence of the term Training* also suggests that training is understood primarily as technical training, both of human operators and of the algorithms themselves. The document frequently uses expressions of concern about the consequences of misuse of AI, particularly in high-risk areas such as education and work, suggesting that AI is experienced more as a tool to be monitored and contained, rather than a catalyst for positive and inclusive transformation.

3 The Qualitative Analysis

It is important to analyze the relation between these words and the text context where they are used and the general context of the law, where other semantic categories appear more in depth.

The qualitative analysis helps to focus on how these words are used. In a crucial turning point of the history of educational technologies, it is important that a European law could offer innovative perspectives on the methodologically correct use of AI in learning environments. If on one hand the law has the merit to underline some critical points (as first of all the risks in the generative AI use), on the other hand it should mark the way of educational-profitable practices.

The cultural heritage of a not very fresh perspective is unable to offer an innovative guidance to enhance learning in the big context of the global European educational field.

Europe has been traditionally more cautious in the adoption and regulation of new technologies, whit a special preoccupation for the risks of new devices and media. The most paradigmatic example is related to the television medium. While in Usa the commercial channels and his economic revenues since the early history of television were the most important focus, in Europe the model was more pedagogical and centered on the public channels. Scared by the risks of television the European nations reserved to the state the right of tv transmissions and used tv as the technology for the cultural promotion of the population avoiding the risk of the new medium. Umberto Eco [14], called this type of television "paleotelevision" opposed to the "neotelevision".

The imprint of the historic sensibility to the technology risks seems to have an impact on the AI Act. Indeed, the text of the AI Act presents a clear risk based approach (as clarified also in the European documents [15] and [16]). The AI Act's main purpose is to avoid the risk of AI. The AI presents a regulatory frame with 4 levels of risks.

So the main aim is the classification of a scale of risks: Unacceptable Risk, High Risk, Limited Risk (AI system with specific transparency obligation), Minimal Risk (Fig. 4).

In the pedagogical related area at the top of the pyramid we find that some use related to education are forbidden. In the 46 *whereas* we read:

Considering the imbalance of power in the context of work or education, combined with the intrusive nature of these systems, such systems could lead to detrimental or unfavorable treatment of certain natural persons or whole groups thereof. Therefore, the

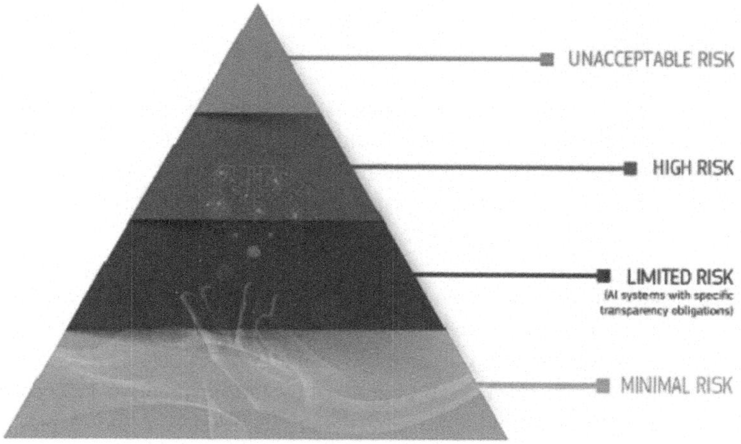

Fig. 4. The Regulatory Framework: the pyramid of 4 levels of risk for AI systems. From [15].

placing on the market, the putting into service, or the use of AI systems intended to be used to detect the emotional state of individuals in situations related to the workplace and education should be prohibited.

So the context of education as a space where AI can determine an unfavorable treatment is seen as the most pedagogic AI related risk. And it is recalled and in particular the capability of detecting the emotional state.

If we go down to the second category, high-risk, we meet another mention of the educational world. The Act indeed underlines the high risk that AI in educational or vocational training could determine the access to education and professional course of someone's life (e.g. scoring of exams). This is put in an important place just after "the critical infrastructures (e.g. transport), that could put the life and health of citizens at risk". These high-risk AI systems have to respect some strict obligation to be put in the market in order to minimize risk (as adequate risk assessment and mitigation systems).

Beyond the mention of education in the first to levels of the pyramid of risks, the Act mentions "education" in a more proactive perspective. It is an important point where the merit of mentioning the crucial role of literacy in the education world emerges.

The Act underlines the importance of AI literacy for a quality education in the future and for the acquisition of the fundamental competencies in the educational and work context [17].

It is clarified yet in the *whereas* (56). Here (56) we can read:

> The deployment of AI systems in education is important to promote high-quality digital education and training and to allow all learners and teachers to acquire and share the necessary digital skills and competences, including media literacy, and critical thinking, to take an active part in the economy, society, and in democratic processes.

In this mention of literacy, we could read an indirect reference to the possibility to build new ways and methodologies for the use of the AI also in learning environments.

But actually, the AI Act doesn't go into detail and immediately after in the same whereas the focus comes back to the risk of a discriminative use of AI in education:

> When improperly designed and used, such systems may be particularly intrusive and may violate the right to education and training as well as the right not to be discriminated against and perpetuate historical patterns of discrimination, for example against women, certain age groups, persons with disabilities, or persons of certain racial or ethnic origins or sexual orientation.

In a global outlook the education perspective is not very present and above all it looks poor in shaping new and innovative pedagogical frameworks for the use of the AI in the educational environment to enhance the education.

The Act presents itself more as a negative law than a positive law, focusing on what can't be done and on forbidden uses. This advice related to the forbidden use in the educational field doesn't present a more specific way to take the advantage of the technology.

The theory of the risks-benefits balance, one of the most ancient and less innovative (cfr [18]), reappears here but in concomitance with a lack of a real proposal for new ways of AI use.

In a global way it appears little able to go beyond a general warning about the AI related. The lack of this focus is impressive because the AI Act contains, in a crucial position, that is in the first pages, an explicit appeal to an "anthropocentric" approach for the use of AI. So the AI Act presents itself as the first AI Act with a anthropocentric approach. Just this "anthropocentric" perspective could have been the starting point to suggest new perspectives also in the pedagogical field.

The adjective "anthropocentric" is inserted in the Italian version and appears more meaningful to express the deep cultural meaning of the Act. In the English version the used expression is "Human centric" while in the Italian version the use of the term "anthropocentric" is more synthetic and semantically pregnant.

The word is composed by "anthropos" (man) and "centric" (centric) and indicates a path to the use of technology guided by human and social development considered primary respect to technological and economic development.

The first time the term appears in the incipit of the AI Act in a very visible place, in the first *whereas* of AI Act where the aims of the Act are declared:

> to promote the uptake of human centric and trustworthy artificial intelligence (AI) while ensuring a high level of protection of health, safety, fundamental rights as enshrined in the Charter of Fundamental Rights of the European Union (the 'Charter'), including democracy, the rule of law and environmental protection, to protect against the harmful effects of AI systems in the Union, and to support innovation.

The same concept is reiterated in a following *whereas* (6) where it is written that "AI should be a human-centric technology" and immediately afterward the text explains the meaning for this sentence, that is "It should serve as a tool for people", with the ultimate aim of increasing human well-being. Also the first article reiterate this same concept.

The expression "human centric" (or the Italian adjective "anthropocentric") is crucial in the AI Act perspective because it shows a very different axiology. The European legal axiology ("axios", "value", and "logos") in fact is based on sustainability from the individual, human and social point of view.

Unfortunately, the "anthropocentric" explicit perspective of the Act is not followed by an explicit focus on pedagogy. It is quite surprising because one of the main disciplines of humanistic and social area is just pedagogy. In this sense is almost overwhelming the absence in the entire text of the word "pedagogy". At the same time also terms as "school" or "university" are absent as many other terms linked to the semantic fields related to the science of education.

Despite a general lack of attention of Act the AI has an impact also in the educational technology sector [19].

This is just the opposite of the USA legal approach, that has been defined "business-centric" because it is more related to industrial and economic development [20]. However, the preoccupation to limit the risk is the same.

The use is even more important in a framework of a larger comparison between the European AI Act and the other worldwide legislations, above all the laws of the USA, the country where the most impactful generative AI comes from.

The qualitative analysis allows a comparison between the European AI Act and the other worldwide legislations, as the USA law. While the *laissez faire* USA approach is more focused on technological and economic development [20], the AI Act is more human-centered and aimed at the protection of citizens' human rights.

So, in the USA the classic *lassez faire* law tendency has led to more flexibility in the use of artificial intelligence with less limits or constrictions. While in Europe the AI Act appears more detailed, in USA the law is more complex: just now there are different proposals to trace a roadmap to the use of AI but a unique AI Act doesn't exist. In any case the main idea is that from an economic point of view it is preferable to let the AI development free to improve the AI industry. As a wave this development is having a huge impact all over the world. Another AI legal global stakeholder, capable of changing the worldwide equilibrium also in the pedagogical area, will be China [21]. This growing worldwide AI stakeholder has an in progress legislation, based on a high politic control, but it appears vague because of a lack of political transparency.

In opposition to other legal approaches, Europe wants to play an important role in managing the power of AI in a global perspective. Just in last years we've seen that this approach has been able to globally influence also the USA industry. The most recent and visible action in the technological field oriented to sustainability is the imposition of Usb-c port of all devices in order to avoid e-waste in a global vision [22].

The AI Act legal comparison is useful in a historical moment where Europe seems to want to play a role in the general technology context projecting its highest profile values (as democracy, openness, versatility, inclusiveness, attention to the social issues, guarantees for the minorities, etc.).

4 Preliminary Conclusions

As a general conclusion, this qualitative and quantitative textual analysis of the European AI Act is useful to trace some general tendencies about the European approach to AI in relation to the pedagogical point of view.

The general appeal to European values and to an anthropocentric use of the AI is an interesting key to propose new points of view about a disruptive technology.

But the shortage of education-related words in the text underlines a general poor consideration of the potential use of AI to enhance learning. A first quantitative analysis shows that the education-related words are a minority in the context of a law that seems to be addressed more to big tech companies rather than to the school or university world.

The frequent risk related semantic occurrences proves a not very innovative perspective to the use of Artificial Intelligence and in general of the new technological tools [23].

It looks like an old risk-benefits paradigm about technologies prevails on the opportunity of offering general guidance in the educational context.

All that in a framework oriented toward the enhancement of learning and a real innovation capable of improving the general education world through technology.

More in general, a pedagogical work will be useful to make us understand the characteristics of the new world we'll meet when the technological transition will be completed. In this way the key will be the AI literacy in teacher education and a reflection about its use in a digital citizenship perspective [24].

Although in this AI law text the pedagogical emphasis is almost absent, we could hope for the future: a general major pedagogical focus could be a crucial point in further legal AI European updates.

The AI pact for instance could provide an opportunity to improve the pedagogical focus. The AI pact, promoted by the European commission, seeks "the industry's voluntary commitment to anticipate the AI Act and to start implementing its requirements ahead of the legal deadline" [25]. In particular the most interesting section could be the pillar 1 that provides for the "Creation and management of a dedicated online space for exchanging best practice". The AI pact could be the starting point to build a platform to recollect all AI-related Pedagogical best practices (Fig. 5):

Another big opportunity in this way could also be the Italian law about AI. The draft law scheme has been published and the mention of literacy paths also in higher education could be promising [26]. But it is still early to evaluate the final AI Italian Act text. The situation will be clearer at the end of the transitional period.

Recovering a metaphor used by Floridi [27], we could affirm that until now the law seems to be as the Athenas's owl that takes flight only when the shadows of night are gathering and innovation has already occurred. Instead of tracing the path to a real pedagogical development, the AI Act seems more interested in containing the social concerns about this technology. Anyway, we are now at the first steps of a radical socio-technological change.

In the future the law, even from a pedagogical perspective, should mark the path toward a new perspective for the methodologically correct use of the actual AI and also with an eye to his future innovation.

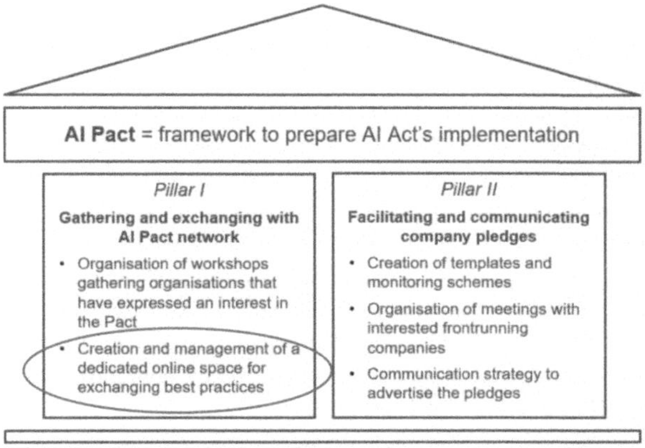

Fig. 5. AI Pact: the Pillar I predicts an online space for best practices (from [25]).

References

1. Eco, U.: Apocalittici e integrati. Milano, Bompiani (1964)
2. Roser, M.: The brief history of artificial intelligence: the world has changed fast—what might be next? Our World Data. (2022). Accessed from https://ourworldindata.org/brief-history-of-ai?ref=morioh.com&utm_source=morioh.com
3. Adeshola, I., Adepoju, A.P.: The opportunities and challenges of ChatGPT in education. Interact. Learn. Environ., 6159–6172 (2023). https://doi.org/10.1080/10494820.2023.2253858
4. Nikolopoulou, K.: Generative artificial intelligence in higher education: exploring ways of harnessing pedagogical practices with the assistance of ChatGPT. Int. J. Changes Educ. **1**(2), 103–111 (2024)
5. Acres, T.: Elon Musk tells Sky News AI is a risk to humanity. Skynews. (2023). Accessed from https://news.sky.com/story/elon-musk-tells-sky-news-ai-is-a-risk-to-humanity-12998024
6. Mohamad, A.F.K., Younis, A.A.: Artificial intelligence and the extinction of humans. Asian Perspect. **13** (2023). https://doi.org/10.21608/sis.2024.229424.1118
7. Murphy, R.R., Woods, D.D.: Beyond Asimov: the three laws of responsible robotics. In: Wallach, W., Asaro, P. (eds.) Machine Ethics and Robot Ethics, pp. 405–411. Routledge, London (2020)
8. Garante per la protezione dei dati personali. Intelligenza artificiale: il Garante blocca ChatGPT. Raccolta illecita di dati personali. Assenza di sistemi per la verifica dell'età dei minori. [Comunicato stampa] (April 13, 2023). Accessed from https://www.garanteprivacy.it/home/docweb/-/docweb-display/docweb/9870847#english
9. De Girolamo, F.: Il Parlamento europeo approva la legge sull'intelligenza artificiale. Attualità Parlamento europeo. (2024). Accessed from https://www.europarl.europa.eu/news/it/press-room/20240308IPR19015/il-parlamento-europeo-approva-la-legge-sull-intelligenza-artificiale
10. Panetta, R.: Ai act: cos'è e come plasma l'intelligenza artificiale in Europa. Agenda digitale eu. (2024). Accessed from https://www.agendadigitale.eu
11. Floridi, L.: The European Legislation on AI: a brief analysis of its philosophical approach. Philos Technol. **34**(2), 215–222 (2021)

12. Laux, J., Wachter, S., Mittelstadt, B.: Three pathways for standardisation and ethical disclosure by default under the European Union Artificial Intelligence Act. Comput Law Secur Rev. **53**(105957) (2024)
13. Laux, J., Wachter, S., Mittelstadt, B.: Trustworthy artificial intelligence and the European Union AI act: On the conflation of trustworthiness and acceptability of risk. Regulat Govern. **18**(1), 3–32 (2024)
14. Eco, U.: La trasparenza perduta. In: Sette anni di desiderio, 1st edn, pp. 163–179. Bompiani, Milano (1983)
15. European Commission. Shaping Europe's digital future. AI act. (2024). https://digital-strategy.ec.europa.eu/en/policies/regulatory-framework-ai. Accessed 8 May 2024
16. Madiega, T.: Artificial intelligence act. European Parliament: European Parliamentary Research Service (2023). Accessed from https://superintelligenz.eu/wp-content/uploads/2023/07/EPRS_BRI2021698792_EN.pdf
17. Sperling, K., Stenberg, C.J., McGrath, C., Åkerfeldt, A., Heintz, F., Stenliden, L.: In search of artificial intelligence (AI) literacy in Teacher Education: a scoping review. Comput. Educ. Open. **100169** (2024)
18. Buckingham, D.: Un manifesto per la media education. Mondadori, Milano (2024)
19. Donadio, V., Rolla, F.: AI act., quale impatto nel settore dell'educational technology? Aiforbusiness (May 10, 2024). Accessed from https://www.ai4business.it/intelligenza-artificiale/ai-act-quale-impatto-nel-settore-delleducation-technology/
20. Cataleta, A., Grillo, A.: Stati Uniti, tutte le leggi sull'intelligenza artificiale: il quadro. Agenda Digitale eu. (2024). Accessed from https://www.agendadigitale.eu/cultura-digitale/leggi-sullintelli…tati%20Uniti%2C%20ad%20oggio%20limiti%20specificamente%20luso
21. Giusti, N.: Verso regole globali sull'AI: occhi puntati sulle mosse della Cina. Agenda digitale eu (February 28, 2024). Accessed from https://www.agendadigitale.eu
22. Fourneaux, A.: The European Union's New USB-C standardization amendment: what does it mean for innovation within the consumer technology industry? Northwestern J. Int. Law Bus. **44**(1), 149–171 (2024)
23. Veale, M., Zuiderveen Borgesius, F.: Demystifying the draft EU artificial intelligence act—analysing the good, the bad, and the unclear elements of the proposed approach. Comput. Law Rev. Int. **22**(4), 97–112 (2021)
24. Panciroli, C., Rivoltella, P.C.: Pedagogia algoritmica. Per una riflessione educativa sull'Intelligenza Artificiale, pp. 1–240. Scholé-Morcelliana, Brescia (2023)
25. European Commission. Shaping European digital future. AI Pact. (2024). https://digital-strategy.ec.europa.eu/en/policies/ai-pact#:~:text...%20Act%20entered%20into.force%20and%20date%20of%20applicability. Accessed 8 May 2024
26. Senato della Repubblica: Disegni di legge. Atto senato n. 1146 XIX legislatura (June 13, 2024). https://www.senato.it/leg/19/BGT/Schede/Ddliter/58262.htm. Accessed 19 Aug 2024
27. Floridi, L.: Etica dell'intelligenza artificiale. Sviluppi, opportunità, sfide. Raffaello Cortina, Milano (2022)

Business Schools Practices: A Websites' Content Analysis

Maria Clara Dicataldo[1(✉)] and Anna Dipace[2]

[1] University of Foggia, 71122 Foggia, Italy
mariaclara.dicataldo@unifg.it
[2] Pegaso University, 80143 Naples, Italy
anna.dipace@unipegaso.it

Abstract. Business and management education must account for an ever changing, dynamic and unpredictable global economy. To prepare work ready graduates, Business Schools (BSs) should adopt innovative approaches, promote Faculty Development and employ educational technologies.

The study intends to identify the Teaching and learning approaches, Educational technologies and Faculty Development (FD) initiatives carried out by the top 100 BSs in the world by conducting a conceptual content analysis on their websites.

Experiential learning is undoubtedly the most used approach by all the BSs analysed; Educational technologies codes present less mentions; FD initiatives codes are quite present but not ubiquitous.

The preliminary results obtained from the content analysis will be further investigated by the administration of an online survey addressed to instructors and deans/directors of the top 100 BSs to gather their opinions and insights about the above analysed themes and their potential impact on MBA students' learning and employability.

Keywords: Business Schools · Teaching and learning approaches · Faculty Development

1 Introduction

1.1 Theoretical Framework

The rapid technological advances of the past decades have led to the fourth industrial revolution, known as Industry 4.0 (I4.0) which has decentralised decision-making processes and disrupted labour markets worldwide, replacing existing occupations and creating new ones [40]. To cope with such changes, companies need personnel with excellent technical and professional competences able to manage such dynamism and the emerging technologies [46].

This article has been developed jointly. Anna Dipace wrote paragraphs 1 and 5, Maria Clara Dicataldo wrote paragraphs 2, 3, 4.

P. Ardimento et al. (Eds.): HELMeTO 2024, CCIS 2468, pp. 199–222, 2025.
https://doi.org/10.1007/978-3-031-93999-0_13

In this vulnerable scenario, Business Schools (BSs), provider of Business Education, must try to educate graduates in a suitable way by equipping them with the necessary skills to thrive in the today's economy, professionally succeed and be employable [6, 7, 10, 24, 38]. There is increasing concern from employers worldwide about graduates' inability to match current and future work's needs [6, 26]. To address this challenge, BSs should adopt innovative approaches, that support creativity, critical thinking, and adaptability, and design curricula that enable global engagement, industry connection and transparency [7, 38]. Furthermore, BSs should improve the teaching standards by promoting Faculty Development (FD) initiatives, given that the quality of the teaching and learning process is positively correlated with students' performance, including student's employability [22]. Lastly, technologies have the potential to empower and enhance the teaching process and student's learning [11].

Considering the theoretical framework outlined above, the study poses the following broader research question:

RQ: How an effective and appropriate use of Teaching and learning approaches; Educational technologies, and Faculty Development (FD) initiatives can enhance students' learning and employability?

To answer this question, the present study intends to carry out:

- a conceptual content analysis on the websites of top 100 BSs in the world aimed at analysing the abovementioned themes and identifying the best practices and the current state of the art;
- an online survey addressed to the instructors and deans/directors of the top 100 BSs in the world to gather their opinions and insights about the above analysed themes and their potential impact on MBA students' learning and employability.

The present paper specifically reports on the results coming from the websites content analysis and provides as answer to the following research questions:

RQ1: Which are the main teaching and learning approaches applied in the MBA courses of the top 100 BSs in the world?

RQ2: Which are the main educational technologies applied in the MBA courses and by the top 100 BSs in the world?

RQ3: Which are the FD initiatives carried out by the top 100 BSs in the world?

2 Methods and Materials

The research sample is given by the "Global MBA 2024"[1] ranking, issued by the Financial Times, that lists the top 100 BSs of the world according to their MBA course. BSs are defined as "organizations that operate according to market principles, management theory, and profit orientation" [35, p. 2]. MBA (Master in Business Administration) is considered the flagship program of BSs worldwide [8, 31] able to provide professional competencies to graduates [27].

The study performed a conceptual content analysis for existence. For the first rounds of coding, structural coding was used to define the websites' sections to be analysed.

[1] https://rankings.ft.com/rankings/2951/mba-2024.

For the further rounds of coding, content analysis coding was used to analyse websites' excerpts. Given the iterative nature of the content analysis method, the websites sections and excerpts went through more rounds of coding. The analysis applied both a deductive and inductive approach, using themes (teaching and learning approaches, educational technologies and faculty development initiative) as units of analysis. For each theme, codes with respective definitions and examples were developed according to the literature and gathered in the codebook (deductive approach). Throughout the analysis, the codebook evolved and developed with inductive codes as well, reaching its definitive form (Appendix 1) at the end of the process. Being a content analysis for existence, only the websites sections and excerpts containing the themes and codes, set out in the codebook, were coded. The website sections browsed, analysed and coded were those tightly related to the research question and were generally named as follow: MBA Program➔ Learning experience/Curriculum; Faculty & Research; Research Initiatives & Centres; Learning Approach/methodology/Teaching/Technology. After having manually browsed and analysed all sections of interest, a general automatic search on each website was performed to increase the systematicity and consistency of the results found, especially when the manual search produced no results. The general search was performed typing the following keywords "Teaching" AND "Learning" AND "Technolog*" AND "Faculty Development". Data coding involved a peer-blind process conducted with the assistance of an independent and impartial external coder. The two coders, each 10 websites, had a peer debriefing to further ensure the reliability and validity of the methodology and findings. Excel was used as main tool to collect and process data, by applying labels and filters to gather excerpts under the respective codes and themes.

The codebook, codes and coding rules guided the whole analysis, being the decisive elements for coding decisions.

3 Results

The results obtained from the analysis are synthetised by the following graphs.

As far as the Teaching and learning approaches are concerned, the most used approach by all the top 100 BSs is Experiential Learning, followed by Collaborative Learning and Coaching, mentoring, modelling. Graph 1 provides an overview of the results.

Educational technologies codes present less mentions in respect to those of Teaching and learning approaches. The most rated codes are Learning tools and Learning Environment. Graph 2 provides an overview of the results.

Faculty Development initiatives codes are quite recurrent on websites, especially those related to Support activities to didactics and Faculty awards. Graph 3 provides an overview of the results.

4 Discussion

RQ1: Which are the main teaching and learning approaches applied in the MBA courses of the top 100 BSs in the world?

As clearly visible from the results section, the teaching and learning approach used in the MBA courses of all the BSs analysed is Experiential Learning (EL). EL is a process

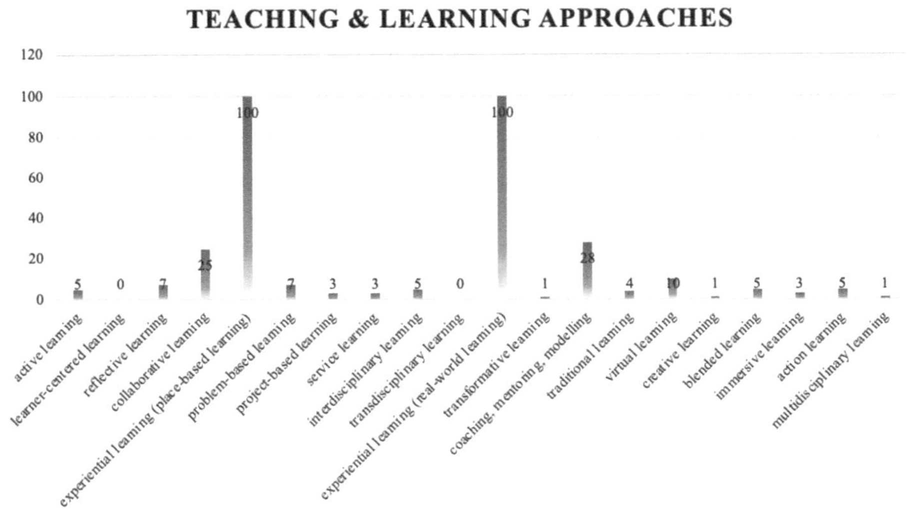

Graph 1. Teaching and learning approaches results

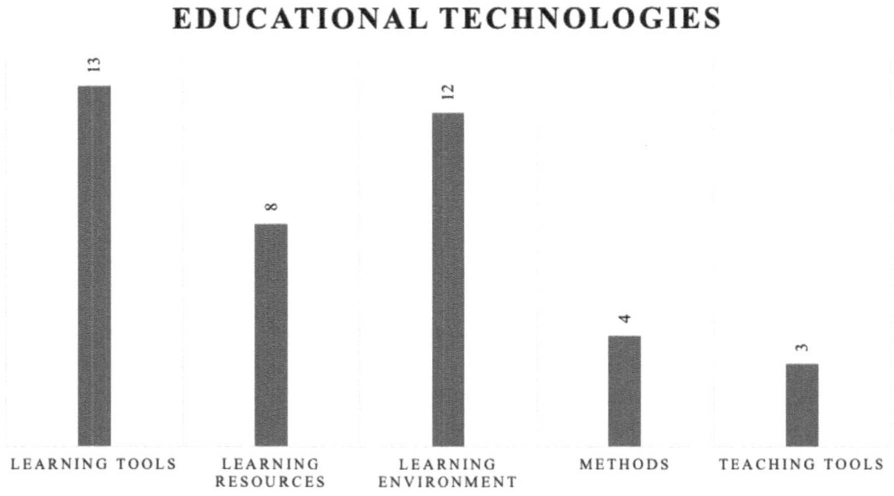

Graph 2. Educational technologies results

through which a learner constructs knowledge, skill, and value from direct experience [21, 47]. According to the Experiential Learning Theory, the learning cycle includes four actions, that is experiencing, reflecting, thinking, and acting. Such activities represent a dynamic cycle through which the learner translates theirs' own direct, immediate experience, observing and reflecting upon the experience and thinking and conceptualizing [44].

For the analysis, the Experiential Learning code embodied real-world learning and place-based learning codes because of the existing commonalities among the approaches.

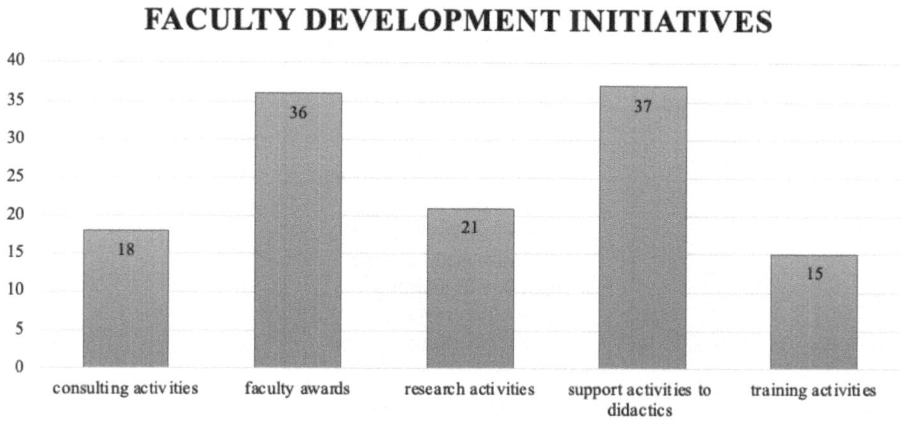

Graph 3. Faculty development initiatives results

Real-world learning and Place-based learning, in fact, are grounded in the educational theory of experiential learning. Placed-based learning is student-centered and permits students to explore topics through hands-on experiences within their community and from their local resources [42]. Real-world learning, as well, implies the use of authentic situations to trigger the learning process. Students learn when they must face complex and difficult problems related to real-life situations for which are required to reflect on possible explanations or solutions. While experiencing authentic learning situations, students learn by doing, acquire new knowledge, competences and life skills such as critical thinking, problem-solving, thinking out of the box, observing, researching, reflecting, collaborating, writing, reading and presenting [13, 39, 44]. In fact, each website mentioned the necessity to interchange traditional lectures with intimate class sizes, peer to peer collaboration, teamwork and group projects to enhance problem solving and decision-making skills, by dealing with often ambiguous and complex issues. These redundant features are present in more than one of the different teaching and learning approaches under study. For this reason, some of them have been gathered under the Experiential learning code (Fig. 1). Indeed, other codes (like problem-based learning, project-based learning, etc.) present far less mentions because most of the excerpts have been coded as EL.

Other recurrent elements are given by hands-on learning experiences, either at university or abroad (internships, exchange programs, study tours, field trips, etc.); and by capstone projects that typically require students to apply the knowledge and skills acquired throughout their academic careers to solve real-world problems.

Despite its old origins, the case study method is the second most used and mentioned approach. The case method story begins at Harvard Law School, where Christopher Columbus Langdell, dean of Harvard Law School from 1870 to 1895, introduced case-based learning around 1890.[2] The case study method is a pedagogical approach that places students at the centre of the learning experience, characterized by the involvement of the participants (teacher-student) in a dialogue and a multidirectional flow of

[2] https://www.exed.hbs.edu/blog/celebrating-100-years-case-method-hbs#.

Experiential Learning

Action learning
Active learning
Collaborative learning
Creative learning
Learner-centered learning
Place-based learning
Problem-based learning
Project-based learning
Real-world learning
Reflective learning
Service learning

Fig. 1. T&L approaches categorization

information (between students-students and students-teacher). The teacher assumes the role of the facilitator of a discussion rather than the sole provider of unidirectional information; while the student assumes an active role, having to face and solve real-world scenarios and problems. By immersing students in the context of a case, the case study method promotes active learning, critical thinking and problem-solving skills [32, 34, 36]. For these reasons, the case method has been considered as an experiential learning approach. In addition, many eastern BSs have their own Case Center dedicated to the publishing activities of their own case studies.

Another constant element is the presence of advisors, mentors and coaches that support students throughout their learning experience. Coaching is often regarded as performance orientated, while mentoring as career orientated. Such programs enable students to take ownership of their learning, improve skills and progress towards their career goals [5]. They may acquire different forms like executive mentors, career coaches, leadership coaches, lifestyle coaches, etc. Career Development Programs are present in all the BSs analysed.

The results found demonstrate the alignment of the MBA educational offer with the labour market's needs and present BSs able to prepare work ready MBA graduates.

Table 1 provides an overview of codes and examples found during the analysis.

RQ2: Which are the main educational technologies applied in the MBA courses and by the top 100 BSs in the world?

Educational technologies are quite less mentioned on the websites with specific reference to the MBA program and Learning approach sections. Of course, the use and presence of educational technologies to enhance the learning process is considered fundamental, predominant and indispensable. Students must be able to effectively use existing and emerging technologies, by adopting associated pedagogies to suit the environment, and recognise technological advances and pedagogical shifts to achieve efficiency and effectiveness [18]. The most recurrent codes were those related to learning tools (like online polling tools, generative AI tools, web-based solutions, interactive assessment tools, learning analytics applications) and learning environment.

Table 1. T&L approaches

Codes	Examples from excerpts
Blended learning	Flipped Classroom
Coaching, mentoring, modelling	Executive mentors, career coaches, leadership coaches
Experiential learning (place-based learning)	Study tours, study trips, study abroad, company visits, practicum, industry treks, internships, field trips, expeditions, intensives, global travel experiences, summer work experience, international exchange program, cultural and global immersions, individual project, Start-up ventures, Board Fellows Programs
Experiential learning (real-world learning)	Case studies, live action cases, computer simulations, executive simulations, role-plays, laboratories, group/field/company/client/consulting/investment/research projects, Company Wikis, Quality Circles, Summer Schools, intensives, workshops, case competitions, venturing projects, business games, design thinking, evidence-based learning, gamification, business creation program, Lean Six Sigma, student investment fund, student asset management, career planning, real-world master's thesis, student organizations and clubs, Hackathon, executive and business challenge, entrepreneurial business incubator, independent study, research paper, business plan, Leadership Fellows Program, assignments, presentations, group discussion, summits, conferences, seminars, guest speakers, interactive and experiential lectures, live events and webinars, testimonials
Immersive learning	VR, AR, XR, Metaverse
Traditional learning	In person, theoretical, face to face lectures
Virtual learning	Online, dual mode, asynchronous, synchronous lectures

The results show that Educational Technologies should receive much more attention in the MBA curriculum design since they have the power to enhance the teaching process and student's learning and train graduates able to manage the technological advancement.

Table 2 provides an overview of codes and examples found during the analysis.

RQ3: Which are the faculty development initiatives carried out by the top 100 BSs in the world?

Faculty development initiatives codes are enough recurrent on the websites' sections. The most present ones are those related to Support activities to didactics and Faculty Awards, presenting less mentions for the remaining codes (Table 3). In the excerpts have been found also two mentions in relation to FD initiatives addressed to the development of the teaching practices of PhD students, yet they haven't been considered in the analysis.

A common element of some BSs is the possession of a dedicated Teaching & Learning Center (T&LC) aimed at supporting and developing the faculty in all their academic

Table 2. Educational technologies

Codes	Examples from excerpts
Learning tools	NameCoach, Seat Gen, Poll Everywhere, Digital Casebook Initiative, Slack, AirMedia, Echo360, Custom, multifunctional lecterns, Feedback Fruits, Miro, Ed Discussion, Google Workspace, Loom, Pool Everywhere, Panopto, Grammarly, Microsoft Copilot, VitalSource, e-portfolios, Slido, Microsoft Forms, Qualtrics, Google Forms, Mentimeter, TurningPoint, Microsoft Teams, Canvas Discussions, FlipGrid, Jamboard, Google Docs, Microsoft OneDrive, Padlet, Mural, Perusall, Hypothesis, MS PowerPoint, Design Ideas, Google Slides, Pear Deck, Prezi, Powtoons, Nearpod, Google Teammates, Canvas New Quizzes, Respondus Lockdown Browser, Crowdmark, Kahoot!, Zoom, OBS, mmHmm, Adobe Premier
Learning resources	eBooks, eJournals, documentary databases, theses, dissertation, digital teaching content repository, MOOCs
Learning environment	Canvas LMS, Zoom, Brightspace, technological university studios
Methods	High-tech and high-touch experiential learning programs, technologies for collaborative and real-world learning
Teaching tools	Teacher Ally, Proctorio, Turnitin, Seat Gen, Google assignment, e-portfolios

practices [25]. T&LC are especially widespread in the USA where they have been established for the first time. Other BSs, instead, possess a Learning Center or Learning Hub aimed at supporting the teaching and learning practices from both the instructor and learner side. During the analysis have been found n. 5 T&LCs and n. 10 Learning Labs.

The development of teaching competences of instructors is a sensitive and actual topic for BSs since it plays a crucial role in training capable and work ready graduates. Despite the awareness about the importance of faculty development initiatives, there is still a long way ahead to be travelled. Business education, indeed, has had limited discussion on professional development for academics and BSs have struggled with integrating it into course design. Professional development in business education requires epistemic and ontological change [50].

The results point out that FD practices need to be further studied and integrated in the MBA curriculum design since the quality of the teaching and learning is positively correlated with students' performance and employability and, thus, represent a crucial aspect for the MBA students' education.

Table 3 provides an overview of codes and examples found during the analysis.

Although the study was conducted with extreme meticulousness, adopting all the methodological measures necessary to avoid research biases, it is appropriate to point out some limitations found. The study sample cannot be considered representative since it does not follow any specific sampling technique. It simply considers the Financial Times ranking of the top 100 BSs in the world defined according to economic indexes. Furthermore, the data analysis method adopted (content analysis), by nature, may be

Table 3. Faculty development initiatives.

Codes	Examples from excerpts
Consulting activities	Instructional coaching, mentorship, teaching observations, mock lectures Course design: learning objectives/outcomes, bloom's taxonomy, backward design, basics of self-paced course design, blended learning essentials (BLE) How To: prepare for class, manage norms call on students, ask effective questions, generate inclusive and accessible teaching and learning, encourage active and interactive participation, teach large courses effectively and efficiently, use educational technologies, use generative artificial intelligence, apply student assessment strategies, provide sound student feedback, get started with case method, flipped classroom, project-based learning, online teaching and learning EdTech consultation
Faculty awards	Teaching and research excellence
Research activities	Integrating research activities in the classroom, case studies publishing, case research center, research to connect teaching to the real world
Support activities to the didactics	Instructional development templates, materials, guidelines, handbooks, teaching plans
Training activities	Training sessions, workshops, seminars

subject to subjectivity of data interpretation and present some inconsistencies. Moreover, the use of structural coding, adopted to define the websites' sections to be analysed, may have missed some data. Nonetheless, the latter limitations were counteracted with a peer blind data analysis and a general automatic search by keywords carried out on each single website.

5 Conclusion and Future Research Directions

Business and management education must account for an ever changing, dynamic and unpredictable global economy. Thus, BSs must equip students with the necessary skills to face the multiple challenges of today's world. BSs should adopt innovative approaches, promote FD and employ educational technologies. The study identified the Teaching and learning approaches, Educational technologies and FD initiatives employed by the top 100 BSs in the world by conducting a conceptual content analysis on their websites. These themes represent crucial aspects for the MBA students' education and may have direct implications on their future professional career. The results show that Experiential learning is undoubtedly the most used approach by all the BSs analysed; Educational technologies codes present quite less mentions in respect to teaching and learning approaches; lastly, FD initiatives codes are quite present but not ubiquitous.

The results obtained from the analysis allow us to draw only preliminary conclusions on BSs practices. In fact, future study intends to carry out an online survey addressed to instructors and deans/directors of the top 100 BSs to gather their opinions and insights about the analysed themes and their potential impact on MBA students' learning and employability. The survey consists of a questionnaire of four sections containing structured questions (dichotomous, multiple-choice, rating scales) and an open-ended question in each section to collect comments and suggestions from the respondents. The survey is currently going through a pilot; after that it will be definitely administered by email using Google Modules. In case of a low response rate, it will be extended to the top 200 BSs in the world.

Disclosure of Interests. The authors have no competing interests to declare that are relevant to the content of this article.

Appendix 1

Themes	Codes	Definitions	Examples
Teaching and learning approaches	active learning	Active learning, focused on instructional strategies such as problem-based learning, small group instruction, and design projects, has been posited as the pedagogical answer to the extensive use of lecture, often presented as the epitome of passive learning instruction, in higher education [14]	Problem-based learning, small group instruction, and design projects [14]

(continued)

(*continued*)

Themes	Codes	Definitions	Examples
	learner-centered learning	Learner-centered learning focuses on the learners' needs, abilities, interests, and learning styles, with the teacher as a facilitator of learning. As a result, the focus is on the needs of the learners rather than the teacher and more on learning than teaching. With learner-centered learning, students are actively engaged in the learning process, encouraged to reflect and think analytically about what they are learning and how they are learning it, motivated by having some control over their own learning, and encouraged to collaborate with others in the learning process [54]	Problem-based learning, project-based learning, and inquiry-based learning. Five characteristics of LCI that can be commonly shown in personalized learning activities and support, social and emotional support, self-regulation, collaborative and authentic learning experiences, and assessment for learning [4]

(*continued*)

(*continued*)

Themes	Codes	Definitions	Examples
	reflective learning	Reflective learning helps students to "turn experience into learning", by analysing and responding to an experience, such as a lecture, then processing this thinking to formulate evaluations and decisions about what has been learnt. It allows a dialogue between the teacher and learner, so that the educator becomes a 'facilitator of learning', focusing on how learners are interacting with the material, rather than how it is being transmitted [23]	Diary and Journals writing, portfolios, reflective learning groups, creativity, Digital Media, Scaffolding [51]
	collaborative learning	collaborative learning as "a collaborative activity of two or more learners who are working on achieving collective goals through the exchange of knowledge, learning and reaching a consensus" [48]	Learning in teams, peer assessment and working in small groups [48] Group work, project work, think pair share, simulation, role play
	experiential learning	Experiential learning is "a process through which a learner constructs knowledge, skill, and value from direct experience" [47]	Internships, studies abroad, field trips, field research, and service-learning projects [47] development of a business plan; providing consulting services to companies; development and implementation of a business; development of projects and activities [29]

(*continued*)

(*continued*)

Themes	Codes	Definitions	Examples
	problem-based learning	In PBL, small student groups work on real-life problems, guided by a teacher PBL's key features are: (a) starting the learning process with a problem to activate students' prior knowledge and interest in learning; (b) student-centered, active learning; (c) small group collaboration (5 to 12 students); (d) teacher guidance; and (e) self-directed learning with adequate self-study time [52]	The problem can be a case, story, visual prompt, or phenomenon that needs explaining [52]
	project-based learning	Through projects students learn a field's central concepts and principles [52]	Projects that are relevant to students' lives, featuring authentic contexts or real-world impact; planning and execution of investigations to answer questions; collaboration with peers, teachers, and sometimes the community; and culmination in a tangible artifact or product [52]
	service learning	Service-learning can be defined as an educational approach where students learn in the classroom while volunteering with an agency (usually a non-profit or service group). Once the service-learning is completed, students usually reflect to deepen their understanding of what was taught [41]	Direct service to individuals: serving meals and participating in community events. Indirect service to people: organizing events, stocking foods at a food pantry, researching information, collecting donations. Advocacy: students actively participate in writing letters or educating others about important topics or causes [41]

(*continued*)

(*continued*)

Themes	Codes	Definitions	Examples
	interdisciplinary learning	Interdisciplinarity refers to activities that unite or combine two or more fields of knowledge. The integration between disciplines is designed to create a meaning, explanation, or product that is more powerful than the sum of its components [16]	Integration of diverse disciplines like ethics, sociology, and environmental science. Interdisciplinary courses that combine disciplines to address sustainability challenges. Interdisciplinary research centers that bring together researchers from different fields to collaborate on sustainability research [28]
	transdisciplinary learning	The transdisciplinary learning advances students' complex thinking skills and utilizes disciplinary depth, draw upon awareness of content from other disciplines and recognize the need to involve community stakeholders for the problem resolution [3]	Integrated learning, problem-based learning, service learning [3]

(*continued*)

(continued)

Themes	Codes	Definitions	Examples
	real-world learning	Real-world learning entails the use of education in authentic situations to trigger a change in knowledge, abilities, mindsets, behaviours and values. Students are called to act in a reflective way in a situation which displays complex and difficult problems related to real-life situations. In such authentic learning situations, students learn by doing, acquiring knowledge and understanding while developing life skills and competences such as critical thinking, problem-solving, thinking out of the box, observation, researching, collaboration, writing, reading and presenting [13]	Case studies, Simulations, Role-plays, Laboratories, Field/company/client/consulting/investment/research projects, Company Wikis, Quality circles, Summer Schools, Intensives, workshops, case competitions, venturing projects, business games
	place-based learning	Placed-based learning utilises students' local environments and communities for teaching and learning. It is student-centered, grounded in the educational philosophy of experiential learning and a recognized approach for inquiry [42]	Study tours, industry treks, internships, field trips, Expeditions, Intensives, Global Travel Experiences, Company visits, Cultural immersions, Individual Project, Work Placement, Start-up ventures, Board Fellows

(continued)

(*continued*)

Themes	Codes	Definitions	Examples
	transformative learning	In transformative learning (TL) individuals learn to reflect on experiences and preconceptions, hidden values and assumptions, to think critically, and to participate freely in rational discourses [53]	
	coaching, mentoring, modelling	Coaching and mentoring nurture professional and personal development by enhancing performance and work satisfaction. Coaching is often regarded as performance orientated, using feedback as essential tool, while mentoring as career orientated. These programmes enable the students to take ownership of their learning, improve skills and progress towards their career goals [5]	Feedback, direct observation, targeted goal-setting, and habits of reflection [5]

(*continued*)

(*continued*)

Themes	Codes	Definitions	Examples
	traditional learning	In traditional learning the instructor is expected to teach exactly the content of the syllabus and conduct assessments provided therein. There is little to no use of technology as all forms of teaching and learning is conducted in a confined location such as a classroom and the students take instructions from the instructor [2]	Lectures, Tutorials, Laboratories, Exams [30]
	virtual learning	Virtual learning refers to an educationally inspired technology that uses electronic or computerized platforms to acquire knowledge at the convenience of both the learners and lecturers. It is invariably associated with the holistic incorporation of modern telecommunication equipment and Information and Communication Technology (ICT) resources into the education system [1]	Distance learning, e-learning and online learning [1] Synchronous, asynchronous and hybrid/blended classes trough internet and IT tools [15] Zoom, Microsoft Teams, Google Hangout (meet), Skype, Bamboo learning, Google class- room, Docebo, WIZIQ, Adobe Captivate, Elucidate and Blackboard Collaborate [1]

(*continued*)

(*continued*)

Themes	Codes	Definitions	Examples
	creative learning	Creative learning has been defined as a "combination of intrapsychological and interpsychological processes that result in new and personally meaningful understandings for oneself and others" [9] Creativity is the capability to develop novel, good explanations for problems that arise through peer interaction and debate [49]	To make students more creative in the classroom, experts recommend that teachers encourage them to ask more questions, think about why, how, and what their observations mean, and come up with more thoughtful questions (Paugh et al., 2010). In other words, by acting as helpful facilitators, instructors should encourage students to take measured risks and develop original solutions to issues [49]
	blended learning	Blended learning combines face-to-face instruction with computer mediated instruction [17]	Flipped classroom
	immersive learning	Immersive learning conceptualizes education as a set of active phenomenological experiences that are based on presence. Immersive learning can be implemented using both physical and digital means, such as virtual reality and augmented reality [33]	AR, VR, XR [33] Metaverse

(*continued*)

(*continued*)

Themes	Codes	Definitions	Examples
	action learning	Action learning is an experiential learning method in which participants learn by doing and then reflecting on what they have done There are several varieties of action learning. In most varieties, the participants work on real tasks in small teams (learning sets). As they do so they learn leadership, teamwork, facilitation and additional skills of value to the organisation [37]	Teamwork, team building, study groups, group assignments
	multidisciplinary learning	Multidisciplinarity is understood as interaction between members from varying disciplines in academia, where the disciplinary boundaries are kept intact. Such collaboration could, for instance, involve a dialogue between critical friends from varying disciplines [12]	Dialogue between critical students and professionals from varying disciplines [12]
Educational technologies	learning tools	Learning tools are those digital and non-digital media used for the purpose to facilitate learning through interactions between people and systems, such as learning applications, multimedia devices [18]	Flash cards, mind maps, blogs, electronic dictionaries, expert systems, Web 2.0 tools, electronic performance support systems (EPSSs), mobile educational apps, table computers, and so on [18]

(*continued*)

(*continued*)

Themes	Codes	Definitions	Examples
	learning resources	Learning resources are materials that can be used to support teaching, learning and research, such as textbooks, course readings, and other learning content [18]	Educational video clips, open educational resources, massive open online courses (MOOCs), and online libraries and repositories [18]
	learning environment	Learning environments refer to the diverse locations, contexts, and cultures in which students learn, such as classroom, cyberspace [18]	Learning environments include traditional classrooms as well as online learning management systems [18]
	method	Method is "a way, technique, or process of or for doing something". (Definition of Method, n.d.) Learning method stands for the way of presentation of the specific contents of a subject that may be properly grasped and understood by learners [18]	Examples include drill and practice, memorization, inquiry-based learning, collaborative learning, competency-based learning, and so on [18]
	teaching tools	Teaching tools support the teacher in the teaching process, facilitate and optimize the tasks	AI tools, Ally, Proctorio, Turnitin, Seat Gen, Google assignment, Steam Platform
Faculty development initiatives	training activities	Training activities aimed at developing lecturers' knowledge and skills about teaching and learning [25]	Workshops, webinars, seminars, conferences and symposia for lecturers, staff and students Structuring MOOCs or online/blended training courses for teachers and students. Designing Faculty Development activities for teachers and new recruits. Supporting the professional development of PhD Students and Research Fellows (Teaching Fellows). Activities related to the development of a Scholarship of Teaching and Learning (SoTL). Training and assistance with educational technology [25]

(*continued*)

(*continued*)

Themes	Codes	Definitions	Examples
	consulting activities	Consulting activities aimed at developing lecturers' knowledge and skills about teaching and learning [25]	Counselling on the creation of a quality feedback for the student. Customised support for teachers to create or re-design a course from the point of view of objectives, methodologies, approaches and assessment. Expert advice on active, interactive and inclusive teaching strategies, methodologies, tools and approaches. Consultancy and professional support for the design, development and evaluation of online and blended courses and programmes [25]
	research activities	Training activities aimed at developing lecturers' knowledge and skills about teaching and learning [25]	Research support and implementation of research projects/programmes aimed at improving teaching practice. Implementation of programmes that foster bridges between teaching, research and professional training Didactic observations and innovative pedagogical solutions Publications and scientific communications. Publications and scientific communications [25]
	support activities to the didactics	Resources aimed at developing lecturers' knowledge and skills about teaching and learning [25]	Collections of academic and tutoring supporting materials, guidelines and resources useful for the professional development of teachers and students. Resources designed to support teaching and the students themselves during the Pandemic (critical situations in general). Supporting the development, use and evaluation of student-centred learning environments Creation and support of Communities of Practice, Faculty Learning Communities and Learning Communities open to teachers and students. Activation of Mentoring and Peer Observation processes [25]
	faculty awards	Acknowledgments to foster the commitment of instructors to the teaching and learning practice [43]	Teaching and research excellence.

References

1. Adesuyi, E.O., et al.: Satisfaction and perceived impact of virtual learning during COVID-19 lockdown: a case study of an online nursing research conference. Nurs. Open. **10**(9), 6215–6227 (2023)
2. Alhassan, S.: A review of blended learning in contrast with traditional learning in Ghanaian universities. arXiv preprint (2023). https://arxiv.org/abs/2309.13045
3. Amelink, C.T., Grote, D.M., Norris, M.B., Grohs, J.R.: Transdisciplinary learning opportunities: exploring differences in complex thinking skill development between STEM and non-STEM majors. Innov. High. Educ. **49**(1), 153–176 (2024)

4. An, Y., Mindrila, D.: Strategies and tools used for learner-centered instruction. Int. J. Technol. Educ. Sci. **4**(2), 133–143 (2020)
5. Atkinson, A., Watling, C.J., Brand, P.L.: Feedback and coaching. Eur. J. Pediatr. **181**(2), 441–446 (2022)
6. Azevedo, A., Apfelthaler, G., Hurst, D.: Competency development in business graduates: an industry-driven approach for examining the alignment of undergraduate business education with industry requirements. Int. J. Manag. Educ. **10**(1), 12–28 (2012). https://doi.org/10.1016/j.ijme.2012.02.002
7. Baldegger, R.J., El Tarabishy, A., Audretsch, D.B., Kariv, D., Passerini, K., Tan, W.L. (eds.): The Future of Business Schools: Purpose, Action, and Impact. Edward Elgar Publishing (2022)
8. Baruch, Y.: To MBA or not to MBA. Career Dev. Int. **14**(4), 388–406 (2009)
9. Beghetto, R.A.: Creative learning. In: The Palgrave encyclopedia of the possible, pp. 286–293. Springer, Cham (2023)
10. Benesova, N.: LEGO® Serious Play® in management education. Cogent Educ. **10**(2), 2262284 (2023). https://doi.org/10.1080/2331186X.2023.2262284
11. Bond, M., Buntins, K., Bedenlier, S., Zawacki-Richter, O., Kerres, M.: Mapping research in student engagement and educational technology in higher education: a systematic evidence map. Int. J. Educ. Technol. High. Educ. **17**(1), 2 (2020). https://doi.org/10.1186/s41239-019-0176-8
12. Brodin, E., Avery, H.: Cross-disciplinary collaboration and scholarly independence in multidisciplinary learning environments at doctoral level and beyond. Minerva. **58** (2020). https://doi.org/10.1007/s11024-020-09397-3
13. Conti, D., Dawson, R.: Real-world learning as a frame for sustainability in education. In: Education for Sustainable Development in Primary and Secondary Schools: Pedagogical and Practical Approaches for Teachers, pp. 55–72. Springer, Cham (2022)
14. Doolittle, P., Wojdak, K., Walters, A.: Defining active learning: a restricted systemic review. Teach. Learn. Inquiry. **11** (2023)
15. Dung, D.T.H.: The advantages and disadvantages of virtual learning. IOSR J. Res. Method Educ. **10**(3), 45–48 (2020)
16. Gero, A., Essami, H.E.B.A., Danino, O., Kornblum, L.: Students' attitudes toward interdisciplinary learning: a high-school course on solar cells. Int. J. Eng. Educ. **38**(4), 1130–1140 (2022)
17. Graham, C.R.: Blended learning systems. Handb. Blend. Learn.: Glob. Perspect. Local Designs. **1**, 3–21 (2006)
18. Huang, R.: Educational Technology a Primer for the 21st Century. Springer Nature Singapore Pte Ltd. (2019)
19. Jones, J., Smith, H.A.: A comparative study of formal coaching and mentoring programmes in higher education. Int. J. Mentor. Coach. Educ. **11**(2), 213–231 (2022)
20. Kolb, D.A.: Experiential Learning: Experience as the Source of Learning and Development. FT Press (2014)
21. Kolb, D.A.: Experiential Learning: Experience as the Source of Learning and Development. Prentice-Hall, Englewood Cliffs (1984)
22. Kowang, T.O., Yew, L.K., Yen, H.W., Hee, O.C., Fei, G.C., Rasli, A., Long, C.S.: Relationship between teaching quality factors and employability among technology management students. Int. J. Eval. Res. Educ. **11**(3), 1154 (2022). https://doi.org/10.11591/ijere.v11i3.21836
23. Leist, E., Lee, J.: Adopting an agile approach for reflective learning and teaching. In: Proceedings of the 46th International Conference on Software Engineering: Software Engineering Education and Training, pp. 46–55 (2024)

24. Livas, C., Karali, N.: Examining the concurrent impact of teaching and assessment format on undergraduate students' academic performance in marketing. High. Educ. Skills Work-Based Learn. **13**(4), 758–771 (2023). https://doi.org/10.1108/HESWBL-02-2022-0039
25. Lotti, A., Serbati, A., Doria, B., Picasso, F., Felisatti, E.: Teaching and learning centre: analysis of key elements. Formaz. Insegnamento. **20**(2), 75–88 (2022)
26. Mantai, L., Calma, A.: Beyond assuring learning: greater challenges ahead for management educators. Int. J. Manag. Educ. **20**(3), 100723 (2022). https://doi.org/10.1016/j.ijme.2022.100723
27. Marino, J., Rivero, A.G., Dabos, G.E.: MBAs and career development: a literature review from the human capital perspective. Cuadernos de Administración (Universidad Del Valle). **35**(64), 110–127 (2019). https://doi.org/10.25100/cdea.v35i64.6392
28. Martins, F., Cezarino, L., Liboni, L., Hunter, T., Batalhao, A., Paschoalotto, M.A.C.: Unlocking the potential of responsible management education through interdisciplinary approaches. Sustain. Dev. **32**(3), 2001–2019 (2024)
29. Motta, V.F., Galina, S.V.R.: Experiential learning in entrepreneurship education: a systematic literature review. Teach. Teach. Educ. **121**, 103919 (2023)
30. Muhammadjonovich, R.M.: Comparative analysis of the use of modern and traditional methods of education in higher education. Periodica J. Mod. Philos. Soc. Sci. Human. **20**, 1–3 (2023)
31. Muposhi, A., Dhurup, M., Martin, R.L., Bhadury, J.: A pilot study of MBA programmes in South Africa. Lond. Rev. Educ. **17**(3) (2019). https://doi.org/10.18546/LRE.17.3.14
32. Musara, M.: Using the case study method in undergraduate entrepreneurship education. Administ. Sci. **14**(4), 60 (2024)
33. Mystakidis, S., Lympouridis, V.: Immersive learning. Encyclopedia. **3**(2), 396–405 (2023)
34. Narzullayev, M., Xoliyorova, S., Pardayev, U., Tilyabov, M.: The method of organizing chemistry lessons using the case study method. Mod. Sci. Res. **3**(5), 119–123 (2024)
35. Randerson, K.: The futures of business schools: Identity, strategies, and imagined futures for a pandemic/post-pandemic world. Futures. **150**, 103175 (2023). https://doi.org/10.1016/j.futures.2023.103175
36. Rebeiz, K.S.: An insider perspective on implementing the Harvard Case Study Method in business teaching. US-China Educ. Rev. A. **5**, 591–601 (2011)
37. Revans, R.W.: The Origins and Growth of Action Learning. Chartwell-Bratt Ltd., Bromley (1982)
38. Riashchenko, V. (Ed.).: Innovative approaches in business education. In: Proceedings of the VII International Scientific Conference Dedicated to The International Day of The Seafarers, "Sustainable Transport Systems and Maritime Logistics" (ISTSML–2023). Batumi Navigation Teaching University Publications (2023)
39. Sala, A., Punie, Y., Garkov, V., Cabrera Giraldez, M.: LifeComp: The European Framework for Personal, Social and Learning to Learn Key Competence (EUR 30246 EN). Publications Office of the European Union, Luxembourg (2020). Accessed 10 May 2021
40. Saleem, S., Dhuey, E., White, L., Perlman, M.: Understanding 21st century skills needed in response to industry 4.0: exploring scholarly insights using bibliometric analysis. Telemat. Informat. Rep. **13**, 100124 (2024). https://doi.org/10.1016/j.teler.2024.100124
41. Schichtl, R., Carroll, K., Sartain, K.: Factors influencing food insecurity empathy: the role of service-learning. Int. J. Home Econ. **15**(2), 151–159 (2022)
42. Soares, L.: Placed-based education for inquiry learning. Int. J. Cross-Discipl. Subj. Educ. **13**(1) (2022)
43. Steinert, Y.: Faculty development: core concepts and principles. In: Faculty Development in the Health Professions: A Focus on Research and Practice, pp. 3–25 (2013)
44. Torres, P., Augusto, M.: The impact of experiential learning on managers' strategic competencies and decision style. J. Innov. Knowl. **2**(1), 10–14 (2017)

45. Turner, R., Cotton, D., Morrison, D., Kneale, P.: Embedding interdisciplinary learning into the first-year undergraduate curriculum: drivers and barriers in a cross-institutional enhancement project. Teach. High. Educ. **29**(4), 1092–1108 (2024)
46. Tushar, H., Sooraksa, N.: Global employability skills in the 21st century workplace: a semi-systematic literature review. Heliyon. (2023)
47. Verma, S.: The effectiveness of experiential learning pedagogy in teaching cross-cultural sensitivity to young management trainees. J. Data Acquisit. Process. **38**(2), 4568 (2023)
48. Vesić Pavlović, T., Đorđević, D.D.: Collaborative learning in ESP classes–an exploration of university students' opinions. In: Jezik–Struka–Nauka–2.1, Zbornik radova sa Pete međunarodne konferencije Društva za strane jezike i književnosti Srbije, pp. 334–349 (2022)
49. Wang, W., Tie, F.H., Omar, I.M.B., Chen, W., Li, P., Shi, C.: An empirical study on the creative learning environment fostering student creativity: a multiple mediation analysis using smart PLS 4. J. Educ. Soc. Res. **13**, 24 (2023)
50. Wardak, D., Huber, E., Zeivots, S.: Towards a conceptual framework of professional development: a phenomenographic study of academics' mindsets in a business school. Int. J. Acad. Dev. **29**(3), 337–352 (2024). https://doi.org/10.1080/1360144X.2023.2183403
51. Weller-Newton, J.M., Drummond-Young, M.: Reflective practice in health professions education. In: Clinical Education for the Health Professions: Theory and Practice, pp. 441–462. Springer, Singapore (2023)
52. Wijnia, L., Noordzij, G., Arends, L.R., Rikers, R.M., Loyens, S.M.: The effects of problem-based, project-based, and case-based learning on students' motivation: a meta-analysis. Educ. Psychol. Rev. **36**(1), 29 (2024)
53. Wolff, L.-A.: Transformative learning. In: Idowu, S., Schmidpeter, R., Capaldi, N., Zu, L., Del Baldo, M., Abreu, R. (eds.) Encyclopedia of Sustainable Management. Springer (2022). https://doi.org/10.1007/978-3-030-02006-4_1135-1
54. Yoshida, F., Conti, G.J., Yamauchi, T., Kawanishi, M.: Learner-centeredness vs. teacher-centeredness: how are they different? J. Educ. Learn. **12**(5), 1–12 (2023)

Faculty Development for the Integration of a Comprehensive Perspective on AI in Higher Education: *LookAIHed*, A Case Study

Juliana E. Raffaghelli[1](✉), Mariana Ferrarelli[2], and Marina de Rossi[1]

[1] University of Padua, Padua, Italy
{juliana.raffaghelli,marina.derossi}@unipd.it
[2] iSalud, Buenos Aires, BA, Argentina
mferrarelli@isalud.edu.ar

Abstract. This article examines the integration of a critical and comprehensive approach to artificial intelligence (AI) in higher education, through the lenses of faculty development spaces and experiences to deal with digital transformation. The study is based on a case, the "LookAIHed" program implemented at the University of Padua, which aimed to enhance faculty understanding of AI as a socio-technical phenomenon. The intervention emphasized critical literacy, ethical awareness, and pedagogical innovation, guiding educators beyond basic tool usage towards reflective and context-sensitive applications of AI. The study employed a mixed-methods approach, involving workshops, collaborative learning design, and scenario analysis.

While initial results showed faculty focusing on content creation and assessment with AI, the program gradually fostered deeper critical engagement. Participants began addressing higher-order thinking skills and ethical considerations, aligning AI use with institutional values such as academic freedom and experimental inquiry.

Findings underscore the importance of supporting critical dialogue on AI integrations, through tactical spaces of faculty development. By prioritizing pedagogical intentions and ethical considerations, the professoriate can avoid AI instrumental usage and engage with technology through situated, strategical and political agency.

Keywords: Faculty Development · Artificial Intelligence · Instrumental Use · Critical Perspective · Ethics

1 Introduction

Until 2022, AIEd had primarily been confined to laboratory development, with discrete integration into everyday teaching and learning activities. The introduction of ChatGPT in November 2022 resulted in extensive media excitement and the pervasive application of the term "AI" for many contexts [1]. Initially, Higher Ed prohibited the use of GenAI-powered chatbots due to apprehensions regarding academic integrity. However,

P. Ardimento et al. (Eds.): HELMeTO 2024, CCIS 2468, pp. 223–234, 2025.
https://doi.org/10.1007/978-3-031-93999-0_14

the discourse rapidly shifted to emphasise the verifiability and authenticity of student and researcher outputs, paralleling the continuing discussion on "academic integrity", to a relevant interest on the potential of AIEd for teaching and learning [2]. The educational practice and research rapidly moved towards investigating and comprehending the applications (more than the implications) of GenAI. This movement critiqued prohibitionism, asserting that the issue resides not in the instrument itself, but in an educational approach rooted in the transmission and reiteration of outdated abstract concepts [3]. Both tendencies neglected to recognise the technological intricacy and relational aspect, wherein the "social life" of AI must be contextualised [4, 5]. Furthermore, the concealed computational framework supporting such an effect was not novel. Research on social media sites such as Google Suite, Amazon, and Netflix has challenged this digital assemblage for its pernicious implications, including monitoring, bias, and epistemic unfairness [6]. Despite the incorporation of a critical perspective into the discourse, following the release of UNESCO and EU critical guidelines for the utilisation of GenAI in education, the concept of "responsible use" was reduced to checklists to be fulfilled prior to implementation, neglecting structural social factors and the significant effects of automated generativity. It may be inferred that higher education institutions are facing challenges in adopting holistic, critical, and complete strategies regarding AI, with most offerings focused on elucidating the capabilities of ChatGPT and other generative AI technologies [7]. This article presents a case that contextualises the institutional endeavours to incorporate AI within the prevailing organisational and faculty development culture, the LookAIHED Programme, in which we participated as facilitators and designers. The planned activity for all freely participating higher education academics aims to comprehend the growing trends of Generative AI to inform agentic and context-specific educational and institutional practices. Our research question was: Is our approach to faculty development effective in dealing with a comprehensive (critical, complex, situated) idea of AI in Higher Education?

2 Background

2.1 The Compelling Need of a Critical Stance on AI in Faculty Development Initiatives

AI-based educational innovations impact on the future consolidation of formal and informal practices of students and faculty [8]. This rapidly evolving scenario calls for deep critical reflection with respect to the changes and the resulting potentialities [9], which cannot be limited to retrospective analysis but must allow for anticipation of future problems and prospects. As boyd and Crawford [10] argue, it is important to develop critical skills with respect to the conscious use and interpretation of data, considering the ethical aspects involved. The university context also plays a crucial role in a critical path toward educational and training models capable of exploiting and developing the potential of AI in a reliable and sustainable way [11].

At this point it is important to draw attention to how crucial the issue of critical literacy in artificial intelligence is, the definition of which is not without complexity as it introduces a number of considerations.

A first consideration concerns the development of systems that have rapidly evolved expanding the very definition of AI because they can perform cognitive tasks, particularly learning and problem solving, thanks to technological innovations such as machine learning, natural language processing, and neural networks [12].

Connected to this is the widespread of applications derived from the availability of cloud computing, which makes AI systems more pervasive in people's lives.

From this follows consideration of the enormous amount of data that each user, often unknowingly, makes available with a strong reminder of the ethical issues on both the design and use of AI [13]. It is now well established that artificial intelligence (AI) ethics is necessary and should help guide technological developments. Indeed, "As AI ethics move from its initial race for enunciating principles (that was mostly focused on issuing general guidelines) to more sustainable, inclusive, and practical guidance, stakeholder engagement and citizen involvement will need to be embedded into the framing of ethical and societal expectations toward this technology and its uses." [13, p. Conclusion].

In this regard, it is necessary to consider the importance of educational and regulatory action at the institutional level in the process of faculty development to guide to understand what AI technology is, its basic functions, social and personal impact and, therefore, also develop reflection on the ethical dimension (use of data to train systems, decision generation, privacy, problem of bias, and others) [1, 4].

Agreeing with Ranieri's [14] synthesis regarding the different definitions of AI critical literacy, four main dimensions can be identified: cognitive (knowing and understanding AI), operational (using and applying AI), critical (evaluating and creating AI) ethical (understanding the ethical implications of AI). In fact, emphasising the importance of going beyond just knowing AI, critical literacy is about acquiring skills that enable teachers to teach AI programs, critically evaluate, communicate, and collaborate effectively with AI in their teaching [15].

The importance of ethics in AI cannot be overlooked as there is a growing need to educate both the general audience, technology experts, and those teaching the younger generation to strengthen their civic responsibility and to address diversity and social inclusion by thinking about AI implementation for the benefit of society and culture. These considerations are part of the overall goals of AI literacy.

Studies have shown that proper training of teachers, especially those without previous AI experience through specific AI literacy courses, can improve tool knowledge, design of appropriate teaching methods, age-appropriate selection of materials for students, understanding of proper use in classroom instruction, management efficiency, and decision-making skills [16–18].

Approaching the recent developments in the field of AI from a critical perspective implies addressing the phenomenon from multiple standpoints that exceed the mere technological or, in the context of higher education, pedagogical stance. As Ferrarelli and Ricaurte [19] sustain, AI can be read as a social, ethical, economic, epistemic and even aesthetic incident extending its ramifications into various fields of knowledge that intertwine. This approach demands the detailed examination of AI's potential to exacerbate existing inequalities, perpetuate biases, and undermine human agency. It calls for a nuanced understanding of AI's impact on labour markets, the politics of knowledge creation, privacy rights, and democratic processes.

The critical perspective we propose interrogates the epistemological foundations of AI, questioning the reliability and transparency of its decision-making processes and content-creation foundations. This approach to AI entails engaging with this technology thoughtfully and critically, considering how it can enhance teaching and learning while we keep an eye on the ways it serves and expands existing power structures. In this context, it is crucial to acknowledge that AI is not neutral but is shaped by the sociotechnical, epistemological, and sociocultural contexts in which it is developed. Consequently, AI not only processes data but also encodes and reproduces existing, values and biases within those data and society at large [20, 21].

Despite this critical literature on AI in Higher Education, there's is growing reliance on AI to generate educational content and make pedagogical decisions. In this scenario, educators may feel pressured to adapt their teaching practices to the context imposed by the popularity of AI systems, a situation which could undermine their professional autonomy and ability to respond to the contextual needs of their students. Therefore, we contend that a critical approach to AI in education necessitates permanent commitment through spaces to engage in discussion and understanding (as forms of professional learning) to evaluate AI's ethical, social, and pedagogical implications. Our case study embraces this approach triggering a particular reflection on the pedagogical implications when the educational aims are brought to the fore.

3 Methodological Approach

Our intervention can be deemed a mixed methods case study since it focuses on a specific intervention in a socio-historical and institutional context [22]. We stem from the idea that AI systems are socio-technical assemblages that require a complex perspective delving into the liaisons between culture, practice, discourse, identities and the technology usages as a relational phenomenon [23, 24]. In this regard, we embrace the "postdigital" stance, which emphasises the complexity and situatedness of any form of digital interaction in datafied and platformised interfaces [25]. Generative AI is the latest and most evident form of a transforming technological landscape. The enthusiastic approach to its outcomes has exacerbated the problems of bias, lack of transparency, universality, neutrality that most technologies have catered to the wider audience [26].

Therefore, we problematized faculty development "to adopt" AI through the postdigital lenses [27], rather than accepting an actual "need" to develop professional skills to adopt AI in Higher Education.

Our "LookAIHEd" approach included the idea of "looking into the future" to find continuity between "who we are" as institutions and academics and "who we could be" with AI. This exercise of imagining possible futures connected to our institutional and professional identity gave us the possibility to delve not only on AI current possibilities of usage, but on AI's impacts in our societies. In this regard, the University of Padua identity as a traditional, ancient university in the Italian landscape (founded in the Middle Ages, 1222) was central. We built over the value given to academic freedom in this history (*Universa Universis Patavina Libertas*, whole freedom for all within the University of Padua) as well as the longstanding tradition initiated by Galileo Galilei about experimental observation and reflection. Over these bases we proposed a programme to understand AI as a situated historical, social and cultural phenomenon. Hence, more than integrating AI-driven activities directly into the classroom, our goal was to inform and support faculty' reflection about the possible impacts of AI in the context of the UNIPD as an Italian university with a singular trajectory.

The approach encompassed a series of progressive stages and approaches with 23 initial faculty members from 8 different disciplines:

- five different phases of interaction (Explore, Understand, Collaborate, Design, Implement/document/share),
- two perspectives on AI (educational or teaching and learning with AI; and promoting AI literacy, or learning about AI);
- and six areas of pedagogical intervention with AI, from the teacher and the student side (Curriculum Design, Learning Design, Content development, Communication, Collaboration and Assessment).

The faculty development programme was tactically organised through a blended approach, with three workshops opening the working phases and assessing the prior work. Table 1 displays the faculty development intervention. We collected data from the trainers' reflection upon the process which lasted 6 months; students' artifacts and narratives; and a final survey from the final group participants, which grew progressively upon the interest generated by the programme (N = 42) with quantitative and quantitative data.

Table 1. LookAIHed programme

Schedule	Online synchronous	Online Asynchronous	Expected Results
Nov–Jan 2023	Introducing LookAIHED Exploring Chatbots and other Gen-AI	Consultation of several sources on AI in Ed Recommendations, Sci Lit, Cases	Improved understanding of AI as a problem, beyond instrumental use
Feb–March 2024	Learning Design with GenAI	Sharing Design Scenarios	Several pedagogical hypotheses (AIED usage)
April–May 2024	Documenting and Sharing	Pedagogical Documentation approaches and cases collection	Cases for reflection Triggering new loops of pedagogical practice

The mixed methods approach could be considered "transformative" [28], as an interventionist sequence of actions leading to qualitative and quantitative data collection. The data collection is opportunistic and aims at representing the processes of change and the way the participants react to the interventions. The qualitative data collection consisted of Pedagogical Documentation based on the learning artifacts generated by the participants along the process, including their learning plans, perspectives and choices made about AI in their classrooms. The qualitative analysis was focused on uncovering the meaning-making process around AI as object of understanding and interaction, in connection to professional praxis, academics and institutional identity and trajectories. The quantitative approach consisted of data collection through a standard survey on the participants' opinion about the activities offered through the LookAIHED Programme. The survey consisted of simple questions to which the participants could respond through a Likert Scale 1–4 (Cronbach's alpha = 0.83 for the whole scale):

- The Topic was relevant to you
- The activities were appropriately organized
- The teaching approach within *LookAIHED* was relevant
- The time devoted to the activities was appropriate
- You believe you will apply to practice what you learnt after this T4L activity

Additionally, we used linear regression to analyse predictors of adopting AI in teaching through a comprehensive approach.

4 Results

We observed low "active" engagement in discussions during the online phases. Each two weeks a topic was launched to prepare participation during the onsite and synchronous phases. In total, five threads were opened, dealing with a) presentation; b) understanding genAI; c) creating content with genAI; d) assessment and evaluation in times of genAI; d) ethical concerns. The participation increased significantly during these last types of activities, which became rich spaces for exchanging opinions, ideas, questions, and practices.

As a matter of fact, the participants came up with relevant results during the session devoted to design learning plans embedding a holistic view of AI.

Out of 18 designs, 16 of them (88%) dealt with topics and practices connected to the instrumental conception of the tools, connected to solving mostly *teacher side* needs and activities (*preparing tests; creating online quizzes; content generation for the slides, case studies creation for the students). Only two cases introduced prompting loops to improve writing skills.*

This initial analysis of documents and recommendations was followed by a second part of the session when participants went on imagining possible scenarios and were invited to work in groups. The generated scenarios predominantly emphasised learning with AI, with only one scenario addressing both aspects, contending that the implementation of the tool for comparing student performance should prompt thought on its use.

In four out of six possibilities, it is the instructor who implements AI in the classroom, while in one scenario both the teacher and students do, and in the final scenario, just the students do. From an educational standpoint, five groups concentrated on assessment, exploring progressive feedback strategies derived from AI-generated quizzes; conversely, one group focused on feedback methodologies for collaboration and group work, utilising self-applied product analysis rubrics.

During the subsequent 2 months (March–April, thus entering the core of the instructional time), the participants concentrated on adhering to the suggestions for enhancing these scenarios; yet they predominantly favoured further understanding of the tools over their use. In the satisfaction questionnaires and reflections following the events, numerous participants indicated a desire to enhance their proficiency and confidence with AI technologies. Also, resources to reflect about the criticalities of adopting AI were provided. As a result, during the third session, the ideas and cases of usage were discussed onsite in the light of the AI complexity. It followed a critical reflection on the application of AI. From this exercise, it was apparent the focus on instrumental AI usage initially. Therefore, the next focus of the discussion was how to move from AI usage to AI that promotes a) active learning, and b) higher order skills.

A relevant element of reflection was that not all AI integration necessarily promote these two elements, central to the T4L (UNIPD)'s values: teaching for learning. We offered cases applied at UNIPD and to an invited institution, to delve on the Bloom's taxonomy levels enacted by the AI practices; the presence of active learning and/or promoting higher order skills and the extent to which the AI usage for good might be interfered by questionable actions by the students (implications of academic integrity). Table 2 displays the reflections carried out during the session, in a thematic synthesis.

Table 2. Synthesis of ideas emerged debating the impact of AI integration according to the scenario's design approach

AI use case	Active Learning/Students' skills	Academic Integrity as a Problem
Automated quizzes creation	No Lower Order	Yes (Student/Teacher side)
Online Forum Analysis with AI	Yes Mid-Lower order	Yes (Teacher side: data ethics)
Argumentative Skills	Yes Higher order	No There is a creative interaction to get the result
Creating an intelligent assistant	No Mid-lower order	No The information can only be used to organise learning
Creating a Generative Twin	Yes Higher order	No There is a progressive creative process of usage and co-design

Therefore, the final session (May 2024) included a discussion of such cases reflecting not only on potential applications, but most importantly, the appropriate approaches to protect data and to communicate with the students about the usage of AI in class. It is possible to observe hence how the different participants moved from instrumental usage to a critical perspective of any AI instrument according to a more comprehensive vision of the educational goals and institutional identity which AI might (or might not) support (Table 3).

We analysed the final Survey on the sessions' quality, including the participants' evaluation of Teaching, Pedagogical Approach, Topic, Time and Organisation. Figure 1

Table 3. Descriptive Statistics - After Training Survey

Variable/Stats	N	Mean	Median	SD	Min	Max
Organisation	42	3.90	4.00	0.297	3	4
Quality	42	2.86	3.00	0.814	2	4
Time	42	2.48	3.00	0.671	1	3
Topic	42	3.60	4.00	0.587	2	4
Teaching	42	3.36	4.00	0.759	2	4
Application - Transfer to Practice	42	2.48	2.00	1.018	1	4
Recommendation to a Third	42	3.14	3.00	0.899	2	4

displays the relationship between the opinion per each area of the survey divided by disciplinary area. We also analysed qualitative responses, which support the interpretation of such results.

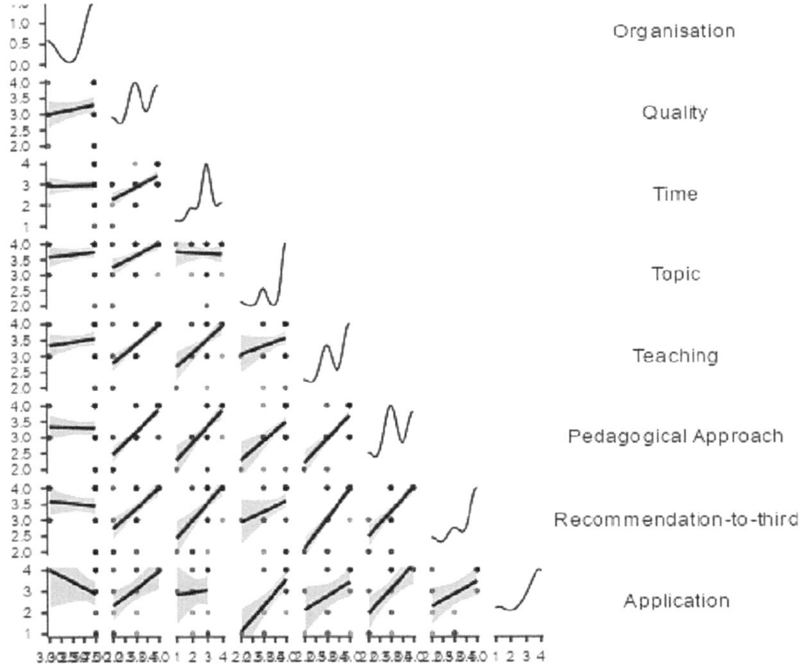

Fig. 1. Matrix of correlations between the variables in the model.

We conclude that though the concatenated, blended activity was positive to raise awareness and engagement in a wider institutional activity, traditional approaches to teaching might lead participants to be rather focused on the instrumental usage of AI.

However, our faculty development approach supported understanding about the relevance of institutional strategies, to embrace both a specific, disciplinary perspective and a wider picture on GenAI in HE institutions.

5 Discussion and Conclusions

The case study "LookAIHEd" effectively highlights the opportunities and challenges of integrating a comprehensive and critical perspective on AI in higher education. The intervention addressed a significant gap by moving beyond instrumental adoption and encouraging faculty to engage with AI as a socio-technical phenomenon, fostering critical awareness and pedagogical innovation. The focus on the cognitive skills being developed and demanded in each case offered a significant entry point to reflection and debate among faculty members. By examining how different AI tools can be used to foster both lower-order and higher-order thinking skills, we promoted discussions on how higher Ed educators can pedagogically harness the power of AI to enhance student learning. This reflective approach let faculty move beyond superficial adoption and delve into the deeper implications of AI for teaching and learning, ultimately leading to the debate of more meaningful and impactful educational proposals.

However, the findings suggest that while participants demonstrated an initial interest in AI tools, their focus remained largely on instrumental uses, such as content creation and assessment tool design. This reflects a broader issue in faculty development, where traditional pedagogical practices and institutional structures often constrain transformative adoption of technology [29]. While offering immediate benefits in terms of experimental approach and eventual productivity, we contend that the instrumental use of technology in general and AI in particular, risks perpetuating outdated pedagogical practices that prioritize knowledge transmission over critical thinking and problem-solving. By focusing on tasks like content creation and assessment design, educators may inadvertently limit the potential of AI reproducing obsolete formats instead of advancing in more meaningful learning experiences. The analysis of the cognitive processes that underlie the proposals designed aimed at discussing the transformative potential of AI in higher education. By exploring diverse examples and alternative use cases, as facilitators we shifted the dialogue to more student-centred design approaches that challenge traditional teaching and learning paradigms.

A key insight from the study is the importance of aligning AI integration with institutional identity and values. By rooting the intervention in the University of Padua's tradition of academic freedom and experimental inquiry, the program fostered a reflective space for exploring AI's implications for teaching and learning from a context-specific perspective. However, the limited transition from instrumental to critical uses underscores the need for deeper engagement with the ethical, environmental, and social dimensions of AI. The program's inclusion of scenarios addressing higher-order skills and active learning was a step in this direction, but broader institutional strategies are needed to ensure these critical perspectives are consistently integrated.

In the context of critical pedagogy and scholarship, an initial unguided approach to integrating technology in education often aligns with traditional teaching practices, perpetuating existing norms rather than fostering transformative pedagogy [25, 30, 31].

While instrumental adoption of EdTech may overlook the pedagogical and critical stance, a progressive and holistic engagement with AI can empower educators and learners by promoting agency in selecting and designing approaches that integrate both qualitative and quantitative insights. Awareness-raising and intentional engagement with AI tools can yield positive outcomes in professional development programs, provided that these initiatives are thoughtfully organized and relevant to participants' needs and institutional culture.

However, challenges remain, including the lack of comprehensive institutional strategies to embed AI meaningfully in higher education. Focused case studies with convenience samples highlight a need for deeper qualitative exploration of educators' intentions to critically embrace generative AI. Moreover, decisive questions arise about the ethical implications of AI usage, such as its carbon footprint and the necessity to balance technological adoption with sustainability concerns [31]. Beyond focusing on how to use AI effectively, there is a pressing need to reconsider the structures and political epistemologies that underpin algorithmic design in educational contexts [4, 32].

These prompts reflection on whether our goal is merely to integrate AI into teaching or to reshape our practices in ways that align with values of social intelligence and ecological responsibility. In essence, the challenge is to live well with a "situated AI," fostering an urgent dialogue that addresses both the pedagogical possibilities and the broader societal implications of these technologies.

References

1. Bond, M., et al.: A meta systematic review of artificial intelligence in higher education: a call for increased ethics, collaboration, and rigour. Int. J. Educ. Technol. High. Educ. **21**(1), 4 (2024). https://doi.org/10.1186/s41239-023-00436-z
2. Tlili, A., et al.: What if the devil is my guardian angel: ChatGPT as a case study of using chatbots in education. Smart Learn. Environ. **10**(1), 15 (2023). https://doi.org/10.1186/s40561-023-00237-x
3. Susnjak, T.: ChatGPT: the end of online exam integrity? (2022). https://doi.org/10.48550/arXiv.2212.09292
4. Raffaghelli, J.E.: (Post)Digital scholarship. Professionalità accademica e trasformazione tecnologica in università. Manoscritto 2.0 in Didattiche, Tecnologie e Media Education. Frontiere per la Sostenibilità. (2024). https://www.pensamultimedia.it/libro/9791255681205
5. Williamson, B.: The social life of AI in education. Int. J. Artif. Intell. Educ. (2023). https://doi.org/10.1007/s40593-023-00342-5
6. Rivera-Vargas, P., Raffaghelli, J., Miño-Puigcercós, R.: Plataformas digitales comerciales en la educación pública: Desafíos emergentes sobre privacidad y protección de datos. Edutec Revista Electrónica de Tecnología Educativa. **87** (2024). https://doi.org/10.21556/edutec.2024.87.3063
7. Bosen, L.-L., et al.: Harnessing the era of artificial intelligence in higher education: a primer for higher education stakeholders. UNESCO-IESALC. (2023). https://unesdoc.unesco.org/ark:/48223/pf0000386670?locale=en
8. Holmes, W.: The unintended consequences of artificial intelligence and education. Int. Res. Educ. (2023) https://www.ei-ie.org/en/item/28115:the-unintended-consequences-of-artificial-intelligence-and-education
9. Pancirolli, C., Rivoltella, P.C., Algoritmica, P.: Per una riflessione educativa sull'Intelligenza Artificiale. Scholé. (2023)

10. Boyd, D., Crawford, K.: Critical questions for big data. Inf. Commun. Soc. **15**(5), 662–679 (2012). https://doi.org/10.1080/1369118X.2012.678878
11. Schneider, G.: L'impatto dell'intelligenza artificiale sull'università tra tutela dei dati personali e diritto all'istruzione. In Intelligenza artificiale e diritto: Una rivoluzione? I Diritti fondamentali, dati personali e regolazione, pp. 413–431. (2022)
12. Zawacki-Richter, O., Marín, V.I., Bond, M., Gouverneur, F.: Systematic review of research on artificial intelligence applications in higher education – where are the educators? Int. J. Educ. Technol. High. Educ. **16**(1), 39 (2019). https://doi.org/10.1186/s41239-019-0171-0
13. Bélisle-Pipon, J.-C., Monteferrante, E., Roy, M.-C., Couture, V.: Artificial intelligence ethics has a black box problem. AI & Soc. **38**(4), 1507–1522 (2022). https://doi.org/10.1007/s00146-021-01380-0
14. Ranieri, M.: Intelligenza artificiale a scuola: Una lettura pedagogico-didattica delle sfide e delle opportunità. Rivista di Scienze dell'Educazione. **62**(1), 123–135. https://flore.unifi.it/handle/2158/1379632 (2024)
15. Sperling, K., Stenberg, C.-J., McGrath, C., Åkerfeldt, A., Heintz, F., Stenliden, L.: In search of artificial intelligence (AI) literacy in teacher education: a scoping review. Comput.Educ.Open. **6**, 100169 (2024). https://doi.org/10.1016/j.caeo.2024.100169
16. Kuhail, M.A., Katheeri, H.A., Negreiros, J., Seffah, A., Alfandi, O.: Engaging students with a chatbot-based academic advising system. Int. J. Hum.–Comput. Interact. **39**(10), 2115–2141 (2023). https://doi.org/10.1080/10447318.2022.2074645
17. Raffaghelli, J.E., Rodríguez, M.E., Guerrero-Roldán, A.-E., Bañeres, D.: Applying the UTAUT model to explain the students' acceptance of an early warning system in higher education. Comput. Educ. **182**, 104468 (2022). https://doi.org/10.1016/j.compedu.2022.104468
18. Sandu, N., Gide, E.: Adoption of AI-chatbots to enhance student learning experience in higher education in India. In: 2019 18th International Conference on Information Technology Based Higher Education and Training (ITHET), pp. 1–5. (2019). https://doi.org/10.1109/ITHET46829.2019.8937382
19. Raffaghelli, J.E., Sangrà, A.: Data, society and the university: facets of a complex problem. In: Raffaghelli, J.E., Sangrà, A. (eds.) Data Cultures in Higher Education: Emergent Practices and the Challenge Ahead, pp. 41–68. Springer (2023). https://doi.org/10.1007/978-3-031-24193-2_2
20. Ferrarelli, M., Ricaurte, P.: Problematizar la IA generativa en educación: metáforas, tensiones y horizontes posibles. In: Martins, L. (ed.) Aspectos éticos y pedagógicos de los datos y la tecnología en educación, pp. 53–94. LMI. (2024)
21. Williamson, B.: Critical keywords of AI in education. Code Acts in Education. (2024). https://codeactsineducation.wordpress.com/2024/11/08/critical-keywords-of-ai-in-education/. Accessed 5 Nov 2024
22. Gerring, J.: Case Study Research: Principles and Practices. Cambridge University Press (2007)
23. Decuypere, M.: The topologies of data practices: a methodological introduction. J. New Approach. Educ. Res. **10**(1) (2021). https://doi.org/10.7821/naer.2021.1.650
24. Passeron, E.: Ciudadania relacional: La convivencia escolar con las tecnologias digitales. Universitat de Barcelona. https://diposit.ub.edu/dspace/handle/2445/212461. Accessed 5 Nov 2024
25. Macgilchrist, F.: Theories of postdigital heterogeneity: implications for research on education and datafication. Postdigit. Sci. Educ. **3**(3), 660–667 (2021). https://doi.org/10.1007/s42438-021-00232-w
26. Suárez-Guerrero, C., Rivera-Vargas, P., Raffaghelli, J.: EdTech myths: towards a critical digital educational agenda. Technol. Pedagog. Educ. (2023). https://doi.org/10.1080/1475939X.2023.2240332

27. Hayes, S.: Postdigital perspectives on the McPolicy of measuring excellence. Postdigit. Sci. Educ. **3**(1), 1–6 (2021). https://doi.org/10.1007/s42438-020-00208-2
28. Creswell, J.W., Clark, V.L.P.: Designing and Conducting Mixed Methods Research. SAGE Publications (2017)
29. Lion, C., Kap, M., Ferrarelli, M.: Universidades desafiadas: Alfabetismos fluidos, hibridaciones y nuevas estrategias de enseñanza. Revista de Educación Superior y Sociedad. **35**(2) (2023). https://doi.org/10.54674/ess.v35i2.768
30. Selwyn, N., Hillman, T., Bergviken Rensfeldt, A., Perrotta, C.: Digital technologies and the automation of education — key questions and concerns. Postdigit. Sci. Educ. **5**, 15–24 (2023). https://doi.org/10.1007/s42438-021-00263-3
31. Selwyn, N.: Lessons to be learnt? Education, techno-solutionism, and sustainable development. In: Technology and Sustainable Development. Routledge (2023)
32. Pasquinelli, M.: The Eye of the Master: A Social History of Artificial Intelligence. Verso Books (2023)

Are You a Left or Right-Brain Type? Persistence of Neuromyths in Italian In-Service Teachers

Andrea Tinterri[1(✉)], Maria Carolina Zarrilli Affaitati[2], Angelo Basta[2], and Anna Dipace[1]

[1] Pegaso Telematic University, Naples 80143, Italy
andrea.tinterri@unipegaso.it
[2] University of Foggia, Foggia 71122, Italy

Abstract. Neuromyths remain pervasive among educators, posing risks to evidence-based pedagogical practices. This study examines the persistence of these myths among Italian in-service teachers, a group critical to effective educational delivery. A structured, anonymous survey was administered to 6679 teachers participating in the 30 CFU qualification program at Pegaso Telematic University. The survey, modeled after Dekker and Jolles (2012), assessed agreement with seven prevalent neuromyths. Alarmingly, 89.7% of participants endorsed the learning styles neuromyth, despite clear evidence refuting its validity (Kirschner, 2017). Additionally, 54.3% believed in hemispheric dominance influencing cognition, while 65.9% accepted that specific exercises could facilitate interhemispheric integration. Even the discredited claim that humans use only 10% of their brain remained prevalent (46.7%). In contrast, neuromyths related to nutrition, such as sugar intake affecting attention (46.5%) and dehydration causing brain shrinkage (23.8%), were less frequently believed. These findings highlight a significant deficit in neuroscientific literacy among teachers, which could hinder the adoption of empirically validated teaching methodologies. The persistence of such neuromyths necessitates a strategic re-evaluation of teacher training curricula to emphasize neuroscientific rigor and critical engagement with research findings. Enhancing scientific literacy within the educational workforce is imperative to mitigate the influence of neuromyths and improve instructional outcomes, aligning educational practices with contemporary neuroscience.

Keywords: Neuromyths · Educational Neuroscience · Evidence based Education

1 Introduction

1.1 Definition

In recent years, there has been a growing dissemination of neuroscience and its applications across various fields, including education. This trend has sparked increasing interest among educators, who perceive neuroscience as a potential tool for developing innovative teaching methodologies. However, over time, there has also been the entrenchment

P. Ardimento et al. (Eds.): HELMeTO 2024, CCIS 2468, pp. 235–246, 2025.
https://doi.org/10.1007/978-3-031-93999-0_15

of misinterpreted concepts known as neuromyths. According to the OECD (2007) these are "misconceptions generated by a misunderstanding, misreading, or misquoting of scientifically established facts from brain research." Unfortunately, such misconceptions often influence educational practices, leading to the adoption of teaching approaches that lack solid scientific support. Several types of neuromyths are commonly discussed in the literature, each of which warrants analysis and consideration.

One such neuromyth is the *learning styles myth*, which posits that individuals learn best through a specific modality (visual, auditory, or kinaesthetic). However, research suggests that learning effectiveness is not dependent on adapting to a particular style but rather on employing diverse, content-based teaching methods (Pashler et al., 2009). Another prevalent neuromyth is the *10% brain myth*, which claims that humans only utilize a small percentage of their brain capacity. However, neuroscientific studies have shown that the majority of the brain remains active, even during routine activities (Raichle et al., 2001). Further misconceptions exist regarding brain plasticity, including the critical periods and *unlimited plasticity* myths. The *critical periods myth* asserts that certain skills must be learned within specific windows during childhood, or they will be permanently inaccessible. In contrast, the *unlimited plasticity myth* suggests that the brain is capable of indefinite adaptation at any age. In fact, brain plasticity is most pronounced during early development and has certain physiological limits (Kolb, Gibb, 2011). Programs such *as Brain Gym* claim that specific physical exercises, like crossing arms and legs, can enhance cognitive abilities. However, there is no strong scientific evidence supporting the notion that such exercises significantly improve learning outcomes (Howard-Jones, 2014). The myth of enriched environments, or the *Mozart effect*, suggests that exposing children to highly stimulating environments, such as listening to classical music, especially Mozart, can boost their cognitive development. However, scientific studies indicate that the effect of music on cognitive function is short-lived and does not lead to lasting improvements in intelligence (Howard-Jones, 2014). The *sugar and hyperactivity myth* claims that sugar consumption leads to hyperactivity in children, a belief commonly held by parents and teachers. However, scientific research has repeatedly debunked this claim. Controlled studies have shown no causal link between sugar intake and hyperactive behavior (Wolraich et al., 1995). This perceived connection may be the result of a placebo effect, where adults' expectations influence their perception of children's behavior. This myth could contribute to misinterpretations of behavior and unnecessary dietary restrictions, without offering any proven benefits for managing hyperactivity. A common neuromyth is the idea that individuals are either "left-brained" or "right-brained," with the left hemisphere associated with logical, mathematical, and linguistic abilities, and the right hemisphere linked to creativity, art, and music. According to this myth, a "left-brained" person would excel in subjects like math and logic, while a "right-brained" individual would be more inclined toward creative pursuits. For example, a teacher might incorrectly categorize a student as "rightbrained" based solely on their interest in drawing, leading to the assumption that the student may struggle with analytical subjects like mathematics. Consequently, the teacher might prioritize creative tasks, potentially overlooking the development of the student's logical and linguistic skills. However, neuroscience has demonstrated that both hemispheres of the brain collaborate and function integratively for nearly all cognitive processes (Howard-Jones, 2014).

Neuromyths represent a significant issue in the realm of education and training among teachers and educational professionals. Numerous studies conducted prior to 2024 consistently demonstrate the widespread belief in neuromyths within the teaching profession, with substantial implications for pedagogical practices. Research indicates that a considerable proportion of educators subscribe to these misconceptions. For instance, a study by Dekker and Jolles (2012) found that 82% of teachers endorsed the *learning styles* myth, and more than 50% believed in the myth that individuals only utilize 10% of their brain capacity. The belief in neuromyths is not confined to general education teachers; it also extends to educators with advanced qualifications. A study by Macdonald et al. (2017) revealed that while neuroscience training can reduce, it does not entirely eradicate belief in neuromyths. Their research showed that a notable number of educators, including those with specialized training, continued to hold misconceptions regarding brain function. Furthermore, neuromyths are prevalent among pre-service teachers. Dündar and Gündüz (2016) reported that 55% of pre-service teachers adhered to *the learning styles myth*, suggesting that such misconceptions emerge early in the professional development of educators. The prevalence of neuromyths varies across countries; however, the overall belief rate remains alarmingly high. For example, Rato et al. (2013) found that 68% of Portuguese teachers believed in neuromyths, such as the existence of critical learning periods in early childhood, and similar findings have been observed in other regions. The widespread acceptance of neuromyths can have detrimental consequences. First, these myths can lead educators to adopt ineffective or scientifically unsupported teaching strategies, such as the learning styles approach, which lacks empirical support (Dekker and Jolles 2012). As Howard-Jones (2014) points out, such beliefs distort educational practices, resulting in methods that are not grounded in scientific evidence. Consequently, educational institutions may invest in neuromyth-based programs or tools, diverting valuable time and financial resources away from practices that are substantiated by scientific research. Second, neuromyths may hinder students' potential. For example, the belief in the myth that only *10% of the brain* is used can negatively impact students' perceptions of their own learning and developmental capabilities, diminishing their motivation and self-efficacy (Macdonald et al., 2017). Moreover, the dissemination of neuromyths within the educational environment not only reinforces misconceptions among students but also among parents and other educators, perpetuating a cycle of misinformation (Rato et al., 2013). This cycle diverts attention away from educational interventions rooted in solid research, thereby undermining the overall effectiveness of education (Howard-Jones, 2014). The persistence of neuromyths can also erode the credibility of scientific research. As Horvath et al. (2017) note, the widespread belief in such myths diminishes trust in neuroscientific findings, as educators may begin to question the validity of scientific research when commonly accepted myths are debunked. Despite efforts by the scientific community to address these misconceptions and promote evidence-based educational practices, neuromyths continue to exert a significant influence on education. Their persistence underscores the gap between neuroscientific discoveries and the teaching practices implemented by educators.

The aim of the present study is to examine the current prevalence of neuromyths among Italian teachers, with the overarching goal of identifying strategies for promoting evidence-based and evidence-informed approaches in teacher training programs. Based on the questionnaire used in the study by Dekker and Jolles (2012), the following research questions have been formulated:

- RQ1: To what extent are neuromyths still prevalent among in-service teachers in Italy?
- RQ2: Are there correlations between different types of neuromyths, and if so, what is the nature and strength of these correlations?

2 Methods

The survey was administered in CAWI modality to a large sample of in-service teachers undergoing the 30 cfu (DPCM August 4th, 2023) teaching qualification course delivered by Pegaso Telematic University in spring 2024. One of the lessons of the course was centered on evidence-based education; thus, the short survey was used to stimulate participation and promote cognitive activation (Trinchero, 2018) in participants. Participation in the short survey was spontaneous and it was administered in CAWI modality using Google Modules. Participants accessed the module by scanning a QR code that was presented onscreen during the lesson. The module did not include any questions concerning the respondent's identity or personal information, as to maximize adhesion to the survey.

The survey were a selection of those published in a previous study by Dekker and Jolles (2012) and translated in Italian. Similar to the original study, participants were asked to indicate whether they agreed with, disagreed with or were not sure about the truthfulness of seven well-known neuromyths. Four concerned factoids about brain functioning and learning:

- We only use 10% of our brain
- People learn better when provided information in their preferred learning style
- Difference in left-right brain hemispheres dominance can explain individual difference,
- Short coordination exercise can improve left-right hemisphere communication Two questions concerned fake knowledge concerning eating and learning, and the last item concerned beliefs concerning cognitive impairment and brain plasticity. Data was collected using Google Modules and then analyzed using Jamovi software (Şahin & Aybek, 2020; Jamovi, 2021). Statistical analysis involved nonparametric correlation analysis (Kendall's tau; Abdi, 2007).

3 Results

On April 5th, 2024, a total of 6.680 teachers answered the survey, thus indicating that the short survey modality was effective in prompting spontaneous response from participants. Of those, 6632 answers came within 15 min of the QR code presentation (that is, before the teacher assessed the results to discuss the topic of neuromyths), and they were thus considered for the analysis.

Concerning the affirmation that we normally use only 10% of our brain, 46.7% of all participants agreed with the notion; 30.8% disagreed and 22.6% were unsure about it. A vast majority of participants also agreed that people learn better when they receive information in their preferred learning style (89.7% agree), a neuromyth known for its pervasiveness (Kirschner, 2017). Only 6.8% of all participants disagreed with this notion and 3.4% were unsure about it. Most of the participants also believe that left-right hemispheric dominance can explain individual differences in learners (54.3% agree) whereas 13.3% disagreed and 32.4% of them were unsure about this statement. Furthermore, 65.9% of participants believed that short sessions of exercise could help the integration of signal from left and right brain hemispheres, whilst 28.4% of them were unsure and 5.6% disagreed with this notion. Participants were slightly less keen to agree with fake notions concerning nutrition: 46.5% of respondents agreed that kids are less attentive after eating or drinking high sugar food, whereas 31.5% of them disagreed and 22.1% were unsure. Furthermore, only 23.9% of participants agreed that drinking less than 8 glasses of water per day could lead to a reduction in brain volume. 38.9% of them were unsure while 37.3% disagreed altogether. Finally, the notion that learning deficits due to differences in neurodevelopment cannot be addressed by education was held true only by 20.4% of participants, while 21.7% of them were unsure and the majority (57.9%) correctly stated it as wrong. Results are summarized in Fig. 1. Thus, these results suggest that neuromyths are still prevalent among in-service teachers, at least within the sample examined, but with significant differences. Myths that refer more directly to neuroanatomical aspects seem to be believed more than myths concerning supposed links between immediate effects of eating and drinking on learning. The learning styles myth, in accordance with previous studies (Dekker and Jolles 2012), remains the most prevalent neuromyth and is still believed by an overwhelming majority of the teachers who participated to the survey.

A second research concerned whether belief in specific neuromyths was correlated to other beliefs, that is, if teachers who agreed on one neuromyth were more likely to believe in another myth. To investigate this issue, we coded the answers provided by teachers (1 = disagree, 2 = not sure, 3 = agree) and performed a Kendall's tau correlation coefficient analysis. The results are shown in Table 1.

As could be expected, most answers present a slight, statistically significant positive correlation, indicating that people who tend to believe in one neuromyth are also slightly keener to believe in other myths. Correlations are overall weak; however, it is interesting to note that the strongest correlation (0.167) is observed for the "sweet drinks affect kids' ability to focus" and "drinking little water can cause brain shrinking", indicating that people who believe in myths concerning nutrition tend to embrace more easily other factoids on the same topic. Other relevant correlations are between the belief that "right-left brain dominance can explain individual differences" and "short coordination exercises can improve left-right brain communication", which is consistent with a simplified view of the relationship between brain anatomy and function. On the other side, it is interesting to note that neuromyths that concern brain functioning are all positively correlated with each other but do not correlate with the belief that neurodevelopmental disorders cannot be addressed through education. This indicates that this belief is held somewhat

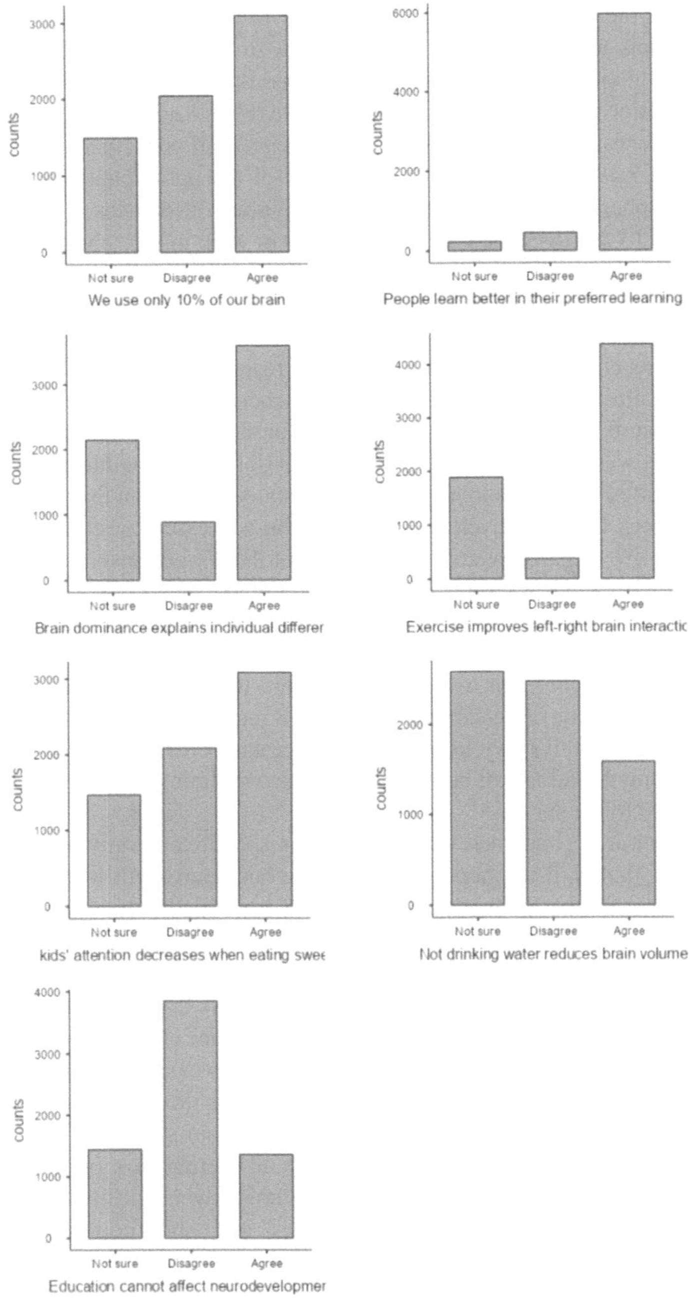

Fig. 1. Summary of teachers' responses on the truthfulness of prevalent neuromyths. Columns represent the number of teachers' responses for each survey question

Table 1. Correlation matrix analysis of teachers' answers. Kendall's tau values and p-values are reported for each cell

		10% brain	Learning Style	Exercise	Left-Right dominance	Sweet drinks affect focus	Water brain shrinking	Neuro development
10% brain	Kendall Tau p-value	— —						
Learning Styles	Kendall Tau p-value	0.058 < .001	— —					
Exercise	Kendall Tau	0.048	0.116	—				
	p-value	< .001	< .001	—				
Leftright dominance	Kendall Tau p-value	0.081 < .001	0.134 < .001	0.138 < .001	— —			
Sweet drinks affect focus	Kendall Tau p-value	0.103 < .001	0.056 < .001	0.108 < .001	0.089 < .001	— —		
Water and brain shrinking	Tau B di Kendall	0.110	0.053	0.119	0.117	0.167	—	
	valore p	< .001	< .001	< .001	< .001	< .001	—	
Neurodevelopment	Tau B di Kendall	0.027	0.035	0.011	0.014	0.060	0.044	—
	valore p	0.017	0.003	0.339	0.206	< .001	< .001	—

independently of the respondent's other beliefs concerning the brain and has more to do with her beliefs on the potential of educational intervention than brain functioning.

4 Discussion

The present investigation makes a significant contribution to the understanding of the persistence of neuromyths among Italian in-service teachers, highlighting not only the extent of the phenomenon, but also its implications on educational practices and professional training. The results obtained, in line with previous international studies such as those by Dekker and Jolles (2012) and Macdonald et al. (2017), show that a considerable number of teachers continue to adhere to pseudoscientific beliefs despite access to uptodate information and dedicated training courses. The methodology adopted in this study, based on a structured survey administered in CAWI mode, allowed for the collection of a large and representative sample, with 6680 participating teachers. The use of a QR code during a lesson on evidence-based teaching encouraged immediate and spontaneous participation, with over 99% of responses collected within 15 min. This innovative approach proved effective in engaging teachers and collecting data quickly, but also has some limitations that deserve attention. However, it must be said that although the sample size is considerable, it does not necessarily guarantee representativeness of the general teacher population, since the participants were enrolled in a specific course on evidence-based teaching at the Pegaso Telematic University. Thus, it is not clear to what extent the sample reflects the entire population of Italian teachers, which includes professionals with different levels of training, work experience and territorial affiliations. Furthermore, the absence of detailed demographic information, such as age, gender, level of education or years of professional experience, further limits the possibility of contextualizing the collected data.

The lack of these variables makes it difficult to analyze possible differences in neuromyth beliefs between specific subgroups, which could be influenced by individual or occupational factors. Furthermore, the scope of the study, which is exploratory in nature, aimed to investigate the prevalence of neuromyths among teachers, but without fully investigating the underlying causes or dynamics. Although the exploratory approach is adequate to provide an initial overview of a phenomenon that has been little studied in the Italian context, it does not investigate the specific reasons why teachers adhere to certain neuromyths or how these beliefs concretely influence their teaching practices. A more in-depth analysis of these aspects could provide useful indications for designing more targeted and effective training interventions.

As the survey was introduced during a lecture focused on evidence-based teaching, participants may have perceived an implicit pressure to provide answers in line with academic expectations, introducing a possible social desirability bias. Furthermore, the anonymous and self-assessment nature of the questionnaire may have led to less thoughtful responses, given the speed with which it was completed. Nevertheless, the results obtained offer significant insights into the prevalence of neuromyths. Analysis of the data reveals a worrying persistence of mistaken beliefs among teachers. The myth of learning styles, for example, was accepted by 89.7% of the participants, confirming its pervasiveness in the Italian educational system. This result is in line with that reported by Dekker and Jolles (2012), who had already highlighted a similar spread of this belief internationally. The adherence to the myth of hemispheric dominance (54.3%) and to the possibility that brief coordination exercises improve communication between the cerebral hemispheres (65.9%) indicates a tendency to simplify complex neuroscientific concepts, making them erroneously applicable to the educational context.

An interesting aspect that emerged from the analysis concerns the correlations between the different beliefs. Although positive correlations were found between some of the neuromyths, these were generally weak. The strongest correlation (Kendall's tau = 0.167) was observed among nutrition-related myths, suggesting that teachers who believe a specific nutrition-related false belief are more likely to accept similar ones. This finding can be interpreted considering that beliefs related to nutrition and behavior are often influenced by non-scientific popular information that is easily accessible through popular media. The limited correlation between neuromyths related to brain functioning and those related to learning deficits suggests that teachers' beliefs are not necessarily interconnected in a linear fashion. This implies that erroneous beliefs may be influenced by several factors, including personal experiences, prior training and cultural influences. For example, the belief that 'learning deficits due to differences in neurodevelopment cannot be addressed by education' was held to be true by only 20.4% of the participants, indicating an increased awareness of the potential of educational intervention in this area.

These findings highlight the need to rethink training strategies for teachers. The persistence of neuromyths, despite participation in courses on evidence-based teaching, indicates that the current training approach may not be sufficiently effective in countering entrenched beliefs. In particular, adherence to myths that offer seemingly intuitive or practical explanations underlines the importance of developing critical skills that enable teachers to assess the scientific validity of information. The literature suggests that a more interactive and critical educational approach could foster greater awareness. Howard-Jones (2014) suggests the integration of hands-on activities and guided discussions that help teachers compare neuromyths with neuroscientific evidence. Furthermore,

Trinchero (2018) emphasizes the importance of cognitive activation in adult learning processes, suggesting that the mere transmission of information is not sufficient to change established beliefs.

Another element to be considered is the role of culture and society in the spread of neuromyths. The pervasiveness of certain beliefs could be influenced by cultural factors specific to the Italian context. For example, the widespread acceptance of the myth of learning styles could be linked to educational models that emphasize the personalization of teaching without a solid scientific basis. This phenomenon underlines the need for educational interventions that consider cultural peculiarities, adapting educational strategies to maximize effectiveness. The adoption of didactic approaches based on erroneous beliefs can limit students' potential by directing educational resources towards ineffective methods. For example, insistence on learning styles may lead teachers to classify students into rigid categories, preventing them from developing competences in areas perceived as unrelated to their supposed style. This limits not only students' educational experience, but also their self-perception and motivation.

5 Conclusions

The present survey makes a useful contribution to understanding the persistence of neuromyths among in-service Italian teachers, highlighting a complex picture that requires systematic and integrated interventions to improve the quality of evidence-based education.

The results show that many now widely disproved neuromyths continue to exert a significant influence among Italian teachers. Myths such as learning styles, hemispheric dominance or the possibility that coordination exercises improve brain communication show worrying adherence rates of 89.7%, 54.3% and 65.9% respectively. This figure is not an Italian anomaly, but reflects a global trend already highlighted in previous studies (Dekker and Jolles 2012; Macdonald et al., 2017). The persistence of these beliefs, despite international efforts to address them, demonstrates the pervasive effect of a pseudoscience that finds a place in educational contexts, popular media and professional training that is not adequately supervised from a scientific point of view. The prevalence of neuromyths is not simply the result of a lack of information, but reflects a complex interaction between cultural, cognitive and structural factors that facilitate the entrenchment of these beliefs in the educational system. A key aspect that emerged from the data is the lack of basic neuroscientific knowledge among teachers, which prevents them from recognizing and deconstructing pseudoscientific concepts. The persistence of neuromyths, such as the idea that we only use 10 per cent of our brain or that certain exercises can improve the connection between the hemispheres, reflects a significant ignorance of the basic principles of brain functioning and their impact on learning. This lack of understanding is not limited to Italian teachers, but has also been found in other international contexts (Rato et al., 2013; Howard-Jones, 2014). However, in Italy, the spread of certain beliefs, such as that of learning styles, seems to be reinforced by a cultural narrative that emphasizes the personalization of teaching without an adequate empirical basis. This gap is not simply the result of an educational gap, but also reflects the complexity of neuroscience, which is often oversimplified to fit practical educational contexts.

Neuromyth-related misconceptions are not harmless, but have a direct impact on educational practices and, consequently, on students' learning experience. Teachers who adhere to pseudoscientific beliefs risk adopting ineffective teaching strategies, such as adapting teaching to supposed learning styles or categorizing students according to hypothetical hemispheric dominance. These approaches not only lack empirical support but may limit students' learning opportunities by reinforcing a static view of their abilities. Moreover, the spread of neuromyths helps perpetuate a cycle of misinformation that extends to students, parents and the educational community, hindering the adoption of evidence-based practices. This phenomenon underlines the urgency of addressing the problem not only on an individual level, but also as a cultural and institutional challenge.

Therefore, considering the findings, the need to integrate cognitive science and neuroscience into teacher education and continuing professional development strongly emerges. It is not enough to convey up-to-date neuroscientific notions; it is crucial to provide teachers with critical tools that enable them to assess the reliability of information and apply it effectively in the educational context. As suggested by Howard-Jones (2014) and Trinchero (2018), training approaches based on interactivity and experiential learning may be promising strategies to stimulate critical reflection and modify established beliefs. Teacher training should include not only theoretical content, but also practical activities and case studies that demonstrate the unfoundedness of neuromyths and the superiority of evidence-based practices. Furthermore, it is crucial that these interventions are part of a continuous and systematic process that integrates moments of verification and periodic updating.

To effectively address the spread of neuromyths, a systemic and multidimensional approach is needed. First, initial teacher training programs should be rethought to include explicit modules dedicated to educational neuroscience and the critical deconstruction of pseudoscientific beliefs. Second, in-service training should also focus on updating knowledge and the practical application of neuroscientific evidence. Furthermore, it is essential to promote greater integration between scientific research and educational practice, encouraging the dissemination of teaching materials that translate research findings into concrete and easily usable tools. Finally, it is necessary to raise awareness not only among teachers, but also among students, parents and the broader educational community to create an evidence-based school culture and to counter the cycle of misinformation that perpetuates neuroscience.

This study highlights a major educational and cultural challenge that requires structural and coordinated interventions to be effectively addressed. Reducing neuromyth adherence is not only a matter of improving teacher training, but represents a fundamental step towards a more equitable, inclusive and effective education system, based on scientific evidence and capable of fully realizing the potential of each student.

Authors' Contributions. This study has been developed collectively by authors. Maria Carolina Zarrilli Affaitati wrote paragraph 1, Andrea Tinterri wrote paragraphs 2 and 3, Angelo Basta wrote paragraph 4, and Anna Dipace wrote paragraph 5.

References

1. Abdi, H.: The Kendall rank correlation coefficient. Encyclopedia Measur. Statist. **2**, 508–510 (2007)
2. Dekker, S., Jolles, J.: Neuromyths in education: prevalence and predictors of misconceptions among teachers. Front. Psychol. **3**, 1–8 (2012)
3. Della Sala, S., Anderson, M. (eds.): Neuroscience in Education: The Good, the Bad, and the Ugly, 1st edn. Oxford University Press, New York (2012)
4. Dündar, S., Gündüz, N.: Misconceptions regarding the brain: the neuromyths of preservice teachers. Mind Brain Educ. **10**(4), 212–232 (2016)
5. Horvath, J.C., Lodge, J.M., Hattie, J.: From the Laboratory to the Classroom: Translating Science of Learning for Teachers, 1st edn. Routledge, London (2017)
6. Howard-Jones, P.A.: Neuroeducation and education: myths and reality. Nat. Rev. Neurosci. **15**, 817–824 (2014)
7. Hughes, B., Sullivan, K.A., Gilmore, L.: Why do teachers believe educational neuromyths? Trends Neurosci. Educ. **21**, 1–8 (2020)
8. Kirschner, P.A.: Stop propagating the learning styles myth. Comput. Educ. **106**, 166–171 (2017)
9. Kolb, B., Gibb, R.: Brain plasticity and behavior in the developing brain. J. Can. Acad. Child Adolesc. Psychiatry. **20**(4), 265–276 (2011)
10. Macdonald, K., Germine, L., Anderson, A., Christodoulou, J., McGrath, L.M.: Dispelling the myth: training in education or neuroscience decreases but does not eliminate beliefs in neuromyths. Front. Psychol. **8**, 1–16 (2017)
11. Nart, A., Biancalana, V., Scarpa, S.: Neuromyths in education: a survey in Italian teachers in the international context. Ital. J. Health Educ. Sports Incl. Didact. **7**(2), 1–15 (2023)
12. OECD: Understanding the Brain: The Birth of a Learning Science, 1st edn. OECD Publishing, Paris (2007)
13. Pashler, H., McDaniel, M., Rohrer, D., Bjork, R.: Learning styles: concepts and evidence. Psychol. Sci. Public Interest. **9**(3), 105–119 (2009)
14. Papadatou-Pastou, M., Haliou, E., Vlachos, F.: Brain knowledge and the prevalence of neuromyths among prospective teachers in Greece. Front. Psychol. **8**, 1–13 (2017)
15. Raichle, M.E., et al.: A default mode of brain function. Proc. Natl. Acad. Sci. USA. **98**(2), 676–682 (2001)
16. Rato, J.R., Abreu, A.M., Castro-Caldas, A.: Neuromyths in education: what is fact and what is fiction for Portuguese teachers? Educ. Res. **55**(4), 441–453 (2013)
17. Şahin, M., Aybek, E.: Jamovi: an easy-to-use statistical software for social scientists. Int. J. Assess. Tools Educ. **6**(4), 1–12 (2020). https://doi.org/10.21449/ijate.661803
18. The Jamovi Project: Jamovi [Software] (2021). https://www.jamovi.org/. Accessed 17 Mar 2025

19. Torrijos-Muelas, M., González-Víllora, S., Bodoque-Osma, A.R.: The persistence of neuromyths in educational settings: a systematic review. Front. Psychol. **11**, 1–18 (2021)
20. Trinchero, R.: Valutazione formante per l'attivazione cognitiva. Spunti per un uso efficace delle tecnologie per apprendere in classe. Ital. J. Educ. Technol. **26**(3), 40–55 (2018). https://doi.org/10.17471/2499-4324/1013
21. Wolraich, M.L., Wilson, D.B., White, J.W.: The effects of sugar on behavior and cognitive performance in children. JAMA. **274**(20), 1617–1621 (1995)

Sensor-Based to Interaction-Based AI Models in Education: The JOINclusion Case Study

Enrique Hortal[1(✉)], Yusuf Can Semerci[1], Annaleda Mazzucato[2,3], and John Christidis[4]

[1] Maastricht University, Minderbroedersberg 4-6, 6211 LK Maastricht, The Netherlands
enrique.hortal@maastrichtuniversity.nl
[2] University of Naples Federico II, Via Porta di Massa, 1, 80133 Naples, Italy
[3] Fondazione Mondo Digitale, Via del Quadraro 102, 00174 Rome, Italy
[4] University of West Attica, Agiou Spiridonos 28, 122 43 Egaleo, Greece

Abstract. The integration of Artificial Intelligence (AI) in education is reshaping traditional learning environments by enabling personalized learning experiences, enhancing accessibility, and providing data-driven insights into student engagement and performance. However, the rise of AI technologies in educational settings brings complex ethical challenges, including concerns over data privacy, transparency, and equity. This paper explores the dual impact of AI on education, examining both its transformative potential and the ethical issues it presents. It discusses the role of AI models that analyse how students use the learning tools as an alternative to sensor-based approaches, which can address privacy concerns while still offering adaptive, personalized support. Furthermore, this study evaluates frameworks for ethical AI implementation, emphasizing transparency, inclusivity, and trustworthiness to support responsible AI deployment in education. By addressing key ethical considerations and regulatory standards, this paper proposes a path toward data-driven tools that enhance educational outcomes without compromising student autonomy or privacy. The findings underscore the importance of aligning AI innovations with educational values, suggesting that an ethically-centred approach to AI can promote trust and effectiveness in diverse learning contexts.

Keywords: Artificial Intelligence in Education · Interaction-Based AI Models · Privacy in Educational Technology · Personalized Learning · Ethical AI

1 Introduction

Artificial intelligence (AI) has rapidly emerged as a transformative force in educational practices, offering tools and methods that promise to enhance learning experiences and optimise teaching strategies. AI's potential in education includes personalised learning paths, adaptive assessment, and real-time feedback, that can significantly improve student engagement and outcomes [1]. However, the integration of AI within educational settings is not without substantial ethical and practical challenges [2]. One primary concern is the reliance on sensor-based data collection, especially when dealing with minors,

P. Ardimento et al. (Eds.): HELMeTO 2024, CCIS 2468, pp. 247–258, 2025.
https://doi.org/10.1007/978-3-031-93999-0_16

where issues of privacy, consent, and data security are crucial [3]. This sensor-based approach, while effective in capturing a range of behavioural and environmental cues, often raises concerns about student autonomy, informed consent, and the risk of surveillance in sensitive educational environments [4].

In contrast, prior research has highlighted the benefits of interaction-based models that prioritize student engagement and learning processes over passive data collection [5–7]. These models harness the natural interactions between students and educational platforms, enabling insights into learning patterns without infringing on personal privacy. Interaction-based AI models capture student actions and preferences data, allowing for real-time adjustments that support learning without requiring invasive monitoring. By focusing on observable interactions and demographic data, these models offer a more ethical and transparent approach, fostering trust among educators, students, and parents [8].

This paper proposes a novel framework that shifts the focus from sensor-based to interaction-based models in AI-powered educational tools. By advocating for an approach that leverages students' interactions and demographic information, the study seeks to establish a foundation for more transparent, ethical, and pedagogically aligned AI integration. Such a shift not only mitigates privacy concerns but also enhances trust among stakeholders, promoting AI as a supportive rather than intrusive component of education. This trajectory towards interaction-based methodologies offers a balanced pathway for AI innovation in education, aligning technology use with fundamental educational values and ethical considerations [9]. The proposed framework thus provides a roadmap for advancing AI applications in a way that prioritizes both effective learning and ethical integrity.

2 Materials and Methods

2.1 Development of the JOINclusion AI Model

To facilitate a shift from sensor-based to interaction-based AI models in a real-world educational context, the JOINclusion application (Fig. 1) was developed as a pioneering tool for inclusive, adaptive learning. This app leverages interaction and demographic data, aiming to create personalized and student-centred learning experiences that respect student privacy and enhance pedagogical priorities. Figure 1 (up) illustrates the two available game modes: Story mode, where students engage in solo activities, and Multiplayer mode, fostering cooperative problem-solving and (down) an example of animation from the collaborative mode.

The JOINclusion AI algorithms are designed to identify and interpret patterns in student interactions with the app to adapt educational resources and support, to meet individual learning needs. The interactions considered included different aspects of the learning process—such as navigation choices (e.g. red arrow in Fig. 2), response times, and engagement with specific content areas including interactions with NPCs, which provide contextual learning challenges designed to enhance social-emotional skills (see dialogue bubbles in Fig. 2). Unlike traditional sensor-based AI, which might rely on ambient sensors to track physiological or environmental cues, the JOINclusion model

Fig. 1. Welcome page showing the game modes (individual experience in the Story mode and cooperative experience in the Multiplayer one) – up; and an example animation used to create an immersive experience - bottom.

focuses on user interactions, minimizing invasiveness while maintaining adaptive functionality. The data collected through these interactions is systematically analyzed and incorporated into a sophisticated recommender and learning support system. This system aids teachers in efficiently managing their students and structuring the delivery of educational materials, thereby streamlining their workload and enriching the learning experience. By providing actionable insights into student preferences, performance, and progress, it empowers educators to tailor learning pathways to individual needs and optimize the educational environment for both engagement and effectiveness.

The development phase involved extensive consultation with educators, AI ethicists, and data privacy experts, to ensure that the model aligns with both educational best practices and rigorous privacy standards. The JOINclusion app was built with flexibility to accommodate diverse learning styles and capabilities, aiming to foster inclusive environments that support each student's unique trajectory without compromising their privacy or autonomy. Throughout this phase, iterative testing with a small group of pilot users allowed for refining the algorithms and adjusting the data-handling protocols to ensure

Fig. 2. JOINclusion game: Interaction with non-player characters and the environment.

that all ethical, security, and pedagogical concerns were addressed prior to large-scale testing.

2.2 Pilot Study Design and Educational Contexts

The evaluation framework for JOINclusion involved a multi-phase pilot study conducted in Italy, Greece, and the Netherlands, leveraging diverse educational settings to explore the app's adaptability and effectiveness across cultural, pedagogical, and institutional contexts. The study focused on how the interaction-based AI model could perform across different age groups, learning needs, and curricula while aligning with the practical realities of classroom instruction.

The pilot was structured in two phases of classroom experimentation, with the app's activities carefully embedded into existing teaching plans and curricular objectives. Prior to these phases, an essential co-design process involved educators, trainers, psychologists, and pedagogues, ensuring the app's development was grounded in psychological models and practical classroom requirements. This collaboration shaped the app's interactive scenarios, aligning them with real-world classroom dynamics to foster empathy, cultural awareness, and social-emotional learning (SEL).

In each country, JOINclusion's activities were tailored to fit national educational goals. Teachers integrated the app into subjects like citizenship education, social studies, humanities, and SEL programs, aligning objectives such as empathy-building, collaboration, and cultural understanding with their lesson plans. These activities aimed to enhance competencies outlined in formal curricula, making the app a complementary teaching resource rather than an add-on. In Italy, the app was implemented as part of lessons on citizenship education and intercultural understanding. Activities encouraged students to reflect on diversity and empathy through role-playing and collaborative problem-solving. In Greece, in the context of humanities classes, JOINclusion supported themes like cultural heritage and social cohesion, helping students improve both interpersonal and linguistic skills. In the Netherlands, in multicultural classrooms, the app addressed challenges such as group cohesion and cultural dialogue, promoting trust and respect in diverse learning environments.

The initial stage of the piloting tested the app in controlled classroom environments to gather feedback on usability, engagement, and relevance. Teachers facilitated the activities, monitoring how well students interacted with the app and each other while linking these experiences to learning objectives. Based on insights from the first phase, the app was refined and reintroduced for broader implementation. The second phase of the pilot emphasised seamless integration into classroom activities, with teachers using the app to meet specific educational goals such as teamwork, conflict resolution, and empathy building.

The primary objectives of the pilot study were to:

- Measure the app's effectiveness in terms of student engagement, learning outcomes, and trust in AI-driven tools.
- Evaluate the ethical and practical implications of using interaction-based AI models in education, ensuring their suitability for diverse classroom settings.
- Assess the app's ability to foster key competencies like empathy, critical thinking, and cultural awareness.

By embedding JOINclusion into structured classroom activities and aligning it with school curricula, the pilot study demonstrated the app's capacity to enhance traditional teaching methods while addressing modern educational challenges. The outcomes revealed that JOINclusion not only engaged students effectively but also encouraged meaningful interactions and fostered trust in AI-driven tools, supporting the creation of inclusive, empathetic learning environments.

2.3 Data Collection and Evaluation Framework

To achieve a comprehensive evaluation, the pilot study incorporated both quantitative and qualitative data collection methods. Metrics were gathered on student engagement and learning outcomes, including frequency and duration of app usage, completion rates of educational activities, and academic performance indicators. Behavioural analytics were employed to track how students interacted with the app, analysing factors such as response accuracy, time spent on tasks, and engagement with adaptive features. Statistical analyses were conducted to assess correlations between interaction data and performance outcomes, allowing for insights into how well the interaction-based model supports individualized learning. To evaluate student trust, perceptions of inclusivity, and the app's perceived value, in-depth interviews and structured surveys were conducted with students, teachers, and parents. Interviews provided qualitative insights into users' experiences, highlighting how the app's non-invasive design affected their comfort and trust levels. Open-ended survey questions enabled students and educators to express their views on how well the app supported learning goals, as well as its usability and ethical considerations.

2.4 Privacy and Security Framework

A distinguishing innovation of the JOINclusion app is its robust focus on privacy and security, designed in alignment with the EU AI Act [10]. In response to the ethical concerns associated with data collection in educational settings, particularly for minors, the

JOINclusion model incorporates several specific privacy safeguards. All interaction data collected by the app is anonymized and aggregated, ensuring that individual users can not be identified. This anonymization process includes stripping identifiable information from records and combining data at a cohort level to allow for meaningful analysis without compromising privacy. JOINclusion operates on a strict, informed consent basis, obtaining explicit permission from students or their guardians before any data is collected. Consent forms are clear and detailed, explaining the purposes of data collection, the types of data collected, and how it will be used to enhance learning. This transparency aims to build trust and ensure that all participants are fully aware of how their information will be utilized. All data collected by JOINclusion is encrypted at multiple stages to prevent unauthorized access. This includes end-to-end encryption during data transmission [11] as well as secure storage protocols that comply with GDPR standards [12]. Data is stored in controlled environments with restricted access, minimizing the risk of data breaches or misuse. The app provides clear, accessible information regarding data collection practices, with a user-friendly dashboard that allows students, teachers, and guardians to view and manage their data. Participants have the option to access their data usage history and, if desired, to delete or modify their data through the app's interface. This level of transparency is intended to empower users and reinforce the ethical commitment of JOINclusion to prioritize data security and user control.

2.5 Analytical Approach

To assess the impact of JOINclusion's interaction-based model, quantitative data on engagement and performance was analysed using statistical methods, such as statistical clustering and regression analysis, to identify patterns and differences across groups. For qualitative data, thematic analysis was conducted on interviews and open-ended survey responses to identify key themes related to trust, engagement, and perceived inclusivity. The mixed-methods approach allowed for a holistic evaluation of JOINclusion's effectiveness in promoting inclusive, personalized learning environments. Overall, this rigorous evaluation framework was designed not only to assess the educational impact of JOINclusion's interaction-based model but also to ensure that ethical principles and privacy standards are upheld throughout the deployment process. By combining robust data analysis with strict ethical protocols, this study aims to present a scalable, ethically sound approach for AI-empowered education tools that prioritize both learning outcomes and user trust.

3 Main Results

The study produced significant findings underscoring the advantages and practicality of interaction-based AI models in educational contexts. These results point to the transformative potential of such models in addressing privacy concerns, fostering trust, and supporting personalized learning—all essential factors for ethical and effective AI integration in education.

One of the standout benefits of the interaction-based model, as demonstrated by the JOINclusion app, is its robust handling of privacy and data security concerns, which are often major barriers to AI adoption in educational settings. Unlike sensor-based models that frequently rely on sensitive biometric or physiological data (e.g., facial expressions, heart rate), the interaction-based approach minimizes ethical risks by avoiding the collection of highly scrutinized data types. Instead, it focuses on anonymized interaction data—such as click sequences, task completion times, and engagement metrics—allowing the AI to adapt without compromising student privacy [13]. This focus on privacy aligned well with both the EU AI Act and GDPR standards, demonstrating the model's feasibility within strict regulatory frameworks. By forgoing physical sensor data, the JOINclusion model not only reduced regulatory burdens but also addressed common ethical concerns voiced by stakeholders regarding the use of AI with minors.

The study noted that parents, educators, and students expressed increased trust in JOINclusion's interaction-based approach, which they viewed as both transparent and minimally intrusive. This trust, in turn, is a critical factor for the broader adoption of AI technologies in educational settings, as highlighted by recent findings [14]. The interaction-based model fostered heightened trust and transparency among key stakeholders, including students, parents, and teachers, which is essential for the ethical deployment of AI in education.

The non-invasive nature of the JOINclusion app—paired with clear communication around data collection and usage—proved effective in building confidence that AI could be used responsibly and ethically within learning environments. Transparency mechanisms, such as the app's dashboard for monitoring data usage and the option to manage personal data, were particularly well-received, as they empowered users to retain control over their information. This increased trust also correlated with higher levels of engagement and willingness to use the app consistently. Teachers and school administrators noted that the JOINclusion model's transparency around data handling reassured them about the AI's compatibility with educational values, paving the way for AI to be integrated as a supportive rather than intrusive tool in education.

A key finding of the study was the demonstrated potential of interaction-based data—when combined with demographic information—to personalize learning experiences effectively. The JOINclusion app's algorithms successfully identified patterns in students' interactions that aligned with self-reported measures of engagement, enjoyment, and academic progress. Specifically, the app could detect behavioural patterns, such as sustained time on tasks, consistent completion of assignments, and increased frequency of participation in activities, which correlated with higher levels of student engagement and satisfaction. This information is available to teachers through a user-friendly dashboard which summarizes the data of their learners at different levels. An example is shown in Fig. 3. In this analysis, three different cohorts (e.g. classrooms in a school) were compared based on their aggregated performance in the game after several sessions (left graph). In this case, the students within each classroom were also divided into two groups based on particular demographic characteristics to evaluate its potential impact (right graph).

These insights enabled the app to adjust content and resources, tailoring learning experiences to individual needs. For instance, students who displayed certain interaction patterns, such as frequent help-seeking or slower task completion times, were

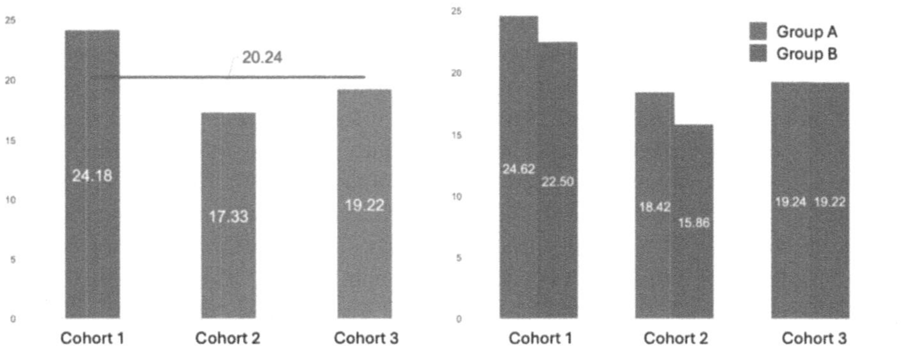

Fig. 3. Example of data evaluation on learner performance from three different cohorts and two different groups per cohort.

provided with additional resources and support through the app's adaptive learning features. This personalization enhanced student engagement, as measured by increased time spent on tasks and self-reported enjoyment, suggesting that interaction-based AI models may indeed be as effective as, if not more effective than, sensor-based models in facilitating personalized learning experiences. The example shown in Fig. 4 shows the identification of three clusters of learners based exclusively on their interactions with the game (no demographic information was considered in this analysis). To facilitate the visualization, t-SNE [15], a tool that reduces high-dimensional data (several features used) into a lower-dimensional space (two-dimensional representation), was utilized. The data-driven algorithm identified three clear groups, mainly characterized by the number of interactions with Non-Player Characters (NPCs) and the frequency of help sought (character button in the top-left part in Fig. 2).

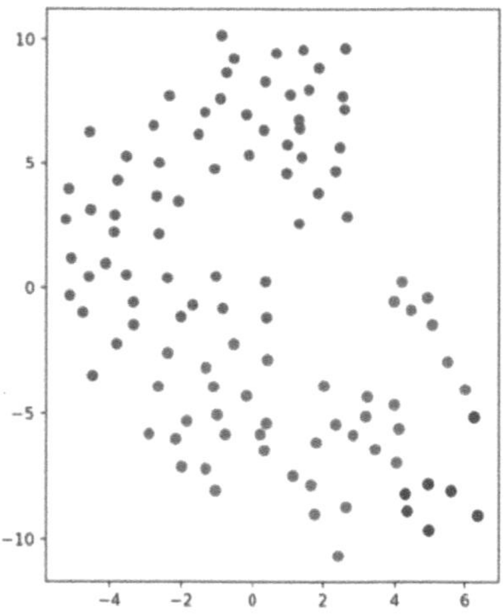

Fig. 4. Example of the clustering technique using learners' interactions. In this graph, the three different clusters of learners are visualized in colors.

Another key outcome was the alignment of the interaction-based model with core pedagogical principles, including inclusivity, accessibility, and learner-centeredness. By focusing on interaction data and steering clear of potentially intrusive biometric inputs, the JOINclusion app effectively supported students with diverse learning needs, many of whom had previously struggled to benefit from traditional sensor-based approaches. This learner-centred design enabled the app to adapt not only to students' academic needs but also to their social and emotional well-being, a balance that is critical for inclusive education. Qualitative feedback from teachers and students revealed that the app's adaptiveness was particularly beneficial for students with varied learning styles and abilities. Teachers observed that students who often felt marginalized in conventional learning environments became more engaged and confident when interacting with the JOINclusion app, thanks to its accessible design and responsiveness to their individual needs. This improvement in engagement was accompanied by notable gains in learning outcomes, especially for students who had difficulty in sensor-based environments where they may have felt observed or judged.

The findings underscored the importance of prioritizing educational goals over technological capabilities in AI design. Unlike many AI systems that focus heavily on data-driven optimization, the JOINclusion model was intentionally aligned with pedagogical objectives from its inception. By concentrating on inclusive, ethical, and learner-centred design principles, the app avoided the pitfalls of over-reliance on data capture and analysis, focusing instead on meaningful educational impact. This approach not only supported educational outcomes but also reinforced the ethical framework necessary for AI in schools. As observed in the study, AI-driven personalization that is grounded in interaction rather than invasive monitoring aligns well with the mission of educational institutions to foster safe, supportive, and inclusive learning spaces. Thus, the JOINclusion model presents a replicable pathway for AI in education, prioritizing student welfare and pedagogical integrity over mere technological sophistication.

4 Conclusions

The findings from this study suggest that interaction-based AI models, exemplified by JOINclusion, have substantial potential as ethical, effective, and trusted tools in educational contexts. By emphasizing privacy, engagement, and inclusivity, the JOINclusion model demonstrates that AI can be developed with a strong focus on ethical standards and student-centred design. These promising results lay a solid foundation for further research and innovation, pointing to an AI-driven future in education that upholds integrity and respects student privacy.

The shift from sensor-based to interaction-based models represents a meaningful evolution in educational AI, addressing both ethical and practical concerns that have long been associated with AI technologies reliant on sensor data. This study confirms that interaction-based models not only circumvent privacy issues but also support a more transparent, adaptable, and pedagogically aligned approach to AI integration. By focusing on students' interactions and learner-centred principles, this model provides a framework that advocates responsible and effective AI use, particularly valuable in online and higher education settings where personalization and engagement are critical. Interaction-based AI's ability to adapt to different learning styles, monitor digital progress, and provide customized feedback makes it a compelling choice for enhancing inclusivity and engagement in dynamic learning environments.

Despite these promising outcomes, the study's pilot phase was limited to a small set of educational contexts, which may influence the generalizability of the results. Future research is necessary to validate these findings across diverse educational settings and to further explore the impact of interaction-based AI on various student learning outcomes. Continued development and testing will help refine these models and ensure that AI tools remain aligned with the ethical and pedagogical values essential to modern education. Additionally, more work towards ensuring AI transparency is crucial for trust in educational applications. While JOINclusion prioritizes ethical data collection, future work should explore integrating explainable AI mechanisms, allowing teachers and students to understand how personalized recommendations are generated. Finally, this study underscores the benefits of interaction-based AI models in education, offering a privacy-conscious alternative to traditional sensor-based approaches. However, while sensor-based models often raise ethical concerns, less invasive technologies—such as smartwatches—could complement interaction-based methods by providing additional contextual insights, like activity levels or engagement patterns. Exploring the synergy between these approaches may enhance adaptive learning without compromising student privacy. Future research should investigate how combining these models can optimize personalization while maintaining ethical and transparent AI integration in educational environments.

Acknowledgments. This research was conducted as part of the JOINclusion project (https://dke.maastrichtuniversity.nl/JOINclusion/),"Joint problem-solving strategy towards social inclusion of children with a migrant background" (Project Reference: 2021-2-NL01-KA220-SCH-000048865), funded by the Erasmus+ program under the 2021 KA220 call.

Appendix

The **Lite version** of the JOINclusion app is available for download on Google Play (https://play.google.com/store/apps/details?id=com.JoinclusionPS.com.unity.template.mobile2D&hl=it). This simplified version of the app is designed to help educators and trainers initiate meaningful activities with students, creating opportunities to explore empathy and cultural understanding in dynamic, interactive ways. JOINclusion Lite offers a series of engaging scenarios that can serve as a springboard for deeper discussions and collaborative experiences in the classroom. For example, teachers can use the app to spark conversations about emotions, cultural differences, and interpersonal relationships, guiding students to think critically about how they perceive and interact with others. The app's scenarios are designed to encourage dialogue, helping students articulate their thoughts and feelings in a safe, structured environment. Beyond discussion, the app fosters collaboration by assigning students challenges that require teamwork and problem-solving. Working together to overcome these challenges helps students develop mutual respect and an appreciation for diverse perspectives, strengthening group dynamics and creating a sense of inclusion. JOINclusion Lite also promotes self-reflection, offering students the chance to explore their own behaviours and choices.

By engaging with the app's interactive activities, they can reflect on how empathy plays a role in their daily interactions and learn to approach real-world situations with greater awareness and sensitivity. Whether used as part of a larger lesson plan or as a standalone activity, JOINclusion Lite is a valuable resource for educators looking to create a more inclusive and empathetic learning environment.

To complement the app, the Fondazione Mondo Digitale offers an online training course through its FMD Academy (Italian version: https://formazione.mondodigitale.org/course/view.php?id=186; English version: https://formazione.mondodigitale.org/course/view.php?id=258), providing educators with the tools and knowledge to make the most of JOINclusion in their classrooms. This course takes a hands-on approach, starting with an introduction to empathy as a core competence and why it is essential for building inclusive learning environments. Teachers learn how to harness the app's potential to engage students effectively, integrating its activities into their teaching practices. Participants are guided step by step on how to use the app in real classroom settings, exploring practical strategies for aligning its scenarios with their curriculum. The course also emphasizes evaluation, equipping educators with methods to assess the outcomes of empathy-building activities and measure their students' progress over time. Through this training, teachers gain valuable insights into fostering an inclusive classroom culture.

References

1. Luckin, R., Holmes, W., Griffiths, M., Forcier, L.B.: Intelligence Unleashed: An Argument for AI in Education. Pearson Education (2016)
2. Mhlanga, D.: Open AI in Education, the Responsible and Ethical Use of ChatGPT Towards Lifelong Learning. SSRN. (2023). https://ssrn.com/abstract=4354422 or https://doi.org/10.2139/ssrn.4354422
3. Holmes, W., Bialik, M., Fadel, C.: Artificial Intelligence in Education: Promises and Implications for Teaching and Learning. Center for Curriculum Redesign (2019)
4. Slade, S., Prinsloo, P.: Learning analytics: ethical issues and Dilemmas. Am. Behav. Sci. **57**(10), 1509–1528 (2013)
5. Celik, I., Dindar, M., Muukkonen, H.: The promises and challenges of artificial intelligence for teachers: a systematic review of research. TechTrends. **66**, 616–630 (2022). https://doi.org/10.1007/s11528-022-00715-y
6. Zhai, X., Chu, X., Chai, C.S., Jong, M.S.Y., Istenic, A., Spector, M., Liu, J., et al.: A review of Artificial Intelligence (AI) in education from 2010 to 2020. Complexity. **2021**, 8812542 (2021). https://doi.org/10.1155/2021/8812542
7. Chen, P., Wu, L., Wang, L.: AI fairness in data management and analytics: a review on challenges, methodologies and applications. Appl Sci. **13**(18), 10258 (2023). https://doi.org/10.3390/app131810258
8. Williamson, B.: Big Data in Education. SAGE Publications (2017). https://doi.org/10.4135/9781529714920
9. Zuo, Z., Watson, M., Budgen, D., Hall, R., Kennelly, C., Al Moubayed, N.: Data anonymization for pervasive health care: systematic literature mapping study. JMIR Med. Inform. **9**(10), e29871 (2021). https://doi.org/10.2196/29871
10. AI Act. https://eur-lex.europa.eu/legal-content/EN/TXT/?uri=CELEX:32024R1689. Accessed 31 Jan 2025

11. Damian, E., Aasebø, I.E.J., Akintoye, S., Knight, W., Karakasidis, A., Mikulan, E., et al.: Pseudonymisation of neuroimages and data protection: increasing access to data while retaining scientific utility. Neuroimage: Reports. **1**(4), 100053 (2021). https://doi.org/10.1016/j.ynirp.2021.100053
12. General Data Protection Regulation. https://eur-lex.europa.eu/eli/reg/2016/679/oj/eng. Accessed 31 Jan 2025
13. Floridi, L., Cowls, J., Beltrametti, M., Chatila, R., Chazerand, P., Dignum, V., et al.: AI4People—an ethical framework for a good AI society: opportunities, risks, principles, and recommendations. Minds Mach. **28**, 689–707 (2018). https://doi.org/10.1007/s11023-018-9482-5
14. Hassija, V., Chamola, V., Mahapatra, A.: Interpreting black-box models: a review on explainable artificial intelligence. Cogn. Comput. **16**, 45–74 (2024). https://doi.org/10.1007/s12559-023-10179-8
15. Van der Maaten, L., Hinton, G.: Visualizing data using t-SNE. J. Mach. Learn. Res. **9**(11) (2008)

Digital Innovation and Internationalisation Through eTwinning: Reimagining Initial Teacher Education

Viviana Vinci(✉)

Foggia University, 71121 Foggia, Italy
viviana.vinci@unifg.it

Abstract. International policies highlight the integration of digital technologies in education to foster skills in digital literacy, collaboration, and internationalization, positioning teacher education at the core of innovation. This exploratory study builds on a 2024 research project at the University of Foggia (Italy) to rethink Initial Teacher Training (ITT) through digital innovation and internationalization, using eTwinning as a transformative platform. In Italy, universities have increasingly promoted eTwinning's integration into Initial Teacher Education (ITE) programs. The main objective was to assess eTwinning's effectiveness in enhancing pre-service teachers' competencies in managing innovative learning environments, focusing on digital and international collaboration. A mixed-methods approach was used, with 204 pre-service teachers completing a Computer Assisted Web Interviewing (CAWI) questionnaire, followed by the analysis of 39 technological artifacts created by participants. The results showed that eTwinning was valued for fostering collaboration, enhancing digital skills, and promoting international networking. Among the key challenges were technical difficulties, language barriers, and time management, while strengths included creativity, adaptability, and teacher support. The study emphasizes the importance of integrating eTwinning into ITT programs to enhance innovation and digital skills. It was noted that eTwinning not only promotes international collaboration but also encourages universities to rethink their training pathways by integrating AI, technological devices, and networking tools. It highlights the value of informal learning and a multi-level educational approach, urging universities to innovate and adapt their curricula and foster digital and cross-cultural competencies. The study's findings highlight the potential of eTwinning to redefine ITT, offering a model that aligns with international trends in digital transformation and educational innovation. These findings contribute to international debates on teacher training, highlighting the need for strategically integrating digital technologies in education.

Keywords: Teacher Education · Digital Innovation · Internationalisation

P. Ardimento et al. (Eds.): HELMeTO 2024, CCIS 2468, pp. 259–275, 2025.
https://doi.org/10.1007/978-3-031-93999-0_17

1 Theoretical Framework

International policy has long emphasised the importance of integrating educational technologies into teaching practices and innovating education systems through the promotion of digital, entrepreneurial, sustainability, personal, social and learning-to-learn skills [1–4]. Technological advancements have inevitably redefined the concept of education and, consequently, the role of professors. Currently, we are witnessing a shift in teaching paradigms, oriented towards collaboration, customization, and interactivity [5]. Additionally, the COVID-19 pandemic has accelerated the implementation of technologies in teaching enhancing, thanks to ICT, a more inclusive teaching-learning process [6–8]. If used strategically ICT can promote the transformation of teaching by adjusting the roles of teachers and students [9]. Furthermore, they enrich didactic mediators by supporting a student needs-based approach [10]. Recent studies [11] highlight how the use of digital technologies spurs active and engaging learning, both in-person and online, requiring an appropriate understanding of learning dynamics and the implementation of innovative pedagogical practices [12]. Not coincidentally, the most widely recognized conceptual frameworks such as TPACK [13], SARM [14], DigCompEdu [15], AI competency framework for teachers [16] and AI competency framework for students [17] agree that focusing exclusively on technical skills is not enough and emphasize the implementation of ICT as a transversal tool in the learning process. Nevertheless, some faculty members remain resistant to continuous professional development programs, which must include technical, pedagogical, and digital skills.

Models for continuing professional development for teachers increasingly focus on co-design and teacher as a designer [18], engaged in the innovation of learning environments [19–20] also under the increasing impetus of information and communication technologies [21]. Using ICT in the supplemented process of teaching/learning, the designer teacher [18], holds a strategic role [22–23]: the technological supplement requires a more accurate didactic design, increasing the complexity of learning processes [24] that creates, as a matter of fact, a community of teachers trained at the reflective practice of the design who at the same time support each other [22–26]. The co-design encourages professional development, increasing the skills and practical design [27], creating a virtuous cycle between work groups and professional development. School networks [28], support innovation, dissemination of good practice and capacity building, offering training opportunities and professional exchanges [29].

Within this evolving educational landscape, the eTwinning program (further described in Subsect. 1.1) aims to enhance teachers' competencies in educational technology, innovation, multilingualism, and global citizenship. It offers customized learning experiences that align with national educational policies.

The experiential learning approach embedded in eTwinning promotes school collaboration and knowledge sharing, distinguishing it from traditional training programs due to its situated and informal learning model [12].

1.1 The eTwinning Approach to Teacher Training

The eTwinning approach to teacher training uses situated and informal learning models and tools, based on the continuous exchange of information/resources though dedicated to collaborative design and intercultural learning. By participating in eTwinning, teachers and students develop digital and transversal skills, while exploring innovative learning methodologies [30]. Official launched in 2005, eTwinning was quickly recognized by European Commission for its educational potential. Over time, increasing participation on the platform allowed the development of more complex projects. Studies on eTwinning efficacy and its national recognition play a crucial role in monitoring educational activities and coordination transnational initiative within the European Union. Therefore, it's important understanding how eTwinning impact teachers' professional development and its broader effects on the educational system. Between 2005 and 2020, more than 94.000 Italian teachers joined eTwinning, making Italy the second largest participating country following Turkey. Originally integrated into the *Lifelong Learning Programme* (LLP) 2007–2013 as a special Action of Comenius, eTwinning shares several objectives with this initiative, including enhancing teacher training quality, promoting ICT use and developing innovative didactic practices, with a specific focus on education sector [31]. The continuous expansion of eTwinning participation in Italy reflects the efficiency of the initiative and the strategy of the National Unit of Italia eTwinning, who has been able to value the two key elements of the Action: the development of electronic twinning and the encouragement of teachers training [32].

The negotiation of the teaching action within the eTwinning approach is proposed as an alternative to the traditional in-service training offer, which is often sporadic and decontextualized from regular teaching practice: it represents a "third space" [33] of active negotiation of situated learning between the first space of informal learning and the second space of formal learning, in which learner agency is enhanced. Practice and theory intertwine thanks to the co-design and to the birth of community of practice where experiences are shared, where new didactic methodologies are experimented and Its right in this *third space* that the teacher develops those skills that can be spend for the innovative education, such as problem-solving and the creative use of technologies. eTwinning stimulates critical reflection, ongoing improvement and at the same time promotes consistent self-assessment process of didactic practices [34]. One of the program's key features is its structured documentation and sharing of educational projects, which encourage the development of innovative teaching methodologies and curricular approaches. These strategies leverage digital transformation and internationalization, fostering creativity and flexibility in educational design [35]. eTwinning subscription allows the access to digital resources and services, making it easy the collaboration between teachers on an international level; moreover, encourages didactive innovation through ICT use and electronic twinning creation, by promoting as consequence the internationalization, multiculturalism, multilingualism. Additionally, it offers continuing professional training and support from NSO, contributing to an updating process and continuing professional development [12].

Therefore, internationalization is a key aspect of eTwinning that encourages students' motivation and enhances teachers' digital competences, by promoting a European dimension of learning and the development of intercultural and multilingual competences. The synergy between documentation, digitalization and internationalization is ensured by a multi-level governance of education that involves European, National and local institutions, and encourages an inclusive and collaborative approach [36]. Coordinated by the

European Commission eTwinning collaboration involves a different entity: the European eTwinning Unit, on the instructions of the European Commission; the National Units; the local units, through collaboration between the Regional School Offices and the network of eTwinning ambassadors; and the schools, which can commit to innovating teaching through digital practice and obtain an eTwinning school certification. This structure allows the diffusion of the best practice and innovative action, aligning central priority with teachers' learning needs. Through multi-level governance [37], eTwinning allows for moving beyond strictly individual learning approaches and aims to promote shared leadership that is a process of social influence aimed at achieving common goals and teamwork. Leadership can be defined as a social influence process finalized for the triggering of the collective efforts for the achievement of specific goals, inspired by a shared vision [38, 39]. In this context eTwinning shows itself useful in the promotion of resilience such as the capacity of turning stressful experiences into opportunities, especially the digital ones through collaboration between schools and students [40]. This study builds upon the analyses conducted using the CAWI methodology [41] and the in-depth investigations into the benefits of ICT integration and the challenges associated with eTwinning [42, 43]. In particular, Mangione et al. [41] highlight the pivotal role of the National Digital School Plan and the continuous professional development initiatives promoted by INDIRE in enhancing teachers' digital competencies. Camilleri [42] underscores how eTwinning fosters global education and intercultural awareness, emphasizing the significance of international collaboration in developing transversal skills. Similarly, Gökbulut [43] examines students' perceptions within eTwinning network countries, revealing a strong correlation between participation in such initiatives and improvements in digital literacy. Collectively, these studies corroborate the notion that international collaboration platforms not only facilitate the acquisition of digital skills but also serve as valuable tools for strengthening project management competencies among future educators.

2 Methods

This study describes the results of a research carried out in 2024 with an exploratory purpose, involving 250 pre-service teachers (*target population*) attending the Qualification in *Scienze della Formazione Primaria* (Primary Teacher Education) at the University of Foggia (Italy). The research focused on their participation in the eTwinning for Future Teachers (ITE). The University of Foggia has actively supported the ITE initiative since its early adoption in 2016, as part of the compulsory seminars within the so called Active Training Internship (TFA) aimed at future secondary school teachers, held by ambassador Brigida Clemente. The primary aim of this inquiry is to analyse the representation of the effectiveness of the eTwinning experimentation. Specifically, the research aims to examine the meanings that trainee teachers attribute to the eTwinning experience and its role in developing the competencies needed to manage innovative learning environments; understand how eTwinning interacts with teachers' continuous professional development; rethink current teacher training models with a stronger focus on media education. The research employed a mixed methods approach, integrating both qualitative and quantitative data collection and analysis techniques. Two phases of inquiry took place: 1) during the course, pre-service teachers (N. 204; *Response Rate*: 81.6%) completed a submitting a Computer Assisted Web Interviewing (CAWI) questionnaire including multiple choice and open questions; 2) in the second phase, 39 technological artifacts developed and analysed from online workgroups on the Moodle platform (all 204 participants in Phase 1 participated in the working groups on Moodle). It is specified that the analysis of the artifacts and open-ended responses is not included in this publication due to space limitations. The results related to these aspects will be presented in a future publication. To inquire about the principal aim regarding the representation of the efficiency of eTwinning experimentation the CAWI questionnaire is articulated in different sections designed to collect data related to perception, engagement and satisfaction of the students in comparison to the experimentation. It's composed of 26 questions, 17 closed-ended answers (with Likert scale) and 9 open-ended questions. The distribution of question types and their purpose are shown in Table 1. 204 student teachers took part in the survey, divided between male (N = 10; 4.88%) and female (N = 194; 94.63%; 1 student preferred not to answer). The age of respondents is distributed with prevalence of people aged between 19–49 (N = 131; 64.2%); the status of the students is, for 63.2% (N = 129), that of attendees; 85.3% (N = 174) have no prior teaching experience. The items focus the attention on both cognitive (perceived effectiveness of activities) and emotional aspects (motivation and satisfaction). Additionally, the study examined the perceived alignment of Didactic technologies with teaching practices, the correlation between enthusiasm and the overall perception of effectiveness, general satisfaction with the educational content, and the quality of support provided by the eTwinning Ambassador and at last concrete suggestions for improving the project were collected. Particularly, there were inquired three specific goals (for reasons of conciseness related to available characters, this contribution only includes a selection of questions from the total 26, organized into three macro-objectives; Table 1). The questions were selected following a criterion of coherence with the proposed study. Furthermore, it was preferred to combine questions with different methodological settings in order to obtain a complete vision of the students' perception.

Table 1. Survey Design: Objectives, Purposes, and Questionnaire Items.

Objectives	Purposes	Questionnaire Items	Type of question
Inquiry Object 1. Understanding the meanings attributed by participants to the experience on its personal and educational value	To understand how the participants perceive and assign value to the eTwinning experience, both from a personal (emotional engagement) and learning perspective (impact on their learning path)	*1. How would you define the eTwinning experimentation?* *2. Write three words you associate with the eTwinning experimentation?* *3. How excited were you about the eTwinning experimentation on a scale from 1 (Not at all) to 10 (Entirely)?* *4. On a scale from 1 (Not at all) to 10 (Entirely), how much do you believe the eTwinning experiment is consistent with the teaching of Educational Technologies?* *5. Express your level of satisfaction on a scale of 1 (minimum) to 10 (maximum) regarding the eTwinning experimentation*	1. Open-ended question 2. Open-ended question 3. Scale Question (1–10, Not at all – Entirely 4. Scale Question (1–10, Not at all - Entirely) 5. Multiple-choice grid question

(*continued*)

Table 1. (*continued*)

Objectives	Purposes	Questionnaire Items	Type of question
Inquiry Object 2. Interaction with Continuous professional development - Professional learning impact	To understand how the eTwinning experience has contributed to the acquisition of skills relevant to the participants' professional journey, with particular focus on collaboration, the use of technologies, and the ability to manage innovative educational projects	*6. On a scale from 1 (Not at all) to 10 (Entirely), how much has the experience so far allowed you to rethink your future role as a teacher?* *7. How has the eTwinning experience influenced or is influencing your learning and your approach to the future profession of a teacher?* *8. What changes have you noticed after the eTwinning experience and at the end of the "Educational Technologies" course?*	6. Scale Question (1–10, Not at all - Entirely) 7. Open-ended question 8. Multiple-answer question (select up two options out of five)
Inquiry Object 3. Rethinking media education models - Innovation in media education models	To understand how the eTwinning experience influences participants' ability to rethink and apply innovative models of media education, promoting a critical and conscious use of digital technologies	*9. In the eTwinning experiment conducted so far, what have been the main strengths and weaknesses?* *10. To appropriately approach the realization of an eTwinning project, which skills do you consider to be the most important? (maximum 3 options)* *11. What would you like to explore further in the continuation of the eTwinning experiment? (e.g., integration into internships, participation in projects, other)*	9. Open-ended question 10. Multiple-answer question (select up three options out of seven) 11. Open-ended question

For aim 1, open-ended questions collect personal opinion, while Likert Scale are used to quantify the degree of perceived impact, therefore providing qualitative and quantitative data on the value attributed to the project. For aim 2 the questions are structured to explore specific skills (for example collaborative and technical) and general aspects of professional development, with the aim of identifying the areas of greatest learning impact. For aim 3 the questions focus on students' perception regarding educational models and their practical application, trying to understand how the experience encourages a critical and creative rethinking in the use of media.

3 Data Analysis and Results

The conducted experimentation provides valuable insights into how collaborative approach and technology integration can transform the learning process in an innovative and inclusive way. The survey responses were analysed using both qualitative and quantitative approaches. The collected data were processed with Microsoft Excel software. This section presents the data analysis of data and outcomes regarding the distribution of the Survey through CAWI questionnaire and the analysis of technological artifacts developed in work groups and uploaded online on Moodle.

The first phase of the study involved the administration of a Computer Assisted Web Interviewing (CAWI) questionnaire, designed to gather both quantitative and qualitative data. From the analysis of the data, it emerged that students perceive the eTwinning platform as an innovative online learning environment capable of enhancing collaboration and networking among European schools, methodologies integrating diverse cultural perspectives, inclusive and accessible teaching materials, and promoting practical and experiential teaching approaches. From the analysis of the questionnaire responses, it appears that the eTwinning experience was perceived by students as engaging and professionally enriching, finding particular value in the practical and theoretical aspects of eTwinning (Figs. 1 and 2).

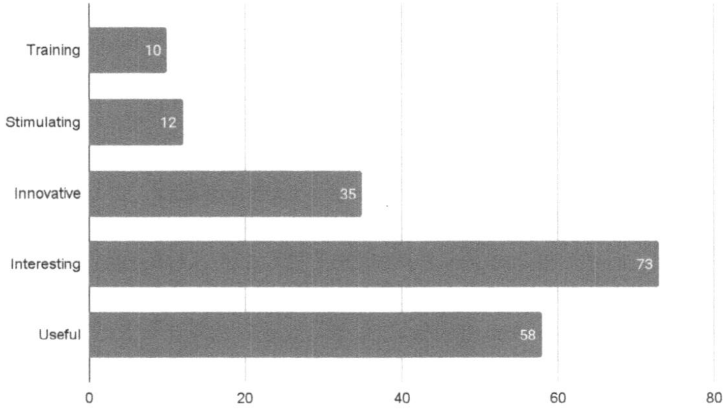

Fig. 1. Item 1: How would you define the eTwinning experimentation?

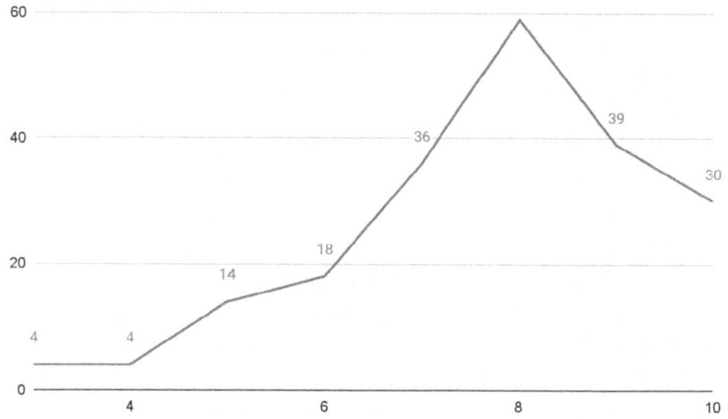

Fig. 2. Item 3: How excited were you about the eTwinning experimentation on a scale from 1 (not at all) to 10 (Entirely)?

The values of Table 2 suggest that most participants rated their excitement at 8, indicating a generally high level of enthusiasm, with some variability in responses as shown by the standard deviation and variance.

Table 2. Excited level regarding the eTwinning experimentation

Mode	Median	Standard deviation	Variance
7.75	8	1.637386	2.681034

The participants give a high rating about the answer "enthusiasm for participating in the eTwinning educational experience" concerning the perceived relationship between the methodology used and Information and Communication Technologies (item 4 – Fig. 3).

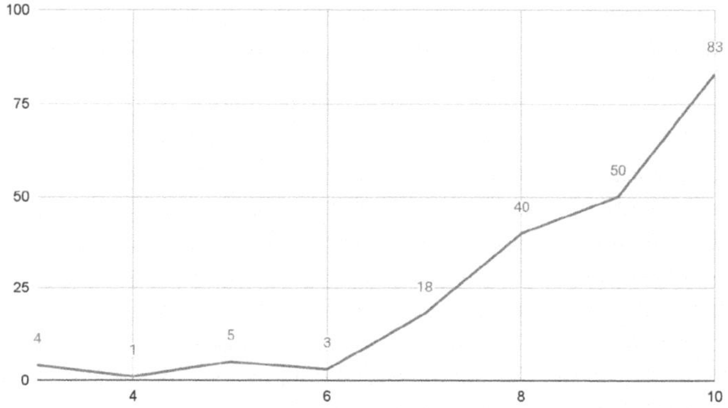

Fig. 3. Item 4: Perceived coherence between eTwinning and ICT

The overall level of satisfaction is high, with over 62% of students positively rating the appropriateness of the content to their educational path. This coherence was further strengthened by the recognition of a clear connection between eTwinning and the use of ICT, indicating a deep understanding of the goals of the methodology (Table 3).

Table 3. Item 5: Perceived average of alignment between eTwinning and the use of ICT

Mode	Median	Standard deviation	Variance
8.743842	9	1.502461	2.257389

Through the use of words such as "collaboration" and "innovative" to describe the initiative, students demonstrated their understanding of this initiative as an opportunity to experience new and international teaching methodologies (Fig. 4). Specifically, the term "innovative" underscores the distinctive nature of eTwinning compared to traditional teaching methods. Furthermore, students recognized this approach as an opportunity to explore new tools and methodologies, perceiving a clear departure from the rigidity of more conventional teaching practices. This element of novelty stimulated curiosity and motivation, encouraging more active and reflection participation.

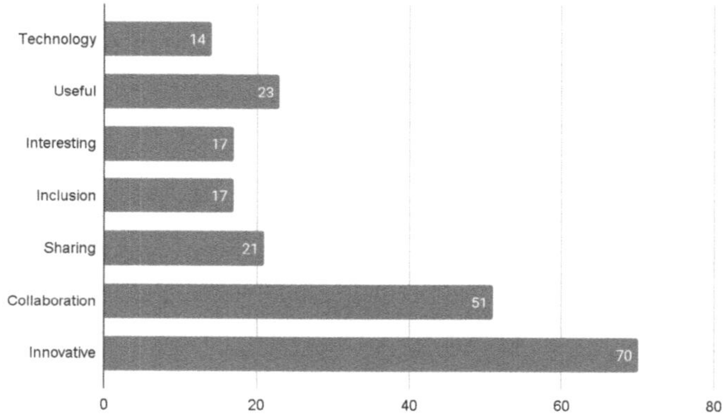

Fig. 4. Item 2: Write three words you associate with the eTwinning experimentation

The use of the terms "collaboration" and "sharing" highlights how peer interaction and co-design represent the core of the experience. eTwinning, in fact, goes beyond simply providing technological tools; it fosters an educational philosophy centred on dialogue and collective effort. Students acknowledged the importance of cultivating meaningful relationships not only within their own group but also through the potential of partnerships with schools in other countries. This international dimension was valued both for its contribution to cultural openness and for understanding different educational contexts. The strong focus on inclusion was evident in both spontaneous comments and the interest in creating accessible teaching materials. Students recognized the value of a methodology that, through ICT, seeks to dismantle barriers and provide equal learning opportunities for all students, regardless of their abilities or starting conditions. The eTwinning experiment had a significant impact on the participants' ongoing professional development. Responses indicated that future teachers have gained a deeper awareness of their skills and abilities to manage innovative learning environments. Moreover, the analysed variables showed a high average lever of reflection on their professional roles, indicating a greater reflection in the more motivated participants.

Of all the items, the graph (Fig. 5) specifically refers to item 5.6, as it contains the most significant data, offering a clearer understanding of the results and proving to be noteworthy (Table 4).

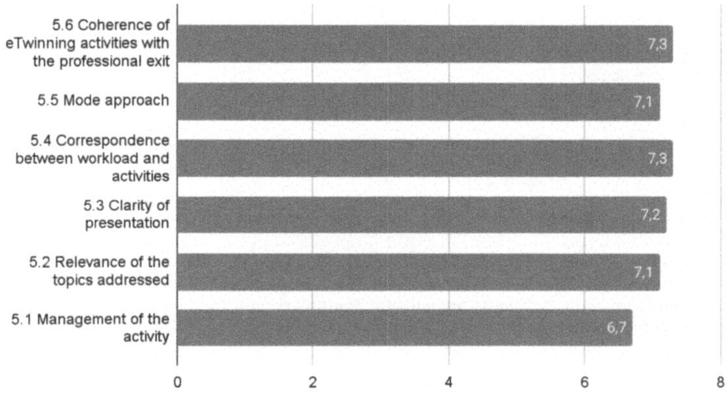

Fig. 5. Expression of the degree of satisfaction with the eTwinning experimentation

Table 4. Item 5: Satisfaction related to the eTwinning experimentation

Express your level of satisfaction on a scale of 1 (minimum) to 10 (maximum) regarding the eTwinning experimentation	Mean	Mode	Median	St. dev.	Variance
5.1 Management of the activity	6.7	8	7	2.6	6.8
5.2 Relevance of the topics addressed	7.1	8	8	2.4	6.1
5.3 Clarity of presentation	7.2	10	8	2.5	6.3
5.4 Correspondence between workload and activities	7.3	10	8	2.4	6.1
5.5 Mode approach	7.1	8	8	2.5	6.2
5.6 Coherence of eTwinning activities with the professional exit profile	7.3	10	8	2.5	6.2

The digital skills and the strengths and weaknesses highlighted by the participants offer ideas for rethinking media education. The skills considered a priority include collaboration and the use of digital tools, while the strengths identify innovation and active participation. The critical areas to improve that emerge are both technical difficulties and time management.

A more detailed analysis of the changes perceived (Fig. 6) by the students shows that 45% reported a more positive attitude towards the use of technology in teaching, while 22% mentioned an increase in specific digital skills. Moreover, 25% of the students developed a greater awareness of the opportunities offered by international school partnerships, demonstrating the potential of eTwinning in promoting global teaching. However, there are areas of concern that require attention, and the main weaknesses identified were: advanced digital skills, team-working abilities, and teaching design skills. This suggests the need for targeted training interventions to bridge these gaps and ensure a more comprehensive and transversal preparation.

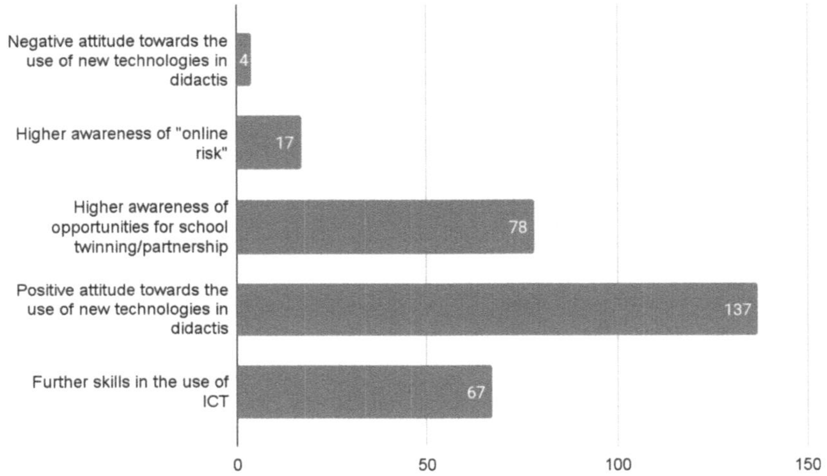

Fig. 6. Item 8: What changes have you noticed after the eTwinning experience and at the end of the "Educational Technologies" course?

3.1 Other Results

The overall analysis of the result (including open-ended questions which are not presented in detail here due to space limitations) revealed: a) *weaknesses and challenges*, such as: technical difficulties, language barriers, challenges in communication and collaboration, complex and time management, lack of tutorials; b) *strengths and opportunities*: international collaboration, development of digital skills, educational innovation; sharing and exchange; creativity; teacher support; adaptability and resilience. The responses highlight a significant interest among participants in advancing and enriching e-Twinning experimentation, encompassing several key areas of focus, for example: integrate e-Twinning into student internship programs; increase participation in collaborative projects with other European schools; deepen digital skills through practical experiences and innovative projects; receive continuous support and training to enhance the use of e-Twinning; engage in workshops and training courses to deepen the use of e-Twinning and educational technologies. The 2023 monitoring report [41] shows that eTwinning is integrated into initial teacher training programmes in different formats, adapting to the needs and contextual factors of training institutions.

This shows that eTwinning offers flexibility and customisation for participating universities. The exploratory study conducted at the University of Foggia will reflect on the role of eTwinning in initial teacher education, and particularly its inclusion in student internships [42].

The analysis of artifacts (during the second phase of survey, whose results are not included in this contribution but will be the subject of a subsequent publication) revealed how the use of specific web tools and AI devices enhances content personalization and creativity. The project work presented by the students highlights a wide range of technological tools used in a conscious and strategic way, representing an openness towards educational innovation. The works are characterized by being highly engaging and interactive. Among the methodologies used, digital storytelling was favoured through the use of avatars, interactive presentations, and geo-contextualization software. The proposed projects were developed on platforms that allow the collaboration of all team members, improving teamwork and idea negotiation skills. The methodologies presented, such as gamification and serious games, have fostered reflection on how technology acts as a transversal mediator of knowledge with enormous inclusive potential. Overall, the results show that the eTwinning experimentation has significantly contributed to the development of digital, collaborative skills and problem solving. Participants have proven a growing consciousness of their role as future teachers, reflecting on how to integrate these skills into their teaching approach. This path has not only favoured the mastery of technological tools but also encouraged deep reflection on the importance of collaborative, creative and future-oriented teaching.

During the experiment, the trainee teachers created an interactive presentation by the use of different applications (e.g.: creation of an avatar using the VIDNOZ or FLIPGRID platform, creation of a shared presentation on the SWAY platform, and others), collaborating in small groups. Each group's task was to illustrate their hometowns with information on the main monuments, history, cultural and culinary traditions. They then integrated the presentation with the Google Earth application, inserting personalized placemarks and multimedia elements. This activity contributed to the development of digital and collaborative skills, promoting an active approach to teaching digital technologies.

4 Conclusion

The eTwinning experimentation has proven to be a successful experience, capable of combining innovation, inclusion, and collaboration in a single methodological approach. The perceptions of the students and the data collected show appreciation for both the methodology and the understanding of its complexity and goals. However, the critical analysis of the results highlights the need to strengthen certain educational aspects, particularly those related to digital and project skills. The interest shown in the international dimension of eTwinning underscores the importance of promoting activities that can connect schools and students from different countries. This cultural openness represents an added value for teaching and also an opportunity to develop fundamental transversal skills, such as the ability to work in multicultural environments and to use technologies for communicative and collaborative purposes.

The results show the need for specific training designed to support teachers' knowledge and skills in adapting teaching materials for augmented learning environments. The international inquiry on teaching and learning (TALIS) conducted in 2018 by the OECD [43] highlighted the training needs of teachers in the countries participating in the survey, such as: improving skills on special educational needs, teaching in multicultural and multilingual contexts, and enhancing methodologies that make use of ICT. Investing in initial training programs focused on the eTwinning methodology proves beneficial, as it offers not only a quality approach but also addresses emerging needs within the teaching profession. There is a significant need to enhance the use of technology – especially AI and augmented learning tools – in innovative learning environments within teacher qualification training courses, highlighting its role as a powerful facilitator and inclusive mediator. This exploratory study underscores the importance of supporting teachers with specific training and promoting awareness of the strategic role of technology and personalization in education. In conclusion, eTwinning serves as a catalyst not only for fostering international collaboration but also for prompting universities to reassess and redesign their teacher training pathways. By integrating AI, technological devices, and networking tools, eTwinning underscores the importance of informal learning and a multi-level educational approach. This approach encourages universities to innovate their curricula and enhance the development of digital and cross-cultural competencies. The findings of the study illustrate eTwinning's to redefine initial teacher training (ITT), offering a model that resonates with global trends in digital transformation and educational innovation. These insights contribute to ongoing international discussions about the future of teacher training [44–46], emphasizing the need for a strategic integration of digital technologies to prepare educators for the challenges of an increasingly interconnected and technology-driven world.

References

1. Punie, Y., Redecker, C.: European Framework for the Digital Competence of Educators: DigCompEdu. Publications Office of the European Union, Luxembourg (2017)
2. Bacigalupo, M., Kampylis, P., Punie, Y., Van den Brande, G.: EntreComp: The Entrepreneurship Competence Framework. Publication Office of the European Union, Luxembourg (2016)
3. Bianchi, G., Pisiotis, U., Cabrera Giraldez, M.: GreenComp. The European sustainability competence framework. In: Punie, Y., Bacigalupo, M. (eds.) EUR 30955 EN. Publications Office of the European Union, Luxembourg (2022)
4. Sala, A., Punie, Y., Garkov, V., Cabrera Giraldez, M.: LifeComp: The European Framework for Personal, Social and Learning to Learn Key Competence. EUR 30246 EN. Publications Office of the European Union, Luxembourg (2020)
5. Väätäjä, H., Ruokamo, H.: Conceptualizing dimensions and a model for digital pedagogy. J. Pac. Rim Psychol. **15** (2021). https://doi.org/10.1177/1834490921995395
6. Perla, L., Felisatti, E., Grion, V.: Oltre l'era Covid-19: dall'emergenza alle prospettive di sviluppo professionale. Excellence and innovation in learning and teaching: research and practices, vol. 5, pp. 18–37. Franco Angeli, Milano (2020). https://doi.org/10.3280/exioa2-2020oa10802

7. Perla, L., Scarinci, A., Amati, I.: Metamorphosis of space into digital scholarship. A research on hybrid mediation in a university context. In: Bridges and Mediation in Higher Distance Education: Second International Workshop, HELMeTO, pp. 226–239. Springer (2021)
8. Pongsakdi, N., Kortelainen, A., Veermans, M.: The impact of digital pedagogy training on in-service teachers' attitudes towards digital technologies. Educ. Inf. Technol. **26**, 5041–5054 (2021). https://doi.org/10.1007/s10639-021-10439-w
9. Díaz Vera, J.-P., Ruiz Ramírez, A.-K., Egüez Cevallos, C.: Impacto de las TIC: desafíos y oportunidades de la Educación Superior frente al COVID-19. Revista Científica UISRAEL. **8**(2), 113–134 (2021)
10. Meisuri, M., Nuswantoro, P., Mardikawati, B., Judijanto, L.: Technology revolution in learning: building the future of education. J. Soc. Sci. Utiliz. Technol. **1**(4), 214–226 (2023). https://doi.org/10.70177/jssut.v1i4.660
11. Timotheou, S., Miliou, O., Dimitriadis, Y., Sobrino, S.V., Giannoutsou, N., Cachia, R., Ioannou, A.: Impacts of digital technologies on education and factors influencing schools' digital capacity and transformation: a literature review. Educ. Inf. Technol. **28**(6), 6695–6726 (2023). https://doi.org/10.1007/s10639-022-11431-8
12. INDIRE. Dati nazionali 2021: cresce la partecipazione a eTwinning. Italia fra i primi paesi in Europa con oltre 100 mila docenti e 3.600 nuovi progetti (2021). https://etwinning.indire.it/news/dati-nazionali-2021-cresce-la-partecipazione-a-etwinning-italia-fra-i-primi-paesi-in-europa-con-oltre-100-mila-docenti-e-3-600-nuovi-progetti/
13. Koehler, M.-J., Mishra, P.: Introducing technological pedagogical content knowledge. In: AACTE Committee on Innovation and Technology (ed.) Handbook of Technological Pedagogical Content Knowledge (TPCK) for Educators, pp. 3–29. Routledge, New York (2008)
14. Puentedura, R.-R.: Transformation, technology, and education in the state of Maine (2006). http://www.hippasus.com/rrpweblog/archives/2006_11.html
15. JRC European Commission Joint Reseanc Center: The changing nature of work and skills in the digital age (2017). https://publications.jrc.ec.europa.eu/repository/handle/JRC111359
16. UNESCO: AI Competency Framework for Teachers. Unesco Open Acces Repository, Parigi (2024)
17. UNESCO: AI Competency Framework for Students. Unesco Open Acces Repository, Parigi (2024)
18. Scott, D., Lock, J.: Teacher as Designer. Springer, New York (2021)
19. OECD: The OECD Handbook for Innovative Learning Environments. OECD Publishing, Paris (2017). http://dx.doi.org/9789264277274-en
20. Paniagua, A., Istance, D.: Teachers as Designers of Learning Environments: The Importance of Innovative Pedagogies, Educational Research and Innovation. OECD, Paris (2018)
21. Limone, P.: Ambienti di apprendimento e progettazione didattica: proposte per un sistema educativo transmediale. Carocci, Roma (2021)
22. Laurillard, D.: Trust the teachers: a collaborative approach to learning design solutions. In: Envisioning the Future of Education Through Design, pp. 119–145. Springer Nature Singapore, Singapore (2024)
23. Laurillard, D.: Teaching as a design science: building pedagogical patterns for learning and technology. Routledge, London (2013)
24. Persico, D., Pozzi, F., Goodyear, P.: Teachers as designers of TEL - Editorial. Br. J. Educ. Technol. **49**(6), 975–980 (2018). https://doi.org/10.1111/bjet.12706
25. Wenger, E.: Comunità di pratica. Apprendimento, significato e identità. Cortina editore, Milano, Cortina (2006)
26. Tondeur, J., Pareja Roblin, N., Van Braak, J., Voogt, J., Prestridge, S.: Preparing beginning teachers for technology integration in education: ready for take-off? Technol. Pedagog. Educ. **26**(2), 157–177 (2017). https://doi.org/10.1080/1475939X.2016.1193556

27. Voogt, J.-M., Pieters, J.-M., Handelzalts, A.: Teacher collaboration in curriculum design teams. Digit. Acad. Repository. (2016) https://pure.uva.nl/ws/files/9593158/Teacher_collaboration_in_curriculum_dsign_teams.pdf
28. Bonometti, S., Ferri, L.: Promuovere l'innovazione didattica e lo sviluppo delle competenze trasversali: una panoramica sul Teaching Learning Center (TLC) dell'Università degli Studi dell'Insubria. CQIA RIVISTA. **14**(42), 36–49 (2024)
29. Sliwka, A.: Networking for educational innovation: a comparative analysis. In: OECD (ed.) Networks of Innovation – Towards New Models for Managing Schools and Systems Schooling for Tomorrow Series, pp. 49–65. OECD, Parigi (2003)
30. Şahin, G., Gökçe, H., Karabulut, H., Kariper, İ.A.: Learning community eTwinning: a literature review. Discov. Educ. **3**(1), 1–13 (2024)
31. Gazzetta Ufficiale dell'Unione Europea. Legislazione 49° anno 20 dicembre 2006. Documenti pubblicati nell'anno 2006. Gazzetta Ufficiale (2006). https://eur-lex.europa.eu/legal-content/IT/TXT/?uri=OJ%3AL%3A2006%3A363%3ATOC
32. EUR-Lex.: Direttiva 2003/98/CE del Parlamento europeo e del Consiglio, del 17 novembre 2003, relativa al riutilizzo dell'informazione del settore pubblico (2003). https://eur-lex.europa.eu/legal-content/IT/TXT/?uri=CELEX:32003L0098
33. Gutiérrez, K.-D.: Developing a sociocritical literacy in the Third Space. Read. Res. Q. **43**(2), 148–164 (2008)
34. Tosi, A., Martinelli, S., Pettenati, M.-C.: Empowering future teachers for a sustainable intercultural and inclusive education. In: The Impact of eTwinning on Continuing Professional Development of Teachers in Italy. Carocci, Roma (2023)
35. Perla, L., Vinci, V., Agrati, L.-S.: The Italian way to the Europeanisation of teacher education: an analysis of reforms and the ongoing experience of digital transformation. Center Educ. Policy Stud. J. (2024)
36. Nucci, D., Tosi, A., Pettenati, M.-C.: eTwinning e la formazione degli insegnanti. Studi, evidenze e prospettive della community italiana, Carocci, Roma (2021)
37. Perla, L., Vinci, V., Agrati, L.: The DidaSco project: a training program for the teachers' professional development. In: Mena, J., Repiso, A.G.V.M., Peñalvo, F.J.G., del Pozo, M.M. (eds.) Search and Research: Teacher Education for Contemporary Contexts, pp. 921–930. Ediciones Universidad de Salamanca (2017)
38. Northouse, P.G.: Leadership: Theory and Practice, 9th edn. SAGE Publications, Thousand Oaks (2021)
39. Reyes, V.C.: What is most important in education reform? The impact of leadership, innovation and partnerships. Int. J. Leadersh. Educ., 1–18 (2023). https://doi.org/10.1080/13603124.2023.2281353
40. eTwinning. Empowering eTwinning Schools: Il programma europeo per il miglioramento delle scuole (2019). https://etwinning.indire.it/wp-content/uploads/2015/11/Empowering-eTwinning-Schools_2019_ITA.pdf
41. Mangione, G.R., Mosa, E., Pettenati, M.C.: Dalla Gelmini alla Giannini. Il Piano Nazionale Scuola Digitale, i PON disciplinari e il ruolo dell'INDIRE nella formazione continua degli insegnanti. Formazione & Insegnamento. **13**(3), 139–166 (2015)
42. Camilleri, R.A.: Global education and intercultural awareness in eTwinning. Cogent Educ. **3**(1) (2016). https://doi.org/10.1080/2331186X.2016.1210489
43. Gökbulut, B.: A study to determine the eTwinning-related views of the Teachers in the eTwinning network countries, and their digital literacy levels. J. Teacher Educ. Lifelong Learn. **5**(1), 18–37 (2023)
44. Unione Europea: L'impatto di eTwinning sulla formazione iniziale degli insegnanti: riflettori puntati sugli insegnanti in formazione e i loro formatori. Ufficio delle pubblicazioni dell'Unione europea, Lussemburgo (2023)

45. Unione Europea eTwinning. Insegnare, creare, innovare. Ufficio delle pubblicazioni dell'Unione europea, Lussemburgo (2023)
46. Teaching and Learning International Survey: Conceptual Framework OECD Education Working Paper No. 187 (2018). https://www.oecd-ilibrary.org/education/teaching-and-learning-international-survey-talis-2018-conceptual-framework_799337c2-en

Developing Assessment Competences in Teacher Education: Insights from Moodle-Based Task

Laura Sara Agrati[1(✉)] and Arianna Beri[2]

[1] Telematic University of Pegaso, Napoli, Italy
laurasara.agrati@unipegaso.it
[2] University of Bergamo, Bergamo, Italy
arianna.beri@unibg.it

Abstract. This paper examines the role of Moodle in the development of assessment competences in student-teachers enrolled in the "Problems and Techniques of Assessment" course at the University of Bergamo. The course, designed for students in the Primary Education Sciences programme, integrates both theoretical and practical learning through the Moodle platform. The study investigates how the online environment supported by Moodle facilitated the creation and analysis of assessment tools by student-teachers, focusing on the development of their assessment skills. The course structure includes 11 lectures, 3 workshops, and several assignments, with a total of 43 student submissions analysed. Findings suggest that Moodle's structured, flexible environment significantly contributed to enhancing student-teachers' competence in designing assessment tools, especially through practical tasks and peer feedback. The results underline the importance of careful planning and the effective use of online resources in teacher training, demonstrating that Moodle can play a key role in fostering assessment skills in future educators.

Keywords: Assessment Competences · Moodle · Training Teachers

1 Student-Teachers' Assessment Competences

Discussing school assessment and, more specifically, teacher training in this area of competence, has often been considered "problematic" [1, 2], as the assessment process crosses relevant technical-operational and ethical-criterial dimensions, which are not always aligned [3].

Although a certain "neglect" of the topic was initially noted [4], teacher training, both initial and in-service, has received increasing research attention in recent years [5, 6]. This renewed interest is also reflected in the wider accountability system [7, 8], which describes teachers' professional learning in the area of assessment as a continuous, career-long pathway that requires adequate support [8].

Teacher assessment competence is considered one of the "professional dimensions that qualify the teacher" [9, 10], as well as "a fundamental part of it" [11, 12], essential for the quality of education in contemporary education systems [13]. In recent years,

P. Ardimento et al. (Eds.): HELMeTO 2024, CCIS 2468, pp. 276–286, 2025.
https://doi.org/10.1007/978-3-031-93999-0_18

the definition of teachers' assessment competence has evolved from being simply the ability to use assessment tools to support and measure students' learning [13], to a negotiated and dynamic competence influenced by contextual factors such as teachers' professionalism, students' learning needs, and the school and cultural context [14].

Although teacher training in assessment has been identified as a priority, research on assessment has mainly been conducted from general perspectives, often without effective links to everyday practice or common standards [15]. Specifically, studies on initial teacher training in assessment have focused on curricula and delivery methods (content, teaching strategies, etc.), on the ways in which specific assessment skills are practised at school and university level (adaptation to disciplines; use of lectures, seminars, workshops [16]). In Italy, assessment competence is part of the overall profile of the teacher and, for this reason, is included in the curricula of qualifying courses [17].

Specifically, for the Degree Course in Primary Education (D.M. 249/2010; Table 1, Art. 6 - LM-85bis; D.M. 259/2017), among the qualifying training objectives, the evaluative field includes:

- the ability to manage the classroom in order to plan the pedagogical and didactic path [...] and to facilitate the school integration of children with special needs;
- possess disciplinary knowledge [...] able to articulate the contents of the disciplines according to the different school levels and the age of the children;
- have the pedagogical and didactic skills to manage the learning process by adapting the timing and modalities to the level of the different pupils.

An explicit reference is made to "assessment techniques", which appears among the knowledge of the graduate profiles in relation to the field of experimental pedagogy, together with research methodologies.

Table 1. Phases and resources of laboratories on Moodle

Phase/modality	Type of activity	Data collection/n	
I presence	Introductory lectures + examples	Questionnaire	
II online	Group work	Open tests, draft (20)	Authentic tasks, draft (23)
III presence	Self- and peer-assessment on drafts		
IV presence	Final individual exame	Open tests, fair copy (125)	Authentic tasks, fair copy (125)

Despite the recognition of the importance of assessment literacy for the teaching profession [18], especially for its obvious impact on learning and teaching processes [19], some critical issues remain:

a) the "assessment literacy abounds" [20], i.e. the gaps in the undergraduate training of student teachers, leading to difficulties in achieving adequate levels of assessment skills, particularly in the construction of open-ended tests [21];

b) a poor understanding of the effectiveness of the training provided, e.g. in relation to evaluation criteria, selection and use of appropriate instruments, and awareness of the functions of evaluation itself [22]. More generally, there is a limited understanding of teachers' evaluative competence in the classroom context [23].

1.1 Use of Moodle in the Student-Teacher's Higher Education

In recent years, particularly in the wake of the Covid-19 pandemic, the education sector has undergone profound changes, especially in terms of tools, modes and teaching environments [24, 25]. The use of integrated online learning management platforms and software has increased considerably, both because of the need for universities to keep education active and because of the benefits of ease of use, openness, sharing and accumulation of knowledge [26]. E-learning has established itself as a functional training modality [27], in terms of cost [28] and space-time flexibility [29]. Among the e-learning platforms - e.g. Schoology, Google Classroom, Edmodo, Zoom Meeting [30, 31] - Moodle (acronym for "Modular Object-Oriented Dynamic Learning Environment") is a learning management system (LMS) developed in 2001, which since its launch has enabled the creation of more than 167,000 university courses and involved almost 400 million users worldwide [32]. These data attest to the effectiveness and widespread adoption of Moodle as a tool for online learning management and planning [33] and as a support for face-to-face teaching [26]. Although the number of specific studies on this topic remains limited [34], some research has explored the impact of online course adaptation on the development of assessment skills of future teachers [35, 36] and proposed models of analysis for the students involved [37].

Several authors [38, 39] have highlighted how assessment strategies are closely linked to the development of teachers' competences.

While some studies point out that "the use of technology often replicates existing assessment practices rather than embracing transformative practices. [...] However, there is little evidence that technology has improved student learning at the tertiary level, and if so, to what extent" [40, p. 2], more recent research confirms, on one hand, that "using the online resources fosters the student teachers' ability to design assessment tools" [35], promoting the development of skills in assessment design and implementation [35]. On the other hand, it underscores the importance of carefully planning the learning environment and selecting digital resources thoughtfully [36, 41].

The use of remote assessment techniques could, in fact, address contemporary challenges thanks to their flexibility and ability to manage a large number of students [42], while also facilitating the generation of "constructive, timely, and 'easy-to-understand' feedback" [40, 43].

Furthermore, students appear to appreciate these methods, particularly when associated with authentic assessment tasks [36].

However, the practical implementation of remote assessment processes risks being less supported by theoretical reflections and empirical research consolidated in the field's literature [36].

2 Study on Student-Teachers' Assessment Competences Development in Moodle Platform

The paper presents a study carried out between February and May 2024 at the B.S. 'Primary Education Science' at the University of Bergamo, with the general aim of learning about student-teachers' learning experiences on the Moodle platform and collecting data on its effectiveness in the development of assessment competences, specifically with regard to the ability to design tools for the assessment of knowledge, skills and competences at school.

The research question was: *Were student-teachers able to design good assessment tools on the Moodle platform? (RQ1)*

2.1 Context, Participants and Survey Design

The study was conducted as part of the 36-h course 'Problems and Techniques of Assessment' held during the second semester of the fifth year of the curriculum. The course consisted of 12 lectures of 3 h each, divided into theoretical lectures focusing on the basics of assessment, assessment terminology and concepts, etc.; thematic seminars focusing on assessment processes/tools for the assessment of skills and competences in schools; group workshop activities on the analysis of standardised tests, development of paper and pencil tools.

The course was delivered synchronously using the Moodle platform, which is accessible via personal login and is useful for the asynchronous exchange of study and in-depth materials as well as student work.

The study involved 125 primary school student-teachers, almost all of them female (95%), with an average age of 27 years and at least two years of work/training experience in primary education.

The 4 workshop activities implemented, totalling 12 h, had as specific training objectives:

- to analyse the characteristics and functions of tools for the assessment of knowledge, skills and competences at school;
- to develop tools for the assessment of knowledge, skills and competences at school;
- to elaborate assessment tools for school competences;
- to critique and revise the developed assessment tools.

The table below (Table 1) shows the alternation of presence/online phases, the types of activities and the methods of data collection during the course.

The study followed a sequential explanatory mixed methods design [37].

The first exploratory phase (quantitative data) generated inferences useful for the second confirmatory phase (qualitative data). The final synthetic meta-inference was made through triangulation (Fig. 1). On the basis of Kirkpatrick's model [43] adapted to the e-learning environment [36], the focus was on the student teachers' aptitudes, i.e. declarative-procedural knowledge and skills.

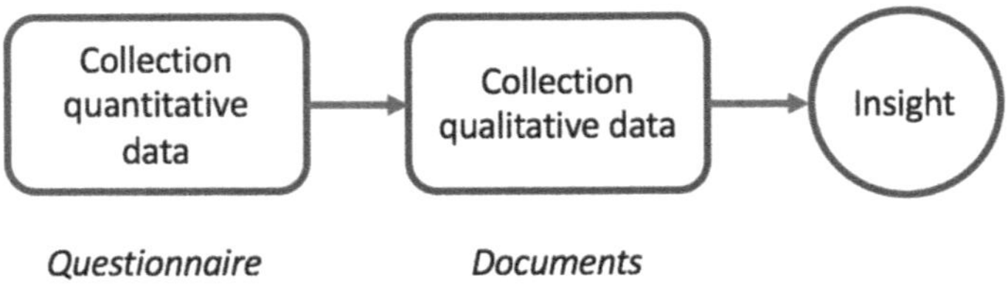

Fig. 1. Explanatory Sequential Design

2.2 Data Collection and Analysis Methods

This study focuses on the skills of the student-teachers derived from the analysis of the documents (tasks) of the paper-and-pencil assessment tools that were processed and uploaded in Moodle during the workshops.

The data were collected by analysing the 43 primary documents [44] produced by the student-teachers during the 4 workshops and uploaded to the platform. The structured analysis of the documents was conducted using criterion-based grids according to predefined types, with their descriptors outlined in the following table [37, 45, 46] - Table 2:

For the analysis of the documents - semi-structured tests and authentic tasks - average scores were calculated by awarding one point for the presence of elements meeting the criterion and summing the points obtained (Table 3).

Figures 2 and 3 show the dimensions and scores between drafts and final copies based on the criteria adopted, respectively for open tasks and the authentic tasks analysed.

2.3 Results, Discussion, and Limitations of the Study

Research question: *were student-teachers able to design good assessment tools on moodle platform? (RQ1)*

Table 3 shows an increase in the overall average for both open tests (0.95, 2.41 - +1.46) and authentic tasks (2.60, 4.06 - +1.46). At the specific level of the criteria adopted for the analysis of the documents, the largest increase concerns "consistency", both for open tests (+0.57) and for authentic tasks (+0.37), the smallest increase concerns "clarity" (+0.40) for open tests and "transposition" (+0.20) for authentic tasks.

The overall average increases allow to confirm the general effectiveness of the pathway implemented through the Moodle platform, as defined above. The trend of the data according to the types of assessment tools developed and the criteria adopted for their analysis provide further indications. The average increase between open tests and authentic tasks was similar - +1.46 and +1.45 respectively. However, the initial average (see draft) was different - open tests (0.95), authentic tasks (2.60), which suggests that the student-teachers involved had a good basic preparation for the development of the authentic tasks, less so for the open tests.

Focusing on the trend by criteria, it can be seen that the criterion "coherence", i.e. the coherence between the required performance and the learning objectives of the curriculum to be assessed, showed the greatest increase compared to the others. This would suggest a sensitivity on the part of student teachers to the overall validity of assessment

Table 2. Criteria and descriptors for document analysis

Assessment Tools	Criteria*	Descriptor
Semi-structured tasks (for knowledge/skills)	Consistency	Coherence between the cognitive/skill-based operation required and the curriculum's knowledge/skills being assessed
	Exhaustiveness	Selection of exhaustive and appropriately predetermined response criteria
	Clarity	Stimuli and any explanatory texts formulated clearly and in language accessible to the user
Authentic tasks (for competences)	Realistic situation	Reference to a plausible area, situation, or context capable of fostering situated knowledge
	Varied solutions	Possibility of different alternatives for solving the task
	Challenges	Complex, dynamic, and combinatorial nature of the knowledge required to solve the task
	Transposition	Adaptation of the problem from specialised disciplinary language to natural language
	Consistency	Coherence between the expected outcome and the key competence selected for structuring the task

instruments - i.e. how well the instrument measures what it is intended to measure, in the way it is intended to measure, without contamination by other characteristics - an important quality parameter of assessment, as well as an indispensable knowledge content of the assessor [47]. It should be noted that the increase in the criterion of 'consistency' occurred as much in the open-tests, to a greater extent (0.57), as in the authentic tasks, to a lesser extent (0.37) and, again, would suggest that the student-teachers at the beginning of the activities were more predisposed to the processing of the authentic tasks, less so than the open-tests.

The documentary analysis carried out thus helps to unveil elements linked to the prior preparation of the student-teachers as well as their learning response to the demands offered by the training course. The student-teachers demonstrate ingress knowledge and skills related to formative assessment processes and tools - such as authentic tasks -, less so to summative assessment tools, such as tests and open-tests. This element could guide course and degree course leaders in the more judicious choice of topics to be addressed in the curriculum.

Table 3. Average scores per criteria for open tests and authentic tasks

Criteria	Draft *m*	Fair copy *m*	Δ
Open tests	n. 20	n. 125	
Consistency	0.20	0.77	+0.57*
Completeness	0.35	0.84	+0.49
Clarity	0.40	0.80	+0.40
Tot.	**0.95**	**2.41**	**+1.46**
Authentic tasks	n. 23	n. 125	
Situation	0.56	0.82	+0.26
Solution	0.43	0.76	+0.33
Challenge	0.52	0.83	+0.31
Transposition	0.60	0.80	+0.20
Consistency	0.47	0.84	+0.37*
Tot.	**2.60**	**4.06**	**+1.45**

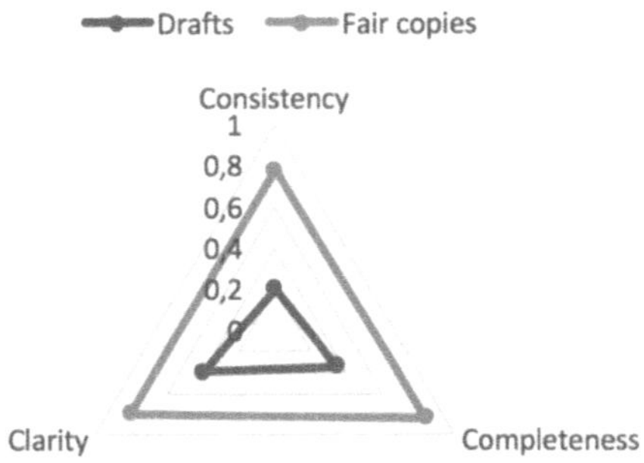

Fig. 2. Scores per criteria, open-tests

The student-teachers first developed draft assessment instruments, then fair copies for the final examination (see Table 1). The process of developing the assessment tools started with the prior analysis of examples provided on the Moodle platform and continued with self-assessment and peer-assessment of the uploaded drafts. The Moodle platform thus offered a space for sharing examples and drafts of assessment tools against which each student-teacher could eventually develop final versions for the examination. Above all, phase III of the self- and peer-assessment of the uploaded drafts, which was carried out both in-presence and online, was probably the most significant moment in the process of the development of the assessment tools, if one considers the average increase of uploaded documents (see Table 3).

A limitation of the study is the small number of student-teachers (see 125), although they represent almost all course participants (89.2%). Further studies involving a larger

Fig. 3. Scores per criteria, authentic tasks

number of student-teachers could either corroborate or challenge the findings. Another limitation is the hybrid (face-to-face/online) nature of the course training situations (see Table 1), which in principle does not allow the actual weight of the Moodle component to be separated from the final averages. However, a relevant element emerges from a comparison of the data on enrolments and uploaded documents. All the student teachers on the course were enrolled in Moodle (140), an average of 40 people participated in the face-to-face activities, 125 final documents were uploaded and analysed (Table 1), with a reasonable average quality (Table 3).

These data suggest that the examples of assessment tools provided in phase I and the drafts uploaded by the groups in phase II were useful learning resources for those who did not attend phases I and III, confirming the usefulness of the Moodle platform as a learning environment for developing complex skills such as the development of school assessment tools.

3 Conclusions

The importance of assessment competence is widely recognised in both academic and policy circles [8, 9]. However, the issue of assessment within teacher training and the development of competences through online courses, particularly through the use of the Moodle platform, has received relatively limited attention so far [23, 34].

The results of the present study are in line with previous literature and confirm the general effectiveness of training using the Moodle platform [33, 35].

It also confirms that students seem to value these modalities, especially when combined with authentic assessment tests [36, 42]. In our study in particular, these tests showed a significant increase, as in the case of open tests.

Notably, there was a significant increase in the 'consistency' criterion, a key element for the quality of assessment work. Furthermore, the work submitted by non-participants showed an improvement due to the spatio-temporal flexibility offered by the platform [27, 29]. This finding suggests that the use of digital tools such as Moodle can effectively support learning processes even in conditions of irregular attendance.

However, there was also a limitation related to the lack of prior preparation for open tests, an aspect already highlighted in the literature [15].

In light of these findings, the study reaffirms the importance of promoting and deepening the reflection on the integration of assessment competences, teacher training, and the use of digital platforms. This integration, when appropriately supported, can serve as a strategic lever to improve the quality of training and learning, thus addressing the challenges posed by contemporary teaching.

References

1. La Marca, P.: Assessment literacy: building capacity for improving student learning. Paper presented at the Council of Chief State School Officers (CCSSO) Annual Conference on Large-Scale Assessment (2006)
2. Scarino, A.: Language assessment literacy as self-awareness: understanding the role of interpretation in assessment and in teacher learning. Lang. Test. **30**(3), 309–327 (2013)
3. Bonazza, V.: Valutazione e scuola. Ideologia, senso comune e cultura della ricerca. Metodologia e organizzazione. Roma, Ancia (2019)
4. Deluca, C., Johnson, S.: Developing assessment capable teachers in this age of accountability. Assessm. Educ. Principles Policy Pract. **24**, 121–126 (2017). https://doi.org/10.1177/0022487113488144
5. Cowie, B., Cooper, B., Ussher, B.: Developing an identity as a teacher assessor: three student teacher case studies. Assessm. Matters. **7**, 64–89 (2014)
6. DeLuca, C., Lapointe-Mcewan, D., Luhanga, U.: Teacher assessment literacy: a review of international standards and measures. Educ. Assessm. Eval. Account. Adv. Online Publ. (2015). https://doi.org/10.1007/s11092-015-9233-6
7. Andrade, H., Heritage, M.: Using formative assessment to enhance learning, achievement, and academic self-regulation. Routledge, London (2018)
8. OECD: Empowering teachers and school leaders in TALIS 2018 Results (Volume II): Teachers and School Leaders as Valued Professionals. OECD Publishing, Paris (2020). https://doi.org/10.1787/b0b7eb40-en
9. Viganò, R.: Qualità e professione docente: la valutazione come risorsa. Edetania. **52**, 269–285 (2017)
10. Agrati, L.S.: Supportare le competenze valutative degli insegnanti in servizio. Primi esiti di un'indagine pilota. Lifelong Lifewide Learning. **19**(42), 146–157 (2023)
11. Brookhart, S.M.: Educational assessment knowledge and skills for teachers revisited. Educ. Sci. **14**(7), 751 (2024)
12. Popham, W.J.: Assessment literacy for teachers: Faddish or fundamental? Theory Pract. **48**, 4–11 (2009)
13. DeLuca, C., Schneider, C., Coombs, A., Pozas, M., Rasooli, A.: A cross-cultural comparison of German and Canadian student teachers' assessment competence. Assessm. Educ.: Princip. Policy Pract. **27**(1), 26–45 (2020)
14. Willis, J., Adie, L., Klenowski, V.: Conceptualizing teachers' assessment literacies in an era of curriculum and assessment reform. Austral. Educ. Research. **40**(2), 241–256 (2013)
15. DeLuca, C., Klinger, D.A.: Assessment literacy development: Identifying gaps in teacher candidates' learning. Assessm. Educ.: Principl. Policy Pract. **17**, 419–438 (2010)
16. DeLuca, C., Chapman-Chin, A.E.A., LaPointe-McEwan, D., Klinger, D.A.: Student perspectives on assessment for learning. Curric. J. **29**(1), 77–94 (2018)
17. Agrati L.S.: La formazione iniziale in area valutativa: prima mappatura dei cds in Scienze della Formazione Primaria. Sessione 2 'La formazione iniziale nella scuola dell'infanzia e primaria'. In: M. Fiorucci e E. Zizoli (a cura di). La formazione degli insegnanti: problemi, prospettive e proposte per una scuola di qualità e aperta a tutti e tutte (pp. 60-64). PensaMultimedia: Roma-Lecce (2022). ISBN volume 978-86-6760-000-0

18. Abell, S.K., Siegel, M.A.: Assessment literacy: what science teachers need to know and be able to do. In: Corrigan, D., Dillon, J., Gunstone, R. (eds.) The Professional Knowledge Base of Science Teaching, vol. 12, pp. 205–221. Springer, Dordrecht (2011)
19. Wilson, S.M., Floden, R.E., Ferrini-Mundy, J.: Teacher Preparation Research: Current Knowledge, Gaps, and Recommendations. University of Washington, Center for the Study of Teaching and Policy, Washington, DC (2001)
20. Stiggins, R.J.: Essential formative assessment competencies for teachers and school leaders. In: Andrade, H.L., Cizek, G.J. (eds.) Handbook of Formative Assessment, pp. 233–250. Taylor & Francis, New York (2010)
21. DeLuca, C., Klinger, D.A.: Assessment literacy development: identifying gaps in teacher candidates' learning. Assessm. Educ.: Princip. Policy Pract. **17**, 419–438 (2010)
22. Agrati, L.S., Beri, A.: Prove di verifica nella scuola primaria. Analisi documentale delle prove carta-e-matita e tratte dai libri di testo. Mizar. Costellazione di pensieri, 18, 24–40 (2023). ISSN 2499-5835.
23. Volante, L., Fazio, X.: Exploring teacher candidates' assessment literacy: implications for teacher education reform and professional development. Can. J. Educ. **30**(3), 749–770 (2017)
24. Xiao, Q.: Using open-source learning platform (Moodle) in university teachers' professional development. J. Phys. Conf. Ser. **1646**(1), 012036 (2020)
25. IAU-UNESCO: Regional/National Perspectives on the Impact of Higher Education. UNESCO House, Paris (2020). https://doi.org/10.1007/978-1-4614-3185-5_32
26. Calderon-Valenzuela, J., Payihuanca-Mamani, K., Bedregal-Alpaca, N.: Educational data mining to identify the patterns of use made by the university professors of the Moodle platform. Int. J. Adv. Comput. Sci. Appl. **13**(1), 321–328 (2022)
27. Koderi, K.G.C.: Moodle E-learning to improve motivation and learning activities at green campus. J. Educ. Technol. **7**(1), 12–24 (2023)
28. Koderi.: Model development of SAVI-based E-module for Arabic instruction at Islamic Junior High School in Bandar Lampung, Indonesia. Humaniora-Binus Univ. ***9***(1), 23–31 (2018). https://doi.org/10.21512/humaniora.v9i1.4136
29. Agbenyegah, A.T., Dlamini, B.I.: Investigating the challenges of E-learning in a developing institution of higher learning: a hypothetical approach. J. Appl. Bus. Res. ***35***(3), 83–96 (2019). https://doi.org/10.19030/jabr.v35i3.10303
30. He, W., Xu, G., Kruck, S.E.: Online is education for the 21st century. J Inform Syst Educ. **25**(2), 101–106 (2018)
31. Ramadayanti, G., Adzima, K.R.: Pengaruh Penggunaan Aplikasi Zoom Meeting Terhadap Kemampuan Pemecahan Masalah Matematika Siswa Pada Pembelajaran Daring Di Kelas V. Jurnal Perseda: Jurnal Pendidikan Guru Sekolah Dasar. **4**(3), 153–158 (2022)
32. Moodle. https://moodle.com/. Accessed 7 Mar 2024
33. Moodle – eLearning. https://www.unibg.it/moodle-elearning. Accessed 7 Mar 2024
34. Agrati, L.S., Vinci, V.: Evaluative knowledge and skills of student teachers within the adapted degree courses. Front. Educ. **7** (2022)
35. Agrati, L.S., Svetlana, K., Valeeva, R., Lazzari, M.: Developing the novice teacher evaluation competence: the challenge of online training. In: Casalino, G., et al. (eds.) HELMeto 2021, CCIS 1542, pp. 1–15. Springer (2022)
36. Hamtini, T.M.: Evaluating e-learning programs: an adaptation of Kirkpatrick's model to accommodate e-learning environments. J. Comput. Sci. **4**, 693–698 (2008)
37. Creswell, J.W., Creswell, J.D.: Mixed methods procedures. In: Research Design: Qualitative, Quantitative, and Mixed Methods Approaches, 5th edn, pp. 213–246. SAGE Publications, Los Angeles (2008)
38. Sullivan, G.M.: A primer on the validity of assessment instruments. J. Grad. Med. Educ. **3**(2), 119–120 (2011)

39. Sweeney, T., West, D., Groessler, A., Haynie, A., Higgs, B.M., Macaulay, J., Mercer-Mapstone, L., Yeo, M.: Where's the transformation? Unlocking the potential of technology-enhanced assessment. Teach. Learn. Inquiry. **5**(1), 1–16 (2017)
40. Pedersen, J.M., Kuran, M.S.: Moodle: practical advices for university teachers. Adv. Intell. Syst. Comput. **681**, 183–190 (2018)
41. Whitelock, D., Watt, S.: Reframing e-assessment: adopting new media and adapting old frameworks. Learn. Media Technol. **33**(3), 153–156 (2008)
42. Lock, J.V., Redmond, P.: Empowering learners to engage in authentic online assessment. In: Koç, S., Liu, X., Wakira, P. (eds.) Assessment in Online and Blended Learning Environments, pp. 21–38. IAP, Charlotte (2015)
43. Kirkpatrick, D., Kirkpatrick, P.: Evaluating training programs, 3rd edn. Berrett-Koehler Publishers, San Francisco (2006). ISBN: 10:1576753484
44. Bowen, G.: Document analysis as a qualitative research method. Qual. Res. J. **9**(2), 27–40 (2009)
45. Domenici, G.: Manuale della valutazione scolastica. Roma, Laterza (2003)
46. De Ketele, J.-M., Gerard, F.-M.: La validation des épreuves d'évaluation selon l'approche par les compétences. Mesure et évaluation en education. **28**(3), 1–26 (2005)
47. Sullivan, M.G.: A primer on the validity of assessment instrument. J. Grad. Med. Educ. **3**(2), 119–120 (2001). https://doi.org/10.4300/JGME-D-11-00075.1

Transversal Competences with AI: Training Implications and Faculty Development Perspectives

Loredana Perla(✉), Annamaria Di Grassi, Raffaella Forliano, and Maria Teresa Santacroce

Università degli Studi di Bari "Aldo Moro", Bari, Italy
{loredana.perla,maria.teresasantacroce}@uniba.it,
{annamaria.digrassi,raffaella.forliano}@unifg.it

Abstract. This paper aims to evaluate the effectiveness of including a transversal skills course on Artificial Intelligence in an academic development programme for doctoral students at the University of Bari. The course, designed to develop advanced digital skills and ethical reflection, provided a basis for integrating technical knowledge with analytical skills for the responsible use of AI in both academic and professional settings. Its main objective was to enable graduate and postgraduate students to understand the tools needed to address the complex challenges posed by artificial intelligence and to reflect on the responsible, conscious and ethical use of such technologies in their own fields and research paths from a human-centered perspective.

Data collected from surveys and feedback from participants indicate a good level of satisfaction and a significant impact on students' research projects. The analysis shows the importance of interdisciplinary courses that promote critical thinking, collaboration and ethical awareness. Findings and recommendations for future course design are presented, highlighting the need to integrate such pedagogies into higher education curricula.

The article uses a detailed analysis of the teaching methods used and the feedback collected from participants to assess the impact of the course on the research skills of doctoral students. It discusses the teaching methods, the results achieved and the challenges faced in integrating this course into the university curriculum. It also reflects on the role of AI in the future of scientific research, highlighting how AI can be an effective tool for innovation and progress in the contemporary research landscape.

Keywords: Artificial Intelligence · Faculty Development · AI Ethics · Higher Education · Soft skills

1 Introduction

The rapid development of Artificial Intelligence and its growing impact on society is challenging higher education to consider how to meet unprecedented challenges and seize unprecedented opportunities. The COVID-19 pandemic had already accelerated

P. Ardimento et al. (Eds.): HELMeTO 2024, CCIS 2468, pp. 287–301, 2025.
https://doi.org/10.1007/978-3-031-93999-0_19

digitalization and increased the use of technology in educational contexts. Today, the emergence of the latest generation of generative artificial intelligence further underlines the need for new pedagogical approaches. These require a move towards more inclusive teaching methods that integrate different pedagogical, technological and organizational skills, a virtuous triangulation between discipline, teaching and research, to which the management and governance dimension is increasingly added [1], elements that are often still lacking in university teacher training programmes. Indeed, lecturers are called upon to be designers, evaluators, resource developers and much more [2]. Innovation, which has become the focus of responses in the field of education, is a complex process that requires investment in multiple directions; it poses significant challenges to universities and requires deep reflection on their role in the education of new generations [3].

Although many universities have launched professional development initiatives aimed at integrating technology into teaching [4], there is still resistance among lecturers, often linked to the perception of technology as a hindrance rather than a help. Currently, training tends to focus on the acquisition of technical skills, neglecting the pedagogical changes that are essential for real and effective technology integration. Moreover, the potential offered by artificial intelligence requires the development of more targeted and specific training approaches to maximise educational impact.

To achieve this, however, it is not enough to facilitate the application of AI in education; it is also crucial to promote and improve AI education and training. Students and citizens need to be equipped with digital skills, including what could be called 'AI literacy', in order to understand, support and contribute to the realization of a sustainable future society [5].

This reflection has focused attention on how to improve the digital literacy of future teachers in higher education and on the need to design targeted educational pathways that prepare students for the challenges of the future. This need has already been highlighted by several established reference models. These include the DigCompEdu framework [6], which identifies a set of digital competences for educators for the profession; DigComp 2.2 [7], which focuses on digital competences for citizens to engage critically and safely with digital technologies and artificial intelligence-driven systems; and TPACK [8], which integrates disciplinary content, pedagogy and technology and promotes the effective use of technology in educational activities. Finally, today, in the light of recent innovations and in particular advances in generative artificial intelligence, several documents have been produced by international organizations such as UNESCO [9–13], the European Union [14] and the OECD [15], proposing a review of digital literacies, including a literacy perspective on and with AI, to respond to the need to equip citizens for a rapidly changing technological environment. It is therefore imperative that universities develop a policy to promote AI literacy [16], defined as the promotion of skills related to the effective, critical and conscious use of and with AI.

2 Background

The university context has a crucial role to play in the critical path towards education and training models capable of exploiting and developing the potential of AI in a reliable and sustainable way [17].

In this direction, research on faculty development [18–25] plays a fundamental role. It is imperative to assess the impact of new applications based on artificial intelligence in academic and societal contexts [26–28], especially in light of the recent agreement on the AI ACT (2024) of the European Union and the urgent guidelines and reports of international organizations [9–13, 15, 29].

Higher education institutions have a responsibility to support, through faculty development activities, the processes of didactic innovation and qualification of teaching staff. University teaching cannot be limited to the mere observation of behaviour or the measurement of micro-skills that can be identified exclusively through approaches based on Evidence Based Education. It takes the form of an ideational and creative process that results in a complex and diverse set of competences that can be promoted through participatory modelling involving the lecturers themselves [30] or future potential lecturers. Among the main areas of teaching competence of university lecturers, a space is occupied by teaching mediation methodologies and technologies. The National Agency for the Evaluation of the University and Research System (ANVUR), which oversees Italy's national public system for assessing the quality of universities and research institutions, has proposed a national framework in its document 'Guidelines for the Recognition and Enhancement of University Teaching' [31] (Fig. 1). This document serves as a solid foundation for the renewal of university teaching in Italy, providing universities with tools to promote more effective, inclusive and student-centred teaching.

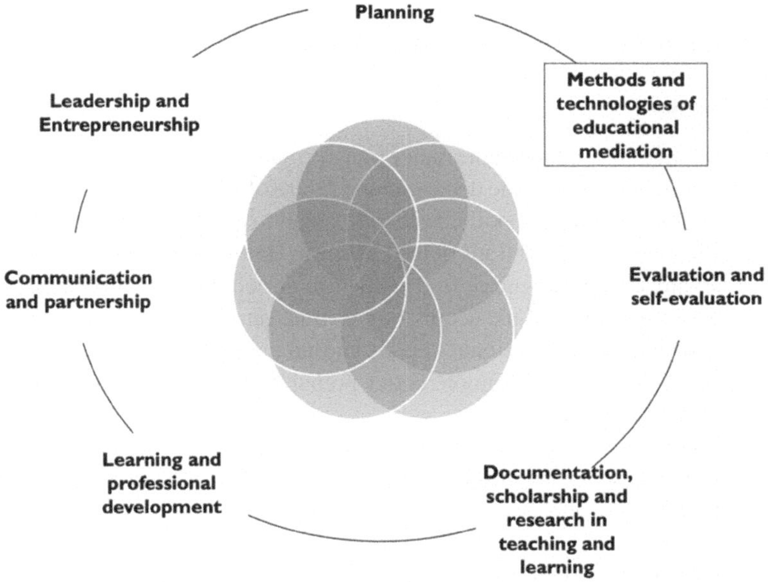

Fig. 1. Proposed national competence framework for university teaching [31]

It defines key areas of teaching competence, referred to as dimensions, which are articulated across three levels of expertise - basic, intermediate and advanced - in terms of values, knowledge, practices, innovative approaches and research orientations. The aim is to provide a framework that enables the reconfiguration of the professional vision of university teachers and enhances academic teaching competences.

Among the key areas of teaching competence in higher education, particular attention is given to the dimension of methodologies and technologies for teaching. This dimension recognizes the ability of university teachers to use strategies, methods, tools and technologies to effectively support teaching and learning processes. It also aims to create conditions for the experimentation and/or validation of innovative methods and tools for teaching and training, and to encourage research and study into teaching and learning methodologies. Ultimately, this will ensure opportunities for professional development and the appropriate training of high-level teaching expertise [32].

According to the ANVUR guidelines, the gradual emergence of artificial intelligence, robotics and machine learning systems calls for a profound transformation of traditional teaching approaches, highlighting their crisis. It is necessary to rethink objectives, practices and learning environments that favour the development of critical-constructive, autonomous and elaborative skills in students. To support this evolution, it is essential to promote communities of teachers engaged in reflection and experimentation with innovative practices based on digital technologies, accompanied by an evaluation of their impact. "If well designed, managed and evaluated, digitally enhanced didactics make it possible to redefine the space-time categories of teaching action, to counteract drop-out, to increase the effectiveness of educational pathways and to support dialogue at national and international levels" [31].

3 Experimenting with Innovative Ways

3.1 Introduction

One of the objectives in the face of the major transformations brought about by the proliferation of AI, which is fuelling the debate on the future of education, is the development of the skills, especially the soft skills, needed to adapt to a world in constant flux.

In line with the recommendations of the European Union [33], every year the University of Bari organizes a catalogue of free courses to enrich the educational offer. These are didactic activities aimed at the acquisition of transversal competences, divided into subject areas, which include optional classes and laboratories integrated into the educational pathway, designed to promote better preparation and widen opportunities for access to the labour market.

These initiatives are open to all students enrolled in three-year degree courses, Master's degree courses, one-cycle Master's degree courses, PhD courses and specialization courses at the University of Bari Aldo Moro, as well as Consortium and National Interest Doctorate courses.

These are microcredit pathways, that is to say, brief, targeted training programmes that permit students to obtain particular skills within a specific field. These pathways are highly flexible and inclusive, thereby enabling them to adapt to the individual learning needs of students and the demands of the labour market. Each pathway is structured to certify concrete and immediately applicable learning outcomes, such as theoretical knowledge, practical skills or transversal competences. Through the micro-credential pathways, students can enrich their professional profile, update existing skills or develop new ones, thus promoting continuous growth in specific areas and in line with technological, social and environmental developments.

In response to these needs, the Department of Education, Psychology and Communication Sciences of the University of Bari has launched an experiment with the formulation of a proposal aimed at improving the training offered to doctoral students through the introduction of a course on transversal skills related to Artificial Intelligence. Inspired by the recent legislation of the European Union [14] and by the guidelines of international organizations, the course, aimed at doctoral students, aims to provide new generations of scientists and professionals with transversal skills capable of integrating AI in a responsible and innovative way in their educational and professional pathways.

3.2 The Project Proposal

In the context of the need for a didactic innovation that guarantees opportunities for professional development and adequate training of expertise, and for strengthening the relationship between research and teaching within doctoral programmes, the interdisciplinary proposal for a course that would meet the training needs of Artificial Intelligence within microcredit courses was born.

The research design is situated within the collaborative learning research framework [34] and is based on a mapping exercise developed around three fundamental pillars.

The first institutional pillar concerns the theoretical framework within which the course is situated. The regulatory framework of faculty development, which aims to promote didactic, methodological and organizational innovation, and the study of national and international documents on literacy in and with AI in higher education contexts, made it possible to 'map' the main trajectories to be followed in order to align the course with the innovations taking place. The second pillar of the research envisaged a series of actions to guide the design development of the pathway. Finally, the third pillar envisaged monitoring and evaluation tools for the training actions.

3.3 Aims and Objectives

The aim of collaborative research training is to transform the educational reality by introducing changes in the reality that it studies. The aim is, on the one hand, to orient students towards a critical reflection on technological innovations (in this case, the development of Artificial Intelligence in educational and research pathways) and, on the other hand, to provide researchers with the tools to identify new pathways for quality professional development, both from a technical and didactic point of view.

The course, entitled 'AI Beyond the Code: Transversal Skills with Artificial Intelligence', directed by Professor Loredana Perla, was aimed at doctoral and postgraduate students at the University of Bari and its consortium universities. It was designed to address a heterogeneous audience of students without specific technical skills and to provide students with interdisciplinary skills and ethical reflection. The course is also part of the consortium's doctoral programme 'Leadership, Empowerment and Digital Innovation in Education and Learning (LEDIEL)'. This doctoral programme aims to train experts and qualified professionals in university educational management and processes related to the Digital Scholarship of Teaching and Learning (TLC and Digital

Hub). The aim is to develop an academic with advanced skills in the field of education, capable of rethinking and innovating practices and professional development. Particular attention is paid to the digital skills and literacies that are essential for the teaching of the future, such as digital literacy, data literacy and AI literacy, which are necessary to design and teach didactics adapted to the needs of the future.

The course, which lasted a total of 42 h and was divided into five thematic modules (Fig. 2), covered a wide range of topics, from the history and theoretical foundations of AI to its practical applications.

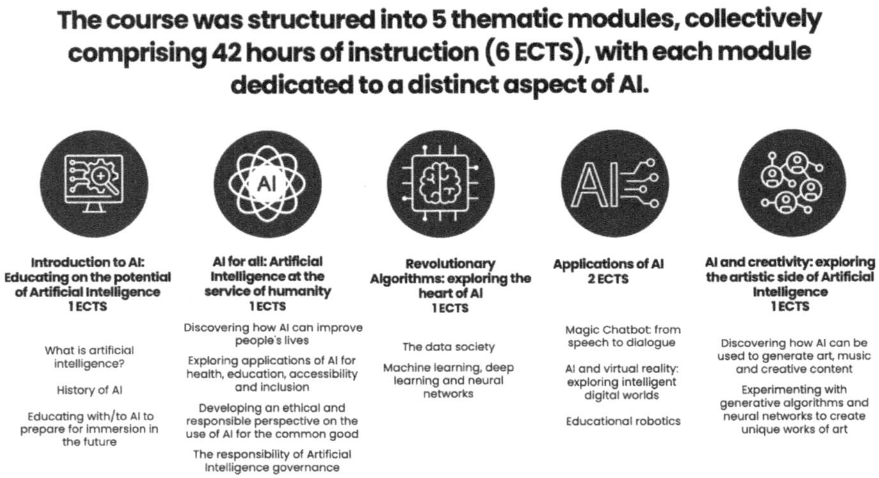

Fig. 2. Course structure

To facilitate the participation of PhD students from the consortium universities, it was decided to deliver the course in a mixed mode (online on the Teams platform and in-presence for Uniba students). The programme explored different aspects of AI, providing advanced insights in areas such as machine learning, natural language processing, data management and computer vision. It also emphasized the development of transversal skills, such as critical thinking and understanding the ethical principles related to the use of AI.

It was delivered by a range of experts in the field, each of whom explored both pedagogical and computer science topics in depth through workshop activities and case studies. The course was attended by 36 PhD students from various doctoral programmes in the humanities.

The structure has been designed to promote a practical and interactive approach, combining workshops, group work and case studies, allowing students to apply their acquired knowledge in an interdisciplinary context. This approach is in line with current educational recommendations, which emphasize the importance of transversal skills to meet the challenges of digitalization and the information society.

3.4 Participants

The course involved 9 lecturers from different backgrounds, including full professors, associate professors, researchers from different fields (pedagogy, computer engineering, robotics) and experts in the field. Thirty-five students participated (87.9% female; 12.1% male), of whom 30 were regularly enrolled in the Esse3 Uniba system and 5 auditors of different ages (Fig. 3), from the University of Bari, other universities in the consortium and national PhDs (Fig. 4). Only 3 enrolled students did not attend lectures.

Digital generations of course participants (the generations and their birth years)	**%**
Gen Z (1996 - 2015)	43,7%
Millennials (1981-1995)	34,4%
Gen X (1966 - 1980)	18,8%
Baby Boomers (1956 - 1965)	3,1%

Fig. 3. Digital generations of course participants

30 course participants + 5 auditors	**The academic profiles of the participants** (doctoral courses attended)
14	Leadership, Empowerment and Digital Innovation in Education and Learning (LEDIEL) - consortium doctorate
7 (1 did not attend)	Public Health, Clinical Medicine and Oncology (SPMCO)
4 (1 did not attend)	Human Relations Sciences
2	Learning sciences and digital technologies (LESDIT) - national doctorate
2	Enrolled in unspecified specialization courses
1	Humanities
1	Humanities, Languages and Arts
1	Teaching & Learning Sciences
1(did not attend)	Machine Learning for wildlife and marine environment conservation
1	Organizational tutor primary education course
1	Forpsicom researcher

Fig. 4. Academic background of participants

3.5 Tools

At the end of the course, a satisfaction questionnaire was administered by sharing a Google Forms link, consisting of closed and open-ended questions. The satisfaction questionnaire was divided into several sections: personal details, soft skills acquired and an area for overall evaluation. Satisfaction was analyzed in three main areas: overall satisfaction with the course, the content covered and the teaching. The last part focused on expectations, critical points and suggestions. In addition to the questionnaire, trainees were asked to complete a final report to assess the impact of the course on participants' research careers. The feedback was voluntary in order to allow the trainees to express themselves freely. The evaluation of the effectiveness of the course was based on three main elements: the satisfaction questionnaire, the final report with qualitative feedback from the participants and the attendance analysis. A total of 21 participants (87.9% female; 12.1% male) with different academic profiles responded (Fig. 5).

Satisfaction questionnaire participant profile	
No.	doctorate course (Uniba - consortium - national doctorates)
10	Leadership, Empowerment and Digital Innovation in Education and Learning (LEDIEL)
4	Public Health, Clinical Medicine and Oncology (SPMCO)
3	Human Relations Sciences
2	Learning sciences and digital technologies (LESDIT)
1	Humanities
1	Teaching & Learning Sciences

Fig. 5. Satisfaction questionnaire participant profile

As students from Uniba doctoral programmes and consortium universities participated in the course, the universities of origin of the course participants are diversified (Fig. 6). As far as the doctoral cycles are concerned, 71.4% of the participants belong to the 39th cycle and are starting their research career for the first time, 19% belong to the 38th cycle and 9.5% to the 37th cycle, which shows an interest that also includes students who are nearing the end of their academic career.

Doctoral candidates' home universities	
15	University of Bari
3	University of Foggia
1	University of Verona
1	University of Urbino
1	University of Macerata

Fig. 6. Doctoral candidates' home universities

The data collection tools used aimed to investigate the relevance of the course content, its effectiveness in strengthening research skills and overall student satisfaction.

Particular attention was paid to the perceived impact on research projects and the ability of the course to stimulate critical thinking and ethical reflection.

4 Results: Analysis and Discussion

4.1 Quantitative Results

The course achieved a high level of overall satisfaction, with trainees predominantly scoring in the 3 and 4 range of the rating scale (from 1 = 'not at all' to 4 = 'very much') on all items: Useful overall - Satisfactory overall - Useful for continuing PhD/specialization - Useful for continuing education - Useful for improving professional skills), with 90.5% of respondents recognizing AI training as essential for their academic development (Fig. 7). In addition, 81% expressed an interest in further study of the content covered, highlighting a growing enthusiasm for AI as an area of advanced study.

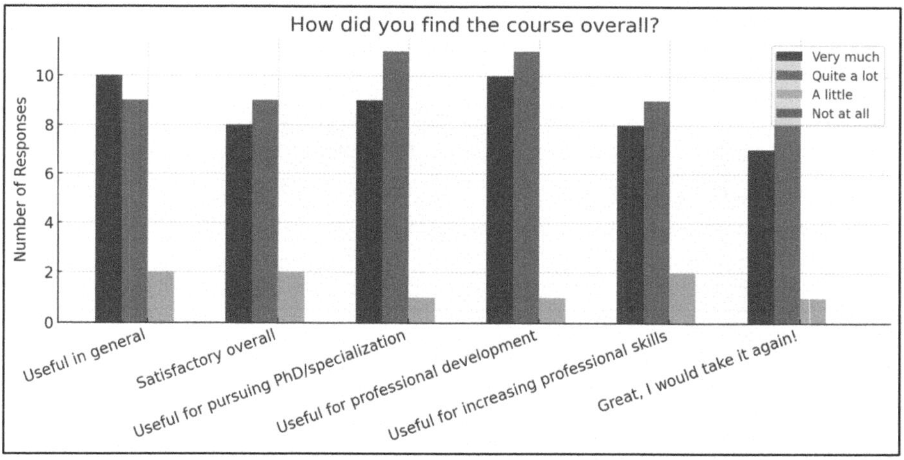

Fig. 7. You liked the course as a whole...

Trainees were asked to evaluate the level of transversal skills they had acquired after attending the course. Trainees commented on their ability to work in a team, relate to the group, critical thinking, professionalism acquired and creativity. The majority of trainees considered that their soft skills had improved to a sufficient extent, with most of them in band 3 of the rating scale (from 1 = "not at all" to 4 = "very much").

In terms of content relevance, 71.4% of students indicated that they were already familiar with the topics proposed, but appreciated the opportunity to explore the issues in more depth. This figure suggests that the course was able to meet the needs of both those approaching AI for the first time and those with previous knowledge, providing a solid foundation and insight.

In terms of research impact, many participants reported that the course had strengthened their theoretical foundations and stimulated critical reflection on ethical aspects, which had positively influenced their PhD research projects. Some students emphasized that the ethical discussions raised during the course were instrumental in improving their research methods, while others appreciated the opportunity to explore new machine learning techniques applicable to their fields of study. This feedback highlights the role of the course not only as a training tool, but also as a catalyst for methodological and theoretical innovation in the academic context.

With regard to the enjoyment of each module (Fig. 8), it is possible to observe a distribution of the preferences expressed by the participants with regard to the modules attended. In order to avoid confusion, it is important to point out that some modules have been divided into groups of lectures entrusted to different lecturers in order to ensure a more specific analysis.

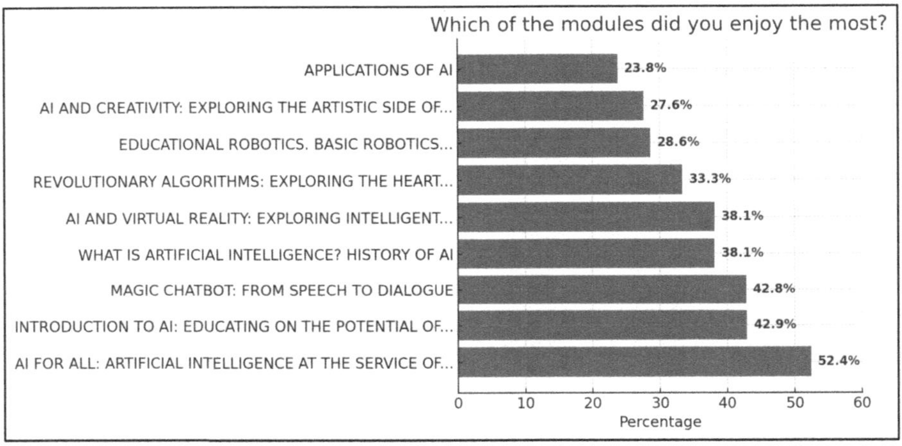

Fig. 8. Which of the modules did you enjoy the most? (max 3 answers)

This is the case of Module 4 on Applications of Artificial Intelligence, divided into Magic Chatbot: from speech to dialogue, AI and Virtual Reality, and Educational Robotics. Among the proposed modules, the most appreciated was the one entitled AI for All: Artificial Intelligence at the service of Humanity, which dealt with the ethical issues of applying AI, with an approval rating of 52.4% of participants, probably indicating an effective combination of content, methodology and perceived relevance.

This was followed by a group of lectures with similar ratings, including the one on education and AI (Introduction to Artificial Intelligence: Educating with/to AI to prepare for immersion in the future) and that on ChatGPT (Chatbot Magic: from speech to dialogue), both at 42.9%; this was followed by a module on the historical excursus of AI (What is artificial intelligence? History of AI) and one on virtual and immersive reality (Discovering how AI and virtual reality combine to create immersive experiences), both at 38.1%, highlighting how participants found several contents meaningful and useful.

Finally, "Revolutionary Algorithms: Exploring the Core of Artificial Intelligence" (33.3%), "Educational Robotics. Basic Robotics Programming and Computational Thinking" and "AI and Creativity: Exploring the Artistic Side of Artificial Intelligence" (28.6% each) and "Exploring AI Applications: Let's get to know OTI BOT" (23.8%) had a lower relative popularity. However, this could reflect not only a subjective preference but also factors such as the specific content or method of delivery. Analysis of these data suggests that while there is a good variety of content, some modules could benefit from further tailoring to participants' needs and interests.

Finally, participants were asked which modules they would like to deepen with further lessons. Of these, the module Chatbot Magic: from speech to dialogue appears to be the most popular, with 42.9% of participants wanting to extend the number of lessons. This result suggests a strong interest in ChatGPT and LLM in general, and suggests that most participants would have benefited from an extension. The results also suggest the possibility of redesigning the course structure to devote more time to topics perceived as more stimulating and relevant.

Regarding the level of satisfaction in relation to the initial expectations of the course participants, most of them expressed a positive level of satisfaction: 42.9% felt that their expectations had been met between 60% and 90%, while a further 38.1% were 100% satisfied. This shows that almost 80% of the participants found that the course met or exceeded their initial expectations, to the extent that 90.5% of the participants felt that this type of training was necessary for their doctoral studies and should be repeated in subsequent years. In addition, 81% of participants felt that the course required further study, suggesting that participants should see the course as a starting point for further educational development. The preparation and competence of the lecturers and trainers in relation to the course content was also rated very positively (Fig. 9). The trainees were almost exclusively in the range of 3 and 4 (1 = "not at all" to 4 = "very much") for all items: *Preparation and competence of lecturers and trainers in relation to course content - Clarity of presentation and depth of teaching skills - Teachers' willingness to engage in dialogue and cooperation - Appropriateness of the teaching methods used - Balance between theoretical lectures and moments of practical activities/exercises - Correspondence between the activities carried out and the professional profile of the course.*

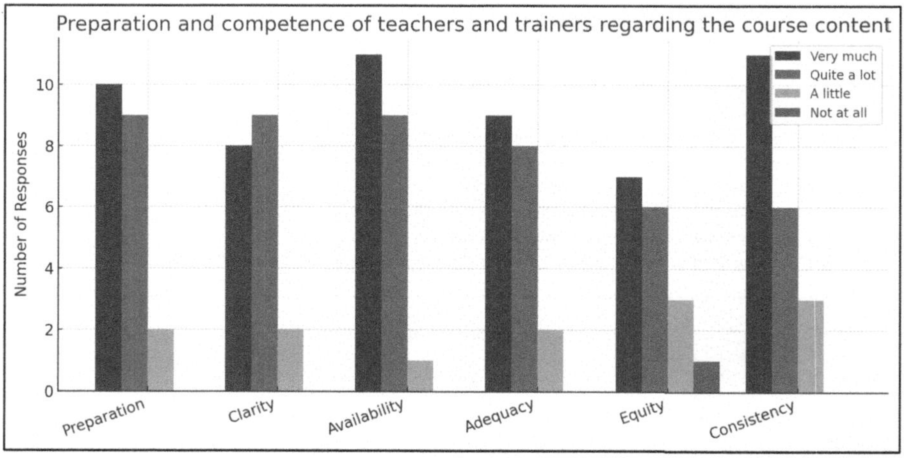

Fig. 9. Lecturers' and trainers' preparation and competence in course content

The almost unanimous positive feedback indicates that the course responded to real and concrete needs of doctoral students, reflecting a strong interest in extending the content or further specializing in certain areas covered during the course.

4.2 Qualitative Results

At the end of the course, participants' opinions, comments and suggestions were also collected (Figs. 10 and 11).

QUALITATIVE DATA (Open questions)

What is the theoretical value of the course lectures and their potential impact on your PhD research project? (some answers)

- In the context of my doctoral research project, which focuses precisely on artificial intelligence, the impact of these lessons is considerable.
- It provided me with a solid conceptual basis that is essential for any advanced research project in this field.
- The knowledge acquired through the lectures helped me to outline a solid theoretical framework for the research project.
- The course lectures were interesting and stimulating for my research project.

Do you consider whether the course lectures could inform the methodology of your research project and enhance its approach?

- Ethical reflections.
- Provided significant insights into how AI and chatbots can be effectively integrated into university teaching.
- Reflection around Artificial Intelligence and its critical application in educational contexts.
- The seminars stimulated my curiosity, opening up further avenues of research, readings, insights.
- The course lectures provided me with a comprehensive understanding of the limitations and advantages of using AI.
- The transversal skills course Ai beyond the code, was an opportunity for me to delve into topics I had never fully approached.

Fig. 10. Open question

Suggestions and comments

- The lecturers were very competent in their subjects.
- The course was well structured.
- I would give the possibility to choose to follow only some meetings.
- The hybrid mode is not very functional, mixed use should be revised.
- It is difficult to follow at the same time as other activities.
- I would have appreciated an insight into the ethics of using artificial intelligence.
- I would like more interactivity between speakers and learners.
- I would have appreciated a focus on the various international documents concerning AI in education.

Fig. 11. Suggestions and comments

The qualitative feedback gathered provided important insights for future improvements. Participants appreciated the competence of the trainers in their respective fields and the well-organized structure of the training, but they also highlighted some critical issues and made suggestions for improvement. Among the main recommendations was the need to increase interactive hands-on and workshop activities by introducing expert panels and face-to-face moments, balancing theory and practice to promote more participatory and engaging learning.

Another request that emerged concerned the flexibility of the course, with the suggestion that individual modules could be attended independently, allowing students to choose the sessions most relevant to their own research paths. This solution would also meet the need to adapt the course to students' academic commitments, making the course more accessible and adaptable. The need to avoid overlap with other teaching activities is also emphasized in order to facilitate participation.

The blended delivery model was seen by some as not very functional, as it was seen as not very inclusive for distance learners. It was suggested that blended delivery should be reviewed. In addition, some recommended that teaching materials be provided in advance to facilitate preparation for and attendance at lectures. One trainee stated that he found some of the training moments inappropriate for his initial level of knowledge.

Several participants expressed the desire for more in-depth study of the ethical and social aspects of AI and the need to devote more attention to the analysis of international documents on the responsible use of AI in educational contexts.

Another area for improvement is the re-organization of the course, with a request to review the division of lectures to allow more time for the most relevant topics.

Finally, specific themes emerge, such as the ethics of using AI in image creation, the introduction of AI applications to support teaching, and a focus on robotics applied to people with disabilities.

5 Conclusion

The integration of an interdisciplinary course in AI into academic programmes has proven its value, providing doctoral students with an opportunity for growth and allowing them to assess the impact of AI on their own research paths. It has provided not only technical skills, but also critical tools to address the ethical and social complexities of AI-driven innovation. This approach responds to the needs of contemporary society, which requires professionals capable of navigating an ever-changing environment where AI-related decisions will have significant and lasting impacts on education and society.

The course emphasized the need for an education that promotes awareness and critical reflection, helping to shape a generation of scholars and professionals capable of positively influencing the direction of technology and society.

There were, of course, some critical questions. The course is in its first edition. Future editions should consider implementing even more interactive activities, offering optional modules focusing on specific topics, and aligning them more closely with the individual research paths of doctoral students.

The results show how the university institution is called upon to provide training opportunities and structured experiences to deal with and competently manage the complexity of scientific, methodological and technological innovation. Innovation is not just about evaluating and reflecting on the results obtained. It is essential to strengthen the human and professional resources already in place and to accompany these interventions with targeted and substantial investments in both structures and educational cultures.

Only in this way is it possible to initiate processes of critical review of consolidated approaches, promoting virtuous cycles of re-elaboration of methodological frameworks and educational practices necessary to face the challenges of contemporaneity in an effective and sustainable way [35].

References

1. Atenas, J., Betta, G., Corbo, F., Corsi, E., Ann Katherine, I., Limone, P., et al.: Linee Guida per il Riconoscimento e la Valorizzazione della Docenza universitaria. ANVUR. (2023)
2. Adamoli, M., Rondonotti, M., Fedeli, L., Scarinci, A., Raviolo, P.: The impact of the digital environment on faculty development: a literature review. In: International Conference on Higher Education Learning Methodologies and Technologies Online, pp. 746–759. Springer, Cham (2024)
3. Felisatti, E.: Innovare la didattica: con quale docente? Il ruolo dei Teaching Learning Center. Strategie per lo sviluppo della qualità nella didattica universitaria. **90** (2023)
4. LN Spilker, M., Prinsen, F., Kalz, M.: Valuing technology- enhanced academic conferences for continuing professional development. A systematic literature review. Profess. Develop. Edu. **46**(3), 482–499 (2020)
5. Stracke, C.M., Chounta, I.A., Homes, W.: Global trends in scientific debates on trustworthy and ethical artificial intelligence and education. In: Olney, A.M., Chounta, I.A., Liu, Z., Santos, O.C., Bittencourt, I.I. (eds.) Artificial Intelligence in Education. Posters and Late Breaking Results, Workshops and Tutorials, Industry and Innovation Tracks, Practitioners, Doctoral Consortium and Blue Sky. AIED 2024 Communications in Computer and Information Science, vol. 2150. Springer, Cham (2024). https://doi.org/10.1007/978-3-031-64315-6_21
6. Punie, Y.: In: Redecker, C. (ed.) European Framework for the Digital Competence of Educators: DigCompEdu, EUR 28775 EN. Publications Office of the European Union, Luxembourg. ISBN 978-92-79-73718-3 (print). 978-92-79-73494-6 (pdf). 10.2760/178382 (print). 10.2760/159770 (online). JRC107466 (2017)
7. Vuorikari, R., Kluzer, S., Punie, Y.: DigComp 2.2: The Digital Competence Framework for Citizens - With New Examples of Knowledge, Skills and Attitudes, EUR 31006 EN. Publications Office of the European Union, Luxembourg (2022). https://doi.org/10.2760/115376, JRC128415. ISBN 978-92-76-48882-8
8. Mishra, P., Koehler, M.J.: Conoscenza dei contenuti pedagogici tecnologici: un framework per la conoscenza degli insegnanti. Teach. Coll. Rec. **108**(6), 1017–1054 (2006)
9. UNESCO, Miao, F., Cukurova, M.: AI Competency Framework for Teachers (2024)
10. UNESCO, Sabzalieva, E., Valentini, A.: ChatGPT and Artificial Intelligence in Higher Education: Quick Start Guide (2023)
11. UNESCO, Holmes, W., Miao, F.: Guidance for Generative AI in Education and Research (2023)
12. UNESCO, Miao, F., Holmes, W., Ronghuai, H., Hui, Z.: AI and Education: Guidance for Policy-Makers (2021)
13. UNESCO. Recommendation on the Ethics of Artificial Intelligence (2021)
14. AI Act (2024). https://data.consilium.europa.eu/doc/document/PE-24-2024-INIT/en/pdf
15. OECD. Governing with Artificial Intelligence: are governments ready? OECD Artificial Intelligence Papers, No. 20. (2024). https://doi.org/10.1787/26324bc2-en
16. Cuomo, S., Ranieri, M., Biagini, G.: Scuola e intelligenza artificiale. Percorsi di alfabetizzazione critica, Carrocci Editore (2024)

17. Schneider, G.: L'impatto dell'intelligenza artificiale sull'università tra tutela dei dati personali e diritto all'istruzione. In: Pajno, A., Donati, F., Perrucci, A. (eds.) Intelligenza artificiale e diritto: una rivoluzione? Volume 1 Diritti fondamentali, dati personali e regolazione. Il Mulino, Bologna (2022)
18. Michelini, M., Perla, L. (eds.): Strategie per lo sviluppo della qualità nella didattica universitaria. Pensa MultiMedia (2023)
19. Perla, L., Vinci, V.: Didattica, riconoscimento professionale e innovazione in Università. FrancoAngeli, Milano (2022)
20. Perla, L., Vinci, V.: Editoriale, Special Issue - Faculty Development and Digital Scholarship: Research issues in higher education. In: Excellence and Innovation in Teaching and Learning, pp. 5–9 (2021)
21. Silva, R.: Faculty Development. Il docente universitario tra ricerca, didattica e management, pp. 1–152. Carocci Editore (2022)
22. Lottti & Lampugnani, P. A.: (a cura di) Faculty Development. Origini, framework teorico, evoluzioni, traiettorie. Faculty Development in Italia: Valorizzazione delle competenze didattiche dei docenti universitari, pp. 171–178. Genova University Press, Genova (2020)
23. Beach, A., Sorcinelli, M.D., Austin, A., Rivard, J.: Faculty Development in the Age of Evidence. Stylus, Sterling (2016)
24. Steinert, Y. (ed.): Faculty Development in the Health Professions: A Focus on Research and Practice, vol. 11. Springer (2014)
25. Sorcinelli, M.D.: Faculty development: the challenge going forward. Peer Rev. **9**(4), 4–9 (2007)
26. Crompton, H., Burke, D.: Artificial intelligence in higher education: the state of the field. Int. J. Educ. Technol. High. Educ. **20**(1), 22 (2023)
27. Chen, L., Chen, P., Lin, Z.: Artificial intelligence in education: a review. IEEE Access. **8**, 75264–75278 (2020)
28. Bond, M., Khosravi, H., De Laat, M., Bergdahl, N., Negrea, V., Oxley, E., et al.: A meta systematic review of artificial intelligence in higher education: a call for increased ethics, collaboration, and rigour. Int. J. Educ. Technol. High. Educ. **21**(1), 4) (2024)
29. EDUCASE. Horizon Report Teaching and Learning Edition. (2024) https://library.educause.edu/-/media/files/library/2024/5/2024hrteachinglearning.pdf
30. Perla, L.: Valutare per valorizzare. La documentazione per il miglioramento di scuola, insegnanti, studenti. Morcellania (2019)
31. Felisatti, E., Perla, L.: Documento Linee Guida riconoscimento e valorizzazione docenza universitaria. ANVUR. (2023) https://www.anvur.it/gruppo-di-lavoro-ric/gruppo-di-lavoro-riconosciment o-e-valorizzazione-delle-competenze-didattiche-della-docenza-universitaria/
32. Felisatti, E., Serbati, A. (eds.): Preparare alla professionalità docente e innovare la didattica universitaria. Milano, FrancoAngeli (2017)
33. European Union. Recommendation on a European Approach to Micro-credentials for Life-long Learning and Employability. (2022). https://data.consilium.europa.eu/doc/document/ST-9237-2022-INIT/en/pdf
34. Perla, L.: I nuovi Licei alla prova delle competenze. Guida alla progettazione nel primo biennio, Pensa MultiMedia Editore (2014)
35. Limone, P., Simone, M.G.: Emergenza, esperienza, riflessione e trasformazione. Verso nuove traiettorie di sviluppo per la professionalità docente. In: Perla L., Vinci, V. (a cura di) Didattica, riconoscimento professionale e innovazione in Università. FrancoAngeli (2022)

The Influence of Online Education and Secondary School Teachers' Views on Digital Competencies

Michele Marangi(✉) and Irene Mauro

eCampus Università, Novedrate, CO, Italy
{michele.marangi,irene.mauro}@uniecampus.it

Abstract. The increasing integration of digital technologies in education has significantly impacted secondary school teachers, challenging traditional pedagogical practices. This study explores Italian teachers' perceptions of digital competencies and their experiences with professional development courses, starting from the perception of teachers enrolled in an online training course training course created by eCampus University to achieve the 30 University Training Credits (CFU or ECTS) necessary to take the exam required for qualification and become tenured teachers in secondary schools, pursuant to the Decree of the President of the Council of Ministers (DPCM) of 4 August 2023. Through a survey of 2400 teachers, the research investigates attitudes toward digital tools, the perceived usefulness of online learning, and the effectiveness of digital teaching methodologies. Findings indicate that teachers recognize digital education as a means to enhance engagement, creativity, and accessibility while also highlighting concerns about the digital divide and the need for continuous professional development. The study underscores the importance of collaborative learning communities, interdisciplinary approaches, and practical digital integration in teaching. Ultimately, the research contributes to the ongoing discourse on digital education, advocating for structured training programs that equip educators with the necessary skills to navigate an evolving technological landscape.

1 Teaching Skills in Digital Education

With the significant increase in the availability of professional development and training courses online, and the growing opportunities to enhance teaching skills using digital technologies at every stage of the learning process [1], secondary school teachers often face a complex challenge. On one hand, many of them express a certain resistance to the transformations brought about by the increasingly pervasive integration of digital technologies in education [2], which can be perceived as destabilizing to traditional practices [3]. On the other hand, there is a growing awareness of the importance of adapting to these innovations, recognizing the urgent need to rethink teaching activities in a refined framework [4]. This process involves not only adopting new tools but also embracing a mindset open to more flexible and future-oriented educational approaches, capable of addressing the needs of a rapidly evolving society [5]. The destabilization

P. Ardimento et al. (Eds.): HELMeTO 2024, CCIS 2468, pp. 302–316, 2025.
https://doi.org/10.1007/978-3-031-93999-0_20

of teachers in integrating digital tools into schools may be rooted in a range of factors, spanning from personal skills to the conditions of the educational institution [6]. Among the key aspects of this phenomenon is certainly the resistance to change exhibited by teachers, often due to a lack of sufficient familiarity with the use of technologies and the fear of undervaluing traditional practices. Another factor that has an impact is the age difference, young teachers seem more available to integrate technologies into teaching [7], even if teaching practices do not always coincide with an ability to manage digital dynamics, especially social media [8].

Some teachers believe that traditional pedagogical methods are more effective compared to new technological tools. Certainly, the lack of specific training programs for teachers also creates a gap between their skills and the requirements for keeping up to date, probably because teachers feel left alone in facing this challenge, which involves rethinking teaching methods [9].

The aim of the research is therefore to investigate teachers' perception of teaching innovation and their perceptions of digital competencies, starting from the perception of teachers enrolled in an online training course training course created by eCampus University to achieve the 30 University Training Credits (CFU) necessary to take the exam required for qualification and become tenured teachers in secondary schools, pursuant to the Decree of the President of the Council of Ministers (DPCM) of 4 August 2023. In Italian schools.

2 Research Context

Before explaining the data collection methodology and the subsequent discussion of the findings and of the evidence, it is important to define the context of the research. The DPCM (Decree of the President of the Council of Ministers) of 4 August 2023 represents a significant step in the regulation of continuous professional development for teachers, with particular focus on the use of digital technologies and the updating of professional skills to meet the needs of an increasingly digital society.

The DPCM of 4 August 2023 is an Italian regulation concerning the professional development of teachers and the system of continuous education. In particular, the decree sets out provisions related to the implementation of training and updating pathways for school teachers, with a focus on the use of digital technologies in education.

Some of the main goals of this DPCM are:

- to guarantee continuous teacher training, because the decree aims to ensure that teachers have the opportunity to participate in continuous professional development courses to update their skills, particularly in relation to the integration of digital technologies in teaching;
- to define the methods by which continuous professional development courses for teachers must be structured, specifying the topics to be covered (such as educational innovation, the use of digital technologies, etc.), as well as the duration and the requirements for earning the credits;
- to support and to promote innovative teaching methods, particularly those that use digital tools and advanced technologies, to address the modern challenges of education.

Shortly after the publication of the decree, several universities have organized themselves to respond to the demand for the organization of these courses, with eCampus Telematic University being one of the first.

The training course organized by eCampus University was entirely online in synchronous mode, lasting a total of 180 h, and saw the participation of teachers from all over Italy and of all levels, enrolled to obtain the teaching qualification by changing school or competition class.

The lessons were held exclusively in synchronous online mode and took place on a dedicated platform with attendance and access control. As stated in Article 7, paragraph 7 of the DPCM of 4 August 2023, to access the final exam, a minimum attendance rate of 70% in the training activities was required.

At the end of the program, a final in-person exam was scheduled, overseen by a committee of four members: two professors from the university, one member appointed by the USR (Regional School Office), and one external expert in training. The final exam consisted of a written part focusing on educational planning, including the use of multimedia technologies, and a simulated lesson lasting up to 45 min.

2.1 Methodology

Since the course included sections on digital technologies and their importance in teaching, the teachers attending the course represented the perfect sample for the research to investigate perceptions of digital technology in Italian schools.

The survey used this representative sample of the professional community of teachers to verify how they approach the use of digital technologies in teaching, based on existing literature [10].

The questionnaire was uploaded and processed on QuestionPro - a SaaS-based survey software focused on customer experience, employee experience, and collecting the pulse of audience through online polls, after online administration in the final module of the course. Semi-structured, it is made up of 18 items which in some cases allow multiple choice responses and in other cases positioning on a Likert scale.

The questionnaire submitted is structured into three sections, which translate the research design. The first, with personal data, allows us to identify, in addition to age and gender, school level and length of service. The second section includes a battery of questions with a Likert scale or multiple choice in a defined set of possible choices, which investigates the perception and interest towards online learning methods. The third section focuses on the concrete experience of the online course they attended, through a series of questions, with a Likert scale, which focuses on the effectiveness, usefulness and possibility of using what they learned in the future. The Likert scale was structured on 6 scores, according to this gradation: 1. not at all, 2. A little, 3. Average, 4. Quite a bit, 5. Very much, 6. Completely.

A total of 2,794 people accessed the questionnaire, with a dropout of 394. Therefore, exactly 2,400 teachers started and completed the questionnaire.

2.2 Research Goals

The research has the following objectives:

- to collect and to measure teachers' perception about digital technologies; this involves investigating their opinions, experiences, and attitudes towards the use of digital tools. The goal is to understand their level of acceptance, usage, and critical reflection on these technologies within the educational context;
- to appraise digital teaching practices; this involves examining how teachers use digital resources in their teaching, how these practices impact student learning, and whether they align with educational goals.
- to provide an overview of the use of technologies in Italian schools; this involves examining how schools integrate technologies into their teaching and learning processes, the types of tools being used.

In fact, the research holds a dual significance. On one hand, it seeks to provide teachers with an opportunity for an initial reflection on their fully online training experience. The focus is not merely on assessing satisfaction or certifying learning outcomes but rather on measuring their stance toward professional development conducted entirely online [11]. On the other hand, the study delves into teachers' perceptions regarding their ability to reflect on their disciplinary knowledge and teaching practices. This reflection is framed in relation to integrating digital technologies into teaching within a learning design perspective [12]. Such an approach updates the concept of Media Education, situating it within a broader and more contemporary framework [13, 14].

The results' overview will highlight trends, challenges, and successes in the use of digital technologies across different levels of education, providing a clear picture of the current state of technology in Italian school.

3 Results

The following section will present some of the quantitative results obtained from the sample's responses. The first analyzed data concern demographic characteristics (gender, school level where teachers work, and years of teaching experience). In the second part of the analysis, the focus will present the impact of digital technology on teachers' perceptions. In the third part of the analysis the focus will be on the teachers' perception of the effectiveness of the course attended online.

3.1 Sample Data

In this short paragraph, we analyze the personal data that help to understand the composition of the sample in reference to objective data on their specificities.

In the analyzed sample, the majority of individuals are female, representing 80.82% of the total. A significantly smaller proportion, 18.07%, consists of male individuals. Lastly, 1.11% of the sample chose not to disclose their gender, indicating a minority that prefers not to identify with traditional gender categories (Fig. 1). These data highlight a predominance of females in the group, with a small but notable percentage maintaining their gender identity private.

With reference to the school levels of teaching, a large majority emerges in secondary school (Fig. 2). In the sample, 1.1% of participants teach in preschool, while 11.55% work in primary school. A larger share, 27.03%, teaches in lower secondary school,

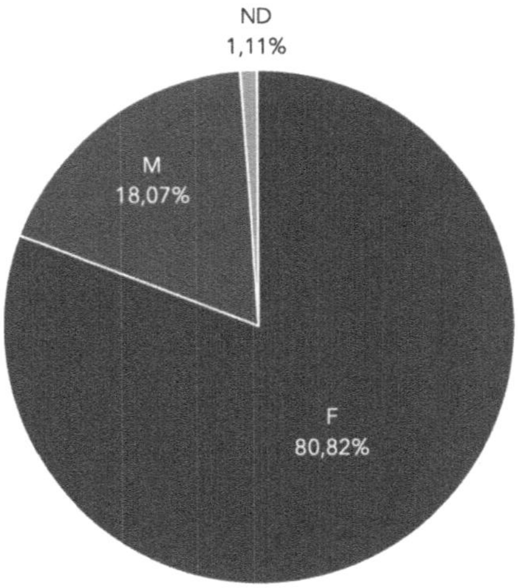

Fig. 1. Sample Gender

but the majority, 53.89%, works in upper secondary school. Finally, 5.92% of the total sample is currently not teaching at any educational level. The data shows that 81% of teachers are already within the school grades required by the type of qualification they will have to obtain. This large percentage therefore denotes an experience already rooted in the teaching universe.

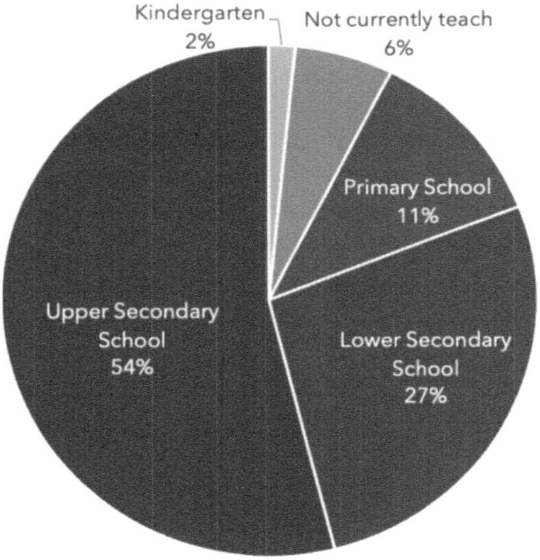

Fig. 2. School Level

The experience already gained in the field also emerges from the data that over half of the participants are already permanent, with 54.22%, while the remaining 45.78% are on a fixed-term contract, not yet permanent.

Two other important pieces of information necessary for developing a more in-depth reflection on the topic were the teachers' years of career experience and whether they had attended any professional training courses prior to the 30 ECTS course they were taking at the time.

In the analyzed sample, 9.44% of teachers have more than 16 years of professional experience, while 9.01% have been teaching for over 21 years. A total of 10.67% reported teaching for 11 to 15 years, and 26.31% have been teaching for 6 to 10 years. The remaining teachers are divided between those with less than two years of experience, representing 17.34% of the sample, and those with 3 to 5 years of experience, accounting for 27.22% (Fig. 3).

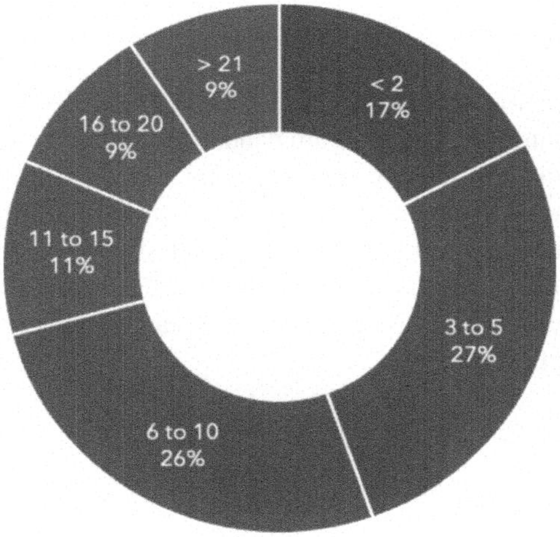

Fig. 3. Years of career experience

Aggregating the data, it emerges that 70% of the participants have been in the world of school for less than 10 years. About half, 44%, have been teaching for less than 5 years. The interest of these percentages lies in the fact that generally most of the teachers competing for the qualification teach and live in a world in which digital technologies are now daily. It will be interesting to take this aspect into account when the subsequent responses referring more specifically to the perception and use of digital in teaching are analyzed.

Regarding the question about attending other professional training courses prior to the 30 ECTS course, 28.33% of the sample reported having never attended any training courses, while the majority (71.67%) stated that they had previously participated in other training programs (Fig. 4). From the data it emerges that the majority of teachers already have experience with online courses, in a proportion of about three out of four, so it will be interesting to consider their "expert" opinion when they evaluate the elements that have most characterized the experience lived online during this training course.

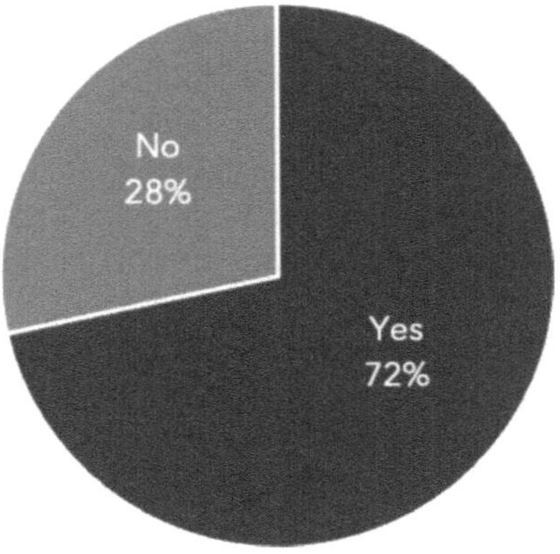

Fig. 4. Attendance of other training courses

3.2 Digital Teaching

In response to the question about how useful they consider distance learning on topics related to digital teaching (such as designing and managing interactive lessons, creating multimedia teaching materials, using apps, etc.), the average score of the teacher sample is 4.64, on a scale ranging from 1 (lowest level) to 6 (highest level).

The second question concerns the usefulness of sharing materials among teacher colleagues. Specifically, in response to the question "How useful do you think it is to share materials and/or tools you have created with your colleagues?", the sample assigns an average score of 5.11 out of 6.

Fig. 5. Perceived usefulness of practices.

The average score of the responses increases when the question relates to collaboration with colleagues. Specifically, in response to the question "How useful do you think it is to collaborate with your colleagues in developing materials and/or tools?", the average score rises to 5.33 out of 6. A similar trend is observed for the question "How useful do you think it is to share experiences and/or practices with your colleagues?", for which the average score is 5.42 out of 6.

The highest score (5.49 out of 6) is reached with the question "How useful do you think it is to give and receive help for solving daily professional problems?", highlighting that one of the most pressing needs for teachers is to be part of a group for sharing tools and best practices.

The answers (Fig. 5) highlight the importance of relationships between colleagues and the centrality of the experiential concreteness of teaching, even when faced with problems. Sharing experiences and practices appears more important than sharing materials and tools, just as the possibility of collaborating operationally with colleagues for the development of teaching materials is highly valued.

All items have decidedly positive values, above 4, including the perception of the usefulness of distance learning on digital teaching topics.

The questionnaire included a question about the impact of digital technology on teaching, allowing respondents to select up to three answers from a range of options. 61.38% of the respondents stated that digital tools make teaching more engaging. Other high percentages include: digital encourages project-based creativity (38%), facilitates the discovery of educational content (35%), and makes teaching more accessible to everyone (37%) (Fig. 6).

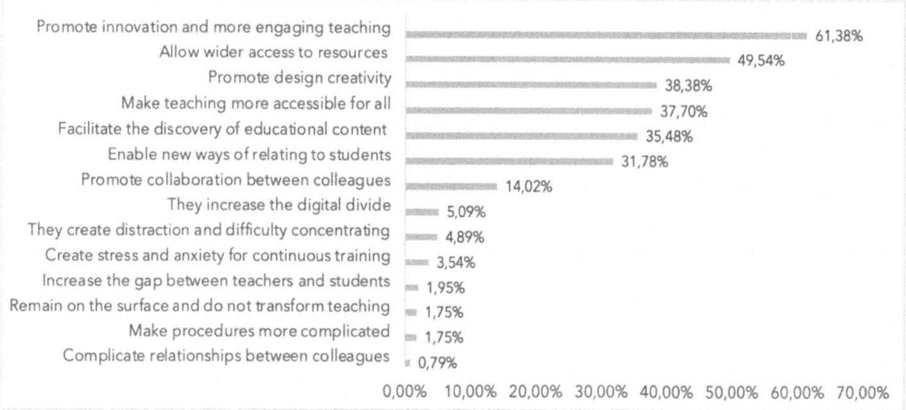

Fig. 6. Aspects of the Impact of Digital Technology on Teaching

Other responses, on the other hand, highlight potential drawbacks of digital technology: the increase in the digital divide between those who know how to use it and those who do not (5%), the rise in stress and anxiety caused by the constant need to stay updated (3.5%), and the complication of procedures (1.7%). However, the aspects of digital technology that can be considered negative account for relatively low percentages of responses.

The participants' choices reward the answers related to two macro areas: on the one hand, that of innovation, discovery and creativity; on the other, that of accessibility and inclusion. Teachers seem particularly sensitive to promoting teaching that is innovative and engaging for students, as emerges in several answers with high results, and to broaden the available resources and the most functional contents for teaching that is also accessible and inclusive. From this perspective, digital no longer seems linked to a purely technological and instrumental dimension, as it might have appeared in an initial phase of about twenty years ago, but rather as innovative and creative design of teaching. It seems emblematic that the values related to the digital divide are very low, to the fact that digital can distract, to stress due to the continuous need for training and above all to the fact that technology is no longer perceived as a divisive factor between students and teachers, confirming the data already mentioned above on the naturalization of digital with respect to a generation of teachers who were born and raised in contexts with a high presence of technologies.

The confirmation of the factors just identified also emerges from the answers to the next question which refers to which aspects learned during the course are more likely to be used in future professional practice (Fig. 7). Also in this case all 8 items are evaluated positively with an overall average of 4.47 on the usual scale with values from 1 to 6. The highest scores are related to planning skills (4.7) and to the acquisition and development of skills in didactic planning and evaluation (4.68). Equal with 4.47 are the discovery of new perspectives to make teaching more engaging and participatory and the maturation with respect to a more professional educational and didactic style, followed by reflective skills (4.45) and the ability to think about teaching in an innovative perspective (4.44). Finally, always with significant values, new knowledge emerges with respect to the topics covered (4.40) and skills on the use of apps and educational technologies (4.19).

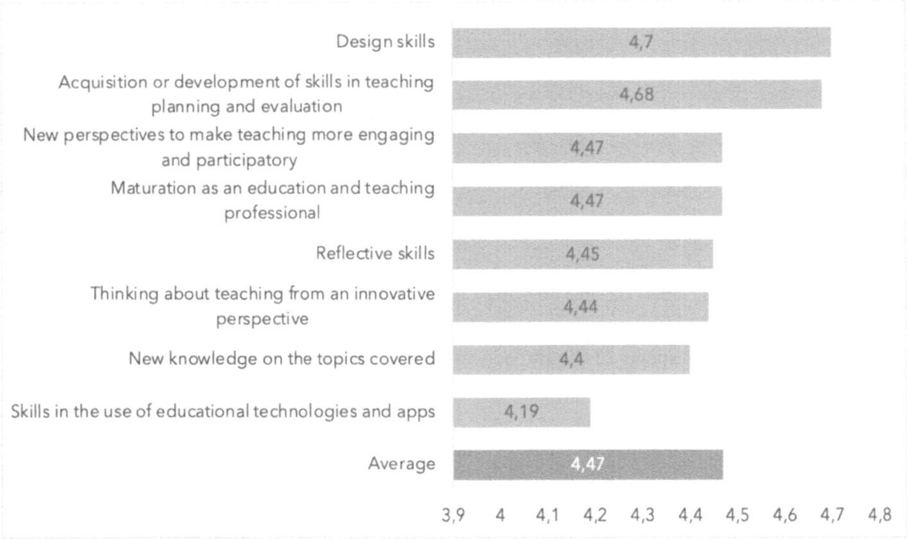

Fig. 7. Usefulness of the online learning experience.

These data further highlight the importance attributed to the development of skills in learning design and the attention to aspects that transform and improve the role of teachers, both in planning and in evaluation. The importance of developing reflective skills, which allow a positive questioning of teaching, appears emblematic, to the advantage of innovative and interactive perspectives with respect to classes, with the theme of participation and involvement that is still very high. Also in this case it is significant that the more specifically technological and applicative skills are in last place, confirming that the use of digital in the teaching field is increasingly less experienced as a purely technical aspect, in favor of an attention linked to the logic of contemporaneity, in a participatory, collaborative and functional perspective to the achievement of accessible and usable results by the whole class.

3.3 An Assessment of the Online Course

In this last part of the data analysis, we will evaluate the answers related to the impact that the students' reflections on the effectiveness of the online course they attended.

The first question (Fig. 8) investigates the reasons why this online course was chosen and not others, both in physical presence and with online alternatives. In this case, 8 answers were proposed with the possibility of choosing only two.

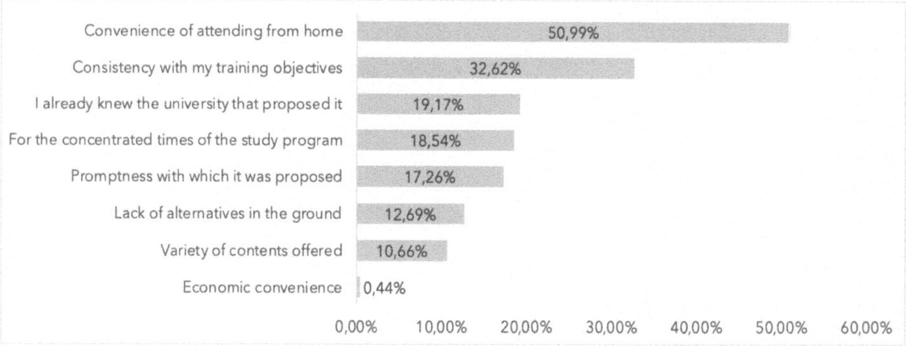

Fig. 8. Reasons for choosing this online course.

The dominant reason, with approximately 51% of the answers, concerns the ease and convenience of being able to follow the course directly from home, without having to travel which presumably would have been problematic for many students. Approximately a third of the students (32.62%) then identified the coherence of the course contents with respect to their educational objectives, while approximately a fifth (19.17%) confirmed their trust in eCampus University which they already knew previously. Elements that were appreciated also concern the concentration of the course program, very tight (18.54%) and the speed and promptness with which the course was proposed (17.26%). The last three usable hypotheses total fewer choices, namely the absence of alternatives in the territory (12.69%), the variety of contents offered (10.66%) and, practically not voted by almost anyone, the economic convenience (0.44%).

From reading these data, some encouraging aspects emerge for eCampus University. First of all, the appreciation for the practicability of the online proposal combined with the immediacy of the launch emerges, even compared to other universities. The fact that the name is already known, and presumably considered reliable, must also be linked to the coherence of the proposed program with respect to the educational objectives and the ability to draw up a study program adequate to the needs, including temporal, of the people who participated.

These aspects are also taken up and explored in greater depth in the following question. Teachers were asked how much they agreed with statements about the 30 ECTS course they were attending, using a scale from 1 (minimum level) to 6 (maximum score) (Fig. 9). The findings reveal that online attendance greatly facilitated participation, as 1471 responses were placed at the highest level on the scale, representing 61% of responses.

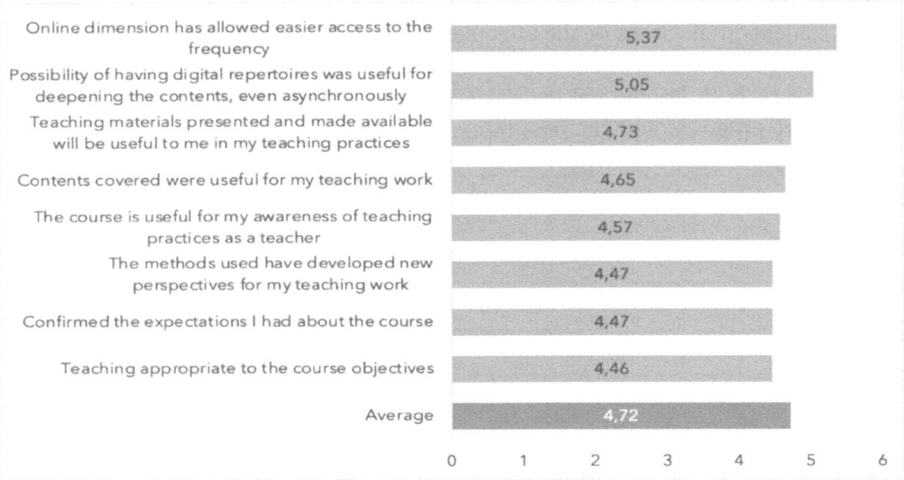

Fig. 9. Statement on the course attended.

Additionally, the availability of a repository of content, accessible asynchronously and thus always available, garnered 42.5% of the sample's responses. Respondents also agreed that the content covered would be useful for their future teaching practice, with 33% selecting level 5 and 27% selecting level 6 on the scale.

The 30% of the sample believed that the methods used opened new professional perspectives, while 34% felt that the materials presented would be useful for their future teaching experiences.

Furthermore, 31% of respondents stated that online teaching was suitable for the course objectives, and 33% considered the online training experience to be a positive one.

Consistently with the answers to the previous question, also in this case the ease of access guaranteed by the online dimension is positioned at the highest level, with a 5.37 which appears to be among the highest values recorded in the entire questionnaire. It seems interesting that the second element of satisfaction, also above 5, is linked to the potential that the course has guaranteed, also thanks to the use of online repertoires and the practicability of the asynchronous dimension, which today appears fundamental in an online learning logic, in the era of MOOCs [15]. Significantly, all the values of this response are very high, above 4.45, and record the appreciation of the materials and contents suitable for concrete use in teaching practices. Also the theme of innovation, already mentioned previously, finds a high level of satisfaction here, with respect to the possibility of transforming the awareness of being a teacher in the digital era and of offering methods that allow teachers to broaden and transform teaching perspectives. Even though they are ranked in the last two places, but with a still high satisfaction of over 4.45, it seems encouraging that the students found the contents of the course consistent with their expectations and with the objectives of the path they attended.

The last question of the survey sought to investigate to what extent the contents learned could actually be used in an operational teaching practice in the immediate future by the students, again using a scale from 1 (minimum level) to 6 (maximum score) (Fig. 10).

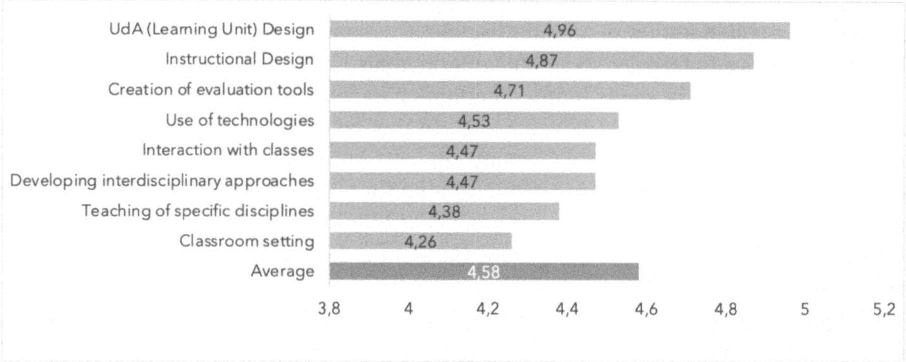

Fig. 10. Future educational use of online learning.

Both top scores, with a value close to 5, have to do with the concept of design, both for the design of the UdA (learning unit) with 4.96, and for the broader design of teaching, with 4.87. In third place is the importance of evaluation (4.71), through the ability to create new tools that respond to logics that are not only canonical and summative, a recurring theme in the training path. Unlike other previous answers, in this case the use of technology is also well valued (4.53), followed equally (4.47) by the ability to be increasingly interactive with classes and to develop interdisciplinary teaching approaches. Less valued, but still with results well above four, are the teaching of a specific subject (4.38) and the management of a class setting (4.26) in the last choices.

The answers to this last question highlight the need for great concreteness on the part of teachers, which however is not attributed to what they already know best, for example their specific discipline or classroom management. Rather, there is an appreciation for one of the key objectives of the training path, namely the transformation of project design, both for learning units (UdA) and for the prospects of didactic development more generally. In this sense, the use of technology also appears closely connected to the attention for the creation of new assessment tools and for an interaction with classes that is increasingly greater and allows for participatory and significant learning. It is also interesting to note how interdisciplinarity still has a high value, confirming a fact that has already emerged in the previous answers, namely the ability to collaborate in a concrete and productive way with teaching colleagues.

4 Conclusion

The study examines the acquisition of digital skills in relation to the primary tasks typically assigned to teachers, particularly in the context of their expertise [16]. It delves into an analysis of how teachers perceive both the teaching and technical affordances of digital tools [17], considering the widespread and growing need to innovate educational practices [18]. The research further explores the potential for integrating digital technologies into teaching environments through the lens of Community Technologies [19], and from the perspective of developing communities of practice [20] among colleagues. These communities, which do not necessarily have to be located in the same physical spaces, foster collaboration in an interdisciplinary manner, extending beyond teaching alone and addressing broader social integration goals [21].

Moreover, the study sheds light on certain characteristics that can be linked to the concept of digital educational poverty [22]. In this context, however, the focus is not on the lack of skills or capabilities among students but rather on the growing need for additional professional development and training for teachers. This highlights a critical gap in the ongoing evolution of teaching practices [23] and the need to empower educators with the necessary digital tools and knowledge to meet the demands of a rapidly changing educational landscape [24].

The survey highlighted some recurring aspects, which we believe to be central to developing the reflection on the use of digital in educational environments [25] and which seem to confirm the greater familiarity and habit of using digital by teachers after the experience with Distance Learning during the Covid-19 epidemic [26]. Beyond the concept of digital divide understood in a purely technological sense [27], the use of digital in teaching is perceived as useful in two fields: methodological innovation and operational creativity; accessibility to content and ever-increasing inclusion.

The choice of an online study or training course requires a balance between convenience and accessibility factors and the quality of the content and consistency with the training objectives. The most appreciated aspects of the course are the online dimension that allows accessibility and attendance, a dimension that also recurs in other research [28]; the contents provided and the tools used, also available in the asynchronous dimension. The course was useful to develop more innovative and engaging teaching perspectives, to strengthen teaching planning skills and evaluation strategies and to increase knowledge on "educational" digital. The main concrete outcomes for the professional practice are: improvement of educational design, new evaluation modalities, possibility of better interaction with the class. Importance of operational concreteness and the ability to be a community of practice: creation and sharing of teaching materials and tools; availability for mutual help, in a peer-to-peer training logic.

Beyond the 30 ECTS course itself, these data can represent a basis for reflection with respect to the fact that online universities are recognized first and foremost for their ability to offer practicable, streamlined and functional alternatives to the educational needs of many people who do not have opportunities in the area or cannot travel, but also for the coherence of the proposed programs and the adopted educational style, while the economic convenience component appears completely irrelevant. It will be interesting to see to what extent and in which aspects there will be major transformations in relation to the ever-widening diffusion of Artificial Intelligence [29]. But it will be useful to dedicate specific research to this.

Author Contributions. The article was designed and developed by both authors. Irene Mauro wrote Sects. 1 and 2, Michele Marangi Sects. 3 and 4.

References

1. Lidolf, S., Pasco, D.: Educational technology professional development in higher education: a systematic literature review of empirical research. Front. Educ. **5**(35), 1–20 (2020)
2. Potter, J., McDougall, J.: Digital Media, Culture and Education. Palgrave MacMillan, London (2017)
3. Gui, M.: L'uso didattico delle ICT. In: Cavalli, A., Argentin, G. (eds.) Gli insegnanti italiani: come cambia il modo di fare scuola. Terza indagine dell'Istituto IARD sulle condizioni di vita e di lavoro nella scuola italiana. Il Mulino, Bologna (2010)
4. Ferri, P.: La scuola 2.0. Verso una didattica aumentata dalle tecnologie. Spaggiari, Parma (2013)
5. Rivoltella, P.C.: Scuola, cultura e società. Cambiamento, rivoluzioni e gattopardismo. In: Mariani, A. (ed.) L'agire scolastico, pp. 165–184. ELS – La Scuola, Brescia (2017)
6. Ranieri, M.: Competenze digitali per insegnare. Modelli e proposte operative. Carocci, Roma (2022)
7. Savarese, G., et al.: Percezione e rappresentazione sull'uso delle tecnologie digitali in docenti esperti e novizi: analisi del contenuto delle interviste. In: Cecchinato, G., Grion, V. (eds.) Dalle Teaching Machines al Machine Learning. Padova University Press, Padova (2020)
8. Petrucco, C., Grion, V.: Insegnanti in formazione e integrazione delle tecnologie in classe: futuri docenti ancora poco "social"? Qwerty. **10**(2), 30–45 (2015)
9. Calzone, S., Chellini, C.: Teachers' training: an empirical study on training needs and digital skills. Form@re - Open Journal Per La Formazione in Rete. **16**(2), 32–46 (2016)
10. Foschi, L.C.: Indagare l'atteggiamento e le percezioni degli insegnanti verso le tecnologie digitali: costruzione, struttura fattoriale e attendibilità di uno strumento. Sirem, Apprendere con le tecnologie tra presenza e distanza. Book of Abstracts. Morcelliana, Brescia (2022)
11. Raviolo, P.: Learning design e software design: analogie e interazioni per l'educazione superiore. Le Società per la società: ricerca, scenari, emergenze. SIRD, vol. 3, pp. 59–66. Pensa MultiMedia, Lecce (2020)
12. Laurillard, D.: Teaching as a Design Science. Building Pedagogical Patterns for Learning and Technology. Routledge, London (2012)
13. Rivoltella, P.C.: Nuovi alfabeti. Educazione e culture nella società post-mediale. Scholé, Brescia (2020)
14. Buckingham, D.: Un manifesto per la media education. Mondadori, Milano (2020)
15. Kent, M., Bennett, R.: Massive Open Online Courses and Higher Education: What Went Right, What Went Wrong and Where to Next? Taylor & Francis, London (2017)
16. Wohlfart, O., Wagner, I.: Teachers' role in digitalizing education: an umbrella review. Educ. Technol. Res. Dev., 1–27 (2022)

17. Raviolo, P.: Online Higher Education Teaching Practices. IC4E Tokyo 2019 Proceedings. ACM, Tokyo (2019)
18. EUA. Learning and Teaching in the European Education Area (2018). https://eua.eu/resources/publications.html
19. Rivoltella, P.C.: Tecnologie di comunità. Morcelliana, Brescia (2017)
20. Wenger, E.: Communities of Practice: Learning, Meaning, and Identity. Cambridge University Press, Cambridge, UK (1999)
21. Rondonotti, M.: Tecnologie, comunità, inclusione sociale. eCampus University Press, Novedrate (CO) (2024)
22. Marangi, M., Pasta, S., Rivoltella, P.C.: Digital educational poverty: construct, tools to detect it, results. Povertà educativa digitale: costrutto, strumenti per rilevarla, risultati. QTimes. J. Educ. Technol. Soc. Stud. **XIV**(4), 236–252 (2022)
23. Nikou, S., Aavakare, M.: An assessment of the interplay between literacy and digital technology in higher education. Educ. Inf. Technol. **26**, 3893–3915 (2021)
24. Lodge, J.M., Kennedy, G., Lockyer, L.: Digital learning environments, the science of learning and the relationship between the teacher and the learner. In: Carroll, A., Cunnington, R., Nugent, A. (eds.) Learning Under the Lens: Applying Findings from the Science of Learning to the Classroom. CRC Press, Abingdon (2019)
25. Pinto, M., Leite, C.: Digital technologies in support of students learning in Higher Education: literature review. Digit. Educ. Rev., 343–360 (2020)
26. Cioci, G.: La DAD ha trasformato le pratiche didattiche? Indagine sull'effettivo utilizzo e sulla percezione del digitale da parte dei docenti. Sirem, Apprendere con le tecnologie tra presenza e distanza. Book of Abstracts. Morcelliana, Brescia (2022)
27. Marangi M., Pensare il Digital Divide come gap educativo, narrativo e creativo, «Scholé», La povertà educativa: quali risposte?, vol. LVIII, 2, Morcelliana, Brescia (2020)
28. Ferranti, C., Petrucco, C.: La competenza digitale del docente: un'analisi delle percezioni emerse nei corsi online PAS e TFA dell'Università di Padova
29. Nirchi, S., Mangione, G.R.J., De Vincenzo, C., Pettenati, M.C.: Indagine esplorativa sulla percezione dei docenti neoassunti circa l'impiego dell'intelligenza artificiale nella didattica: punti di forza, ostacoli e prospettive. J. Educ. Cult. Psychol. Stud. (ECPS J.). **30**, 151–180 (2025)

Author Index

P. Ardimento et al. (Eds.): HELMeTO 2024, CCIS 2468, pp. 317–318, 2025.
https://doi.org/10.1007/978-3-031-93999-0

The manufacturer's authorised representative in the EU is Springer Nature Customer Service Centre GmbH, Europaplatz 3, 69115 Heidelberg, Germany. If you have any concerns regarding our products, please contact ProductSafety@springernature.com

Printed and bound by CPI Group (UK) Ltd, Croydon, CR0 4YY
30/09/2026
02225585-0003